A QUALIFIED HOPE

The Indian Supreme Court is widely seen as a vanguard of progressive social change. Yet there are no systematic studies of whether its progressive decisions actually improve the lives of the relatively disadvantaged. This book presents the first collection of original empirical studies on the impact of the Indian Supreme Court's most progressive decisions. Combining original datasets with in-depth qualitative research, the chapters provide a rigorous examination of the conditions under which judicial decisions can make a difference to those in need. These studies reveal that the Indian Supreme Court, like its US counterpart, is largely constrained in its efforts. Yet, through its procedural innovations, its institutional independence, and the broad sweep of constitutional rights in the Indian Constitution, the Indian Supreme Court can sometimes make a difference to the lives of those most in need.

Gerald N. Rosenberg is Associate Professor of Political Science and Lecturer in Law at the University of Chicago. He is the author of *The Hollow Hope: Can Courts Bring About Social Change?* (2008) which was awarded the Laing Prize by the University of Chicago Press and the Wadsworth Award from the American Political Science Association.

Sudhir Krishnaswamy is on the faculty of Azim Premji University, Bangalore. He has served as the Dr. B.R. Ambedkar Visiting Professor of Indian Constitutional Law at Columbia University Law School and as the Director of the School of Policy and Governance at Azim Premji University in Bangalore.

Shishir Bail is completing a PhD in Anthropology at Columbia University. He has served as a law-clerk to Justice Anil R. Dave of the Supreme Court of India and as a Research Associate at the School of Policy and Governance at Azim Premji University.

T0381567

COMPARATIVE CONSTITUTIONAL LAW AND POLICY

Series Editors

Tom Ginsburg, *University of Chicago*
Zachary Elkins, *University of Texas at Austin*
Ran Hirschl, *University of Toronto*

Comparative constitutional law is an intellectually vibrant field that encompasses an increasingly broad array of approaches and methodologies. This series collects analytically innovative and empirically grounded work from scholars of comparative constitutionalism across academic disciplines. Books in the series include theoretically informed studies of single constitutional jurisdictions, comparative studies of constitutional law and institutions, and edited collections of original essays that respond to challenging theoretical and empirical questions in the field.

Books in the Series

Constitution-Making and Transnational Legal Order Edited by Tom Ginsburg, Terence C. Halliday, and Gregory Shaffer

Hybrid Constitutionalism Eric C. Ip

The Politico-Legal Dynamics of Judicial Review Thenuis Roux

The Invisible Constitution in Comparative Perspective Edited by Rosalind Dixon and Adrienne Stone

Constitutional Courts in Asia: A Comparative Perspective Edited by Albert H. Y. Chen and Andrew Harding

Judicial Review in Norway Anine Kierulf

Constituent Assemblies Edited by Jon Elster, Roberto Gargarella, Vatsal Naresh, and Bjorn Erik Rasch

The DNA of Constitutional Justice in Latin America: Politics, Governance, and Judicial Design Daniel M. Brinks and Abby Blass

The Adventures of the Constituent Power: Beyond Revolutions? Andrew Arato

Constitutions, Religion and Politics in Asia: Indonesia, Malaysia and Sri Lanka Dian A. H. Shah

Canada in the World: Comparative Perspectives on the Canadian Constitution Edited by Richard Albert and David R. Cameron

Courts and Democracies in Asia Po Jen Yap

Proportionality: New Frontiers, New Challenges Edited by Vicki C. Jackson and Mark Tushnet

Constituents before Assembly: Participation, Deliberation, and Representation in the Crafting of New Constitutions Todd A. Eisenstadt, A. Carl LeVan, and Tofigh Maboudi

Assessing Constitutional Performance Edited by Tom Ginsburg and Aziz Huq

Buddhism, Politics and the Limits of Law: The Pyrrhic Constitutionalism of Sri Lanka Benjamin Schonthal

A Qualified Hope

THE INDIAN SUPREME COURT AND PROGRESSIVE SOCIAL CHANGE

Edited by

GERALD N. ROSENBERG
University of Chicago

SUDHIR KRISHNASWAMY
Azim Premji University, Bangalore

SHISHIR BAIL
Columbia University

CAMBRIDGE
UNIVERSITY PRESS

CAMBRIDGE
UNIVERSITY PRESS

University Printing House, Cambridge CB2 8BS, United Kingdom

One Liberty Plaza, 20th Floor, New York, NY 10006, USA

477 Williamstown Road, Port Melbourne, VIC 3207, Australia

314-321, 3rd Floor, Plot 3, Splendor Forum, Jasola District Centre, New Delhi - 110025, India

103 Penang Road, #05-06/07, Visioncrest Commercial, Singapore 238467

Cambridge University Press is part of the University of Cambridge.

It furthers the University's mission by disseminating knowledge in the pursuit of
education, learning and research at the highest international levels of excellence.

www.cambridge.org
Information on this title: www.cambridge.org/9781108464802
DOI: 10.1017/9781108565530

First published 2019
First paperback edition 2022

A catalogue record for this publication is available from the British Library

Library of Congress Cataloging in Publication data
NAMES: Rosenberg, Gerald N., editor. | Krishnaswamy, Sudhir, editor. | Bail, Shishir, editor.
TITLE: A qualified hope : the Indian Supreme Court and progressive social change / edited by
    Gerald N. Rosenberg, University of Chicago; Sudhir Krishnaswamy, Azim Premji University, Bangalore;
    Shishir Bail, Azim Premji University, Bangalore.
DESCRIPTION: Cambridge, United Kingdom ; New York, NY, USA : Cambridge University Press, 2019. |
    Series: Comparative constitutional law and policy | "This book emanates from a pair of academic conferences
    organized in 2015 which examined the ability of the Indian Supreme Court to act as an effective agent
    of progressive social change. The first Conference was held at the Columbia University Law School,
    New York, on the 25th and 26th of September, 2015. The second Conference was held at the University
    of Chicago Center in New Delhi, India on the 11th and 12th of December, 2015."–ECIP Introduction. |
    Includes bibliographical references and index.
IDENTIFIERS: LCCN 2018061492 | ISBN 9781108474504 (hardback : alk. paper) |
    ISBN 9781108464802 (pbk. : alk. paper)
SUBJECTS: LCSH: India. Supreme Court–Congresses. | Political questions and judicial power–India–
    Congresses. | Social change–India–Congresses. | Law–Social aspects–India–Congresses. | Law–Economic
    aspects–India–Congresses.
CLASSIFICATION: LCC KNS3466.A67 .Q35 2019 | DDC 347.54/035–dc23
    LC record available at https://lccn.loc.gov/2018061492

ISBN 978-1-108-47450-4 Hardback
ISBN 978-1-108-46480-2 Paperback

Contents

Notes on Contributors

Shishir Bail is a PhD student in the Department of Anthropology at Columbia University. Between 2012 and 2017 he was a research associate at the School of Policy and Governance at Azim Premji University, prior to which he was law-clerk to Justice Anil R. Dave on the Supreme Court of India. He holds a B.A-L.L.B from the West Bengal National University of Juridical Sciences.

M. Mohsin Alam Bhat is an assistant professor of law and the executive director of the Centre for Public Interest Law, at Jindal Global Law School, O.P. Jindal Global University (India). He works on legal and empirical dimensions of equality and exclusion, law and religion, and minority rights. He received his doctoral degree from Yale Law School and was a Peter and Patricia Gruber Fellow in Global Justice (2016–2017). He has previously served as the law clerk to the former Chief Justice P. Sathasivam, Supreme Court of India.

Alyssa Brierley is the executive director of the Centre for Equality Rights in Accommodation and a doctoral candidate in the Department of Political Science at York University. Her dissertation investigates how Indian social activists have used litigation to influence food policy. Prior to her PhD, Brierley completed a Juris Doctor at Osgoode Hall Law School, an MA in political science at York University, and a BA in economics and political science at the University of Waterloo. She also served as a research and policy advisor to the UN Special Rapporteur on the Right to Food, as the director of policy to Ontario's Minister of Economic Development and Infrastructure, and as the health, social and justice policy advisor to the president of the Treasury Board of Ontario.

Aparna Chandra is an assistant professor of law and the research director of the Centre for Constitutional Law, Policy and Governance, National Law

University, Delhi. She works on constitutional law, human rights, gender and
the law, and judicial process reform. Chandra has previously worked as a tutor
in law at Yale Law School and has been on the faculty of the National Judicial
Academy, Bhopal, and the National Law School, Bangalore. She holds a BA
LL.B (Hons.) degree from National Law School Bangalore and LL.M and
JSD degrees from Yale Law School.

Poorvi Chitalkar is the manager of analysis at the Global Centre for
Pluralism (Ottawa, Canada) where she leads the Centre's research on the
sources of inclusion and exclusion in diverse societies and policy and normative responses to diversity. Her current research interests include diversity and
pluralism, public interest litigation, and the role of courts in advancing social
and economic rights. She holds an LL.B. from Symbiosis University (India)
and an LL.M. from the University of Toronto (Canada). She serves on the
editorial board of the *African Conflict and Peacebuilding Review*. Prior to the
Global Centre for Pluralism, she worked at the International Development
Research Centre, the Ombudsman of Ontario, and practiced Law at the
Bombay High Court, India.

Rishad Chowdhury is an advocate-on-record at the Supreme Court of
India, and a New Delhi-based partner with the Indian law firm VERUS. He
holds an undergraduate degree in law from the National University of Juridical Sciences, Kolkata and LL.M. and JSD degrees from the University of
Chicago Law School. His area of research interest is Indian and comparative
constitutional law.

Rosalind Dixon is a professor of law at the University of New South Wales,
Faculty of Law, and previously served as an assistant professor at the University
of Chicago Law School and has been a visiting professor at the University of
Chicago, Columbia Law School, Harvard Law School, and the National
University of Singapore. Her work focuses on comparative constitutional
law and constitutional design, constitutional democracy, theories of consti-
tutional dialogue and amendment, socioeconomic rights, and constitutional
law and gender, and has been published in leading journals in the USA,
Canada, the UK, and Australia. She was recently elected as copresident of the
International Society of Public Law.

Marc Galanter is Professor of Law Emeritus at the University of Wisconsin,
Madison. He was previously a Fulbright Scholar at the University of Delhi, a
Fellow of the American Institute of Indian Studies, and consultant on legal
services to the Ford Foundation in India. He has taught South Asian Law,
Law and Social Science, Legal Profession, Religion and the Law, Contracts,
Dispute Processing, and Negotiations. He has authored numerous books and

articles related to law, the legal profession, and the provision of legal services in India.

Varun Gauri is a senior economist in the Development Economics Vice Presidency of the World Bank. He coleads the Mind, Behavior, and Development Unit (eMBeD), which integrates behavioral science into the design of anti-poverty policies worldwide. He was the codirector of the *World Development Report 2015: Mind, Society, and Behavior* and serves on the editorial boards of the journals *Behavioral Public Policy* and *Health and Human Rights*. He has also been a member of the World Economic Forum Council on Behavior, the Advisory Board of Academics Stand Against Poverty, and the Board of the Behavioral Economics Action Research Centre at the University of Toronto. His research has appeared in journals spanning the fields of economics, philosophy, political science, and law, and has been covered in the *New York Times*, *The Economist*, the *Washington Post*, *Forbes*, *The Hindu*, and *Frontline*, among others. He has published three books: *Courting Social Justice*, *School Choice in Chile*, and *Bringing Law to Life*.

William H. J. Hubbard is a professor of law and Ronald H. Coase Teaching Scholar at the University of Chicago Law School. His scholarly work involves empirical studies of courts and economic analysis of civil procedure and litigation, and he serves as an Editor of the *Journal of Legal Studies*. He received his JD with high honors from the University of Chicago Law School in 2000, where he was executive editor of the *Law Review*. He then clerked for the Hon. Patrick E. Higginbotham of the US Court of Appeals for the Fifth Circuit, practiced law as a litigation associate at Mayer Brown LLP in Chicago, and completed a PhD in economics at the University of Chicago. Before joining the faculty in 2011, he was a Kauffman Legal Research Fellow and a lecturer in law at the Law School.

Sital Kalantry is a clinical Professor of law at Cornell Law School where she founded the International Human Rights Clinic and cofounded the Avon Global Center for Women & Justice. Her scholarly work focuses on using quantitative approaches to understand and promote the enforcement of international human rights law. She received a Fulbright-Nehru Senior Research Scholar grant to conduct research in India. Her works have been published in, among other places, the *Human Rights Quarterly*, the *National Law Journal*, and the *Stanford Journal of International Law*. Her book *Women's Human Rights and Migration: Sex-Selective Abortion Law and Politics in the United States and India* was published in 2017.

Sudhir Krishnaswamy is the director of the School of Policy and Governance at Azim Premji University. Previously he was the Dr. B. R. Ambedkar Visiting Professor of Indian Constitutional Law at Columbia Law School, and a professor of law at the West Bengal National University of Juridical Sciences, Kolkata, India, where he taught constitutional law and jurisprudence. He has engaged with the government at various levels, including the Prime Minister's Committee on Infrastructure and the Kasturirangan Committee on Bangalore's Governance. Krishnaswamy has published widely in various academic and non-academic journals and newspapers. His book *Democracy and Constitutionalism in India* was published in 2009. His research interests include constitutional law, administrative law, and intellectual property law, as well as reform of the legal system, legal profession, and legal education in India.

Robert Moog is Associate Professor Emeritus of Political Science at North Carolina State University, and ex-Chair of that department. His research, reflecting interests in both law and South Asia, includes the book *Whose Interests Are Supreme? Organizational Politics in the Civil Courts in India*, as well as numerous articles on India's courts and alternative dispute resolution fora. He also jointly edited the June 2012 issue of the *Election Law Journal*, which focused on the Indian electoral system. Additionally, he has published articles on judicial selection and trial rates in the USA. Professor Moog has received two Fulbright awards among other fellowships to conduct research in India and acted as a consultant on justice system reform projects in India, Nepal, and Afghanistan.

Arindam Nandi is a senior fellow at the Center for Disease Dynamics, Economics & Policy, Washington, DC. His research focuses on the long-term effects of early childhood interventions on cognitive, educational, and labor market outcomes in low- and middle-income countries. His past work has evaluated the economic benefits of various health interventions and policies in India, and the political economy of gender, particularly sex-selective abortions, in India and the USA. In the past, he has been the associate director of research of the Data Centre for Development at the University of Chicago and a visiting scholar at the Public Health Foundation of India. He received his PhD in economics from the University of California, Riverside.

Vasujith Ram is a graduate of the LL.M. program at Harvard Law School. He completed his B.A-L.L.B degree from the National University of Juridical Sciences in Kolkata, India.

Karthik Rao-Cavale is an assistant professor at Ahmedabad University and obtained his doctoral training from the Department of Urban Studies and Planning at the Massachusetts Institute of Technology (MIT). His theoretical interests lie in heterodox political economy and historical geography. He is currently working on a social history of regional road networks, regimes of circulation, and rural development in southern Tamil Nadu in the early twentieth century. His earlier work has been published in leading journals such as *Transportation Research Record* (2012) and *Landscape and Urban Planning* (2017). He has also edited an issue of *Projections: MIT Journal of Urban Planning* (June 2016), with articles exploring the intersection between law and urban planning.

Nick Robinson is a legal advisor at the International Center for Not-for-Profit Law (ICNL). Prior to joining ICNL, Robinson was a lecturer and fellow at Yale University and before that a post-doctoral research fellow at the Center on the Legal Profession at Harvard Law School. He spent seven years in South Asia, where he served as a clerk to the Chief Justice of the Indian Supreme Court, worked at Human Rights Law Network in New Delhi, taught at law schools in India and Pakistan, and was a senior fellow at the Center for Policy Research. His research has been published in a number of leading academic journals. His writing has focused on the judiciary, the legal profession, and public law in South Asia, as well as on occupational licensing and the legal profession in the USA. He holds a JD from Yale Law School and a BA from the University of Chicago.

Gerald N. Rosenberg teaches political science and law at the University of Chicago. He has taught at Yale University, Northwestern University School of Law where he served as the Jack N. Pritzker Distinguished Visiting Professor of Law, at the Law School of Xiamen University in China as a Fulbright Professor, and at the National Law School of India University in Bangalore. In the 1995–1996 academic year he was a visiting fellow in the law program of the Research School of Social Sciences at the Australian National University in Canberra, Australia. He holds a BA from Dartmouth College, an MA in politics and philosophy from Oxford University, a law degree from the University of Michigan, and a doctorate in political science from Yale University. His work focuses on the interaction between courts, social movements, and the society and culture in which they are embedded. His work has appeared in numerous law reviews and journals. He has contributed to multiple edited collections and is the author of *The Hollow Hope: Can Courts Bring About Social Change?* (1991, 2nd edition 2008, 3rd edition forthcoming, 2020) and a textbook on American government.

Shylashri Shankar is a senior fellow at the Centre for Policy Research in New Delhi. She is the author of *Scaling Justice: India's Supreme Court, Anti-Terror Laws and Social Rights* (2009), coauthor, with Raghav Gaiha, of *Battling Corruption: Has NREGA Reached India's Rural Poor?* (2013), both published by Oxford University Press, coeditor, with Mirjam Kunkler and John Madeley, of *A Secular Age beyond the West: Religion, Law and the State in Asia, the Middle East and North Africa* (Cambridge University Press 2018), and author of *A Moveable Indian Feast: A Food Biography* (Speaking Tiger,

2019). She has held academic positions at the University of Texas at Austin and the Center on Religion and Democracy, University of Virginia. She was a Bellagio Fellow, a co-convener of an international research cluster at ZiF, University of Bielefeld, and a co-coordinator of CORD, Collaboration of Research on Democracy, a research network.

Siddharth Swaminathan is a professor at Azim Premji University. He earned his MA and PhD in political science from the Claremont Graduate University. His research focuses on political demography, voter behavior, citizenship, and urban governance in India. Prior to joining Azim Premji University he held faculty positions at the Institute for Social and Economic Change, La Sierra University, and California State University.

Foreword

Cambridge University Press has made a considerable contribution to comparative jurisprudence by its series on comparative constitutional law and policy studies. It is a privilege to be associated with this painstaking work engaged with the wondrous, and often miraculous, itineraries of the Supreme Court of India. The judicial peregrinations have, overall, made impressive normative and socially progressive contributions. However, we do not know precisely what the impact may be of judicial governance, or of demosprudential adjudicatory leadership, across seven decades.

This work accentuates contributions that empirical and quantitative research may yet bring to global studies of Indian constitutionalism. The editors rightly maintain (in the Introduction) that a special focus on the American experience marks a new research pathway in binational constitutionalism spheres that enhances comparative constitutional analyses. They have brought home a wealth of empirical reasons why American judicial action does not bring about widespread social changes, despite lofty constitutional aims and aspirations.

The learned editors rightly maintain that "courts are constrained institutions" but that "there are three important reasons to suggest that the Indian Supreme Court might be less constrained and, therefore, more effective at bringing about progressive social change than its United States counterpart." The notion of a "less constrained" apex court fascinates; so does the sister notion of types of constraints. The Indian story is interesting because what were once perceived to be historical constraints are now regarded as normative opportunities for social action by the apex court. The Indian landscape presents three features: a "broad sweep of constitutional rights," "the procedural improvisations," and high degree of "formal independence of the Court." The diverse studies here assembled reinforce, in fine detail, these structural aspects of adjudicatory leadership of the nation.

But the editors also note three potential "roadblocks." The first is a syndrome that I have described in my *Courage, Craft, and Contention: The Indian Supreme Court in Mid-Eighties* as "independence-within-dependence" – the fact that the orders and directions of the Court depends on state agencies for enforcement. Second, the Indian justices do not merely lack the US-style life tenure but have a relatively short presence in the Supreme Court. Third, "there are tremendous variations in the history, culture, and capacity of the individual states that make up the national unit." The first and third factors are well-nigh universal but I suspect that these affect the constitutional unfolding in the USA as well. The striking differences in their playing out would, I think, advance more than a binational exploration,

Quantitative and empirical studies of judicial action for social change have great potential to expose the impact of judicial action, as this fine work demonstrates. There are broadly four outcomes: (1) no change in behaviors or values; (2) episodic behavioral changes; (3) structural changes in behavior; (4) sustained changes in behavior as well as values. Of course, what the agents intend as change matters, as do those people whose behaviors and values are sought to be transformed and their capacity to retard or resist change. This work studies these transformations (though under a range of different rubrics) and directs attention to contexts that provide many variables. It also archives the ways in which demosprudential adjudicatory leadership may consist of transforming constraints into opportunities for action. One hopes that a sister volume will eventually provide equally valued insights into the interfaces between activist adjudication and social movements.

Upendra Baxi
Emeritus Professor of Law
University of Warwick and Delhi

Acknowledgments

This book owes its genesis to a dinner conversation in a restaurant in Bangalore, India, in April 2014. Sudhir Krishnaswamy had invited Gerald Rosenberg to give a talk at Azim Premji University on whether the US Supreme Court can further the interests of the relatively disadvantaged. After the talk there was a dinner attended by the editors and some of Krishnaswamy's colleagues and students. The question arose as to whether Rosenberg's argument applied to the Indian Supreme Court. We were intrigued by the question. After further conversation we determined that there was no published collection of empirical studies of the ability of the Indian Supreme Court to help the relatively disadvantaged. This led to our organizing two conferences, one in the USA and one in India, to address the question. The result is this volume.

For their generous financial support we thank Azim Premji University, Bangalore, India; the University of Chicago Center in New Delhi, India; and the Center for Constitutional Governance and the Dr Ambedkar Chair in Indian Constitutional Law at Columbia University Law School. In particular, we thank Professor Gillian Metzger of Columbia Law School for her support, wisdom, and good humor. Furthermore, we are very grateful to the paper presenters at the two conferences. To a person they presented serious scholarly studies. We regret that we couldn't include more of them in this volume.

Professor Tom Ginsburg of the University of Chicago Law School provided continual support and counsel. He, along with John Berger of Cambridge University Press, demonstrated remarkable patience in seeing this project to completion. We are grateful for their understanding. We are also grateful to the thoughtful suggestions for revisions from the anonymous reviewer engaged by Cambridge University Press.

We thank the authors of the studies included in this volume for responding in thoughtful ways to our suggestions for revisions of their conference papers and chapter drafts.

Gerald Rosenberg thanks Sudhir Krishnaswamy for providing the speaking invitation and dinner that led to this volume. He especially thanks Shishir Bail for his deep and unfailing commitment to both the two conferences and this edited collection. Without Bail's tireless work there would be no book.

Shishir Bail thanks Azim Premji University and Sudhir Krishnaswamy for giving him a home for five years, as well as the opportunity to work on this book. He especially thanks Gerald Rosenberg for his optimism and dedication to seeing this project to completion.

Introduction

The Indian Supreme Court and Progressive Social Change

GERALD N. ROSENBERG, SUDHIR KRISHNASWAMY, AND SHISHIR BAIL

There is a widely held belief among Indian academics, political and civil society activists, and public-spirited citizens that the Indian Supreme Court is both capable and uniquely structured to help the relatively disadvantaged. The broad scope of rights granted by the Indian Constitution and the relative institutional independence of the Indian Supreme Court bolster this optimistic view of the Court.[1] This view also draws support from the perceived inability of the Indian political system to respond to chronic denials of human rights. Political infighting, corruption, inert bureaucracies, and an ossified yet resilient cultural system render the political system structurally incapable of decisive and progressive social change. In contrast, the Indian Supreme Court is free from these constraints.

The optimistic view of the Indian Supreme Court extends to debates in comparative constitutional law where the Court is increasingly seen as an exceptional agent of progressive social change and an authentic expression of "Global South" constitutionalism.[2] Sandra Fredman argues that the Indian Supreme Court, through its Public Interest Litigation (PIL) docket, has played a vital, if not entirely unproblematic, role in the expansion of the positive freedoms of Indian citizens.[3] Daniel Bonilla Maldonado, in a more recent

---

[1]   See, e.g., Vijayashri Sripati, *Human Rights in India – Fifty Years after Independence*, 26 DENV. J. INT'L L. & POL'Y 93 (1997); Upendra Baxi, *Taking Suffering Seriously: Social Action Litigation in the Supreme Court of India*, in JUDGES AND THE JUDICIAL POWER: ESSAYS IN HONOUR OF JUSTICE V.R. KRISHNA IYER (Rajeev Dhavan et al. eds. 289, NM Tripathi 1985); Nick Robinson, *Expanding Judiciaries: India and the Rise of the Good Governance Court*, 8 WASH. U. GLOBAL STUD. L. REV. 1 (2009).

[2]   CONSTITUTIONALISM OF THE GLOBAL SOUTH: THE ACTIVIST TRIBUNALS OF INDIA, SOUTH AFRICA AND COLOMBIA (Daniel Bonilla Maldonado ed. Cambridge University Press 2013).

[3]   "By recognizing the inherent inequalities in the adversarial court system, the Court has adapted its processes so that the voices of the poor and disadvantaged can be heard ... The result has been a transformation of the role of the Court in protecting and promoting the actual

contribution, argues that the Indian Supreme Court, along with the high courts in South Africa and Colombia, has "played an important role in the protection of the rule of law and the realization of individuals' constitutional rights." Further, he argues, its actions "present modern constitutionalism's basic components in a new light, or at least rearrange them in novel ways" and, therefore, "have something to contribute to the ongoing global conversation on constitutionalism."[4] Most recently, Mark Tushnet and Madhav Khosla have described the work of the Indian Supreme Court as an example of how countries can respond to the challenges of the "unstable constitutionalism" characteristic of South Asian jurisdictions. They posit that the Indian Supreme Court functions as an effective bridge between the normative commitments and empirical realities of South Asian society and politics.[5]

These views of the Indian Supreme Court as an effective agent of progressive social change, and as a bastion of constitutional values, are premised on the idea that decisions of the Indian Supreme Court actually improve the lives of the relatively disadvantaged. However, as Gerald Rosenberg demonstrated in the case of the United States,[6] there are reasons to be skeptical of this claim. To put it simply, if decisions of the Indian Supreme Court are unable to tangibly improve the lives of the relatively disadvantaged, then its most progressive pronouncements stand the risk of being hollow, as do its most delicate acts of constitutional mediation. There is, therefore, a need to empirically examine the effects of Supreme Court decisions on the lives of India's marginalized citizens. That is the aim of this volume.

Most work on the Indian Supreme Court is doctrinal with very few empirical studies.[7] Some of the earliest empirical investigations of the work of the Indian Supreme Court were undertaken by George Gadbois and Rajeev Dhavan. Both these early attempts, however, trained their empirical attention

---

enjoyment of human rights, particularly the right to life." SANDRA FREDMAN, HUMAN RIGHTS TRANSFORMED: POSITIVE RIGHTS AND POSITIVE DUTIES 124 (Oxford University Press 2009).

[4] Daniel Bonilla Maldonado, *Introduction: Toward a Constitutionalism of the Global South*, in Daniel Bonilla Maldonado ed. *supra* note 2 at 23.

[5] Mark Tushnet & Madhav Khosla, *Unstable Constitutionalism*, in UNSTABLE CONSTITUTIONALISM: LAW AND POLITICS IN SOUTH ASIA 5–11 (Mark Tushnet & Madhav Khosla eds. Cambridge University Press 2015); See also Pratap Bhanu Mehta, *The Indian Supreme Court and the Art of Democratic Positioning*, in id.

[6] GERALD N. ROSENBERG, THE HOLLOW HOPE. CAN COURTS BRING ABOUT SOCIAL CHANGE? (University of Chicago Press 1991; 2d ed., 2008; 3d edition forthcoming, 2020).

[7] This is the general problem described by Jayanth Krishnan in his article on perceptions of the Indian Supreme Court. See Jayanth Krishnan, *Scholarly Discourse and the Cementing of Norms: The Case of the Indian Supreme Court – and a Plea for Research*, 9 J. APP. PRAC. PROCESS (2007). The subject of perceptions of courts in India, and the Supreme Court specifically, is dealt with by Sudhir Krishnaswamy and Siddharth Swaminathan in this volume.

on the institutional character of the Supreme Court; neither broached the question of the impact of its decisions. Gadbois' work devoted substantial attention to the composition of judges in the Supreme Court, revealing them to be markedly socially homogeneous,[8] while Dhavan's early studies of the Supreme Court's docket revealed it to be creaking under the strain of pending cases ("arrears," as he describes them).[9]

The first call to look past doctrinal analyses of Indian Supreme Court decisions to their actual impact was made by Upendra Baxi in 1982.[10] In his provocatively titled article "Who Bothers about the Supreme Court," Baxi lamented the complete absence of attention to what happened to the decisions of the Court once they were made. His article presented two important analytic clarifications for the study of judicial impact in India. The first was the need to identify the different ways in which judicial decisions could affect behavior.[11] The second was the need to identify "Impact Constituencies" so that the effects of judicial decisions could be accurately measured.[12] Baxi's call for empirical investigation of the effects of Indian Supreme Court decisions could have inaugurated a wave of judicial impact studies. Unfortunately, such studies were not undertaken.

The timing of Baxi's early account is crucial because it arrived around the time that, post the Indian Emergency (1975–1977), the Indian Supreme Court sought to reclaim some legitimacy by instituting powerful procedural innovations through the device of "Public Interest Litigation" (PIL) (or as Baxi described it, Social Action Litigation).[13] In essence, PIL opens the courts to

---

[8] George Gadbois, *Indian Supreme Court Judges: A Portrait*, 3 L. & Soc'y Rev. Special Issue Devoted to Lawyers in Developing Societies with Particular Reference to India (1969).

[9] Rajeev Dhavan, The Supreme Court Under Strain: The Challenge of Arrears (NM Tripathi Pvt. Ltd 1978).

[10] Upendra Baxi, *Who Bothers about the Supreme Court? The Problem of Impact of Judicial Decisions*, 24 J. Indian L. Inst. (1982). Baxi's article was a follow-up to Stephen L. Wasby's work on the impact of US Supreme Court decisions. Stephen L. Wasby, *The Supreme Court's Impact: Some Problems of Conceptualization and Measurement*, 5 L. & Soc'y Rev. (1971).

[11] Baxi argued that as opposed to mere "compliance," which would simply mean whether or not a judicial decision was implemented by the persons or authorities whose job it was to do so, "impact" was a broader category. He further argued that a decision could have expected (or intended) impacts as well as unexpected (or unintended) impacts. Baxi argued that studies of judicial impact should enquire as to whether judicial decisions achieved their expected impact (or intended result) or not, and if not, to identify the reasons for this. See id. at 851.

[12] Baxi defined impact constituencies as follows: "human groups whose behavior is sought to be influenced in a definite manner by the court through its explicit decisions." Supra 10 at 852.

[13] This argument is most elaborately developed by Baxi in Upendra Baxi, The Indian Supreme Court and Politics (E. Book 1980). It also features in Upendra Baxi, *Taking Suffering Seriously: Social Action Litigation in the Supreme Court of India*, 4 Third World Legal

disadvantaged individuals and groups who have historically been unable to access them. The institution of Public Interest Litigation in India is responsible for some of the broadest expansions of the guarantees in the Indian Constitution and inaugurated an unprecedented wave of judicial activity on behalf of the relatively disadvantaged.[14] In turn, this wave of judicial activity was greeted by a veritable efflorescence of academic literature, both laudatory and critical.[15] Some scholars saw the rise of PIL as a clear sign of judicial overreach into the domains of the legislature and the executive.[16] Others were more optimistic, for instance assessing the Supreme Court's new role as filling a vital gap created by the governance failures of other state institutions.[17] What is undeniable, however, is that the judicial activity of the Indian Supreme Court, especially through the institution of PIL, has been, and continues to be, prominent. Yet very few of the contributions to this literature have taken

---

STUD. (1985), and Jamie Cassels, *Judicial Activism and Public Interest Litigation in India: Attempting the Impossible?* 37 AM. J. COMP. L. (1989).

[14] The use of the term "judicial activism" to describe the activity of the Indian Supreme Court has, unsurprisingly, been controversial. See Upendra Baxi, *The Avatars of Indian Judicial Activism: Explorations in the Geographies of [In]Justice*, in FIFTY YEARS OF THE SUPREME COURT OF INDIA: ITS GRASP AND REACH (S. K. Verma & Kusum Kumar eds. Oxford University Press 2000); S. P. SATHE, JUDICIAL ACTIVISM IN INDIA (1st ed. Oxford University Press 2002); SUDHIR KRISHNASWAMY, DEMOCRACY AND CONSTITUTIONALISM IN INDIA (1st ed. Oxford University Press 2009); Madhav Khosla, *Addressing Judicial Activism in the Indian Supreme Court: Towards an Evolved Debate*, 32 HASTINGS INT'L COMP. L. REV. (2009) for diverse accounts of the judicial "activism" of the Indian Supreme Court.

[15] Cf. P. P. Craig & S. L. Deshpande, *Rights, Autonomy and Process: Public Interest Litigation in India*, 9 OXFORD J. LEGAL STUD. (1989)(on the rise of PIL and its implication for the constitutional structure in Parts III and IV of the Indian Constitution); G. L. Peiris, *Public Interest Litigation in the Indian Subcontinent: Current Dimensions*, 40 INT'L COMP. L.Q. 66 (1991)(on the maturing of PIL in India to align with the separation of powers in India); Christine M. Forster & Vedna Jivan, *Public Interest Litigation and Human Rights Implementation: The Indian and Australian Experience*, 3 ASIAN J. COMP. L. 1 (2008)(on the importance of PIL for the implementation of human rights in India and Australia).

[16] Pratap Bhanu Mehta, *The Rise of Judicial Sovereignty*, 18 J. DEMOCRACY (2007)(on the appropriation by the Indian Supreme Court of many of the powers of both the legislature and the executive branches of government); Pratap Bhanu Mehta, *India's Judiciary: The Promise of Uncertainty*, in PUBLIC INSTITUTIONS IN INDIA: PERFORMANCE AND DESIGN (Pratap Bhanu Mehta & Devesh Kapur eds. Oxford University Press 2005). More recently, Anuj Bhuwania has delivered a sharp critique of PIL because of its tendency to remove all procedural safeguards and place overwhelming power in the hands and whims of individual judges. He describes this as a form of "panchayati justice." Bhuwania's critique is explicitly focused on PIL's impact on fidelity to legal process in Indian law and society, rather than its effect on substantive social outcomes. ANUJ BHUWANIA, COURTING THE PEOPLE: PUBLIC INTEREST LITIGATION IN POST-EMERGENCY INDIA (Cambridge University Press 2016).

[17] See Vijayashri Sripati *Supra* note 1; Jeremy Cooper, *Poverty and Constitutional Justice: The Indian Experience*, 44 MERCER L. REV. 611 (1993).

seriously Baxi's earlier call to study the impact rather than only the content, coherence, or constitutional validity of judicial decisions.[18] There remains an urgent need to understand whether decisions of the Indian Supreme Court, and its (in)famous judicial activism, tangibly improve the lives of the relatively disadvantaged. Exploring this question requires rigorous empirical study.

In the United States, Gerald N. Rosenberg's *The Hollow Hope* undertook an in-depth empirical study of the effects of several of the US Supreme Court's most famous decisions aimed at improving the lives of the relatively disadvantaged.[19] Based on careful empirical investigation, Rosenberg argued that in the absence of a small set of unusual enabling conditions, judicial decisions aimed at helping the relatively disadvantaged, by themselves, were unable to bring about the widespread change for which they are celebrated. In large part, Rosenberg argued, this is the result of three constraints that limit courts; the lack of fundamental rights embodied in the US Constitution; the general unwillingness of courts to order changes not supported by other governmental institutions or the people; and the lack of tools at the Court's disposal to implement its decisions.

Since its initial publication, *The Hollow Hope* has provoked a range of reactions.[20] However, its central insight, that courts are constrained institutions, has enduring appeal. Contemporary attempts to study judicial impact must at least address these insights, even if they find them less applicable to the court under study. In India, there are three important reasons to suggest that the Indian Supreme Court might be less constrained and, therefore, more effective at bringing about progressive social change than its US counterpart:

The broad sweep of constitutional rights in India: Unlike the limited, largely negative rights contained in the US Constitution, the Indian Constitution

---

[18] There have been attempts to assess the effects of Supreme Court decisions in particular subject areas, especially the environment. See, e.g., Armin Rosencranz & Michael Jackson, *The Delhi Pollution Case: The Supreme Court of India and the Limits of Judicial Power*, 28 COLUM. J. ENVTL. L. 223 (2003); Lavanya Rajamani, *Public Interest Environmental Litigation in India: Exploring Issues of Access, Participation, Equity, Effectiveness and Sustainability*, 19 J. OF ENVTL. L. 293 (2007). More recently, Gautam Bhan and Anuj Bhuwania have published two important studies on the impact of Supreme Court decisions on the city of Delhi, especially on slum demolition and the lives of slum dwellers. See GAUTAM BHAN, IN THE PUBLIC'S INTEREST: EVICTIONS, CITIZENSHIP AND INEQUALITY IN CONTEMPORARY DELHI (Orient Blackswan 2016); Anuj Bhuwania *supra* note 16. These attempts are focused on particular areas of court intervention and stop short of systematically exploring the question of whether Indian Supreme Court decisions impact the lives of the relatively disadvantaged, and if so under what conditions.

[19] Rosenberg, *supra* note 6.

[20] For a selected list of reviews, and Rosenberg's response to them, see http://press.uchicago.edu/books/rosenberg/index.html.

contains both positive as well as negative rights.[21] Part III of the Indian Constitution, dealing with Fundamental Rights, sets out a range of civil and political rights that protect citizens from oppressive state action.[22] These rights are judicially enforceable, and citizens can petition the higher judiciary to set aside any law or administrative action that violates them.[23] At the same time, Part IV of the Indian Constitution, dealing with Directive Principles, lays out a number of positive socioeconomic goals of state action.[24] These provisions have been described as setting forth "the humanitarian socialist precepts that were, and are, the aims of the Indian social revolution."[25] Crucially, these provisions are technically not judicially enforceable.[26] However, the Indian Supreme Court has, in several decisions,[27] held that the positive obligations contained in the Directive Principles supply the substantive content of various Fundamental Rights, and are, therefore, integral to the securing of the latter.[28] As a result, the fundamental rights of citizens under the Indian Constitution have been imbued with a much more expansive positive content. Thus, the Indian Constitution is arguably a weaker constraint on the Indian Supreme Court's ability to help the relatively disadvantaged than is the US Constitution on the US Supreme Court.

The procedural improvisations of the Indian Supreme Court: Unlike its US counterpart, the Indian Supreme Court has introduced a range of procedural

---

[21] It must be emphasized that the distinction drawn here between positive and negative rights is merely heuristic. There is a powerful line of scholarship which argues that this distinction is unhelpful, and masks the requirements for "positive" state action even to secure ostensibly "negative" rights. Cf. David P. Currie, *Positive and Negative Constitutional Rights*, 53 U. Chi. L. Rev. 864 (1986); Cass Sunstein, The Partial Constitution 69–71 (Harvard University Press 1993).

[22] See Indian Const. Arts. 12–35.

[23] See Indian Const. Art. 13. See also M. P. Jain, Indian Constitutional Law 834–836 (5th ed. reprint LexisNexis Butterworths Wadhwa 2009).

[24] See Indian Const. Arts. 36–51.

[25] Granville Austin, The Indian Constitution: Cornerstone of a Nation 75 (1st ed. 2d impression Oxford University Press 1974).

[26] Indian Const. Art. 37.

[27] Cf. *State of Kerala* v. *NM Thomas* (1976) 2 SCC 310; *Bandhua Mukti Morcha* v. *Union of India* (1984) 3 SCC 161; *Olga Tellis* v. *Bombay Municipal Corporation* (1985) 3 SCC 545.

[28] Craig and Deshpande make precisely this observation and argue that the Supreme Court has "construed the *substantive* rights which are protected by Part III as entailing certain minimum social and economic rights which flow from Part IV." See Craig and Deshpande *supra* note 15 at 365 (emphasis in original). Gautam Bhatia makes a similar point, *inter alia*, when he argues that the Directive Principles "play a structuring role in selecting the specific conceptions that are the concrete manifestations of the abstract conceptions embodied in the Fundamental Rights chapter." Gautam Bhatia, *Directive Principles of State Policy*, in The Oxford Handbook of the Indian Constitution 661 (Sujit Choudhry, Madhav Khosla, & Pratap Bhanu Mehta eds. Oxford University Press 2016).

changes that give it the potential to more effectively implement decisions furthering the rights of the relatively disadvantaged. First among these are the mechanisms of PIL itself. Emerging in the context of severe problems with access to justice,[29] PIL greatly reduces standing requirements to potentially allow diverse and traditionally excluded constituencies to approach the Supreme Court and the High Courts.[30] Sometimes, this access is facilitated simply through a letter mailed to the Court, through what is called its "epistolary jurisdiction."[31] Similarly, *suo motu* litigation enables the Indian Supreme Court to intervene on its own motion whenever it believes a violation of fundamental rights exists, even without being petitioned by an aggrieved claimant or party.[32] Another notable innovation is the *continuing mandamus* process that the Supreme Court has evolved. This device allows the Supreme Court to continually oversee the implementation of its orders rather than having to wait for parties to file new cases alleging non-compliance.[33] This means that *continuing mandamus* cases often remain open for years on end, while the Court oversees the progress made on implementing its decisions.[34] All these procedural innovations potentially give the Indian Supreme Court a greater ability to implement its decisions than the U.S. Supreme Court.

The formal independence of the Indian judiciary: Rosenberg's *constrained court* account of the US Supreme Court takes a qualified view of the Court's independence, because, as he writes: "Judges do not select themselves."[35] According to this view, the fact that appointments to the US Supreme Court are made by politicians means that judges are likely to be nominated for their

---

[29] See Marc Galanter & Jayanth Krishnan, *"Bread for the Poor": Access to Justice and the Rights of the Needy in India*, 55 HASTINGS L.J. 789, 795–797 (2004) for a discussion of Public Interest Litigation in the context of access to justice.

[30] For a rigorous examination of this question see Ashok H Desai & S Muralidhar, *Public Interest Litigation: Potential and Problems*, in SUPREME BUT NOT INFALLIBLE: ESSAYS IN HONOUR OF THE SUPREME COURT OF INDIA 162–165 (B. N. Kirpal et al. eds. Oxford University Press 2011).

[31] For some examples of cases initiated in this manner, see *Sunil Batra (II) v. Delhi Administration* (1980) 3 SCC 488, *Dr Upendra Baxi v. State of UP* (1983) 2 SCC 308, *Veena Sethi v. State of Bihar* (1982) 2 SCC 583.

[32] See Marc Galanter and Vasujith Ram, chapter 4, *infra*.

[33] The first notable instance of *continuing mandamus* was Vineet Narain's case (1998) 1 SCC 226, where the Court oversaw a criminal investigation into corruption and black money in the central government.

[34] *Continuing mandamus* was also used in one of the best-known environmental cases before the Supreme Court of India, *T.N. Godavarman v. Union of India* (1997) 3 SCC 312, which was filed in 1995 and is still pending before the Court. It has been heard by the Court 223 times to date. For a critical account of the Court's involvement in this case, see Armin Rosencranz & Sharachchandra Lele, *Supreme Court and India's Forests*, 43 ECON. POL. WKLY. 11 (2008).

[35] Rosenberg, *supra* note 6 at 13.

adherence to particular (partisan) "judicial philosophies."[36] This, therefore, reduces their chances of issuing opinions requiring change that is politically unpalatable. This is a powerful consideration. It is, therefore, noteworthy that the opposite is true in India: judges do indeed select themselves. This position emerges from three decisions of the Supreme Court itself.[37] These decisions were delivered after the Indian Emergency, when the Executive was widely seen to have paid little respect to judicial independence.[38] Under the current system, a collegium of judges, led by the Chief Justice along with the four most senior judges, recommends appointments to the Supreme Court. Similarly, High Court judges are appointed on the recommendation of the Chief Justice of India, the two most senior Supreme Court judges, and the Chief Justice of the High Court concerned. These recommendations are always followed, and in no circumstances can the judiciary be bypassed or overruled.[39] Thus, owing to its remarkable insulation from executive influence, the Indian higher judiciary might be uniquely placed to order emancipatory social change against the political mainstream.

It must be emphasized that this formal independence is not without problems. The first of these is that judges in the Indian higher judiciary are a remarkably homogeneous group, and generally emerge from the upper echelons of India's highly stratified caste and class structure.[40] It is unclear

---

[36] Id.

[37] *SP Gupta v. Union of India* (1981) Supp SCC 87; *Supreme Court Advocates-on-Record* *** *Association v. Union of India* (1993) 4 SCC 441; *Re Special Reference No 1 of 1998* (1998) 7 SCC 739.

[38] Nick Robinson, *Judicial Architecture and Capacity*, in The Oxford Handbook of the Indian Constitution 345 (Sujit Choudhry, Madhav Khosla, & Pratap Bhanu Mehta eds. Oxford University Press 2016).

[39] Id. at 346. In recent years, there have been attempts by the legislature and the executive to gain a measure of influence in the appointment of judges, through the creation of a National Judicial Appointments Commission (NJAC). The creation of this commission was, however, struck down by the Supreme Court as unconstitutional on October 16, 2015. The justices argued that the commission was detrimental to the independence of the judiciary, and hence violated the "basic structure" of the Indian Constitution. For two critical views, see Suhrith Parthasarthy, *Assessing the NJAC Judgment*, 3 J. Nat'l L. U. Delhi (2015–2016), and Rehan Abeyratne, *Upholding Judicial Supremacy in India: The NJAC Judgment in Comparative Perspective*, 49 George Wash. Int'l L. Rev.(2017). At the very least, this exchange demonstrates the Supreme Court's continuing ability and willingness to defend its own independence.

[40] George Gadbois' portrait of "the archetypal judge" is instructive on this point. See George H Gadbois, Jr, Judges of the Supreme Court of India: 1950–1989 at 376–377 (Oxford University Press 2011). Gadbois' account traces this history until 1989, and the collegium system was truly established only in 1993. A more recent empirical account is provided by Abhinav Chandrachud, who finds a similar lack of diversity continues to prevail among judges of the Indian Supreme Court. Abhinav Chandrachud, The Informal Constitution: Unwritten

how their elite backgrounds condition their inclination towards widespread progressive social change. The second constraint is that unlike in the United States, judges in the Indian Supreme Court and High Courts do not have life tenure. This means that there is increasingly a politics of post-retirement appointment on government tribunals and commissions.[41] There is also a general sense that judges sometimes become more sympathetic to government or corporate interests as they approach retirement.[42] That being said, the complete autonomy of the Indian higher judiciary in questions of appointment is an exceptional arrangement, and does point to the possibility of progressive action against the vested interests of the political mainstream. Overall, these features of the Indian Supreme Court suggest that it might be more able to bring about progressive social change than its US counterpart.

In addition, there are potentially powerful constraints on the Indian Supreme Court that are missing in the United States. The bulk of these draw on the Indian Supreme Court's inability, in keeping with judicial institutions the world over, to implement its own orders. It thus depends on the other institutions of the state, both at central and subnational levels, to see that its orders are implemented. This dependence is typically less apparent when courts stick to making declarations on negative rights: the more traditional common law position. However, when courts seek to intervene directly in positive social policy, as the Indian Supreme Court has done repeatedly, the ability (and willingness) of other state institutions to implement becomes a particularly pressing consideration. Here, there are a few potential roadblocks. First, the Indian Supreme Court has not always maintained a cordial relationship with the national government.[43] Indeed, it is often seen as competing with the executive and legislature for legitimacy, particularly through exercising PIL jurisdiction.[44] In these conditions, the inclination of state authorities to implement Supreme Court decisions is better seen as highly contingent in each case, rather than a more or less stable background assumption. Second, even in cases where they are inclined to act, the capacity of state authorities to implement broad and potentially expensive judicial remedies is likely limited by the resources at their disposal. The Indian state has many fewer resources

---

CRITERIA IN SELECTING JUDGES FOR THE SUPREME COURT OF INDIA (Oxford University Press 2014).

[41] Gadbois, at 370–375.

[42] Nick Robinson, *supra* note 38 at 346–347.

[43] See. UPENDRA BAXI *supra* note 13; Rajeev Dhavan, *Law as Struggle: Public Interest Law in India*, 36(3) J. INDIAN L. INST.303 (1994) for two illustrative accounts.

[44] See Pratap Bhanu Mehta *supra* note 5; Anuj Bhuwania *supra* note 16.

than, for instance, its US counterpart.[45] In this situation, it is probable that the state will in certain cases simply be *unable* to fully comply with the directions of the Court, to the extent that they prescribe expensive state action.[46] Third, there are tremendous variations in the history, culture, and capacity of the individual states that make up the national unit. This has been clearly demonstrated by, among others, scholars of development who have studied the greatly varying outcomes achieved by the Indian states.[47] Since a large part of the implementation of Indian Supreme Court orders depends on the actions of individual state governments, these governments can either be a help or a hindrance to the prospects of progressive Supreme Court orders. Lastly, Supreme Court orders are articulated in the context of deep-seated cultural practices, beliefs, and cleavages in Indian society. At one level, these may form powerful barriers to the implementation of Supreme Court orders.[48] At another level, ostensibly neutral Supreme Court orders may have the unintended effects of emboldening reactionary social and political groups when placed in their social context.[49]

---

[45] The difference between the per capita gross domestic product (GDP) of India and the United States is dramatic: in 2015 India's per capita GDP (purchasing power parity) was $6,161, while the equivalent figure for the United States was $55,805. INT'L MONETARY FUND, WORLD ECONOMIC OUTLOOK DATABASE (Int'l Monetary Fund 2016), goo.gl/2mZcYf (last visited May 5, 2017). Per capita GDP is widely seen as a useful measure of bureaucratic and administrative capacity. In his study measuring state capacity in the context of civil conflict, Cullen Hendrix writes: "GDP per capita is highly correlated with a variety of measures of bureaucratic/administrative capacity and may be plausibly considered both a cause and effect of bureaucratic quality and strong state institutions." Cullen S Hendrix, *Measuring State Capacity: Theoretical and Empirical Implications for the Study of Civil Conflict*, 47 J. PEACE RES. 273, 277 (2010).

[46] The links between state capacity and the implementation of judicial decisions, though merely suggested here, are more fully explored in Vinay Sitapati's unpublished dissertation. Vinay Sitapati, After Judgment Day: Under What Conditions Are Court Decisions Implemented? PhD Dissertation, Princeton University, 2016.

[47] Cf. ASEEMA SINHA, THE REGIONAL ROOTS OF DEVELOPMENTAL POLITICS IN INDIA: A DIVIDED LEVIATHAN (Indiana University Press 2005); Pradeep Chhibber & Irfan Nooruddin, *Do Party Systems Count? the Number of Parties and Government Performance in the Indian States*, [37 (2)] COMP. POL. STUD. 152 (2004); Suraj Jacob, *Towards a Comparative Subnational Perspective on India*, 3 STUD. INDIAN POL. 229 (2015).

[48] A 2018 example is the pushback against a Supreme Court order permitting women to enter a temple that was earlier only open to males. When women sought to enter the temple pursuant to the Supreme Court order, they were chased away by angry mobs, which themselves contained many women. Suhasini Raj & Kai Schultz, *Religion and Women's Rights Clash, Violently, at a Shrine in India*, N.Y. TIMES, Oct. 18, 2018 at, https://nyti.ms/2CwwJYR (last visited Oct. 20, 2018).

[49] Cf. Flavia Agnes on the discursive and political effects of Indian Supreme Court orders on Uniform Civil Code in FLAVIA AGNES, LAW AND GENDER INEQUALITY: THE POLITICS OF

A powerful example of both the capacity of the Indian Supreme Court to help the relatively disadvantaged and the obstacles to its effectively doing so is gay rights. On September 6, 2018, a five-judge bench of the Indian Supreme overturned a nineteenth-century British law criminalizing same-sex sexual relations.[50] This is clearly an example of the Court interpreting the Indian Constitution to further the rights of the relatively disadvantaged, in this case gays and lesbians. Although prosecutions under the law were "relatively rare," in 2016 there were 2,187 complaints filed and over 1,600 cases sent for trial. In the words of Meenakshi Ganguly, the South Asia director for Human Rights Watch, "This ruling is hugely significant."[51] Yet at the same time that gays and lesbians are now free from the fear of criminal prosecution, they still face powerful social and cultural barriers to leading normal lives. As Geeta Pandey notes, "it will still be a while before attitudes change and the community finds full acceptance."[52]

The analysis above provides a mixed account of the potential of Indian Supreme Court decisions to bring about progressive social change. If the broad scope of Indian constitutional rights, the procedural innovations of the Indian Supreme Court, and its strong independence from the government provide cause for optimism, the generally low and unevenly distributed state capacity in India and the strength of traditional cultural values provide reasons for pause. What is clear is that an account of the Indian Supreme Court's ability to bring about social change is likely to look substantially different from Rosenberg's account of the US Supreme Court. This is the account that this volume seeks to provide.

ORGANIZATION OF THE BOOK

This book is the first attempt to collect and organize empirical studies of whether Indian Supreme Court decisions actually improve the lives of the relatively disadvantaged, and if so under what conditions. The first section of this introduction described the analytic context in which the actions of the

WOMEN'S RIGHTS IN INDIA 112–121 (Oxford University Press 2001), and Shylashri Shankar on judgments relating to religious conversion, in this volume.

[50] *Navtej Singh Johar & Ors. v. Union of India*, Writ Petition (Criminal) No. 76 of 2016, decision at www.sci.gov.in/supremecourt/2016/14961/14961_2016_Judgement_06-Sep-2018.pdf, (last visited Oct. 24, 2018)

[51] Jeffrey Gettleman, Kai Schultz, & Suhasini Raj, *India Gay Sex Ban Is Struck Down. "Indefensible," Court Says*. N.Y. TIMES, Sept. 6, 2018. https://nyti.ms/2CnBJQR.

[52] Geeta Pandey, "Recognising everyone's right to love," BBC News, Delhi, India, Sept. 6, 2018. www.bbc.com/news/world-asia-india-45429664.

Indian Supreme Court may be understood. This section describes the approaches that the chapters in this book take to answering its central question. All the chapters described here are united by a desire to empirically examine the effects of Supreme Court decisions. However, the particular empirical strategies they adopt are diverse. While some chapters take recourse to extensive and original quantitative data sets, others discuss the results of long-term qualitative and ethnographic research. Each of these chapters throws light on a different facet of the Supreme Court's functioning, and we discuss them individually below.

The book is organized into four parts. The chapters in Part I present background information about the institutional character of the Indian Supreme Court. In Chapter 1 Nick Robinson sets out its basic structure and operation. Chapter 2 by Aparna Chandra, William Hubbard, and Sital Kalantry presents the results of a pioneering new data set analyzing more than 5,000 decisions of the Indian Supreme Court from 2010 to 2015. This throws light on a range of previously ignored questions such as who approaches the Indian Supreme Court, why, and to what end. The data set allows a move away from the relatively infrequent "high-profile" cases, to the study of the mass of cases that occupy the Court on a day-to-day basis. In uncovering the kinds of cases and parties that come before the Supreme Court, and how the Court is structured to deal with them, these two chapters provide an initial picture of whether the Court's docket is indeed one that allows for the possibility of considered, progressive social action, or is instead one that is too mired in everyday disputes to contemplate broader interventions.

Chapters 3 and 4 examine two of the most eye-catching procedural reforms implemented by the Indian Supreme Court: PIL and *suo-motu* hearing of cases. In Chapter 3, Chitalkar and Gauri focus on PIL, by far the most salient example of the Indian Supreme Court's judicial activism. PIL deserves close scrutiny in order to see if the Court's interventions have indeed brought about progressive social change. Chitalkar and Gauri examine the kinds of parties and cases that the Court usually patronizes through this mode of extraordinary jurisdiction. Their results suggest that rather than an avenue for the socially disadvantaged, the PIL jurisdiction of the Indian Supreme Court has slowly morphed into a forum for the mobilization of elite and otherwise vested interests, thereby casting doubt on its acting as an agent for progressive social change.

In Chapter 4, Galanter and Ram examine the practice of *suo moto* jurisdiction by which the Indian Supreme Court and State High Courts initiate and hear cases on their own accord without any prior litigation being filed by claimants or parties. *Suo moto* jurisdiction is a well-known but poorly understood procedural innovation by the Indian judiciary. This chapter provides some much-needed analytic texture to understanding precisely what this innovation entails. This inquiry is accompanied by a detailed illustrative account of one *suo moto* case, and the manner of the Supreme Court's intervention therein. Galanter and Ram's chapter raises important questions relating to the symbolic impact of procedures such as *suo moto*, and, by extension, PIL itself. They argue that these interventions prioritize spectacular, immediate, and palpable interventions by India's highest judicial institutions, but sometimes have the effect of belittling the operation of the lower level executive and judicial institutions charged with everyday administration of the law, impeding long-lasting change.

Chapter 5, the final chapter in Part I, focuses on how the Court, and other judicial institutions in India, are perceived by members of the Indian public. An important part of understanding the Court's ability to bring about social change is understanding the degree of institutional trust placed in it by citizens. Thus, Krishnaswamy and Swaminathan ask how much Indians trust the Indian Supreme Court and other judicial institutions in the country. The answers they provide suggest that the Indian Supreme Court has been at least modestly successful in convincing the Indian citizenry of its potential for positive action.

The chapters in Part II focus on how disadvantaged groups have used litigation to protect their livelihoods from governmental action, extend the reach of governmental benefits, and, crucially, to mobilize social movements to further their aims. Chapter 6 by Karthik Rao-Cavale examines the nature of judicial action to protect the rights of street vendors, a ubiquitous part of Indian social life. Through a careful historical study of street vendor politics in two major Indian cities, Rao-Cavale places street vendors' resort to courts in the context of complex long-term negotiations with the state for legal status and the right to practice their trade. Perhaps most interestingly, Rao-Cavale demonstrates that rather than substantive judicial victories, street vendor groups have most benefited from litigation when they have been able to exploit the procedural lacunae endemic to the Indian legal system, enabling them, as he puts it, to "buy time."

Chapter 7 by Mohsin Alam Bhat examines how the language of Supreme Court decisions can be used by disadvantaged groups as a tool for political mobilization and negotiation. He demonstrates that legal discourse can improve these groups' chances of success when engaging with state authorities to secure benefits. Specifically, Bhat studies the case of *Dalit* (formerly "untouchable") Muslim mobilization subsequent to a landmark Supreme Court decision on backward classes in India (the *Indra Sawhney* case). Bhat argues that the Indian Supreme Court's discussion and treatment of caste in this case brought new forms of awareness and visibility to the plight of *Dalit* Muslims. This enabled them to generate political support, negotiate with state authorities, and eventually mount a constitutional challenge of their own. Bhat argues that the intervention of the Supreme Court led the *Dalit* Muslim movement to adopt styles of mobilization that strengthened its chances of emancipatory social, political, and, finally, judicial action.

Chapter 8 by Alyssa Brierley provides another telling instance of a Supreme Court decision providing the impetus for large-scale social mobilization to improve the lives of the relatively disadvantaged. Brierley studies the *PUCL* case, also known as the Right to Food case, which was a response to starvation deaths across the country. This case, which has been litigated for over 15 years and is still ongoing, was responsible for the initiation and growth of the "Right to Food movement," a broad-based coalition of state and civil society actors across the country working to secure the right to food for all Indian citizens. By comparing this case to an earlier case dealing with similar questions, and conducting in-depth interviews with activists, Brierley draws out the peculiar conditions and contextual features that allowed this case to have wide impact, while the earlier case only achieved modest results.

The chapters in Part III of the book are united in a focus on measuring the *direct* impact of Supreme Court decisions. The first example of this is Chapter 9 by Rosalind Dixon and Rishad Chowdhury, which looks at the same case as Brierley in Part II. However, the focus of their analysis is distinct. While Brierley maps out the discursive and mobilizing effects of the Supreme Court decision through interviews with actors in the "Right to Food movement," Dixon and Chowdhury are more squarely concerned with whether or not the Court decision improved nutritional outcomes. After a careful study of nutritional outcomes which finds improvement, Dixon and Chowdhury focus on whether the Court's "Right to Food" decisions contributed to these changes. While acknowledging the challenges of identifying causal influence, Dixon and Chowdhury find that the Court decisions indeed did play a role in the improvement of nutritional outcomes.

Chapter 10 by Robert Moog turns to one of the most notable decisions of the Indian Supreme Court, the *Delhi Pollution Case*. In this case, the Court took the unprecedented action of ordering all petrol and diesel-powered public transport vehicles in the sprawling city of Delhi to be shifted to Compressed Natural Gas (CNG) fuel overnight. This case has been variously read as an example of concerted judicial action to overcome a recalcitrant executive and as an egregious example of judicial overreach. Moog, however, leaves these constitutional questions to one side, and instead points out that in this particular instance the Supreme Court was surprisingly successful in having its orders implemented: all public transport vehicles in Delhi were indeed converted to CNG. He, therefore, shifts the analysis to the factors that enabled this kind of impact, and outlines two main sets of factors: the first dealing with the impact of monitoring agencies, and the second dealing with a range of contextual peculiarities such as the specificity of court orders, the credibility of the court, publicity, etc.

In Part IV, the focus turns to the Indian Supreme Court's approach to cases involving discrimination on the grounds of caste and gender, and the impact of these interventions. Chapter 11 by Shylashri Shankar uses the example of Supreme Court judgments on religious conversions to make two broad and powerful arguments. The first is that Indian Supreme Court interventions are limited, or mediated, by existing contradictions in India's constitutional structure. This is evident in the case of *Dalit* and Scheduled Tribe converts to religions such as Christianity or Islam. The Supreme Court has repeatedly declared Scheduled Caste Hindus or Scheduled Tribe members ineligible for the benefits of affirmative action ("reservations") as soon as they convert to another religion, such as Christianity or Islam. Therefore, exercising their rights to religious expression and dignity causes these individuals to become materially worse off, through their exclusion from affirmative action. Shankar's second argument demonstrates how the effects of Supreme Court decisions are mediated by political actors and mobilization, and, as a result, can often have unintended consequences. She studies how Supreme Court judgments on religious conversion have been mobilized by members of the Hindu nationalist Right to advance their exclusionary political agenda, ostensibly with the imprimatur of India's highest judicial institution.

Chapter 12 by Sital Kalantry and Arindam Nandi explores the impact of Supreme Court interventions on the practice of sex-selective abortion in India. In this case, the Supreme Court was petitioned simply to order the implementation of already existing national legislation, which had until then remained un-implemented. The question in this case was whether the Supreme Court could do a better job at securing implementation than the legislature and executive. Kalantry and Nandi point out that while the Supreme Court was successful in generating more attention and dialogue for the issue of sex-selective abortion, it was unable to change behavior. Examining data on male–female population ratios and their change over time, they argue that Indian Supreme Court decisions stand less of a chance of being implemented when they deal with deeply held personal beliefs and familial preferences, such as son preference in the Indian context.

In the conclusion the editors reflect on what we've learned about the Indian Supreme Court's ability to further the interests of the relatively disadvantaged.

The conclusion explores how the findings both confirm and challenge the existing literature on the role of courts in furthering the interests of the relatively disadvantaged.

BACKGROUND TO THE BOOK

This book emanates from a pair of academic conferences organized in 2015 which examined the ability of the Indian Supreme Court to act as an effective agent of progressive social change. The first conference was held at the Columbia University Law School, New York, on September 25 and 26, 2015. The second conference was held at the University of Chicago Center in New Delhi, India on December 11 and 12, 2015. The conference in New York was funded jointly by the Center for Constitutional Governance and the Dr. Ambedkar Chair in Indian Constitutional Law at Columbia University Law School. The conference in New Delhi was jointly funded by the University of Chicago Center in New Delhi and Azim Premji University in Bangalore, India.

These conferences brought together scholars from both North America and India engaged in cutting-edge empirical research on the impact of judgments of the Indian Supreme Court on the lives of marginalized citizens. Each scholar was invited to present an empirical paper on an Indian Supreme Court case in his or her area of expertise. In addition, a small number of participants at the conference held in New Delhi were invited on the basis of a highly competitive call for papers across India: a total of 147 papers were submitted, seven of which were selected for presentation at the conference.

The chapters that follow present a fascinating examination of the Indian Supreme Court and its role in helping the relatively disadvantaged. By exploring the conditions under which Indian courts are more or less able to further the interests of the relatively disadvantaged, the chapters in this volume speak directly to arguments raised by Rosenberg, Michael McCann,[53] Siri Gloppen,[54] and others. As far as we know, this volume presents the first empirically based collection of studies of the Indian Supreme Court and social change. The chapters that follow shed new light on the Indian Supreme Court, Indian government and politics, and social, cultural and economic inequality in India.

---

[53] MICHAEL M. MCCANN, RIGHTS AT WORK: PAY EQUITY REFORM AND THE POLITICS OF LEGAL MOBILIZATION (University of Chicago Press, 1994).

[54] ALICIA ELY YAMIN & SIRI GLOPPEN (eds.), LITIGATING HEALTH RIGHTS: CAN COURTS BRING MORE JUSTICE TO HEALTH? (Harvard University Press, 2011).

REFERENCES

Abeyratne, Rehan, *Upholding Judicial Supremacy in India: The NJAC Judgment in Comparative Perspective,* 49 GEORGE WASH. INT'L L. REV. (2017).

AGNES, FLAVIA, LAW AND GENDER INEQUALITY: THE POLITICS OF WOMEN'S RIGHTS IN INDIA (Oxford University Press 2001).

AUSTIN, GRANVILLE, THE INDIAN CONSTITUTION: CORNERSTONE OF A NATION (1st ed. 2d impression, Oxford University Press 1974).

Baxi, Upendra, *Taking Suffering Seriously: Social Action Litigation in the Supreme Court of India.* In JUDGES AND THE JUDICIAL POWER: ESSAYS IN HONOUR OF JUSTICE V.R. KRISHNA IYER. Rajeev Dhavan et al. eds. (NM Tripathi 1985) 289.

Taking Suffering Seriously: Social Action Litigation in the Supreme Court of India, 4 THIRD WORLD LEGAL STUD. (1985).

The Avatars of Indian Judicial Activism: Explorations in the Geographies of [In]-Justice. In FIFTY YEARS OF THE SUPREME COURT OF INDIA: ITS GRASP AND REACH (S. K. Verma & Kusum Kumar eds. Oxford University Press 2000).

BAXI, UPENDRA, THE INDIAN SUPREME COURT AND POLITICS (Eastern Book Co. 1980).

Who Bothers about the Supreme Court? The Problem of Impact of Judicial Decisions, 24 J. INDIAN L. INST. (1982).

BHAN, GAUTAM, IN THE PUBLIC'S INTEREST: EVICTIONS, CITIZENSHIP AND INEQUALITY IN CONTEMPORARY DELHI (Orient Blackswan 2016).

Bhatia, Gautam, *Directive Principles of State Policy.* In THE OXFORD HANDBOOK OF THE INDIAN CONSTITUTION 661 (Sujit Choudhry, Madhav Khosla, & Pratap Bhanu Mehta eds. Oxford University Press 2016).

BHUWANIA, ANUJ, COURTING THE PEOPLE: PUBLIC INTEREST LITIGATION IN POST-EMERGENCY INDIA (Cambridge University Press 2016).

Bonilla-Maldonado, Daniel (ed.), CONSTITUTIONALISM OF THE GLOBAL SOUTH: THE ACTIVIST TRIBUNALS OF INDIA, SOUTH AFRICA AND COLOMBIA (Cambridge University Press 2013).

Cassels, Jamie, *Judicial Activism and Public Interest Litigation in India: Attempting the Impossible?* 37 AM. J. COMP. LAW. (1989).

Chandrachud, Abhinav, THE INFORMAL CONSTITUTION: UNWRITTEN CRITERIA IN SELECTING JUDGES FOR THE SUPREME COURT OF INDIA (Oxford University Press 2014).

Chhibber, Pradeep and Irfan Nooruddin, *Do Party Systems Count? the Number of Parties and Government Performance in the Indian States,* 37 (2) COMP. POL. STUD. 152 (2004).

Cooper, Jeremy, *Poverty and Constitutional Justice: The Indian Experience,* 44 MERCER L. REV. 611 (1993).

Craig, P. P. and S. L. Deshpande, *Rights, Autonomy and Process: Public Interest Litigation in India,* 9 OXFORD J. LEGAL STUD. (1989).

Currie, David P., *Positive and Negative Constitutional Rights,* 53 U. CHI. L. REV. 864 (1986).

Desai, Ashok H. and S. Muralidhar, *Public Interest Litigation: Potential and Problems.* In SUPREME BUT NOT INFALLIBLE: ESSAYS IN HONOUR OF THE SUPREME COURT OF INDIA (B. N. Kirpal et al. eds. Oxford University Press 2011).

Dhavan, Rajeev, The Supreme Court Under Strain: The Challenge of Arrears (NM Tripathi Pvt. Ltd 1978).

Dhavan Rajeev, *Law as Struggle: Public Interest Law in India,* [36(3)] J. Indian L. Inst. 303 (1994).

Forster, Christine M. and Vedna Jivan, *Public Interest Litigation and Human Rights Implementation: The Indian and Australian Experience,* 3 Asian J. Comp. L. 1 (2008).

Fredman, Sandra, Human Rights Transformed: Positive Rights and Positive Duties (Oxford University Press 2009).

Gadbois, George H, Jr, Judges of the Supreme Court of India: 1950–1989 (Oxford University Press 2011).

Gadbois George, *Indian Supreme Court Judges: A Portrait,* 3 L. & Soc'y Rev. Special Issue Devoted to Lawyers in Developing Societies with Particular Reference to India (1969).

Galanter, Marc and Jayanth Krishnan, *"Bread for the Poor": Access to Justice and the Rights of the Needy in India,* 55 Hastings L.J. 789, 795–97 (2004).

Gettleman, Jeffrey, Kai Schultz, and Suhasini Raj, *India Gay Sex Ban Is Struck Down. "Indefensible," Court Says.* N.Y. Times Sept. 6, 2018, https://nyti.ms/2CnBJQR.

Hendrix, Cullen S., *Measuring State Capacity: Theoretical and Empirical Implications for the Study of Civil Conflict,* 47 J. Peace Res. 273 (2010).

Jacob, Suraj, *Towards a Comparative Subnational Perspective on India,* 3 Stud. Indian Pol. 229 (2015).

Jain, M. P., Indian Constitutional Law (5th ed. reprint LexisNexis Butterworths Wadhwa 2009).

Khosla, Madhav, *Addressing Judicial Activism in the Indian Supreme Court: Towards an Evolved Debate,* 32 Hastings Int'l Comp. L. Rev. (2009).

Krishnan, Jayanth, *Scholarly Discourse and the Cementing of Norms: The Case of the Indian Supreme Court – and a Plea for Research,* 9 J. App. Prac. Process (2007).

Krishnaswamy, Sudhir, Democracy and Constitutionalism in India (1st ed. Oxford University Press 2009).

McCann, Michael M., Rights at Work: Pay Equity Reform and the Politics of Legal Mobilization (University of Chicago Press 1994).

Mehta, Pratap Bhanu, *India's Judiciary: The Promise of Uncertainty.* In Public Institutions in India: Performance and Design (Pratap Bhanu Mehta & Devesh Kapur eds. Oxford University Press 2005).

The Indian Supreme Court and the Art of Democratic Positioning. In Unstable Constitutionalism: Law and Politics in South Asia (Mark Tushnet and Madhav Khosla eds. Cambridge University Press 2015).

The Rise of Judicial Sovereignty, 18 J. Democracy (2007).

Pandey, Geeta, *"Recognising everyone's right to love,"* BBC News, Delhi, India, Sept. 6, 2018. www.bbc.com/news/world-asia-india-45429664.

Parthasarthy, Suhrith, *Assessing the NJAC Judgment,* 3 J. Nat'l L. U. Delhi (2015–2016).

Peiris, G. L., *Public Interest Litigation in the Indian Subcontinent: Current Dimensions,* 40 Int'l Comp. L.Q. 66 (1991).

Raj, Suhasini and Kai Schultz, *Religion and Women's Rights Clash, Violently, at a Shrine in India,* N.Y. Times, Oct. 18, 2018. https://nyti.ms/2CwwJYR (last visited Oct. 20, 2018).

Rajamani, Lavanya, *Public Interest Environmental Litigation in India: Exploring Issues of Access, Participation, Equity, Effectiveness and Sustainability*, 19 J. ENVTL. L. 293 (2007).

Robinson, Nick, *Expanding Judiciaries: India and the Rise of the Good Governance Court*, 8 WASH. U. GLOBAL STUD. L. REV. 1 (2009).

Judicial Architecture and Capacity. In THE OXFORD HANDBOOK OF THE INDIAN CONSTITUTION 345 (Sujit Choudhry, Madhav Khosla & Pratap Bhanu Mehta eds. Oxford University Press 2016).

ROSENBERG, GERALD N., THE HOLLOW HOPE. CAN COURTS BRING ABOUT SOCIAL CHANGE? (University of Chicago Press 1991; 2nd ed. 2008; 3rd edition forthcoming 2020).

Rosencranz, Armin and Michael Jackson, *The Delhi Pollution Case: The Supreme Court of India and the Limits of Judicial Power*, 28 COLUM. J. ENVTL. L. 223 (2003).

SATHE, S. P., JUDICIAL ACTIVISM IN INDIA (1st ed. Oxford University Press 2002).

SINHA, ASEEMA, THE REGIONAL ROOTS OF DEVELOPMENTAL POLITICS IN INDIA: A DIVIDED LEVIATHAN (Indiana University Press 2005).

Sitapati, Vinay, After Judgment Day: Under What Conditions Are Court Decisions Implemented? PhD Dissertation, Princeton University, 2016.

Sripati, Vijayashri, *Human Rights in India – Fifty Years after Independence*, 26 DENV. J. INT'L L. POL'Y 93 (1997).

SUNSTEIN, CASS, THE PARTIAL CONSTITUTION (Harvard University Press 1993).

Tushnet, Mark and Madhav Khosla, *Unstable Constitutionalism.* In UNSTABLE CON-STITUTIONALISM: LAW AND POLITICS IN SOUTH ASIA (Mark Tushnet and Madhav Khosla eds. Cambridge University Press 2015).

Wasby, Stephen L., *The Supreme Court's Impact: Some Problems of Conceptualization and Measurement*, 5 L. & SOC'Y REV. (1971).

Yamin Alicia Ely and Siri Gloppen (eds.), LITIGATING HEALTH RIGHTS: CAN COURTS BRING MORE JUSTICE TO HEALTH? (Harvard University Press 2011).

CASES

Bandhua Mukti Morcha v. *Union of India* (1984) 3 SCC 161.
Dr Upendra Baxi v. *State of UP* (1983) 2 SCC 308.
Navtej Singh Johar & Ors. v. *Union of India*, Writ Petition (Criminal) No. 76 of 2016.
Olga Tellis v. *Bombay Municipal Corporation* (1985) 3 SCC 545.
Re Special Reference No 1 of 1998 (1998) 7 SCC 739.
SP Gupta v. *Union of India* (1981) Supp SCC 87.
State of Kerala v. *NM Thomas* (1976) 2 SCC 310.
Sunil Batra (II) v. *Delhi Administration* (1980) 3 SCC 488.
Supreme Court Advocates-on-Record Association v. *Union of India* (1993) 4 SCC 441.
T.N. Godavarman v. *Union of India* (1997) 3 SCC 312.
Veena Sethi v. *State of Bihar* (1982) 2 SCC 583.
Vineet Narain & Ors. v. *Union of India and Anr.* (1998) 1 SCC 226.

PART I

The Supreme Court of India –
An Institutional Overview

The Structure and Functioning of the Supreme Court of India

NICK ROBINSON

The Indian Supreme Court is crowded. The parapeted open-air hallways that ring the side of its building buzz with lawyers talking business and small talk while waiting for their cases.[*] Exasperated litigants rush to find their hearings amongst the building's 15 courtrooms, while lawyers' clerks jostle to their seats carrying armfuls of disheveled briefs.

The Court, which can have up to 31 judges, sits in panels and will hear tens of thousands of cases each year. Admission day, held on Monday and Friday, is known by court insiders as the "fish market" for its fast-moving and frequently raucous exchanges. On these days, benches of two judges listen to dozens of admission matters from a deep line of black-jacketed lawyers, each arguing why their case should be accepted for regular hearing. Leaning down from their bench a judge will question advocates skeptically, frequently cutting them off abruptly, while the lawyers beseech their "lordships" just to hear them out.[1]

Generally the advocates' pleas will prove futile. In 2013 only about 17.2 percent of cases were accepted for regular hearings, which are on Tuesday, Wednesday, and Thursday.[2] During these longer hearings, panels of typically two or three judges will hear drawn-out arguments as lawyers painstakingly lead them through a case, sometimes for hours, and even days, at a time.

---

[*] This chapter has been adapted from extracts of Nick Robinson, *Structure Matters: The Impact of Court Structure on the Indian and U.S. Supreme Courts*, 61(1) AM. J. COMP. LAW 173 (2013). All views are the author's alone.

[1] Observations of the scene at Supreme Court are based on the author's experience as a judicial clerk to Chief Justice Sabharwal in 2006–2007 and in repeated visits thereafter; INDIAN CONST. Art. 145 (4) (Stipulating, "No judgment shall be delivered by the Supreme Court save in open Court").

[2] 2013 SUPREME COURT ANNUAL STATEMENT (on file with author).

Given its frequently discussed reputation for being so central to Indian political life, outsiders are often struck that the Supreme Court hears so many seemingly routine matters. Stepping into a courtroom one might find an Indian administrative officer from Tamil Nadu arguing he should have been ranked in a higher seniority grade, two neighbors from Nagpur disputing ownership over land from a deal gone bad in the 1990s, or a Delhi business-man pleading he has been taxed at the wrong rate. Indeed, to accommodate all these diverse cases the Court is open for hearings Monday to Friday from 10.30 a.m. to 4.00 or 5.00 p.m. (with just an hour's lunch break) about 190 days a year.[3] In addition, during Court vacations, a vacation bench often sits to hear urgent matters. The Court is rarely closed for business.

Despite the range of matters before it, or perhaps partly because of it, the Indian Supreme Court has become well known for both its interventionism and creativity. This combination of activism and accessibility has caused it to alternatively be dubbed a "people's court,"[4] the "last resort for the oppressed and bewildered,"[5] and the "most powerful court in the world."[6] The chapters in this volume, in part, explore whether such laudatory titles for the Court are justified, but this perception has become a significant part of the Court's narrative.

A full synopsis of the Court's major judgments or role in Indian political life is not possible here.[7] Still, it is worth noting major political controversies of the day routinely come through the Court's doors, whether it is permissible levels of reservations based on caste, high-profile corruption cases, or determining whether a chain of shoals between India and Sri Lanka is part of a mythical bridge that Rama, a Hindu deity, crossed in the days when gods walked the country.[8]

---

[3] For example, in 2017 the Court was in session 190 days of the year. Supreme Court of India Calendar – 2017, www.supremecourtofindia.nic.in/calendar.

[4] Paari Vendhan, *What Lady Justice Can't See*, TEHELKA, May 23, 2011 (one of many popular media references to the court as being perceived as a "people's" court).

[5] *State of Rajasthan* v. *Union of India* (1979) 3 SCC 634 at 670 (per J. Goswami); Rajeev Dhavan, JUSTICE ON TRIAL: THE SUPREME COURT TODAY (1980).

[6] Alexander Fischer, *Higher Lawmaking as a Political Resource* in SOVEREIGNTY AND DIVERSITY 186 (Miodrag Jovanović & Kristin Henrard eds. 2008) (noting both Upendra Baxi and S. P. Sathe refer to the Indian Supreme Court as the "most powerful in the world").

[7] For a useful overview see B. N. Kirpal et al. (eds.), SUPREME BUT NOT INFALLIBLE: ESSAYS IN HONOUR OF THE SUPREME COURT OF INDIA (2001); Lavanya Rajamani and Arghya Sengupta, *The Supreme Court of India: Power, Promise, and Overreach* in THE OXFORD COMPANION TO POLITICS IN INDIA (2010); Pratap Bhanu Manu Mehta, *India's Judiciary: The Promise of Uncertainty* in Devesh Kapur and Pratap Bhanu Mehta (eds.) PUBLIC INSTITUTIONS IN INDIA (2005).

[8] Dhananjay Mahapatra, *Adam's Bridge Was NDA Decision: Govt*, TIMES OF INDIA, Sept. 11, 2007.

The Court has also frequently asserted itself in public policy, perhaps because the government is often seen to have abdicated or mismanaged many of its governance functions. For example, in a case on the right to food, its orders directed the implementation of many of India's core social welfare schemes from 2001 to 2017.[9] The Court has ordered smoking be banned from public spaces, penned sexual harassment guidelines for the workplace, and directed taxis, buses, and auto rickshaws to convert to natural gas in the country's capital to help curtail spiraling pollution.[10]

The Indian Supreme Court has extended its perceived guardianship role from beyond public policy, or promoting good governance, to also supervise Parliament's constituent powers. After standoffs with Parliament during the Court's early years, it pioneered the "basic structure" doctrine. Under this judge-made doctrine the Court has struck down constitutional amendments that violate the Constitution's "basic structure," which it has found includes commitments to democracy, secularism, federalism, and judicial review.[11]

I. HISTORY

Yet the Court wasn't always so central to Indian political life or overloaded with cases. Today's teeming hallways of the Supreme Court were not part of the original vision for the Court, but rather an unintended consequence of it. The Supreme Court first sat in 1950 with just eight sanctioned judges, who typically presided in panels of five and three. Looking back on the Supreme Court's early years Justice B. P. Singh recounts, "Only five to six lawyers would be present in the Court Hall and one could only hear the Counsel addressing the Court ... The proceedings were consequently solemn, virtually dull, when compared to what is witnessed in the Court Halls nowadays."[12]

What then accounts for this transformation not only in the Court's work-load, but also its very structure? In short: access. The Indian Supreme Court is one of the most accessible highest courts in the world, and as a result has become one of the most sprawling.

---

[9] Apurva Vishwanath, *What Are the Lessons Learnt from the Right to Food Case?*, MINT, Mar. 20, 2017.

[10] For more details on these cases, *see* Nick Robinson, *Expanding Judiciaries: India and the Rise of the Good Governance Court*, 8 WASH. UNIV. GLOBAL STUDIES L. REV. 1 (2009).

[11] *Id.*

[12] Justice B. P. Singh, *Supreme Court – As I Saw It Then* in THE ANNUAL REPORT OF THE SUPREME COURT OF INDIA 2006–07.

A. *The court's founding*

History played a key role in this story. During most of the British Raj, the
decisions of the High Courts (which were based in Allahabad, Bombay,
Calcutta, Lahore, Madras, and Patna) could only be appealed to the Privy
Council in London as there was no highest court in India.[13] Litigants complained such appeals to the Privy Council were costly, took too much time,
and that the judges in England were not well versed in India's laws.[14]

The 1935 Government of India Act, which would later significantly influence
the design of the Indian Constitution, created a new Federal Court in New
Delhi. This Federal Court had original jurisdiction in disputes between states,
provinces, or the Federation[15] and took appeals from high courts if a high court
certified the matter involved a substantial question of law under the 1935 Act.[16]
The Privy Council though continued to take certified and special leave petitions
from the Federal Court, meaning judges in London retained ultimate control.[17]

Many of India's leading politicians had unsuccessfully lobbied for a Federal
Court with broader jurisdiction, including allowing appeal even if a
High Court did not grant a certificate.[18] With its narrower jurisdiction, the
Federal Court decided only 100 cases in its entire 11-year existence.[19] Although
the 1935 Act allowed the Court up to seven judges, with such a small docket it
began with just three and ended with only six.[20]

When independence came in 1947, India's constituent assembly members
finally had the moment to create the national court with wide access for all
Indians that they had long advocated. The new Supreme Court was seen as
transferring the powers of the Privy Council to the Federal Court, and since
the Privy Council had allowed appeals at its discretion through special leave,
the new Supreme Court would too.[21] The Supreme Court would also have
original jurisdiction for fundamental rights cases, meaning litigants could
directly approach the Court to enforce these rights without first going to the
lower courts (the 1935 Government of India Act hadn't granted any

---

[13] M. V. Pylee, THE FEDERAL COURT OF INDIA 68 (1996).
[14] *Id.* at 73–74.
[15] Government of India Act, 1935, Section 204.
[16] *Id.* at Section 205.
[17] *Id.* at Section 207; See also Raj Kumar, ESSAYS ON LEGAL SYSTEMS IN INDIA 110 (2003).
[18] Rajeev Dhavan, THE SUPREME COURT UNDER STRAIN – THE CHALLENGE OF ARREARS
5 (1978).
[19] Pylee, *supra* note 13 at 132.
[20] *Id.* at 83.
[21] Dhavan, *supra* note 18 at 10.

fundamental rights). Finally, litigants could still bring cases to the Supreme Court if they were certified from a High Court.

Pandit Thakur Das Bhargava embodied much of the assembly's spirit of promoting wide access when he argued that "we should liberalise the jurisdiction, we should see that in all cases, in all fit and proper cases, the ordinary man gets full justice."[22] Dr. B. R. Ambedkar, the lower-caste leader considered by many the father of the Indian Constitution, called the ability of citizens to directly petition the Supreme Court for violation of their fundamental rights "the very soul of the Constitution and the very heart of it" without which the Constitution "would be a nullity."[23] The Supreme Court, with its wide jurisdiction, was to be the final protector of all Indians' rights. A court whose decisions would help unite an exceedingly diverse and often politically splintered country.

Despite this ambitious vision, little concerted debate went into how many judges would be required to staff the Court.[24] Ultimately, it was decided there would be eight, with the judges of the old Federal Court becoming the Supreme Court's first judges. The Constitution requires that a constitution bench of at least five judges sit to hear substantial questions of constitutional law; this presumably left three judges to hear other matters.[25]

B. *The court's expansion*

In crafting its jurisdiction, few of the constituent assembly members seemed to have foreseen the dominant role the standard leave petition (SLP) would take on in the Court's caseload, believing the Court would only exercise this

---

[22] Pandit Thakur Das Bhargava, Constituent Assembly Debates (hereafter CAD), June 3, 1949 (Bhargava made this statement during a debate over whether certified criminal cases should be able to be appealed to the Supreme Court. Bhargava, a noted criminal lawyer, charged that resistance to allowing certified criminal cases arose because the assembly was "full of civil lawyers").

[23] Dr. Ambedkar, CAD, Dec. 9, 1948 (Vol. VII p. 953) (Dr. Ambedkar did not claim that the Supreme Court would fully hear cases involving fundamental rights under its original jurisdiction, but rather that it could grant interim relief in appropriate cases).

[24] One early draft of the Constitution provided for 10 judges, who would sit in two equal divisions, while another proposed to continue with the Federal Court's allocated strength of seven. Committee appointed in pursuance of the Resolution of the Assembly of April 30, 1947, Report on the Principles of the Union Constitution reported in the Constituent Assembly Debates July 21, 1947; Dhavan, *supra* note 18 at 13.

[25] Constit. of India Art. 145(3). Although not as common as today, in the Court's early years some matters were heard by just two judges. However, it was felt by many then that two judges were a "weak bench" (P. N. Sapru speaking during the Rajya Sabha Debate of Supreme Court (number of judges) bill, 1956 p. 3315 – Sept. 4, 1956) and that benches should have "at least three judges as a rule" (K. K. Basu speaking in Lok Sabha Debate, p. 3809 Supreme Court (number of judges) bill Aug. 20, 1956.

discretionary jurisdiction if there was a "serious breach" of justice.[26] This oversight would seem glaring in hindsight. An original member of the Court and its third Chief Justice, Mehr Chand Mahajan, recounted: "We were soon flooded with applications for special leave to appeal wherever a litigant could afford the high cost of such a proceeding in the Supreme Court."[27]

The Court's liberal interpretation of its jurisdiction led to an ever-ballooning increase in work. According to the Supreme Court's Annual Report, in its first year of operation in 1950 over 1,000 cases were filed with the Court, by 1960 almost 2,000, by 1970 over 4,000, by 1980 this had jumped to over 20,000, and by 2000 it was over 30,000. The number of regular hearing matters it disposed of tracked a similar curve, rising from 227 in 1951 to 2,433 in 1980 and 4,320 in 2000.[28] In 2015, almost 70,000 admission matters were filed with the Court, while it disposed of 11,329 regular hearing matters.[29]

This increase in work was not only driven by the wide jurisdiction originally given to the Court, but how Parliament, the public, and the judges themselves perceived the Court. During its first 25 years, the Supreme Court was often painted as protecting elite interests and playing spoiler to the government's nationalization and property redistribution policies.[30] Although wary of the Court's interventions in economic affairs, Parliament steadily increased the Court's jurisdiction as part of its efforts to address the perceived needs of ordinary Indians. For example, Parliament eased and eventually eliminated monetary restrictions on civil appeals and minimum sentences for criminal appeals.[31]

When Indira Gandhi's government declared an emergency in 1975–1977, the Supreme Court was widely seen as being unable to stand up to the government's worst abuses, damaging its reputation. In the exuberance of the revitalization of democratic institutions in post-Emergency India the Supreme Court recast itself as a "people's court," responsive to the people's

---

[26] Prof. Shibban Lal Saksena, Constituent Assembly Debates, June 6, 1949 (Vol. VIII).

[27] Mehr Chand Mahajan, Looking Back: The Autobiography of Mehr Chand Mahajan, Former Chief Justice of India 196 (1963); For a discussion of Court's initial and later interpretation of SLP jurisdiction see 14th India Law Commission Report 47; Dhavan, *supra* note 18, at 21–24.

[28] It was 1,271 matters in 1960 and 2,569 in 1970. Supreme Court of India Annual Report 2015–2016, pp. 53–55.

[29] *Id.*

[30] Gregory Alexander provides a nuanced account of this showdown over property in Gregory Alexander, the Global Debate Over Constitutional Property: Lessons for American Takings Jurisprudence (2006).

[31] In 1970 Parliament removed the monetary limit for appeals to the Supreme Court in certified civil cases and reduced the limits for appeal in criminal cases to any sentence over 10 years (eventually even this restriction would be dropped). Dhavan, *supra* note 18 at 39.

needs through such tools as public interest litigation (PIL).[32] The Court's often far-reaching PIL orders were made possible in part by the Court expanding *locus standi* to allow public-spirited individuals to bring petitions for the violations of constitutional rights of those who may not be able to approach the Court directly.[33] During this period, the Court also expanded access by instituting a policy of treating letters to the Court by citizens complaining of fundamental rights violations as petitions[34] and also hearing cases *suo moto*, where judges themselves could start a case based on the report of a rights violation in a newspaper article or other source.[35]

Parliament's response to the Supreme Court's ever-increasing docket has generally been to simply add more judges.[36] Parliament increased the size of the Court from its original 8 judges to 11 in 1956, 14 in 1960, 17 in 1977, 26 in 1986, and finally to 31 in 2008.[37] During debates over these increases, Members of Parliament or judges themselves rarely, if ever, recommend the Court's jurisdiction should be restricted or that the Court should accept significantly fewer cases for regular hearing.

C. *The appointment process and insularity*

Despite the Court's populist reputation, its judges are highly insulated from democratic accountability. While under the Constitution, it is the President

---

[32] For a brief synopsis of some important Public Interest Litigation cases see I. P. Massey, ADMINISTRATIVE LAW 453–457 (2008).

[33] See, for example, *Fertilizer Corpn. Kamgar Union v. Union of India* 1 SCC 568 (1981) (Justice Iyer discussing how locus standi for petitioners must be liberalized because when "corruption permeates the entire fabric of government" public spirited individuals must not be barred from bringing cases to correct the use of public power).

[34] In actual practice, few of these letters are actually read by judges, but rather by the registrar. See Nick Robinson, A *Quantitative Analysis of the Indian Supreme Court's Workload*, 10(3) J. EMPIRICAL LEGAL STUDIES 570, 599 (2013).

[35] For more on the Court's use of its *suo moto* jurisdiction, see Marc Galanter and Vasujith Ram, *Suo Motu Intervention and the Indian Judiciary* (in this book).

[36] This is not to suggest that the Supreme Court never took steps to limit its jurisdiction. For example, the Supreme Court has suggested curtailing its SLP jurisdiction and in *P.N. Kumar v. Municipal Corpn of Delhi* 4 SCC 609 (1987) the Court directed that where writ petitions (cases invoking its fundamental rights jurisdiction) could be filed before a High Court the parties should not approach the Supreme Court first.

[37] Supreme Court (Number of Judges) Act 1956, Supreme Court (Number of Judges) Amendment Bill 1960, Supreme Court (Number of Judges) Amendment Bill 1977, Supreme Court (Number of Judges) Amendment Bill 1986, Supreme Court (Number of Judges) Amendment Bill 2008. The original increases in judges were in increments of three judges so as to add more three judge benches, but as two judge benches became more frequently used this arithmetic made less sense. INDIA LAW COMMISSION 14TH REPORT 54–55 (1958).

who appoints Supreme Court judges in consultation with the judiciary, in practice the Supreme Court has had a controlling hand in appointments. Through its orders in the 1980s and 1990s in what is collectively known as the Three Judges Cases,[38] the Court evolved new rules for the appointment and transfer of judges in the upper judiciary in order to guard against what it perceived as undue influence from the executive. Under this jurisprudence a collegium of the Chief Justice of India and the four most senior other judges recommends appointments to the Supreme Court. These recommendations are almost always followed and the judiciary cannot be bypassed in the appointment process. The general principal of judicial control of appointments was reaffirmed in *Supreme Court Advocates-on-Record Association v. Union of India* in 2015. At issue in this case, Parliament passed a constitutional amendment in 2014 to replace the judges' collegium with a national judicial appointments commission, which would have three judicial and three non-judicial members. In its judgment, the Court struck down the amendment as violating the basic structure of the Constitution, finding that such a commission would undercut the independence of the judiciary.

Despite having so much control over the appointment of their fellow judges, Supreme Court judges are actually on the Court for a relatively limited period of time, limiting their ability to accrue oversized personal influence. Supreme Court judges are generally selected by the collegium from among senior high court judges, where the retirement age is 62. In November 2017, the typical judge on the Supreme Court had been appointed at about the age of 59.[39] Supreme Court judges must retire at the age of 65 under the Constitution. As a result, a typical tenure of a judge on the Supreme Court is only around six years.

II. THE IMPACT OF THE COURT'S STRUCTURE

A. Access

Wide access to the Indian Supreme Court has historically been accepted as a largely unquestioned good, and as a result the Court has added additional judges and panels to accommodate this value. As has already been hinted, the

---

[38] *SP Gupta v. Union of India* AIR 1982 SC 149; *Supreme Court Advocates-on Record Association vs Union of India* AIR 1994 SC 268; and *In re Special Reference 1 of 1998*, AIR 1999 SC 1.

[39] Averaging of the ages of the 25 current judges on the Supreme Court on Nov. 6, 2017. At the time, the judge who was appointed when youngest was 56 and the oldest was 61. Chief Justice & Judges, Supreme Court of India: www.supremecourtofindia.nic.in/chief-justice-judges (accessed Nov. 6, 2017).

roots of this tradition are both idealistic and pragmatic. The idea that anyone who has had their constitutional right violated – from the poorest villager in the tribal areas of Jharkhand to the wealthiest businessman in a high rise in Bombay – can appear before a panel of the Supreme Court to have their case heard has deep democratic resonance. It is a legitimizing idea infused with a populist spirit that carries added weight in a country wracked by sharp class, religious, caste, and ethnic divisions. An often distant and rigid government is suddenly made personal and (potentially) responsive at the pinnacle of judicial power. The Court's interpretation of the law will be shaped not just by the privileged few, but by the petitions of a wide cross-section of the Indian population.

India's constitution was meant to be transformative. The Constitution, and by extension the judiciary, was charged with changing a country rooted in hierarchy into one that internalized the liberal values of equality and freedom of expression for all its citizens. Arguably, a Supreme Court active in many cases has more opportunities to act as this sort of democratic schoolmaster, working to instill these values in a society still frequently resistant.

Wide access also has clear practical benefits. Take the practice of open admission day, when all cases filed before the Court are briefly heard. It is a product of the strong oral tradition in India and the general weakness of written briefs. Judges find that they can often determine more efficiently whether a case should have a regular hearing through a short verbal exchange with a lawyer than by reading an often wandering brief that may not adequately represent the issues at stake.

More importantly, accepting more cases for regular hearing allows the Indian Supreme Court to actively police the high courts and lower judiciary. Both the Supreme Court and many members of the public seem to distrust these lower courts, fearing that they might be incompetent or corrupt, or that local parochial interests unduly influence decisions.[40]

It also strengthens the Supreme Court's check on the executive and legislature; allowing it to make its presence known on a wide range of matters that might escape the attention of a less active court. This is particularly relevant in India where many perceive that the legislature has abdicated some of its governing responsibilities and the executive frequently abuses some of its powers. Access then seems a more desirable feature where a Supreme Court is building legitimacy with a large, poor population, still distant from the

---

[40] Nick Robinson, *Too Many Cases*, FRONTLINE, Jan. 3–16, 2009.

values in its constitution, and there is distrust of the lower courts' ability and integrity, as well as the executive's and legislature's.

Yet there are clear costs to this approach. By accepting so many cases, delay has become a serious problem. A typical case takes on average about two years to be heard as an admission matter and approximately another two to be decided as a regular hearing matter. It would currently take the Supreme Court about three years to clear its existing docket if it accepted no more cases. This backlog also means judges are generally overworked and the quality of their opinions suffers.

Constitution bench matters, which involve a substantial question of constitutional law, require at least five judges to be heard and generally have lengthy argument. Among the mass of other matters, these larger benches have become difficult to schedule and have declined in number.[41]

Litigation in such a system is not only longer, but also more expensive. Those with money, the government (whose officers don't bear the cost of appeal), and appellants geographically situated closer to New Delhi are all far more likely to appeal a case to the Supreme Court.[42] A group of leading lawyers have emerged whose perceived high "face value" with judges and success in getting orders, especially for admission of cases, allows them to charge around $10,000 an appearance. Several of these lawyers make between $2 million and $10 million a year.[43]

With no real opinion survey data, it is unclear how much the general public actually values wide access to the Supreme Court. Both the bar and bench reiterate this value, often claiming it to be a public one, but they arguably have a vested interest in perpetuating this view.[44]

Yet there is reason to believe that wide access does tap into some larger societal value. Over the years, Members of Parliament, particularly those from

---

[41] In the first decade of the 2000s there were on average only nine five-judge or larger benches a year compared with about a hundred such benches a year in the 1960s. Nick Robinson et al., *Interpreting the Constitution: Supreme Court Constitution Benches Since Independence,* XLVI(9) Ec. Pol. Weekly 27 (2011).

[42] Nick Robinson, *Hard to Reach,* Frontline Jan. 30–Feb. 12, 2010 (finding that parties in Delhi are four times more likely to appeal their case to the Supreme Court than the national average, and the farther one is from Delhi the less likely a case will be appealed).

[43] Marc Galanter and Nick Robinson, *India's Grand Advocates: A Legal Elite Flourishing in an Age of Globalization,* 20(3) Int'l J. Legal Profession (2013). The Court's many panels empower these lawyers, as smaller benches are arguably easier for them to impress and sway.

[44] Although Supreme Court judges may have a bias towards believing that the answer to the Supreme Court's backlog is more judges like themselves, they do not have a material interest in expanding the Court. However, the more matters heard before more benches the more business is created for lawyers since they typically charge by appearance.

the South, have made pleas for having benches of the Court sit across the country to decrease costs for litigants from those regions.[45] In effect, these MPs argue having wider, more equitable access to the Court by continuing to open up its structure is more important than limiting access to keep its structure intact and keep down the number of cases that it hears.[46]

B. *Cohesiveness and polyvocality*

Speaking of *the* Indian Supreme Court is in many ways a misnomer. There is no one Court that speaks with a single voice in the way one might think of, say, the US Supreme Court. Instead, the separate panels of the Court usually number no more than two or three judges. It is a polyvocal court. Any given bench has a slightly different interpretation of the law than another bench, and sometimes a starkly different interpretation.

The Court's polyvocality is present from admission day. Some judges are well known for accepting certain types of cases for regular hearing or denying others. Some simply accept far more cases for regular hearing than others, believing the Court should leave its doors more widely open.

During regular hearings, differences between benches can also become stark. In public interest litigation certain judges are known for intervening aggressively when they see lapses in governance, while others rarely sanction intervention. Cases involving the death penalty are another clear example. In the first decade of the 2000s, Justice Pasayat was well known for supporting the death penalty for serious and heinous crimes such as rape and murder, and his bench frequently upheld death sentences.[47] On the other hand, Justice Sinha stressed the death penalty's arbitrariness and his bench interpreted India's death penalty jurisprudence so that it almost never applied.[48] Meanwhile, Marc Galanter and Alex Fischer have recorded how the Court's ever-controversial caste-based reservation decisions have become increasingly conflicting as the Court has increased in size.[49]

---

[45] LAW COMMISSION OF INDIA, REPORT NO. 229 (Aug. 2009).

[46] Resisting such a move, a full meeting of the judges unanimously rejected the 2009 Law Commission recommendations, claiming such a change would adversely affect the Court's institutional cohesiveness. J. Venkatesan, *Supreme Court Again Says 'No' to Regional Benches*, THE HINDU, Feb. 21, 2010.

[47] *Supreme Court Judge Pasayat Retires*, THE HINDU, May 10, 2009; *Child Rapist Deserves Death Penalty: Retd Justice*, TIMES OF INDIA, Dec. 6, 2009.

[48] Tarunabh Khaitan, *Justice Sinha's Legacy: Strict Scrutiny, Death Penalty, Counter-majoritarianism*, LAW AND OTHER THINGS, Aug. 6, 2009. Justice Sinha's stance against the death penalty ironically strengthened his claim that it was arbitrarily applied.

[49] Marc Galanter and Alex Fischer, New Introduction to *Competing Inequalities* (forthcoming).

Differences in opinion between benches are usually subtler than these examples, but they still exist. As a result, lawyers frequently will hunt for the most favorable bench. When a matter is before a judge who they think will give an unfavorable ruling they may try to delay the hearing until either the case is transferred to another bench or the judge retires. On other occasions they will try to bring the case before the Chief Justice to be relisted as an urgent matter, so that different judges are assigned to it.

These differences between benches confuse doctrine. The resulting uncertainty arguably motivates more cases to be brought to the Supreme Court.[50] Litigants realize even if their appeal is not strong that with a sympathetic bench they could get a better ruling. Meanwhile, lower court judges, let alone Indian citizens, sometimes cannot distinguish which Supreme Court judgments represent settled law, adding uncertainty into a wide array of social and economic relations.

C. Precedent, experimentation, and chief justice dominance

This polyvocal structure of the Supreme Court may seem baffling to an outsider (and even some insiders). Yet it should not be understood as incoherence, as the opinions of the judges are unified by a set of rules governing precedent and judicial discipline. The Court's polyvocal nature also has benefits that could not be achieved otherwise.

The Supreme Court's rules governing precedent rein in the most extreme outlier decisions. Under current case law benches are bound to follow the precedent of benches of the same or greater size.[51] In theory, a bench cannot question the decision of a larger bench, but only ask the Chief Justice to place the matter before an even larger bench.[52]

Seniority plays a unifying role as well. Most benches are composed of only two judges, but despite this even number there is rarely a split decision because tradition dictates that the junior judge generally defers to the opinion of the senior.[53] This means that fewer judges routinely express their individual

---

[50] Richard Posner makes a similar argument about how the increase in the size of the US Courts of Appeal increased appeals to them since there was more uncertainty in the law. Richard Posner, *The Federal Courts: Challenges and Reform* 120–122 (1999).

[51] *See Central Board of Dawoodi Bohra Community* v. *State of Maharasthra* 2 SCC 673 (2005) (also noting that Chief Justice Pathak thought there would be greater consistency and certainty in the law if the entire court sat together, but that workload prohibited this).

[52] *Id.* The Chief Justice can also independently place a matter before any size bench.

[53] In the USA a number of scholars have shown the effect of ideological dampening and amplification on panels of the federal courts of appeal. A judge's voting becomes more liberal

opinion decreasing the number of voices, and chances for conflict, on the Court. A junior judge will generally dissent though if they believe that the senior judge is expressing an opinion that is clearly against past precedent, a check which results in a one–one split and a referral to another bench.

The most senior judge on the Court has traditionally been the Chief Justice. He plays a strong role not only in deciding which cases are heard by larger benches, but also which cases are heard by which judges. These powers have led to the development of a Chief Justice-dominated Supreme Court, where the Chief Justice polices the system and helps unify doctrine.

Normally, a computer system assigns cases to different benches for hearing. The Chief Justice, however, can override this automated system and explicitly assign cases to his own or another's bench. He can speed up the hearing of cases or hold up a politically sensitive case for years (given that backlog provides an ample excuse for delaying a hearing). He also creates the composition of benches, meaning he can effectively punish judges for outlier decisions. For example, he can place a non-conforming judge on a two-judge bench where he or she is the junior judge (meaning they will rarely be speaking for the bench) or not include them on the larger and more powerful constitution benches of five or more judges.

Since independence, the Chief Justice has been about 6.5 times less likely to be in dissent than another judge on constitution benches.[54] Presumably, this is at least in part because he can place like-minded judges on the same bench. In research on the Court's earlier history, George Gadbois found that K. Subba Rao, Chief Justice from 1966 to 1967, with his stark anti-government bias, was in dissent 48 times when he was a Supreme Court judge (more than any other judge up to that point). However, he was never in dissent after he became Chief Justice. Perhaps more tellingly, during his tenure the entire Supreme Court gave more anti-government decisions than at any other point up to that time, suggesting the Chief Justice used his bench-setting power to affect cases he didn't even hear.[55]

Justices also typically come from very similar backgrounds, leading to more uniformity in their decisions. Judges are traditionally all former High Court

---

or conservative depending on how many democratic or republican appointed judges are on the same panel with them. Cass R. Sunstein et al., ARE JUDGES POLITICAL? AN EMPIRICAL ANALYSIS OF THE FEDERAL JUDICIARY (2006); Frank B. Cross, DECISION MAKING IN THE U.S. COURTS OF APPEALS (2007) In India, Supreme Court judges do not have clear political party affiliations. A culture of dissent aversion, spurred on by high workloads, may instead result in an ideologically dampening of Indian judges' opinions.

54 Robinson et al., *supra* note 41 at 31.
55 George H Gadbois Jr, *Indian Judicial Behaviour*, 3(5) EC. POL. WEEKLY 149 (1970).

judges, who come from backgrounds of relative privilege, including fluency in the English language.[56] Unlike their US counterparts, these judges are rarely seen as overtly favoring the political philosophy of one political party over another. This internal selection method and their relative homogeneity adds to a sense of brotherhood, which encourages judges to reach consensus when possible, although vocal dissents still frequently occur on the larger and rarer constitution benches.[57]

Finally, the Supreme Court has intermittently created special benches to hear certain types of matters, such as for tax, criminal, or social justice cases.[58] The smaller number of judges hearing cases on these specialized benches helps create more uniformity across the case law.

Therefore, what initially appears as a haphazard system of almost anarchic polyvocality has clear controls, such as theoretically strong precedent rules and a dominant Chief Justice. From this perspective, the typical Indian Supreme Court bench of two judges frequently does not look like the highest court of a country. It more closely resembles a High Court, unable to overrule Supreme Court benches of even the same size.[59]

Despite these constraints that push the Court's jurisprudence towards uniformity, individual judges or small groupings of like-minded judges have significant space to innovate. After all, a two-judge judgment is still a Supreme Court ruling and binding on the parties unless a larger bench overrules it (which only occurs relatively rarely). The Supreme Court's polyvocality may be limited and regulated, but it has consequences that make it different from if it sat as a unified bench.

For example, the development of public interest litigation would have been far less likely without the Court's panel structure. Judicial entrepreneurs such as Justices Bhagwati, Iyer, and Verma played a leading role in developing PIL in the 1980s and 1990s, frequently issuing decisions from smaller benches on which they were the senior judge. The detailed orders and long hearings in public interest litigation cases were made possible on a widespread basis at

---

[56] Supreme Court Advocates on Record Ass'n vs. Union of India (AIR 1994 SC 258); For an overview of Supreme Court judges' backgrounds, see GEORGE H. GADBOIS JR., JUDGES OF THE SUPREME COURT OF INDIA: 1950–1989 (2011); Abhinav Chandrachud, *An Empirical Study of the Supreme Court's Composition*, 46(1) EC. POL. WEEKLY (2011).

[57] Robinson et al., *supra* note 41 at 28 (finding that dissent rates have climbed above 20 percent on constitution benches in recent years).

[58] Shreeja Sen, *Supreme Court sets up new benches for tax, criminal cases*, MINT, Feb. 24, 2015.

[59] Dhavan, *supra* note 18 at 36 (finding that by the end of the 1950s "In dealing with many appellate matters the Supreme Court was acting just like the High Courts. It was manned by judges who came from the High Courts. It decided cases in fragmented bench structures. It did not sit and think as a court. It was merely a collection of judges").

Supreme Court level by having a large number of smaller benches with the capacity to commit the time necessary to hear these cases.

When judges on smaller benches create new innovations such as public interest litigation it enters a feedback loop. The press, public, and bar react with favorable or unfavorable views. Based on these inputs the rest of the judges can then reflect on the merits of this turn in the Court's jurisprudence. If there is a largely favorable reception, an expectation is created that other judges should follow a similar line of reasoning. Allowing smaller benches to first experiment with new paths in jurisprudence also allows other benches of the court to better understand the feasibility and real-world implications of its judgments. Like the "laboratories of experimentation" argument for American federalism,[60] the whole is not necessarily committed to the innovations of one bench, but instead the rest of the Court can assess the success of the orders of a particular bench to determine if they want to follow a similar path.

Finally, having precedent more regularly reinterpreted through different Supreme Court benches may be a strength in a country where there is less national consensus on many political issues, from caste-based reservations to economic liberalization. The judge can use their discretion to navigate the particularities of a specific case rather than try to impose a more cohesive jurisprudence. In this way, the Court's controlled pluralism can be seen as a tool, conscious or not, to keep the law and the Court as an open recourse to different social forces with divergent views.

D. *Image and expertise*

Given their virtual self-selection, judges on the Indian Supreme Court are viewed as less partisan than in some other countries, such as the United States. The panel structure of the Court also prevents clear ideological blocks from being perceived by the public (even if there are more "activist" or "conservative" judges). Partially as a result, there is not the sense that all the judges have to assemble together for a decision to be legitimate or fair in the eyes of the public.

Quite the opposite, the large size of the Court and the authority of the Chief Justice to assign judges to panels are frequently defended on the ground that judges bring different expertise or backgrounds that should be selectively utilized. As Pandit Sharma pointed out in Parliament when he advocated expanding the Court in 1960, "It is not possible for a Judge to know everything," and so more judges would ensure that "the final law for the land is to

---

[60] *New State Ice Co. v. Liebmann*, 285 U.S. 262 (1932).

be laid down by Judges specialized in a particular branch of law."[61] If judges gain legitimacy from expertise in interpreting the law,[62] having specialized judges arguably produces stronger, more legitimate judgments. The more judges and panels on the Supreme Court the more expertise it can draw upon.

Indian identity politics may also play a role when creating benches. As Abhinav Chandrachud has documented, there seems to be an unwritten rule that at any given point there should be geographic diversity on the Court with a judge from each major state or region.[63] Similarly, there has almost always been a Muslim on the Court, as well as a couple of other non-Hindu judges (Sikh, Christian, or Parsi). While it is difficult to definitively track lower-caste judges they do seem to be represented more frequently and purposively in recent years, with the first lower-caste Chief Justice serving from 2007 to 2010.[64] Such selection is done not only to give the overall Court more legitimacy, but also for specific benches for certain cases. For example, in a constitution bench case concerning religious discrimination against Muslims in the state of Assam, the Chief Justice might decide to assign a judge from Assam, another who is Muslim, one who is an expert in religious discrimination jurisprudence, a judge well known for his opinion writing skills, and himself. It is noteworthy that up until 2017 only six women had served on the Indian Supreme Court and none had been Chief Justice, perhaps indicating that, at least until recently, the Court did not see women judges as necessary for its legitimacy.[65]

Larger benches carry more weight both in precedent value[66] and seemingly in the eyes of the public. As such, it is perhaps not surprising that the largest bench of the Indian Supreme Court (13) sat for *Kesavananda Bharati*. This case laid down the foundational principles of the basic structure doctrine, which allows the Court to strike down constitutional amendments. So many judges heard the case not just to be able to overturn past precedent on this issue, but the

---

[61] Pandit Sharma, Lok Sabha debate April 27, 1960, over Number of Judges Bill, 14150; interview with former Chief Justice Verma (on file with author) (commenting that the Chief Justice can place judges with special expertise on different benches).

[62] Roscoe Pound, *The Courts and the Crown* in THE SPIRIT OF THE COMMON LAW (1921) (arguing judicial independence was originally founded in part upon the idea that judges had a certain expertise in understanding the law that the sovereign did not).

[63] Chandrachud, *supra* note 56 (noting that there is a tradition of having at least four non-Hindu vacancies on the Court in recent years).

[64] Chief Justice Balakrishnan was the first lower-caste Chief Justice.

[65] As of 2017, four women had served on the Court: Justices Beevi, Manohar, Pal, and Misra. The last of these, Justice Misra, retired in April 2014. Supreme Court of India, Chief Justice and Judges of the Supreme Court, www.supremecourtofindia.nic.in/chief-justice-judges.

[66] See *supra* note 52 (describing how under Indian case law smaller benches cannot overrule benches of equal or greater strength).

sheer number of judges added extra legitimacy to a judgment directly challenging a core power of Parliament.

The overall image of the Court as a guardian institution is fostered by its structure. The Court is widely perceived as a group of regularly revolving, mostly apolitical, judicial experts that provides a backstop for governance failures committed by the other branches of government. Its large size gives the Court an almost impersonal nature that helps foster this sense of expertise, even while its ability to take on many cases creates a more populist image at the same time.

III. RELATIONSHIP TO THE REST OF THE JUDICIARY

Finally, the Supreme Court sits not in isolation, but in relationship to the rest of the Indian judiciary. Fuller descriptions of the structure and functioning of the Indian judiciary can be found elsewhere.[67] In brief, though, the Supreme Court and the country's 24 High Courts (each of whose jurisdiction covers either a single or multiple states) act as India's constitutional courts. As a result, cases will frequently begin in the High Courts themselves, including public interest litigation. The country's district courts are courts of first instance for both criminal and civil cases. In many cases, litigants will appeal the decisions of district courts to the High Courts. To lessen the load on, and sometimes bypass, India's notoriously backlogged courts, specialized tribunals have proliferated, including for tax, environmental, and government service matters.

The Indian Supreme Court uses several tools to exercise control over the functioning of the rest of the Indian judiciary. The most direct way is through appeal, where the Supreme Court may overturn lower court decisions and set precedent for the rest of the judiciary to follow. The Supreme Court can also exercise indirect administrative control over other courts. From an administrative perspective, the High Courts supervise the district courts in their respective states, including deciding on the promotion of judges. However, the Supreme Court, through the collegium system, has significant influence over the functioning of the High Courts, and so indirectly over the district courts, through its ability to appoint and transfer High Court judges, as well as appoint High Court judges to the Supreme Court.[68]

---

[67] For a brief summary of the architecture of the Indian court system, see Nick Robinson, *Judicial Architecture and Capacity*, in THE OXFORD HANDBOOK ON INDIAN CONSTITUTIONAL LAW, ed. Sujit Choudhry, Madhav Khosla & Pratap Mehta (2016).

[68] Judges are appointed to High Courts through a collegium of the Chief Justice of India, the two next most senior Supreme Court judges, and the Chief Justice of the respective High Court.

The Supreme Court also spreads information and norms through the National Judicial Academy in Bhopal and by regularly hosting a conference of the chief justices of High Courts to coordinate administrative goals across the judiciary.

Today, India is investing more resources in its courts, including the subordinate judiciary. While nothing should be taken away from the Supreme Court and High Courts' efforts to be more responsive to the needs of ordinary Indians, if the Indian judiciary is to truly be democratized it will be in the subordinate courts. It is only judges at a more local level who can systematically ensure that a citizen unfairly imprisoned by the police or a shopkeeper attempting to enforce a contract receives justice.

The evolution of the rest of the judiciary will continue to affect the functioning and structure of the Supreme Court itself. If the subordinate courts become perceived, by both the public and the upper judiciary, as less corrupt and more competent, then the High Courts may become less likely to hear appeals from the subordinate judiciary, and so more cases may begin and end in the subordinate courts. Similarly, if the Supreme Court has more confidence in the High Courts and subordinate judiciary it may decrease the number of appeals it hears. Reducing the number of cases the Supreme Court hears would then directly affect how many benches are necessary and whether those benches spend their time hearing rather ordinary appeals or select cases chosen for their precedential value or political salience.

In whatever manner the rest of the judiciary evolves, it is clear that the Indian Supreme Court is significantly shaped by both its own structure and that of the Indian judiciary more broadly. Mapping this larger architecture helps us understand how both judges and litigants navigate this system and the context in which the law and the Constitution are ultimately interpreted and realized in India.

REFERENCES

Alexander, Gregory, *The Global Debate Over Constitutional Property: Lessons for American Takings Jurisprudence* (2006).
Chandrachud, Abhinav, *An Empirical Study of the Supreme Court's Composition*, 46(1) Ec. POL. WEEKLY (2011).
Central Board of Dawoodi Bohra Community v. *State of Maharasthra* 2 SCC 673 (2005).
Child Rapist Deserves Death Penalty: Retd Justice, TIMES OF INDIA, Dec. 6, 2009.

CONSTITUTION OF INDIA

Cross, Frank B., *Decision Making in the U.S. Courts of Appeals* (2007).

Dhavan, Rajeev, *Justice on Trial: The Supreme Court Today* (1980).

THE SUPREME COURT UNDER STRAIN – THE CHALLENGE OF ARREARS 5 (1978).

Fertilizer Corpn. Kamgar Union v. Union of India 1 SCC 568 (1981).

Fischer, Alexander, *Higher Lawmaking as a Political Resource*, in SOVEREIGNTY AND DIVERSITY 186, ed. Miodrag Jovanović & Kristin Henrard 2008).

Gadbois, George H. Jr., *Indian Judicial Behaviour*, 3(5) EC. POL. WEEKLY 149 (1970).

JUDGES OF THE SUPREME COURT OF INDIA: 1950–1989 (2011).

Galanter, Marc and Nick Robinson, *India's Grand Advocates: A Legal Elite Flourishing in an Age of Globalization*, 20(3) INT'L J. LEGAL PROFESSION (2013).

GOVERNMENT OF INDIA ACT, 1935

INDIA CONSTITUENT ASSEMBLY DEBATES (1946–1948).

INDIA LAW COMMISSION, REPORT, No. 14 (1958).

INDIA LAW COMMISSION, REPORT NO. 229 (Aug. 2009).

In re Special Reference 1 of 1998, AIR 1999 SC 1.

Khaitan, Tarunabh, *Justice Sinha's Legacy: Strict Scrutiny, Death Penalty, Counter-majoritarianism*, LAW AND OTHER THINGS, Aug. 6, 2009.

Kumar, Raj, ESSAYS ON LEGAL SYSTEMS IN INDIA 110 (2003).

Mahajan, Mehr Chand, LOOKING BACK: THE AUTOBIOGRAPHY OF MEHR CHAND MAHAJAN, FORMER CHIEF JUSTICE OF INDIA (1963).

Mahapatra, Dhananjay, *Adam's Bridge Was NDA Decision: Govt*, TIMES OF INDIA, Sept. 11, 2007.

Massey, I. P., ADMINISTRATIVE LAW (2008).

Mehta, Pratap Bhanu Manu, *India's Judiciary: The Promise of Uncertainty* in PUBLIC INSTITUTIONS IN INDIA (Devesh Kapur and Pratap Bhanu Mehta eds, 2005).

New State Ice Co. v. Liebmann, 285 U.S. 262 (1932).

P.N. Kumar v. Municipal Corpn of Delhi, 4 SCC 609 (1987).

Posner, Richard, THE FEDERAL COURTS: CHALLENGES AND REFORM (1999).

Pound, Roscoe, *The Courts and the Crown* in THE SPIRIT OF THE COMMON LAW (1921).

Pylee, M. V., THE FEDERAL COURT OF INDIA 68 (1996).

Rajamani, Lavanya and Arghya Sengupta, *The Supreme Court of India: Power, Promise, and Overreach* in THE OXFORD COMPANION TO POLITICS IN INDIA (2010).

Robinson, Nick, *Expanding Judiciaries: India and the Rise of the Good Governance Court*, 8 WASH. UNIV. GLOBAL STUDIES L. REV. 1 (2009).

Too Many Cases, FRONTLINE, Jan. 3–16, 2009.

Hard to Reach, FRONTLINE, Jan. 30–Feb. 12, 2010.

et al., *Interpreting the Constitution: Supreme Court Constitution Benches Since Independence*, XLVI(9) EC. POL. WEEKLY 27 (2011).

Structure Matters: The Impact of Court Structure on the Indian and U.S. Supreme Courts, 61(1) AM. J. COMP. LAW 173 (2013).

A Quantitative Analysis of the Indian Supreme Court's Workload, 10(3) J. EMPIRICAL LEGAL STUDIES 570, 599 (2013).

Robinson, Nick, Judicial Architecture and Capacity, in *The Oxford Handbook on Indian Constitutional Law* , ed. Sujit Choudhry, Madhav Khosla, & Pratap Mehta (2016).

Sen, Shreeja, *Supreme Court Sets up New Benches for Tax, Criminal Cases*, MINT, Feb. 24, 2015.

Singh, Justice B. P., *Supreme Court – As I Saw It Then*, in THE ANNUAL REPORT OF THE SUPREME COURT OF INDIA 2006–07.

SP Gupta v. *Union of India* AIR 1982 SC 149.

State of Rajasthan v. *Union of India* (1979) 3 SCC 634.

Sunstein, Cass R. et al., ARE JUDGES POLITICAL? AN EMPIRICAL ANALYSIS OF THE FEDERAL JUDICIARY (2006).

SUPREME BUT NOT INFALLIBLE: ESSAYS IN HONOUR OF THE SUPREME COURT OF INDIA (B.N. Kirpal et al. eds., 2001).

Supreme Court Advocates-on Record Association vs Union of India AIR 1994 SC 268.

SUPREME COURT OF INDIA ANNUAL REPORT 2015–2016.

Supreme Court of India Calendar – 2017, www.supremecourtofindia.nic.in/calendar.

Supreme Court of India website, Chief Justice & Judges, Supreme Court of India, www.supremecourtofindia.nic.in/chief-justice-judges.

Supreme Court judge Pasayat Retires, THE HINDU, May 10, 2009.

Supreme Court Advocates on Record Ass'n vs. Union of India (AIR 1994 SC 258).

Vendhan, Paari, *What Lady Justice Can't See*, TEHELKA, May 23, 2011.

Venkatesan, J., *Supreme Court Again Says 'No' to Regional Benches*, THE HINDU, February 21, 2010.

Vishwanath, Apurva, *What Are the Lessons Learnt from the Right to Food Case?*, MINT, March 20, 2017.

2

The Supreme Court of India

An Empirical Overview of the Institution

APARNA CHANDRA, WILLIAM H. J. HUBBARD,
AND SITAL KALANTRY

I. INTRODUCTION

The Indian Supreme Court has been called "the most powerful court in the world" for its wide jurisdiction, its expansive understanding of its own powers, and the billion-plus people under its authority.[1] Yet, for an institution that exercises immense public power and enjoys a high degree of legitimacy, no broad account exists of who approaches the Court, for what purposes, and with what levels of success.[2] Both owing to its fragmented bench structure (where cases are usually decided by only two or three out of 31 judges) as well as the large volume of cases, scholars and policy makers have a very uneven picture of the court's functioning: deep knowledge about the more visible, "high-profile" cases and near-absolute silence about more mundane, below the radar, but often equally important, decisions.[3]

This imbalance is particularly relevant to the central question addressed in this book: To what extent does (or can) the Supreme Court of India promote progressive social change? Observers of the Court see the Court as self-consciously seeking to give justice to the common person not only through

---

[1] See George Gadbois, *Supreme Court Decisionmaking*, 10 BANARAS L. J. 1 (1974); V. R. Krishna Iyer, OUR COURTS ON TRIAL 18 (1987). This assessment has been widely echoed in subsequent academic works on the Indian Supreme Court. See, e.g. Shylashri Shankar, *India's Judiciary: Imperium in Imperio?, in* Paul Brass ed., ROUTLEDGE HANDBOOK OF SOUTH ASIAN POLITICS 165 (2010); Alexander Fischer, *Higher Lawmaking as a Political Resource, in* Miodrag Jovanović and Kristin Henrard eds., SOVEREIGNTY AND DIVERSITY 186 (2008).

[2] An initial effort to flesh out this picture was made in Nick Robinson, *A Quantitative Analysis of the Indian Supreme Court's Workload*, 10 J. EMPIRICAL LEGAL STUD. 570 (2013) (using "the hodgepodge of data that is either publicly available or that can be acquired from the Supreme Court").

[3] See generally Nick Robinson, *Structure Matters: The Impact of Court Structure on the Indian and U.S. Supreme Courts*, 61 AM. J. COMPARATIVE L. 101 (2013).

high-profile cases asserting or expanding rights for the disadvantaged, but also by exercising its discretionary jurisdiction to admit and decide each year thousands of low-profile cases, usually involving individuals asserting mundane legal claims.[4] Thus, much of the current practice of the Court cannot be understood simply by studying its landmark judgments. The Court devotes the lion's share of its energy to smaller cases, and these smaller cases are part of its strategy of providing access to justice for the disadvantaged.

But is the Court succeeding in this aspect of its mission? The Indian judiciary as a whole, and the Supreme Court in particular, has come under increased attack for being unable to fulfill its mandate of providing access to justice for the common person. Concerns about large backlogs, long delays, and barriers to access have eroded the legitimacy of the judicial system and have led to calls for systemic reforms. However, there is little consensus on the nature of the judicial dysfunction, its causes, and paths to reform. While some believe that the Supreme Court has witnessed a "docket explosion," which has limited the Court's ability to provide timely and just resolution of disputes,[5] others argue that the core concern with the Court's functioning is "docket exclusion," whereby the Court is increasingly accessible only for the rich and powerful.[6] Both narratives — that of explosion and exclusion — agree, however, that the Court is increasingly limited in its ability to achieve the lofty ideals of providing succor and justice to "the butcher, the baker and the candle-stick maker . . . the bonded labour and pavement dweller."[7]

To address these concerns, various proposals for reforming the direction and functioning of the Supreme Court have been advocated. These include proposals to abolish two-judge benches;[8] to set up special benches such as the recently established social justice bench;[9] to set up regional benches;[10] to bifurcate the Court's constitutional court function from its appellate court

---

[4]   See Aparna Chandra, William H.J. Hubbard, and Sital Kalantry, *The Supreme Court of India: A People's Court?*, 1 INDIAN L. REV. 145 (2017).

[5]   Rajeev Dhavan, LITIGATION EXPLOSION IN INDIA (1986).

[6]   G. Mohan Gopal, *Justice and the Two Ideas of India*, FRONTLINE, May 27, 2016, www.frontline .in/cover-story/justice-and-the-two-ideas-of-india/ article8581178.ece (accessed Aug. 29, 2018).

[7]   *Moti Ram v. State of Madhya Pradesh* (1978) 4 SCC 47.

[8]   Abolish Two Judge Benches: Fali Nariman, INDIAN EXPRESS, Apr. 10, 2014.

[9]   See Masoodi, Ashwaq, and Monalisa, *Supreme Court Sets Up Social Justice Bench*, LIVE MINT (Dec. 4, 2014) (describing notice issued by the Supreme Court on establishing the social justice bench); Utkarsh Anand, *Allocate More Time to Social Justice Bench, say experts*, INDIAN EXPRESS, Dec. 13, 2014.

[10] See Law Commission of India, 229th Law Commission Report, *Indiankanoon* (August 2009), https://indiankanoon.org/doc/24442307/ (accessed Aug. 29, 2018).

function;[11] and so on. However, in the absence of rigorous empirical study of the Court, many of the current reform proposals are based on impressionistic and anecdotal evidence of the Court's functioning.

Little empirical data exists on the functioning of the Supreme Court. In the early years of the Court George Gadbois undertook such an exercise.[12] More recently, Nicholas Robinson has provided empirical insights into the functioning of the Court.[13] The Vidhi Centre for Legal Policy has also begun empirical studies of the Court.[14] However, much remains to be done in mapping the functioning of the Court.

In this chapter we provide a descriptive account of the functioning of the Court through an empirical analysis of all cases decided by the Supreme Court between 2010 and 2015. The objective of this chapter is to understand the social identity of the litigants that approach the court, the types of matters they bring to the court, the levels of success that different groups of litigants have before the Court, and the decision patterns of the various judges of the Supreme Court. Our approach is quantitative and comprehensive, based on a data set of information drawn from all judgments rendered by the Supreme Court during the years from 2010 through 2015. Our data set contains information on judgments in over 6,000 cases, decided in over 5,000 published opinions issued during this time period. Each of the Court's opinions was hand coded for information on a wide range of variables, allowing us to compile the largest and most detailed data set on the Court's judgments ever collected.

This data provides information about all of the cases decided by Supreme Court judgments during this period (as reported in the *Supreme Court Cases* reporter), including facts about the parties before the Court, where the cases arose, what claims are at issue, what kind of legal representation the parties

---

[11] Id.

[12] George H. Gadbois, Jr., *The Supreme Court of India: A Preliminary Report of an Empirical Study*, 4 J. Const. Parliamentary Stud. 34 (1970). Nonetheless, several authors have used empirical data generated largely by the Court itself to identify trends and the workings of the Court. Rajiv Dhavan used data extensively to observe the litigation explosion in Indian courts. See, e.g., Rajeev Dhavan, Litigation Explosion in India 60–61 (1986).

[13] See, e.g., Nick Robinson, *A Court Adrift*, Frontline, May 3, 2013, www.frontline.in/cover-story/a-court-adrift/article4613892.ece (accessed Aug. 30, 2018).

[14] See, e.g., Alok Prasanna Kumar, Faiza Rahman & Ameen Jauhar, *Vidhi Ctr. for Legal Pol'y, Consultation Paper: The Supreme Court of India's Burgeoning Backlog Problem and Regional Disparities in Access to the Supreme Court* (2015), https://static1.squarespace.com/static/551ea026e4b0adba21a8f9df/t/560cf7d4e4b092010fff89b1/1443690452706/29092015_Consultation+Paper+on+the+Supreme+Court%27s+Burgeoning+Backlog+Problem.pdf (accessed Aug. 30, 2018).

have, how the Court hears the cases and how long the Court takes to decide, who wins, and which justices write the opinions of the Court. In this chapter, we summarize this treasure trove of information with the goal of establishing a set of basic facts about the Court. These facts, we hope, will prompt new research questions and inform existing descriptive and normative debates about the role of the Court in promoting progressive social change. At the very least, this chapter provides a foundation of empirically grounded background facts to inform and contextualize the chapters in this volume.

In the sections that follow, we provide a brief background on the Supreme Court of India and a description of the creation of our data set before presenting our findings. While the aspiration of this chapter is descriptive, not normative, we offer in a short, concluding section some initial thoughts about potential implications of the findings we report.

II. BACKGROUND ON THE SUPREME COURT OF INDIA

The Indian Supreme Court is the apex court for the largest common law judicial system in the world. Set up in 1950 under the Constitution of India, the Court began its existence with eight judges. Over the years, the Court has changed dramatically in size and structure. At present it has 31 seats.[15] It entertains over 60,000 appeals and petitions,[16] and issues approximately 1,000 judgments per year.[17] Court rules do not require judges to sit *en banc*. Judges ordinarily sit in benches of two or three, and sometimes – increasingly rarely – in larger benches.[18] Decisions of all benches of the Court are binding on all lower courts within the territory of India.[19]

Judges of the Court are technically appointed by the President in "consultation" with the Chief Justice of India.[20] In practice, as a result of judicial interpretations, appointments to the Court are made by a "collegium" of the most senior judges of the Court, who choose the Court's new members.[21]

---

[15] INDIAN CONST. Art. 124, § 1.

[16] Supreme Court of India, ANNUAL REPORT 2014, at 79.

[17] JUDIS, the official e-reporter of the Supreme Court of India records 900 judgments for 2014.

[18] Nick Robinson et al., *Interpreting the Constitution: Supreme Court Constitution Benches since Independence*, 46 ECON. POL. WKLY. 27, 28 (2011). (Finding that the number of cases heard and disposed of by five judge benches has decreased from 15.5 percent in the 1950s to 0.12 percent in the 2000s.) A single judge sits for "chamber matters," a set of designated procedural matters, such as bail applications pending appeal.

[19] INDIAN CONST. Art. 141.

[20] INDIAN CONST. Art. 124, § 2.

[21] Special Reference No. 1 of 1998, (1998) 7 SCC 739; *Supreme Court Advocates on Record Ass'n v. Union of India* (1993) 4 SCC 441; *S. P. Gupta v. Union of India*, AIR 1982 SC 149.

Appointees tend to be senior judges, often chief justices, from the high courts.[22] Judges of the Supreme Court must retire at 65 years of age.[23] Consequently, most judges serve on the Supreme Court for short durations, and generally for not more than five years.[24] In its 68 years of existence, more than 230 judges have served on the Court.[25] The Chief Justice of India is the most senior judge of the Supreme Court as measured by the date s/he was appointed to the Court.[26]

The Supreme Court has broad jurisdiction. It performs a dual function: as a court of original jurisdiction on certain matters such as those relating to the enforcement of fundamental rights;[27] and as a final court of appeals against decisions and orders passed by subordinate courts and tribunals.

Article 32 of the Constitution guarantees the right to move the Supreme Court for enforcement of fundamental rights. A distinctive component of this jurisdiction is public interest litigation (PIL), a judicially created innovation of the 1970s. Through PILs the Court reformulated standing rules to allow any member of the public to seek relief from the Court on behalf of a person or people whose fundamental rights had been violated but who could not, "by reason of poverty, helplessness or disability or socially or economically disadvantaged position," come before the Court for relief themselves.[28]

The Court also has discretionary appellate jurisdiction over any order passed by any court or tribunal across the country.[29] A party seeking such

---

[22] The high courts are the next-highest courts to the Supreme Court in the hierarchy of the Indian court system.

[23] INDIAN CONST. Art 124, § 2.

[24] *See* T. R Andhyarujina, *The Age of Judicial Reform*, THE HINDU, Sept. 1, 2012, www.thehindu .com/opinion/lead/the-age-of-judicial-reform/article3845041.ece (accessed Aug. 30, 2018).

[25] SUPREME COURT OF INDIA, www.sci.gov.in (accessed Aug. 30, 2018) (data gathered from adding up the lists of sitting and retired justices).

[26] *See* Abhinav Chandrachud, *Supreme Court's Seniority Norm: Historical Origins*, 47 ECON. POL. WKLY. 26, 26 (2012).

[27] This is not the limit of the Court's jurisdiction. The Supreme Court has original jurisdiction with respect to interstate disputes and over certain election matters. INDIAN CONST. Art. 132 & 711. The President may also refer any matter to the Court for its advisory (non-binding) opinion. INDIAN CONST. Art. 143.

[28] *S. P. Gupta* v. *Union of India*, AIR 1982 SC 149. The Court's own data reveals, however, that even among cases admitted for merits hearing, PILs constitute only 1 percent of the Court's cases. Nick Robinson, A *Quantitative Analysis of the Indian Supreme Court's Workload*, 10 J. EMPIRICAL LEGAL STUD. 570, 590, 598 (2013).

[29] INDIAN CONST. Art. 136 ("Special leave to appeal by the Supreme Court. (1) Notwithstanding anything in this Chapter, the Supreme Court may, in its discretion, grant special leave to appeal from any judgment, decree, determination, sentence or order in any cause or matter passed or made by any court or tribunal in the territory of India.").

discretionary review files a Special Leave Petition (SLP). In recent years, on average about 68,000 cases are filed annually before the Supreme Court,[30] most of which are SLPs.

Apart from SLPs, the Court can also hear cases certified for appeal by high courts.[31] Further, many statutes provide for a statutory right to appeal to the Court.[32] Appeals as of right are defined by statute for certain claims heard by lower courts as well as for the review of decisions by specialized tribunals – adjudicatory bodies separate from the Indian court system that resolve statutory claims in specialized fields, such as electricity regulation, customs and excise, or statutory consumer protection.

Cases filed before the Court are processed in two stages: an initial admissions stage to decide which cases to admit for hearing and a regular (merits) hearing. Judges sit in benches of two every Monday and Friday to decide which cases to hear.[33] The admissions hearing is an *ex parte* proceeding, and the Court denies most SLPs at the admissions stage. However, if the Court is inclined to admit a case, it ordinarily does so only after issuing notice to the other side to appear. A party can also preemptively file a caveat in the Court, requesting that no petition be admitted in which it is a respondent without the presence of such party. In such cases, a matter is listed for admission only after notice is served to the other party. Very rarely does the Court admit a matter *ex parte*. Of the matters in which notice is issued, the Court may dispose of the matter at the admissions stage itself (called "final disposal" matters). In such cases, after a brief hearing, if the Court admits the matter, it allows or denies the SLP as part of the same order. Where the Court finds the need for a more extensive hearing, the case is listed for a "regular" merits hearing.

---

[30] Supreme Court of India, ANNUAL REPORT 2014, at 76–79 (average of cases filed in 2010–2014).

[31] INDIAN CONST. Art. 132, 133, 134. Although the Court's jurisdiction can be invoked through procuring a certificate of appeal from the high court, this practice is rarely used. One possible reason for the low use of the "Certificate of Appeal" jurisdiction is that while ordinarily a petitioner has 90 days to file a SLP, the limitation for filing a SLP after the high court has refused a certificate of appeal is 60 days. Some experts suggested during interviews and interactions with us that lawyers do not invoke the certificate of appeal process so as to give themselves more time to file in the Supreme Court.

[32] Supreme Court of India, ANNUAL REPORT 2014, at 59–63.

[33] Supreme Court of India, PRACTICE AND PROCEDURE: A HANDBOOK OF INFORMATION 35 (2010) (herein SC HANDBOOK).

III. DATA PROCESSING

Our study is based on a comprehensive data set of all opinions of the Court from 2010 to 2015, as published in the case reporter *Supreme Court Cases* (SCC). The data set contains 5,699 judgments from 2010 to 2015 (dealing with 6,857 cases).[34] Our methodology for creating this data set involved five roughly sequential elements: (1) selection of source material for Court opinions; (2) initial development of a template for hand-coding, and pilot testing, review, and revision of the template; (3) comprehensive hand-coding of all cases within the sample frame; (4) processing and quality control; and (5) creation of the final database for analysis.

First, we selected SCC as the source material for our data set because it is the most cited reporter by and before the Supreme Court.[35] Since SCC is a private reporter, it is under no obligation to publish every decision given by the Supreme Court. However, it is easily accessible, has extensive headnotes, and unlike other reporters, records many details, including the names and designations of lawyers involved.

We began our research by running a pilot of the project at Cornell Law School. At this stage, students at Cornell Law School coded cases based on an initial template. After review of the pilot effort, the template was overhauled. To ensure internal consistency within the final data set, we discarded the results of the pilot coding phase.

We then assembled a team of nearly two-dozen students from National Law University (NLU), Delhi, who then took up the task of coding cases. The team read judicial opinions from the SCC Reporter and completed Excel templates. The NLU, Delhi team hand-coded all cases reported in SCC in its volumes for the years 2010 to 2015. Cases reported in these volumes that were decided prior to 2010 were excluded from consideration. Each case was coded for 66 variables (although we do not discuss all coded variables below).

The team of coders at NLU, Delhi then worked with a team of researchers at the University of Chicago Coase-Sandor Institute for Law and Economics to identify coding errors and variables that required recoding. This iterative process involved statistical analysis of the coded data to identify inconsistencies

---

[34] Cases that raise similar issues or revolve around the same facts are tagged and heard together by the Court. Hence, one judgment may dispose of more than one case.

[35] Rakesh Kumar Srivastava, *A Guide to India's Legal Research and Legal System*, GLOBALEX (Apr. 2014), www.nyulawglobal.org/globalex/india_legal_research.htm#_10._Law_Reporting (Chief Librarian of the Supreme Court, stating that this reporter is used around 60 percent of the time before the Supreme Court itself).

in coding patterns across variables. This primarily consisted of items being entered inconsistently by coders, owing to spelling errors or the use of abbreviations by some coders but not others.[36] These inconsistencies were documented by the research team and corrected through an automated recoding process to make codes consistent across cases.[37]

Finally, the cleaned and processed data was converted to the Stata database format for statistical analysis. The data set includes all Court judgments from 2010 through 2015 that have been published in the SCC, with the exception of orders from one-judge benches.[38]

IV. A QUANTITATIVE OVERVIEW OF THE COURT, 2010–2015

In this section, we present a series of descriptive analyses roughly corresponding to the sequence of events in the life of a case decided by the Court. We address, in sequence, the following topics: the characteristics of the cases, including their subject matter, procedural history and the time elapsed in the judicial process; characteristics of the litigants bringing the cases or being brought to court; characteristics of their attorneys; characteristics of judges deciding these cases; and finally trends and patterns of the decisions themselves. In our Conclusion, we provide tentative discussion of potential implications of some of our empirical findings.

A. *Case characteristics*

i. Subject matter categories

We begin by looking at the subject matter of the cases that the Court is deciding. Table 2.1 shows the distribution of subject matters, using the categories employed by the Court itself.[39] Criminal cases are the single largest category, while civil cases are spread over 40 separate categories, none of

---

[36] For most variables, such discrepancies were avoided through use of pre-filled drop-down menus that allowed coders to choose among multiple options. Some variables needed to have an option for coders to enter unique text, however.

[37] Computer code documenting these corrections is available upon request.

[38] We excluded one-judge benches because they generally deal with procedural matters, such as certain types of minor interim applications, which do not generate merit judgments (although they occasionally generate orders that appear in SCC).

[39] See SC HANDBOOK. However, the judgments themselves do not indicate under which subject matter category the Court registry has placed individual cases. We have therefore used the Court's categories but categorized the cases ourselves.

TABLE 2.1 *Subject matter categories*

Subject matter category	Share (%)
Criminal matters	29.1
Service matters	11.2
Ordinary civil matters	10.4
Land acquisition & requisition matter	6.2
Constitutional matters	5.3
Indirect taxes matters	3.8
Letter petition & PIL matters	3.1
Direct taxes matters	2.7
Compensation matters	2.6
Family law matters	1.9
Matters relating to judiciary	1.9
Mercantile laws, commercial transactions, etc.	1.9
Labour matters	1.8
Arbitration matters	1.8
Land laws and agricultural tenancies	1.5
Environmental matters	1.3
Contempt of court matters	1.3
Academic matters	1.2
Appeal against orders of statutory body	1.2
Rent act matters	1.1
Election matters	1.1
Matters relating to leases, govt. contracts, etc.	1.1
Matters relating to consumer protection	1.0
Mines, minerals and mining leases	1.0
Company Law, MRTP & allied matters	0.8
Admission/transfer to engineering and medical colleges	0.8
Matters pertaining to armed forces	0.6
Admission to educ. inst. other than med. & eng.	0.4
Establishment and recognition of educ. inst.	0.4
Personal law matters	0.3
Simple money & mortgage matters, etc.	0.3
Habeas corpus matters	0.2
Statutory appointments	0.2

(*continued*)

TABLE 2.1 *(continued)*

Subject matter category	Share (%)
State excise—trading in liquor	0.2
Religious & charitable endowments	0.2
Human rights matters	0.1
Admiralty and maritime laws	0.1
Reference under right to information	0.1
Other (three categories)	0.0
Total	100.0

which consumes the lion's share of the Court's attention. The largest category among civil cases is "Service Matters," which covers employment-related disputes in government service.

Note that Constitutional Matters comprise 5.3 percent of the entire output of the judiciary, and PIL matters comprise an additional 3.1 per cent. Thus, less than 10 percent of the Court's attention (as measured by number of cases) focuses on case categories most associated with the protection of human rights and the interests of the disadvantaged. Of course, while the volume of these cases is relatively low, this says nothing about the time, effort, and energy of the Court that these matters take. Furthermore, criminal matters, which disproportionately affect the most vulnerable populations, make up a large share of the Court's output.

ii. Procedural history

Our data enables us to trace the procedural history of cases. Most cases decided by the Court come to it as appeals from lower courts and tribunals. Only about 12 percent of judgments are for proceedings within the Court's original (rather than appellate) jurisdiction. See Table 2.2.

Of those cases that came to the Court through appeal or special leave petition (SLP), the vast majority (about 85 percent) came from courts rather than tribunals. Interestingly, 6.2 percent of the appeals involved an interlocutory appeal, that is, an appeal from an order other than the final decision of a court below. See Table 2.3.

Examining the cases coming up to the Supreme Court on appeal from high courts, we find that high courts are unevenly represented in our data set, with over 600 cases from the High Court of Punjab and Haryana and no cases from

TABLE 2.2 *Case origins: nature of proceeding*

Variable	All (%)	Civil (%)	Criminal (%)
Appeal/SLP	88.1	86.2	92.7
Writ petition	8.2	9.7	4.9
Other original jurisdiction	3.2	3.4	2.0
Review or curative	0.6	0.7	0.4
N	6,850	4,659	2,174

TABLE 2.3 *Case origins: source of case*

Variable	Count	Total (%)	N
Referred from smaller bench	131	1.9	6,806
Originated in court rather than tribunal	5,806	85.4	6,799
Interlocutory appeal	428	6.2	6,854
Continuing mandamus	383	5.7	6,724

the High Court of Manipur or the High Court of Tripura (which may not be surprising, since these courts were created only in 2013). See Table 2.4. These patterns largely track what we might expect, based on factors such as the per capita gross domestic product (GDP) of the states within the jurisdiction of each high court (see Figure 2.1), the size of the various courts' jurisdictions and their geographical proximity to the Supreme Court.[40]

iii. Case duration

Next, we examine how long the cases in our data took to reach judgment. Litigation in India is notoriously slow. Our data allow us to quantify how long cases remain pending in the Supreme Court before the Court hands down judgment. See Table 2.5. On average, cases take about 10 years from filing in the court of first instance to judgment in the Supreme Court. About one-third of that time was spent in the Supreme Court itself.

The data also permit, to a limited extent, a comparison of case duration in the Supreme Court, the high courts, and courts of first instance. For 170 cases, we have detailed information on filing and judgment dates for all three levels

---

[40] Robinson, *A Quantitative Analysis of the Indian Supreme Court's Workload*, 10 J. EMPIRICAL LEGAL STUD. 570 (2013).

TABLE 2.4 *Case origins: High Court appealed from*

Rank	High Court	Number	Reversal rate (%)
1	High Court of Punjab & Haryana	646	62
2	High Court of Bombay	607	56
3	High Court of Delhi	530	55
4	High Court of Allahabad	502	54
5	High Court of Madras	368	60
6	High Court of Karnataka	367	61
7	High Court of Andhra Pradesh	301	59
8	High Court of Madhya Pradesh	289	64
9	High Court of Rajasthan	262	62
10	High Court of Calcutta	261	60
11	High Court of Kerala	233	49
12	High Court of Gujarat	198	61
13	High Court of Patna	171	64
14	High Court of Uttarakhand	121	63
15	High Court of Orissa	94	73
16	High Court of Gauhati	91	54
17	High Court of Jharkhand	88	65
18	High Court of Himachal Pradesh	73	56
19	High Court of Chhattisgarh	56	65
20	High Court of Jammu & Kashmir	39	44
21	High Court of Sikkim	8	75
22	High Court of Meghalaya	1	62
23	High Court of Manipur	0	0
24	High Court of Tripura	0	0
	Total	5,306	59

of the court system, which allows us to compare, for the very same cases, how much time they spent in each level of the court system. Table 2.6 indicates that on average cases that travel all the way to the Supreme Court are likely to take longer in the Supreme Court than in the lower courts, including the court of first instance where the case was tried. Although a significant amount of energy is devoted to resolving delays in the trial courts, our data indicates that the problem is present throughout the system, and in fact may be more acute in the higher levels of the judiciary.

TABLE 2.5 *Date and duration*

Variable	Mean	Median	Max	Min	N
Year filed in court of first instance	2002	2004	2015	1905	3,937
Year decided in court of first instance	2003	2005	2014	1964	1,381
Year of decision appealed from	2008	2008	2015	1976	5,500
Year filed in Supreme Court	2009	2010	2015	1968	6,853
Year decided by Supreme Court	2012	2012	2015	2010	6,856
Duration in court of first instance (days)	1,466	858	9,372	1	180
Duration in court below (days)	1,784	987	16,574	5	1,278
Duration in Supreme Court (days)	1,569	1,296	12,404	0	5,461

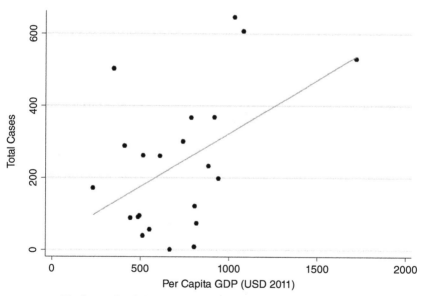

FIGURE 2.1. Total cases decided and per capita GDP, by High Court jurisdiction

Table 2.7 indicates that at the Supreme Court itself civil and criminal cases take on average approximately the same amount of time to be decided. Writ petitions to the Court take longer – as is to be expected given that the court has to hear the case afresh and cannot rely on case records from the courts below.

TABLE 2.6 *Cases with complete duration data*

Variable	Mean	Median	Max.	Min.
Duration in court of first instance (days)	1,424	847	9,372	0
Duration in court below (days)	2,082	880	11,966	18
Duration in Supreme Court (days)	1,456	1,207	4,372	30

TABLE 2.7 *Duration (days) in the Supreme Court, by case type*

Variable	Mean	Median	Max.	Min.	N
Civil	1,582	1,212	12,404	0	3,440
Criminal	1,533	1,411.5	8,993	0	1,812
Constitutional challenge	1,610	1,140.5	12,404	0	194
Writ petition	1,937	1,492.5	12,404	81	34
Case originated in court	1,541	1,277.5	12,404	0	4,542
Case originated in tribunal	1,721	1,441	11,078	0	909

Interestingly, cases originating in tribunals take longer for disposal in the Supreme Court than cases originating in courts. One of the goals behind setting up tribunals is to speed up the disposal of cases. If such cases are likely to face long pendency in the Supreme Court, this purpose gets defeated.

Breaking down case durations by subject matters reveals wide variation in the speed with which different types of cases are resolved by the Court. Table 2.8 shows that some (albeit small) categories of cases take upwards of seven or eight years on average, while others take much less. (Eight years is 2,922 days, and four years is 1,461 days, so the category of Admiralty and Maritime cases exceeds eight years in duration on average, and 20 additional categories exceed four years in the Supreme Court alone.) Only one category, habeas corpus, averages resolution in less than one year.

B. *Litigant characteristics*

Next, we consider the configuration of the parties in the cases in our data. We use the terms plaintiffs and defendants to refer to the original status of parties in the court of first instance. Plaintiffs and defendants are about evenly represented among appellants.[41] A large fraction of cases involves multiple

---

[41] For simplicity, we use "appellant" to refer to the party who sought review in the Supreme Court, regardless of whether by special leave petition or appeal.

TABLE 2.8 *Average duration (days) in the Supreme Court, by subject*

Rank	Subject matter category	Duration
1	Admiralty and maritime laws	3,050
2	Religious & charitable endowments	2,776
3	Indirect taxes matters	2,261
4	State excise—trading in liquor	2,133
5	Direct taxes matters	2,116
6	Land acquisition & requisition matters	2,021
7	Land laws and agricultural tenancies	1,990
8	Human rights matters	1,801
9	Family law matters	1,796
10	Matters relating to commissions of enquiry	1,763
11	Matters pertaining to armed forces	1,691
12	Labour matters	1,663
13	Environmental matters	1,651
14	Simple money & mortgage matters, etc.	1,643
15	Contempt of court matters	1,610
16	Constitutional matters	1,593
17	Mercantile laws, commercial transactions, etc.	1,546
18	Criminal matters	1,544
19	Matters relating to consumer protection	1,526
20	Ordinary Civil matters	1,499
21	Service matters	1,469
22	Appeal against orders of statutory body	1,460
23	Arbitration matters	1,450
24	Compensation matters	1,438
25	Rent act matters	1,378
26	Company law, MRTP & allied matters	1,356
27	Personal law matters	1,343
28	Mines, minerals and mining leases	1,284
29	Letter petition & PIL matters	1,280
30	Academic matters	1,193
31	Matters relating to judiciary	1,188
32	Matters relating to leases, govt. contracts, etc.	1,077
33	Establishment and recognition of educ. inst.	888

(continued)

TABLE 2.8 (*continued*)

Rank	Subject matter category	Duration
34	Statutory appointments	863
35	Election matters	735
36	Admission to educ. inst. other than med. and eng.	631
37	Eviction under the public premises	592
38	Reference under right to information	538
39	Admission/transfer to eng. and med. colleges	390
40	Habeas corpus matters	190

TABLE 2.9 *Plaintiffs and defendants: summary statistics*

Variable	Mean (%)	N
Appellant is plaintiff	46.3	5,894
More than one plaintiff	38.2	5,892
More than one defendant	55.9	5,890
Plaintiff is male (among individual plaintiffs)	83.2	2,756
Defendant is male (among individual defendants)	90.9	2,475
Plaintiff is Indian	99.7	5,888
Defendant is Indian	99.8	5,887

plaintiffs or multiple defendants (or both). To the extent that the lead plaintiff or defendant is a natural person, parties are overwhelmingly male. (Only 16.8 percent of the plaintiffs are female and 9.1 percent of the defendants are women. Males are a higher share of defendants than plaintiffs because in our data criminal defendants are about 95 percent male.) See Table 2.9. Perhaps the most notable statistics in Table 2.9, though, are the shares of all parties (including natural persons, governments, and institutional entities such as corporations) who are Indian. Unlike the US Supreme Court, which like the US court system as a whole, entertains a substantial number of claims by or against foreign parties, the Supreme Court of India appears to be a forum almost exclusively engaged with disputes between Indian nationals.

Focusing specifically on civil cases, the majority of plaintiffs are individuals (i.e., natural persons), and government is the defendant more often than not. Not surprisingly, then, the most common configuration of parties in our data set is an individual plaintiff versus a government defendant. See Table 2.10.

TABLE 2.10 *Pairings of parties in civil cases, shares by status*

		Defendant		
		Individual (%)	Government (%)	Institution (%)
Plaintiff	Individual	17.0 (N = 662)	32.9 (N = 1,284)	11.6 (N = 453)
	Government	4.4 (N = 172)	0.9 (N = 34)	3.4 (N = 131)
	Institution	2.7 (N = 104)	20.1 (N = 783)	7.1 (N = 277)

TABLE 2.11 *Appellants in civil and criminal cases*

Share of appellants	Civil cases (%)	Criminal cases (%)	Total (%)
Individual	46.1	84.9	58.4
Government	23.9	10.9	19.8
Institution	30.0	4.2	21.8

(We do not separately present results for criminal cases, where the configuration is usually the government against an individual defendant.)

Looking instead at the appellant/appellee relationship rather than the plaintiff/defendant relationship, we find that individuals make up the largest group of appellants in both the civil and criminal context. See Table 2.11. In criminal appeals this implies that the vast majority of the Court's criminal judgments involve individuals appealing against conviction and/or sentence, rather than the state appealing an acquittal. This data is consistent with the premise that the Court tends to take up the cause of the individual against corporations or the government.

As Table 2.11 indicates, before the Supreme Court the Government is the appellant in roughly 20 percent of the cases. Of these, service matters, tax matters, and criminal matters form the largest share of the cases that the government brings to Court. See Table 2.12. Interestingly, in tax matters, the government wins in only half the cases that the Court admits. This might indicate both over-appealing weaker cases by the Government and relaxed admission scrutiny for such cases by the Court. Paired with the finding in Table 2.11, that tax matters take amongst the longest to dispose of, these statistics point to the need for the Court and the Government to review their approach to tax litigation.

TABLE 2.12 *Government appellants, top subject matter and reversal rates*

Rank	Subject matter category	Share (%)	Reversal rate (%)
1	Service matters	19.2	67.3
2	Criminal matters	17.3	56.8
3	Indirect taxes matters	10.8	50.3
4	Ordinary civil matters	8.9	66.4
5	Direct taxes matters	6.9	48.4
6	Land acquisition & requisition matters	6.4	74.1
7	Constitutional matters[42]	5.5	100
8	Academic matters	2.3	13.8
9	Arbitration matters	2.1	65.5
10	Appeal against orders of statutory body	2.1	72.4

C. Attorneys

There are two tiers in the Supreme Court bar in India: advocates and senior advocates. "Senior advocate" is a status conferred upon an attorney by the Court itself. Senior advocates are an exclusive group. As of April 2015, there were 349 senior advocates designated by the Supreme Court of India,[43] but these lawyers obtain a great share of the advocacy work at the Court. As Table 2.13 indicates, advocates and senior advocates are about evenly represented in our data set, (with only a tiny number of unrepresented parties). In criminal cases, most attorneys (for both sides) are advocates, while in civil cases, a majority are senior advocates.

Notably, there are more cases pairing senior advocates against each other than other pairings of attorneys. See Table 2.14.

Further, in a small fraction of cases (3.9 percent) the Court appoints an *amicus curiae*, typically a senior or otherwise well-respected lawyer, to act as a friend of the court, and assist the Court in the matter. The *amicus* does not represent either party. S/he is supposed to assist the court in an impartial manner. Amicus curie are generally appointed in PILs or in criminal appeals

---

[42] Note that the reversal rate for constitutional matters is 100 percent because there is only one observation with non-missing information on reversal.

[43] *List of Senior Advocates Designated by Supreme Court (as on 23/04/2015)*, SUPREME COURT OF INDIA, www.sci.nic.in/outtoday/List%20of%20Sr.%20Advocates%20.Designated%20by%20Supreme%20Court%20as%20on%2023%2004%202015.pdf (accessed Aug. 30, 2016).

TABLE 2.13 *Counsel, by party and case type*

Counsel	Appellant			Respondent		
	Total (%)	Criminal (%)	Civil (%)	Total (%)	Criminal (%)	Civil (%)
Advocates	51.1	64.0	45.1	46.9	58.5	41.4
Senior advocates	47.5	35.2	53.3	52.9	41.2	58.3
Other[44]	1.4	0.8	1.6	0.3	0.4	0.3
N	6,041	1,960	4,058	5,978	1,956	3,999

TABLE 2.14 *Pairings of counsel for appellant and respondent, civil cases*

		Respondent	
		Advocate N (%)	Senior advocate N (%)
Appellant	Advocate	1,098 (28.5)	659 (17.1)
	Senior advocate	513 (13.3)	1,582 (41.1)

where the defendant is represented and the Court feels the need for additional assistance over and above what the defense lawyer can provide.

D. *Decision characteristics*

i. Bench size

We now turn from the characteristics of the cases to how the Court decides them. First, we examine bench size. Nearly 90 percent of cases in our data set were decided by a two-judge bench and nearly all the rest were decided by three-judge benches. Only 91 cases out of 6,856 in our data were decided by a five-judge bench – and in this six-year period there were no benches larger than five judges. See Table 2.15.

As one would expect, to the extent we see five-judge benches in the data, they are disproportionately devoted to cases within the original jurisdiction of the Court. While over 90 percent of decisions from two-judge benches arose

---

[44] "Other" refers to "party in person" (i.e., *pro se* party) or legal aid representation.

TABLE 2.15 *Summary statistics, by bench size*

Bench size	2	3	5	All
Total cases	5,971	794	91	6,856
Share of total (%)	87.1	11.6	1.3	100.0
N with PIL	187	71	4	262
Share with PIL (%)	3.1	9.0	4.4	3.8
Share of PIL (%)	71.4	27.1	1.5	100
N with const. challenge	349	65	32	446
Share with const. challenge (%)	5.8	8.2	36.4	6.5
Share of const. challenge (%)	78.3	14.6	7.2	100

TABLE 2.16 *Summary statistics, case categories, by bench size*

Bench Size	2 (%)	3 (%)	5 (%)
Appeal/SLP	91.4	66.4	56.7
Writ petition	5.7	24.2	28.9
Other original jurisdiction	2.3	8.8	12.2
Review or curative	0.6	0.5	2.2
Total	100	100	100

out of appeals and SLPs, only about half from five-judge benches did. See Table 2.16.

More surprising is the distribution of cases involving challenges to the constitutionality of laws or government action. Given that substantial questions of law as to the interpretation of the constitution are required by law to be decided by constitution benches of five or more judges,[45] one would expect cases involving challenges to the constitutionality of legislation or government action to be concentrated in five-judge benches. However, as Table 2.15 shows, more than 78 percent of all such questions are decided by two-judge benches. Less than 8 percent of constitutional challenges are decided by benches of five or more. There were even fewer cases disposed by five or more judge benches (0.12 percent) from 2005 to 2009 than in our data set.[46]

---

[45] INDIAN CONST. Art. 145.

[46] Nick Robinson et al., *Interpreting the Constitution: Supreme Court Constitution Benches since Independence*, 46 ECON. POL. WKLY. 27, 28 (2011).

TABLE 2.17 *Summary statistics, indicator variables*

Variable	Mean (%)	N
Reversed	59.4	6,278
Reversed, civil cases	61.4	4,195
Reversed, criminal cases	55.3	2,066
Referred to larger bench	1.7	6,386
Plaintiff wins	50.0	5,632
Parties to bear own costs	90.3	2,468

In contrast, in the period from 1950 to 1954, 15.5 percent of disposed cases were by five or more judge benches.[47] A sharp decline in bench size occurred from the early 1960s to the late 1960s.[48]

A similar pattern appears for PILs. Given their broad reach, intended social impact, and fundamental rights implications, one might expect the Court to decide such cases in larger benches. Yet over 71 percent of all PILs are heard by two-judge benches.

ii. Outcomes

We turn now to outcomes. How does the Court resolve the cases in our data? Table 2.17 provides some data on outcomes. We find an overall reversal rate of nearly 60 percent. The reversal rate in criminal cases (about 55 percent) is lower than in civil cases (about 61 percent). In other work, we interpret this difference as reflecting a willingness of the Justices of the Court to admit criminal appeals with weaker grounds for appeal (and therefore with a lower probability of an eventual reversal).[49] This is consistent with Justices being more concerned about correcting errors in criminal proceedings; they may admit borderline criminal appeals but dismiss borderline civil appeals.

Interestingly, despite reversing lower court decisions in only 60 percent of the cases admitted for a merits hearing, the Court, by and large, does not impose costs on parties. In 90.3 percent of the cases it directs parties to bear their own costs.

---

[47] Id.
[48] Id.
[49] See Aparna Chandra, William H. J. Hubbard, and Sital Kalantry, *The Supreme Court of India: A People's Court?*, 1 INDIAN L. REV. 145 (2017).

TABLE 2.18 *Summary statistics, by bench size*

Bench size	2 (%)	3 (%)	5 (%)	All (%)
Share of PILs successful	50.0	69.2	100	53.8
Share of const. challenges successful	51.5	55.6	60.0	52.7
Share overruling precedent	0.9%	5.2	19.8	1.7

TABLE 2.19 *Summary statistics, nature of constitutional challenge*

Reason	N	N Successful
Constitutional amendment/legislation: basic structure	21	6
Legislation: fundamental rights	77	16
Legislation: other	52	31
Executive action: basic structure	12	4
Executive action: fundamental rights	224	125
Executive action: other	55	34
Total	441	216

Following on from the discussion about bench sizes, Table 2.18 presents the success rates of PILs and constitutional challenges in the Supreme Court, by bench size.[50] Although larger benches are more willing to declare something unconstitutional or grant relief in a PIL, benches of all sizes show willingness to reach these conclusions.

Table 2.19 provides further information on constitutional challenges. The majority of constitutional challenges are against executive action rather than legislation or constitutional amendments. The success rate of challenges to executive action is higher than challenges to legislation as well. Table 2.20 provides details of the success rates of the various types of constitutional challenges, by bench size.

Another action that should be reserved for judgments by larger benches is the overruling of precedent. This is because decisions of coordinate and larger benches are binding on subsequent benches. If the judges on a subsequent bench disagree with the ruling of a previous coordinate bench, or find contradictory precedents from larger benches, they are required to refer the

---

[50] We code a PIL successful if the plaintiff is the prevailing party in the Supreme Court. We code a constitutional challenge as successful if the challenged government law or action is struck down or altered by the judgment.

TABLE 2.20 *Number (number successful) of constitutional challenges, by bench size and nature of challenge*

Bench size	2	3	5
Const. amend./legislation: basic structure	4 (3)	7 (1)	10 (2)
Legislation: fundamental rights	57 (10)	18 (4)	2 (0)
Legislation: other	48 (29)	2 (0)	2 (2)
Executive action: basic structure	10 (2)	0	2 (2)
Executive action: fundamental rights	183 (98)	32 (21)	9 (6)
Executive action: other	42 (26)	6 (4)	7 (4)
Total	344 (168)	65 (30)	32 (16)

matter to the Chief Justice of India for reference to a larger bench.[51] In our data, we coded a judgment as overruling precedent if the SCC headnote so indicated.[52] Indeed, we find that larger benches and especially five-judge benches are much more likely to overrule precedent in the course of their decisions. See Table 2.18 above. Notably, though, half (56 of 115) of all overrulings are announced by two-judge benches, in disregard of rules of precedent.

We also find variation in the reversal rates of different high courts and other courts and tribunals from which the cases originated. Table 2.21 ranks the high courts, tribunals, and special courts by their reversal rates. Most rates are in a band roughly around the overall reversal rate of about 59 percent. Although there are some outliers far from the average, we advise caution in interpreting the outlier values, as many of them involve courts with relatively small numbers of cases (there are only eight cases from the High Court of Sikkim, for example), and thus the difference may be due to variation arising from small sample sizes.

Our data also show that individual, government, and institutional appellants are likely to win at roughly the same rates. See Table 2.22.

---

[51] *Central Board of Dawoodi Bohra v. State of Maharashtra* (2005) 2 SCC 673.
[52] The Chief Editor of the SCC informed us that the SCC headnote editors also flag cases that impliedly overrule precedents. Such implied overrulings are therefore also part of this data.

TABLE 2.21 *Reversal rate: adjudicatory body appealed from*

High Court	Reversal rate (%)	N[53]
High Court of Sikkim	75.0	8
High Court of Orissa	73.3	94
High Court of Jharkhand	65.1	88
High Court of Chhattisgarh	64.8	56
High Court of Madhya Pradesh	64.1	289
High Court of Patna	64.0	171
High Court of Uttarakhand	62.7	121
High Court of Punjab & Haryana	62.3	646
High Court of Rajasthan	62.1	262
Special Court	61.5	13
High Court of Gujarat	61.3	198
High Court of Karnataka	60.9	367
High Court of Madras	59.9	368
High Court of Calcutta	59.7	261
High Court of Andhra Pradesh	59.2	301
High Court of Himachal Pradesh	56.2	73
High Court of Bombay	55.7	607
High Court of Delhi	54.7	530
High Court of Allahabad	54.4	502
High Court of Gauhati	53.9	91
Tribunal	50.3	254
High Court of Kerala	49.1	233
High Court of Jammu & Kashmir	43.6	39
High Court of Meghalaya	0.0	1
Total	58.5	5,573

Finally, we studied whether concurring judgments by lower courts (i.e., the courts of first and second instance reached the same outcome) would have an impact on the reversal rate before the Supreme Court. As set forth in Table 2.23, we find, as expected, that the Supreme Court is more likely to reverse a decision when lower courts disagree on the outcome than when the lower courts agree.

---

[53] Number of cases includes cases for which information on reversal is missing.

TABLE 2.22 *Appellant win rates, by party status*

Appellant status	Win rate (%)	N
Individual	58.0	3,728
Government	61.2	1,277
Institution	61.4	1,261
Total	59.3	6,266

TABLE 2.23 *Reversal rate, by lower court agreement*

Outcomes in lower courts/tribunals	Agreement (%)	Disagreement (%)	N
Criminal appeals from High Courts	49.8	58.0	1,384
Civil appeals from High Courts	60.3	63.7	1,142
Civil appeals from appellate tribunals	59.6	73.8	600

TABLE 2.24. *Total judgment length*

Variable	Mean	Median	Max.	Min.	N
No. of pages in opinion	8.7	6	268	1	5,547
No. of pages in opinion, const. challenge cases	17.9	11	268	1	269

E. *Opinion characteristics*

We conclude the survey of our data on the Court with a look at the judgments themselves – the opinions that are the work product of the justices of the Court. The first thing to note is that the Supreme Court of India is prolific! It produces nearly 1,000 opinions per year. As these opinions average almost nine pages in length, the Court generates over 8,000 pages of new law for the bench and bar to digest each year.[54] See Table 2.24.

---

[54] Data in prior sections were organized by judgment—each case decided by the Court is treated as separate, even if two cases were decided in a single opinion. In this section, we treat opinions, rather than judgments, as the unit of analysis. Thus, if a judge writes a single opinion deciding two consolidated cases, we treat that as a single observation.

TABLE 2.25 *Authorship summary statistics, by bench size*

Bench size	2 (%)	3 (%)	5 (%)	All (%)
Share with signed opinion	74.4	61.9	80.7	73.2
Share with concurrence	0.8	2.7	5.3	1.0
Share with dissent	0.3	1.4	5.3	0.5

Nearly all of this output takes the form of unanimous judgments. Most opinions take the familiar form of an opinion authored by a single justice (what we are calling "signed opinions"), although a large share of opinions are *per curiam* (i.e., not attributed to a specific justice). Separate opinions, whether concurring or dissenting, are extremely rare. See Table 2.25. Even five-judge benches, which presumably hear the most difficult and contentious cases, produce a separate opinion (dissenting or concurring) barely 10 percent of the time.

Among signed opinions, opinion-writing duties do not fall evenly among justices. Table 2.26 lists the judges in our data, with the total number of opinions of the court (as opposed to concurring opinions or dissenting opinions) each justice has authored and the total number of cases in which each justice has participated.[55] The number of opinions authored by justice varies widely (from none to 236). This is largely owing to variation in the number of cases decided by the justices, of course, but there is also substantial variation in how often a justice writes after hearing a case. In Table 2.26, we use bold typeface to mark the three highest rates (Banumathi, Kabir, and Sirpurkar, JJ) and three lowest rates (Joseph, Agrawal, and Misra, JJ) of opinion writing as a percentage of all cases in which the justice participates. Justice Banumathi writes the opinion of the court nearly two-thirds (64.4 percent) of the time she participates in the case; Justice Joseph did so less than one-in-20 times (4.4 percent).[56]

As noted above, concurrences and dissents are exceedingly rare in our data. The few separate opinions we do find are largely the product of a minority of justices. As Table 2.27 indicates, only 10 justices have authored more than one concurring opinion in our data; 37 have authored zero. But even among those

---

[55] The "other" justices not separately listed are Justices Arijit Pasayat, B. N. Kirpal, Y. K. Sabharwal, G. B. Pattanaik, and V. Ramaswami, each of whom served during only a tiny segment of our sample period and thus are not well represented in the data.

[56] For purposes of identifying outliers in opinion-writing rates, we focus only on judges who have participated in at least 25 judgments. Justices who have heard only a handful of cases, of course, may have very high or very low rates simply because of small sample size, so to speak.

justices most likely to write a concurring opinion (Lokur, Chelameswar, and Thakur, JJ), they do so rarely.

So too with dissenting opinions. Table 2.28 reveals that only five justices have authored more than one dissenting opinion in our data; 46 have

TABLE 2.26 *Opinion authorship: opinions of the court*

Justice	Opinions of the court	Total cases	Rate (%)
B. S. Chauhan	236	495	47.7
P. Sathasivam	227	511	44.4
G. S. Singhvi	184	494	37.2
K. S. P. Radhakrishnan	178	450	39.6
T. S. Thakur	176	403	43.7
Dipak Misra	167	438	38.1
Altamas Kabir	160	252	63.5
R. M. Lodha	151	348	43.4
R. V. Raveendran	139	295	47.1
A. K. Patnaik	133	397	33.5
Swatanter Kumar	112	300	37.3
S. J. Mukhopadhaya	111	307	36.2
Ranjan Gogoi	100	253	39.5
A. K. Ganguly	96	246	39.0
Aftab Alam	95	299	31.8
A. K. Sikri	95	239	39.7
V. Gopala Gowda	95	231	41.1
Mukundakam Sharma	89	201	44.3
C. K. Prasad	86	337	25.5
Anil R. Dave	85	364	23.4
S. S. Nijjar	83	288	28.8
Ranjana Prakash Desai	78	204	38.2
D. K. Jain	75	170	44.1
M. Y. Eqbal	75	160	46.9
H. L. Dattu	72	373	19.3
F. M. I. Kalifulla	68	212	32.1
H .L. Gokhale	61	244	25.0
J. S. Khehar	61	176	34.7
V. S. Sirpurkar	56	98	57.1
Dalveer Bhandari	53	193	27.5

TABLE 2.26 CONT.   *Opinion authorship: opinions of the court (cont.)*

Justice	Opinions of the court	Total cases	Rate (%)
Madan B. Lokur	49	187	26.2
R. Banumathi	47	73	64.4
Kurian Joseph	45	124	36.3
Jasti Chelameswar	44	219	20.1
Vikramajit Sen	43	139	30.9
S. H. Kapadia	37	225	16.4
J. M. Panchal	37	110	33.6
Markandey Katju	36	152	23.7
Chockalingam Nagappan	36	134	26.9
P. C. Ghose	36	110	32.7
H. S. Bedi	35	174	20.1
Gyan Sudha Misra	34	267	12.7
B. Sudershan Reddy	31	107	29.0
Adarsh Kumar Goel	31	64	48.4
Prafulla C. Pant	28	59	47.5
Shiva Kirti Singh	27	91	29.7
N. V. Ramana	26	92	28.3
Rohinton Fali Nariman	24	69	34.8
Deepak Verma	23	164	14.0
U. U. Lalit	20	51	39.2
Abhay Manohar Sapre	20	50	40.0
S. A. Bobde	17	122	13.9
Tarun Chatterjee	11	21	52.4
K. G. Balakrishnan	10	74	13.5
Arun Mishra	9	37	24.3
Amitava Roy	9	22	40.9
Cyriac Joseph	5	113	4.4
R. K. Agrawal	2	38	5.3
5 others	3	7	42.9
Total	4,172	12,073	34.6

TABLE 2.27 *Opinion authorship: concurring opinions*

Justice	Concurring opinions	Total cases	Rate (%)
Madan B. Lokur	8	187	4.3
T. S. Thakur	6	403	1.5
Jasti Chelameswar	5	219	2.3
K. S. P. Radhakrishnan	4	450	0.9
Dipak Misra	4	438	0.9
C. K. Prasad	4	337	1.2
Altamas Kabir	3	252	1.2
A. K. Ganguly	3	246	1.2
Gyan Sudha Misra	3	267	1.1
A. K. Sikri	2	239	0.8
G. S. Singhvi	1	494	0.2
R. M. Lodha	1	348	0.3
Swatanter Kumar	1	300	0.3
Aftab Alam	1	299	0.3
Mukundakam Sharma	1	201	0.5
Ranjana Prakash Desai	1	204	0.5
F. M. I. Kalifulla	1	212	0.5
H. L. Gokhale	1	244	0.4
J. S. Khehar	1	176	0.6
R. Banumathi	1	73	1.4
Kurian Joseph	1	124	0.8
Vikramajit Sen	1	139	0.7
S. H. Kapadia	1	225	0.4
B. Sudershan Reddy	1	107	0.9
Rohinton Fali Nariman	1	69	1.4
Cyriac Joseph	1	113	0.9
37 others	0	5707	0
Total	58	12073	0.4

authored zero. Table 2.28 indicates that Justices Banumathi, Misra, and Chelameswar write dissents at the highest rates. When considering the prospects for the Supreme Court of India to serve as a catalyst for social change, it may be worth contemplating whether the extremely low rates of concurring and dissenting opinions indicate a norm of agreement, or perhaps even conformity, within the Court. If so, a norm of agreement might empower

TABLE 2.28 *Opinion authorship: dissenting opinions*

Justice	Dissenting opinions	Total cases	Rate (%)
Gyan Sudha Misra	6	267	2.2
Jasti Chelameswar	4	219	1.8
V. Gopala Gowda	3	231	1.3
H. L. Gokhale	2	244	0.8
R. Banumathi	2	73	2.7
P. Sathasivam	1	511	0.2
K. S. P. Radhakrishnan	1	450	0.2
Altamas Kabir	1	252	0.4
A. K. Patnaik	1	397	0.3
Ranjan Gogoi	1	253	0.4
Aftab Alam	1	299	0.3
Anil R. Dave	1	364	0.3
S. S. Nijjar	1	288	0.3
F. M. I. Kalifulla	1	212	0.5
V. S. Sirpurkar	1	98	1.0
Dalveer Bhandari	1	193	0.5
H. S. Bedi	1	174	0.6
46 others	0	7,548	0
Total	29	12,073	0.2

the Court to speak in a united way when making bold pronouncement, or it may prevent the Court from taking bold steps in the first place.

V. CONCLUSION

In this chapter, we present a wide range of findings from our analysis of the largest, most detailed data set of Supreme Court of India judgments ever constructed. These findings should help establish basic facts about the Court that can inform and perhaps provoke future research.

Evaluating the potential of the Supreme Court of India to instantiate social change requires identifying the current capabilities and limitations of its current practices. In this respect, our chapter has identified many facts about the Court that may be relevant. Here, we will simply note a few of them and offer some speculations about their relevance for the larger project of understanding how the Court functions and which directions for potential reform are the most promising.

First, the large number of cases decided by the Court, large number of criminal cases, and large number of cases involving individual appellants are consistent with the Court's oft-stated self-conception as a "people's court" determined to provide broad access to litigants. Yet handling the crush of thousands of routine cases surely detracts from the time and energy that the Court can devote to high-profile cases or the elaboration of broad rules to govern Indian society. There are clearly trade-offs here. One way in which the Court has created a greater capacity to hear large numbers of cases has been its increasing reliance on two-judge benches, to the point in our study period that nearly 90 percent of cases are being decided by only two judges. Yet decisions overruling existing precedent are required to be heard by benches of three or more judges and important constitutional challenges by benches of five or more (although, as we observed, this rule appears to be honored in the breach). The Court's ability to speak with a unified voice (or at least to speak in groups larger than two) on questions of jurisprudential or constitutional import suffers as the resources of the Court are spread thinner and thinner to hear more and more cases. Thus, a crucial question is whether the Court would benefit from striking a different balance. In other work,[57] we explore this question further.

Second, and closely related, we see that public interest litigations constitute less than 4 percent (262 of 6,856) of the cases in our data, and most PILs are handled by two-judge benches. Yet PILs are the consummate legal actions for promoting progressive social change. Do the small numbers relative to the whole belie a disproportionate impact (and disproportionate effort and attention from the Court)? Or does this call for a reassessment of the Court's commitment to PILs? Our data alone cannot answer these questions.

Third, while our focus and the focus of this volume is on the role of the Court, our data raises questions about the role of attorneys in setting India's agenda for social change. Accounts of the influence of so-called grand advocates abound.[58] Is there a way to see whether they affect the outcomes of

---

[57] See Aparna Chandra, William H.J. Hubbard, and Sital Kalantry, *The Supreme Court of India: A People's Court?*, 1 INDIAN L. REV. 145 (2017).

[58] Robinson and Galanter describe an even smaller group of lawyers in the top echelon of the Indian legal profession whom they dub "Grand Advocates." Marc Galanter and Nick Robinson, *India's Grand Advocates: A Legal Elite Flourishing in the Era of Globalization* 2 & 11 (HLS Program on the Legal Professional Research Paper No. 2013–5, 2013). These elite lawyers charge eye-popping fees ($10,000 for a few minutes of argument) and represent only the "uber-rich, major multinational corporations, and the country's political class." Id. Robinson and

cases? Preliminary work by Vidhi suggests that they most certainly do.[59] If elite advocates have substantial influence over which cases the Court exercises its discretion to hear, this raises the question of the agenda-setting power of advocates vis-à-vis the Court itself.

Fourth, the data on case duration suggests that delays in adjudication are substantial in the Supreme Court and are distributed throughout the appellate hierarchy as well. Many questions remain. How long are the delays faced by the cases that *aren't* in our data, which are pending but not yet decided? At what levels of the court system can delays be most easily remedied? How are delays affecting the delivery of justice? Most importantly for the agenda of this book, how does pervasive delay affect the ability of the Indian Courts to deliver aid to the disadvantaged or instantiate legal and social change? Delay, by its very nature, preserves the status quo.

It is inevitable that there are countless more questions we have not even identified. Our hope is that the data we have presented here will provide a starting point for research that identifies, and ultimately answers, these questions.

REFERENCES

Anand, Utkarsh. 2014. Allocate More Time to Social Justice Bench, Say Experts. *Indian Express*. Dec. 13. Accessed Aug. 29, 2018. https://indianexpress.com/article/india/india-others/allocate-more-time-to-social-justice-bench-say-experts/.

Andhyarujina, T. R. 2012. The Age of Judicial Reform. *The Hindu*. September 1. Accessed Aug. 30, 2018. www.thehindu.com/opinion/lead/the-age-of-judicial-reform/article3845041.ece.

Central Board of Dawoodi Bohra v. *State of Maharashtra*. 2005. 2 SCC 673 (Supreme Court of India).

Chandra, Aparna, William H. J. Hubbard, and Sital Kalantry. 2017. *The Supreme Court of India: A People's Court?* INDIAN L. REV. 1(2):145–181.

Galanter further argue that "the presence of so many benches, and the resulting pervasive (though mild) indeterminacy of precedent, increases the chances that representation by a grand advocate may make a difference in outcome. At least it is perceived to possibly make a difference by significant numbers of clients with deep pockets engaged in controversies where the stakes make irrelevant the size of legal fees." Id. at 9.

[59] Amok Prasanna Kumar, *The True Worth of a Senior Advocate: Senior Counsels Seem to Wield Disproportionate Influence on How the Supreme Court of India Exercises Its Jurisdiction*, LIVE MINT (Sept. 16, 2015). Vidhi randomly selected 378 SLPs out of the 34,500 civil SLPs filed in 2014 where there was a lawyer appearing only for the petitioner. They found that a senior advocate appeared in 38 percent of the cases and notice was issued (i.e., the senior advocate was successful) in 60 percent of those cases. When a non-senior advocate appeared, the success rate was 33 percent.

Chandrachud, Abhinav. 2012. *Supreme Court's Seniority Norm: Historical Origins.* ECON. & POL. WEEKLY 47(8):26–30.

Dhavan, Rajeev. 1986. LITIGATION EXPLOSION IN INDIA. N.M. Tripathi.

Fischer, Alexander. 2008. *Higher Lawmaking as a Political Resource.* In SOVEREIGNTY AND DIVERSITY, Miodrag Jovanović and Kristin Henrard eds. Eleven International Publishing.

Gadbois, George H. 1970. *The Supreme Court of India: A Preliminary Report of an Empirical Study.* J. CONST. & PARLIAMENTARY STUD. 4:34.

Gadbois, George. 1974. *Supreme Court Decision Making.* BANARAS L. J. 10:1–49.

Galanter, Marc, and Nick Robinson. 2013. India's Grand Advocates: A Legal Elite Flourishing in the Era of Globalization. November. Accessed Aug. 30, 2018. file:/// Users/sumridhikaur/Downloads/SSRN-id2348699.pdf.

Gopal, G. Mohal. 2016. Justice and the Two Ideas of India. *Frontline.* May 27. Accessed Aug. 29, 2018. www.frontline.in/cover-story/justice-and-the-two-ideas-of-india/article8581178.ece.

Iyer, V. R. Krishna. 1987. OUR COURTS ON TRIAL. B.R. Publishing Corporation.

Kumar, Alok Prasanna. 2015. The True Worth of a Senior Advocate. Sept. 16. Accessed Aug. 30, 2018. www.livemint.com/Politics/FFgFOFnzN8rqvRNWTTgugM/The-true-worth-of-a-senior-advocate.html.

Kumar, Alok Prasanna, Faiza Rahman, and Ameen Jauhar. 2015. Vidhi Ctr. for Legal Pol'y, Consultation Paper: The Supreme Court of India's Burgeoning Backlog Problem and Regional Disparities in Access to the Supreme Court. 2015. Accessed Aug. 30, 2018. https://static1.squarespace.com/static/551ea026e4b0adba21a8f9df/t/560cf7d4e4b092010fff89b1/1443690452706/29092015_Consultation+Paper+on +the+Supreme+Court%27s+Burgeoning+Backlog+Problem.pdf.

Law Commission of India. 2009. 229th Law Commission Report. Indiankanoon. August. Accessed Aug. 29, 2018. https://indiankanoon.org/doc/24442307/.

Masoodi, Ashwaq, and Monalisa. 2014. Supreme Court sets up social justice bench. *Live Mint.* Dec. 4. Accessed Aug. 31, 2018. www.livemint.com/Politics/vUH4B7kKPH4WcSFbnfhRKP/SC-sets-up-social-justice-bench-to-deal-with-social-issues.html.

Moti Ram & Ors. v. *State of M.P.* 1978. 4 SSC 47 (Supreme Court of India, Aug. 24).

Nariman, Fali. 2014. Abolish Two Judge Benches. Indian Express. Apr. 10.

Robinson, Nick. 2013. A Quantitative Analysis of the Indian Supreme Court's Workload. J. EMPIRICAL LEGAL STUD. 10(3):570–601.

2013. A Court Adrift. *Frontline.* May 03. Accessed Aug. 30, 2018. www.frontline.in/cover-story/a-court-adrift/article4613892.ece.

2013. *Structure Matters: The Impact of Court Structure on the Indian and U.S. Supreme Courts.* AM. J. COMPARATIVE L. 61(1):173–208.

Robinson, Nick, Anjana Agarwal, Vrinda Bhandari, Ankit Goel, Karishma Kakkar, Reeba Muthalaly, Vivek Shivakumar, Meera Sreekumar, Surya Sreenivasan, and Shruti Viswanathan. 2011. Interpreting the Constitution: Supreme Court Constitution Benches since Independence. ECON. & POL. WEEKLY 46(9):27–31.

S.P. Gupta v. *Union of India.* 1982. AIR 1982 SC 149 (Supreme Court of India).

Shankar, Shylashri. 2010. India's Judiciary: *Imperium in Imperio.* In ROUTLEDGE HANDBOOK OF SOUTH ASIAN POLITICS, ed. Paul R. Brass. Routledge.

Shrivastava, Rakesh Kumar. 2014. Update: A Guide to India's Legal Research and Legal System. *GlobaLex*. April. Accessed Aug. 30, 2018. www.nyulawglobal.org/globalex/India_Legal_Research1.html.

Special Reference No. 1 of 1998. 1998. 7 SCC 739 (Supreme Court of India).

Supreme Court Advocates on Record Association v. Union of India. 1993. 4 SCC 441 (Supreme Court of India).

Supreme Court of India. 2014. *Annual Report 2014.* New Delhi: Supreme Court of India. Accessed Aug. 30, 2018. www.sci.gov.in/pdf/AnnualReports/annualreport2014-15.pdf.

Supreme Court of India. 2010. Practice and Procedure: A Handbook of Information. Supreme Court of India.

Supreme Court of India. n.d. List of Senior Advocates Designated by Supreme Court (as on 23/04/2015). Accessed Aug. 20, 2016. www.sci.nic.in/outtoday/List%20of%20Sr.%20Advocates%20   Designated%20by%20Supreme%20Court%20as%20on%2023%2004%202015.pdf.

Supreme Court of India. n.d. Supreme Court of India. Accessed Aug. 30, 2018. www.sci.gov.in/.

3

The Recent Evolution of Public Interest Litigation in the Indian Supreme Court

POORVI CHITALKAR AND VARUN GAURI

Starting in the 1970s, the Indian Supreme Court has used public interest litigation (PIL, or social action litigation) to significantly expand the scope of fundamental rights under the Constitution.[*] The Court's original agenda was to expand access to justice for the poor and marginalized, and to improve the well-being of the socially and economically disadvantaged segments of Indian society. In a series of landmark social justice judgments, the Court advanced the rights of prisoners,[1] bonded laborers,[2] and pavement dwellers,[3] among other groups. To achieve its ambitions, the Court relaxed rules of standing, adopted innovative judicial remedies, and often acted *suo motu*. But in the 1990s, the Court began to include other topics in its PIL agenda, including urban pollution,[4] corruption,[5] and the sexual harassment of women.[6] More recently, the Court has both permitted and encouraged the use of PIL to address issues in governance, urban lifestyles, property rights, and cultural preservation.

As a result of this evolution, and despite the real achievements of PIL, especially its historical role in expanding access to justice on the part of the poor and disenfranchised, several critiques are now widespread. Critics have

---

[*] The findings and views expressed in this chapter do not necessarily represent those of the Global Centre for Pluralism or its Board of Directors or those of the World Bank or its Executive Directors. The authors would like to thank Anindita Chatterjee, Iman Sen, Siddharth Sonkar, and Tejas Popat for their research assistance in the preparation of this chapter.
[1] *Sunil Batra* v. *Delhi Administration* AIR 1978 SC 1675 and *Upendra Baxi* v. *State of Uttar Pradesh* (1983) 2 SCC 308.
[2] *Bandhua Mukti Morcha* v. *Union of India* AIR 1984 SC 802.
[3] *Olga Tellis* v. *Bombay Municipal Corporation* AIR 1986 SC 180.
[4] *M.C. Mehta* v. *Union of India* (*Delhi Vehicular Pollution*) AIR 1991 SC 1132.
[5] *Vineet Narain* v. *Union of India* AIR 1998 SC 889.
[6] *Vishaka* v. *State of Rajasthan*, AIR 1997 SC 3011.

argued that PIL is subject to increasing misuse and is often a vehicle for private disputes, which can be brought to the Supreme Court and the High Courts in the garb of PIL. Others question the effectiveness of PILs and cite the lack of enforcement of many of the Court's rulings, especially on social and economic rights issues, which result in sweeping directives with little real impact. A number of criticisms relate to the separation of powers, and question the prudence and appropriateness of the Court's incursions into complex policy areas, such as environmental, social, and economic domains. From this perspective, much of PIL constitutes judicial overreach or activism. Finally, there are critiques stemming from concerns about inequality, which ask, given the evolution of PIL over the decades, whether it continues to benefit the poor and marginalized, or whether it has become a route for the middle classes to advance their own interests.[7]

The last critique is the main concern of this chapter. It is not surprising that *some* of the benefits of litigation, even PIL, accrue to individuals who are relatively advantaged in their societies. After all, in most societies the distribution of legal resources tends to follow the distribution of economic, social, and political resources. But has the Indian Supreme Court, and in particular its PIL jurisdiction, permitted, or even exacerbated, inequality in the country?

Before examining the data, it is worth distinguishing this question from two related, and sometimes conflated, ways of posing it.[8] First, some writers believe that the very entry of courts into areas of social and economic policy, and the constitutional provisions on which those incursions are often based, are dubious. In addition to raising separation of powers concerns, judicial involvement in policymaking, some argue, results in higher levels of inequality, compared to the counterfactual in which constitutions do not provide for that involvement and courts do not get involved, because judges usually reflect elite interests when making policy decisions. In the Indian context, this would be tantamount to saying that Indian society would be more equal had the constitution not included social and economic rights in the directive principles or had the Court maintained the non-justiciability of social and economic rights. Some scholars disagree with this point of view and argue that constitutional provisions on social and economic rights create opportunities for civil society and political parties to mobilize on behalf of the poor and

---

[7]   See generally A. K. Thiruvengadam (2009), "Evaluating Contemporary Criticisms of 'Public Interest Litigation': A Progressive Conception of the Role of the Judge," Paper presented at the 2009 Lassnet Conference, New Delhi, India.

[8]   For a discussion of these issues, see D. M. Brinks and V. Gauri (2014), "The Law's Majestic Equality? The Distributive Impact of Judicializing Social and Economic Rights," *Perspectives on Politics*, 12 (2), 375–393.

marginalized. According to this argument, Indian society would be more equal today had PIL and social and economic existed from the beginning, from 1947. The counterfactual presents a challenging set of questions, and to date the empirical literature on it is limited, though there have been efforts to use cross-national time series in order to correlate constitutional textual language with social indicators, such as educational attainment.[9] Whatever the answer to that question, the main point here is that the question of *constitutional inequality*, or what would have happened had the courts not intervened in policymaking, or had not been allowed to intervene, is more expansive and more difficult to assess, because the counterfactual is so difficult to identify, than the simpler question of whether, in the current constitutional setup, poor and marginalized individuals are the main beneficiaries of litigation.

A second way of addressing the question is to assess the impact of PIL and fundamental rights litigation by determining, of the share of total beneficiaries, how many are poor or marginalized, relative a reasonable benchmark, or, alternatively, what fraction of the total benefits, standardized according to a common metric, go to poor and marginalized individuals. Here, the analysis aims to uncover who benefits, and who does not, from litigation in these domains. The analysis can include not only the direct effects of court rulings, but also indirect effects, which occur when the results of rulings are generalized through judicial precedent, abstract constitutional review, informal influence, or other judicial mechanisms, as well as through extrajudicial channels, including social mobilization, new legislation, and changes in policy formulation and implementation. Because the effects of judicial involvement depend, in this analysis, on the distribution of beneficiaries in various policy domains (e.g., improvements in university education would tend to benefit rich beneficiaries more than poor beneficiaries), this can be referred to as *policy area inequality*. Brinks and Gauri (2014) assess the impact of social and economic rights litigation on policy area inequality in five countries, including India. They find that, in India, the large majority of beneficiaries from health and education rights litigation are disadvantaged individuals.

The third approach, the one undertaken in this chapter, is the most common. *Beneficiary inequality*, or the extent to which the disadvantaged are able to take advantage of existing legal opportunities, examines who gets into court (rich people or poor people), and who wins and who loses. Although more limited than the other ways of posing the question (unlike

---

[9] For example, see S. Edwards and A. G. Marin (2015), "Constitutional Rights and Education: An International Comparative Study," *Journal of Comparative Economics*, 43(4), 938–955.

policy area inequality it does not assess the indirect effects of litigation), it can be a useful benchmark, particularly in jurisdictions or dockets where the benefits of litigation tend not to generalize through judicial or extrajudicial channels.

This chapter focuses on beneficiary inequality. It updates a previous analysis of public interest and fundamental rights litigation in the Indian Supreme Court from 1961 to 2008.[10] That paper found that win rates for fundamental rights claims were, in the first decade of the new century, significantly higher when the claimant came from an advantaged social group than when he or she came from a marginalized group, which constituted a social reversal both from the original objective of PIL as well as from the relative win rates in the 1980s. The present chapter examines whether that trend continued into the second decade of the twenty-first century.

I. METHODS

The authors conducted a search for all Indian Supreme Court cases from 2009 to 2014, published in the Manupatra database, which met the same search criteria used in Gauri (2011):

1. Supreme Court cases involving fundamental rights and related to women's and children's rights, whether or not explicitly admitted as PILs;

2. Supreme Court cases involving fundamental rights and related to issues regarding Scheduled Castes/Scheduled Tribes or Other Backward Classes (SCs/STs/OBCs), whether or not explicitly admitted as PILs; and

3. All Supreme Court Cases explicitly called "public interest litigation."

The overall search, using a number of search terms, yielded 414 cases.[11] Table 3.1 shows the 220 "in sample" cases, meaning that the cases met the

---

[10] V. Gauri (2011), "Fundamental Rights and Public Interest Litigation in India: Overreaching or Underachieving?" *Indian Journal of Law and Economics*, 1(1), 71–93.

[11] For the set of cases involving women and children's rights, these search terms were used: "women," "children," and "abuse"; "violence," "women" and "neglected children"; "juvenile justice" and "Article 21"; "trafficking," "women," and "Article 21"; "labor," "children," and "Article 14"; "custodial violence" and "children"; "education," "fundamental right," and "Article 14"; "gender and fundamental right"; "prison rights and children"; "rape" and "Article 21"; "emancipation" and "women and children." The SC/ST/OBC search used the terms "scheduled caste" and "fundamental right"; "scheduled tribe" and "fundamental right"; "other backward classes" and "fundamental right" "scheduled caste" and "Article 21"; "scheduled

TABLE 3.1 *Topic areas of litigation*

Topic area of litigation (220 cases, Supreme Court of India, 2009–2014)			
Women's rights	Children's rights	Caste	PILs
22	22	19	177

Note: Some cases cover more than one topic area.

search criteria listed above. When examined by issue, 22 cases related to women's rights, 22 related to children, 19 related to SCs/STs/OBCs. There were 177 PIL cases in the sample.

A. *Beneficiary inequality*

In order to examine the data regarding the beneficiaries of PIL, the selected cases were coded according to the social class of the litigant. For the purposes of coding, a member of the "advantaged" classes included a professional (doctors, teachers, members of the armed forces, etc.), a landowner or businessperson, or someone otherwise in the global middle class (including formal sector workers and civil service employees not designated as workers or laborers). Those coded as "disadvantaged" included individuals belonging to an SC, ST, or an OBC (unless otherwise designated as a member of an advantaged class), peasants, laborers, and those detained in the criminal justice system. Where the class of the litigant could not be determined, the cases were coded according to the general social class of the individuals whose interests were being advocated or defended. And if the benefits of the litigation accrued to a diffuse class of individuals, the cases were coded as "diffuse" (e.g., cases concerning food adulteration, the criminalization of politics, and environmental issues).

Of the 220 cases in the sample, 28 were brought by litigants categorized as "disadvantaged" (13 percent), and 116 by those categorized as "advantaged" (53 percent). In 42 cases, the social class of the litigant was "diffuse" (19 percent). And in the remaining 35 cases (16 percent), it was not possible to determine the social class of the litigant.

Limiting the cases to the 177 PILs in the sample, 91 represented litigants from the advantaged classes (51 percent), 16 from disadvantaged classes

tribe" and "Article 21t"; "other backward classes" and "Article 21"; "scheduled caste" and "Article 14"; "scheduled tribe" and "Article 14"; "other backward classes" and "Article 14."

TABLE 3.2 *PIL cases only: beneficiary inequality*

Year	Advantaged litigants	Disadvantaged litigants	Diffuse litigant class	Unknown/not applicable	Total
2009	4	1	6	3	14
2010	9	2	6	4	21
2011	16	6	3	8	33
2012	10	3	5	7	25
2013	25	2	8	7	42
2014	27	2	7	6	42
2009–2014	91	16	35	35	177

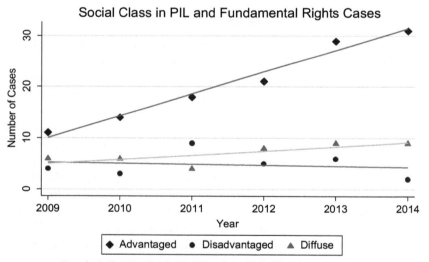

FIGURE 3.1 **Trends in the social class of PIL and fundamental rights litigants**

(9 percent), and 35 were on behalf of the diffuse litigant class (20 percent). See Table 3.2.

The data suggest that the Court's docket involving advantaged classes, in the areas of PIL and fundamental rights cases involving women, children, and caste, has been increasing steadily in recent years, while the share of the docket involving disadvantaged litigant classes, as well as diffuse litigant classes, has been more or less flat (see Figure 3.1).

Table 3.3 shows that in 2014 the litigant's class was disadvantaged in only 2 of the 48 cases in which the social class could be identified. Among cases

TABLE 3.3 *All cases: beneficiary inequality*

Year	Advantaged litigants	Disadvantaged litigants	Diffuse litigant class	Unknown/not applicable	Total
2009	10	4	6	3	23
2010	14	3	6	4	27
2011	18	9	4	8	39
2012	15	4	7	7	33
2013	28	6	9	7	50
2014	31	2	9	6	48
2009–2014	116	28	41	35	220

with individual litigants whose social class could be identified, advantaged litigants were almost 15 times as common as disadvantaged litigants. This represents an apparent increase in the share of advantaged litigants, compared with the first decade of the 2000s. In a similar sample of 68 cases from 2000 to 2008, 31 (46 percent) were from advantaged classes and 36 (53 percent) were not. While suggestive, it is possible that this is a result of a change in reporting practices on the part of the Court.[12]

The cases were also examined to determine whether they were brought by an non-governmental organization (NGO) or a cooperative group, as cases involving an NGO or cooperative may be more likely to involve the concerns of the poor than the middle class, and, importantly, they are also more likely to result in generalized benefits to individuals beyond the original litigants. Of the 177 PIL cases, it was possible, in 109 cases, to determine whether or not the case was brought by an NGO. Of these 109 cases, 32 were brought by NGOs (29 percent) while 77 were brought by individuals (71 percent). In the previous analysis, the numbers were 15 percent by NGOs and 80 percent by individual litigants. In the 2009–2014 sample, cases brought by NGOs and groups related largely to litigants whose social class was either diffuse or unclear (58 percent).

---

[12] The samples for 2000–2008 and 2014 were selected using nearly identical criteria for valid, in sample cases. However, in the 2000–2008 sample only 3 of the 68 cases were explicitly labeled as a PIL. In contrast, 45 of the 56 cases in the 2014 sample were explicitly labeled as a PIL by the Court. This change in reporting practices by the Court may be driving the results. Of the 11 cases that were not PILs in 2014, there were 3 advantaged litigants and 4 litigants who were not advantaged. Of the 65 non-PIL cases in the 2000–2008 sample, 29 were from advantaged class litigants and 36 from disadvantaged. It appears that there may have been more disadvantaged litigants in the past, but the samples are drawn from different populations with different underlying distributions.

TABLE 3.4 *Win–loss rates*

	Number of cases with clear result	Litigant won	Litigant lost
Advantaged litigant	97	48	49
Disadvantaged litigant	23	22	1
Diffuse class	31	25	6
Unknown litigant	27	13	14
Suo moto	1	1	0
PIL	143	81	62
Women's rights	20	16	4
Children's rights	19	16	3
Caste	16	8	8
All cases	179	109	70

Note: Some cases fall in more than one category. The table only includes cases that resulted in a clear winner or loser.

Only 5 of the 32 (16 percent) PIL cases brought by an NGO related to a disadvantaged class litigant. The examination reveals that while NGOs appear to be using PILs more, they are using it to take on issues such as corruption, criminalization in politics, and police investigations rather than issues that directly address poor, disadvantaged, or marginalized populations (more on this later).

What are the win–loss rates for claimants, both generally and disaggregated by the social class of the litigants? The overall win rate in the sample of cases in which the outcome was clear was 61 percent. In the remaining cases, there was no clear decision as to win or loss (e.g., they were referred back to the High Court for consideration, or to a constitutional bench).

The win rates were notably higher for disadvantaged litigants. The win rate for disadvantaged litigants was 96 percent and 49 percent for advantaged litigants. In other words, unlike in the 2000–2008 sample, disadvantaged litigants, though a minority of the docket, appear to have a much higher chance of winning. In the current sample, the Court appears much more active in cases involving advantaged litigants, but when it did take a case involving the disadvantaged, the disadvantaged litigant was much more likely to prevail. Notably, the win rate when the social class of the litigant was diffuse was also high (81 percent). See Table 3.4.

The win–loss rates were also examined by issue area. There were a total of 22 "in sample" cases related to women's fundamental rights, with the overall win rate for women's rights cases being 73 percent. Adding back "out of sample cases" involving women (in addition to explicit "fundamental rights" claims), there were a total of 46 cases that addressed women's issues in the Indian Supreme Court during this period. Of these, 40 cases (87 percent) were related to violence against women (including rape, murder, kidnapping, sexual harassment, and dowry deaths). This in itself is noteworthy: the Court was focused on violence against women, rather than women's economic empowerment or civil and political rights. Among these 46 cases involving women's issues, the win rate was 63 percent and the loss rate 7 percent. Lower win rates in cases involving violence might be explained by the fact that a vast majority of these were criminal in nature, requiring higher standards of proof and more strict evidentiary requirements. The Court's focus on violence against women may have arisen, at least in part, from the greater attention to the issue in society triggered by the high-profile Delhi gang rape case in December 2012, which was accompanied by calls for stricter legislation and punishment for rape.

On the other hand, in cases related to caste, the win rate was 50 percent, notably lower than win rates for children's rights and women's rights cases. This is consistent with the widespread impressions that, in recent years, judges may have become more favorably disposed to women and children's issues than to SC/ST/OBC claims.

B. *Public interest litigation*

Consistent with the impression that the Court's PIL docket has continued to turn away from the rights of the poor and disenfranchised, which it addressed during its "heroic" years in the 1970s and 1980s, the Court's PIL cases were largely, during the period studied in this chapter, focused on "diffuse" interests or the interests of advantaged litigants. The most prominent issues included corruption (e.g., related to coal block allocations, telecom spectrum allocations, and anti-corruption legislation), challenges to construction projects on environmental grounds, police investigations (requests for independent investigations where police investigations were perceived to be flawed), regulation of business, and service matters.

In one case examined, the Court itself took note of this shift:

> it may be stated that public interest litigation was initially used by this Court as a tool to take care of certain situations which related to the poor and under-privileged who were not in a position to have access to the Court. Thereafter, from time to time, the concept of public interest litigation expanded with the

change of time and the horizon included the environment and ecology, the atrocities faced by individuals in the hands of the authorities, financial scams and various other categories including eligibility of the people holding high offices without qualification.[13]

In a 2010 case, the Court reflected on the evolution of PIL and described three phases of its PIL jurisdiction. By the Court's description, Phase 1 of PIL dealt with the protection of fundamental rights of marginalized groups and sections of the society who, because of extreme poverty, illiteracy and ignorance, cannot approach the Courts. Phase 2 dealt with the cases relating to protection, preservation of ecology, environment, forests, marine life, wildlife, mountains, rivers, historical monuments, etc. The Court described Phase III (present) as dealing the maintenance of probity, transparency, and integrity in governance.[14]

The data on the topic areas of PILs back support this interpretation. Out of 177 PILs, there were 3 related to child trafficking and abuse and only 1 related to untouchability. In contrast, there were 17 cases on regulation of commerce, 17 on issues related to service matters, 13 in the area of corruption, and 11 addressing environmental issues (see Table 3.5).

From some quarters, one criticism of PIL is that it largely involves judicial activism, in which the courts encroach on policy issues that are better left to the other branches of government. To what extent is this true? We coded PIL cases on whether they addressed issues of general public policy. In the sample, individual issues, as opposed to policy concerns, constituted the majority of PILs in the Supreme Court (65 percent). Still, broader policy issues PILs comprised a significant share of the docket (35 percent). The win rates in individual and policy cases were virtually identical (45 percent in individual cases and 48 percent in policy cases, though in 25 percent of the policy cases the win–loss outcome was unclear or could not be determined from the material in our sample.

To what extent was the Court indicating deference to the other branches in its PIL cases? Cases in which the Court specifically noted that the legislative or executive branch was better equipped or more appropriate to address an issue or referred the case to an executive authority for decision were coded as exhibiting "deference." Of the 61 PILs that addressed policy issues, the possibility of expressing deference to the other branches was relevant to 29 of these cases. In these 29 cases, the Court exhibited deference in 17 of

[13] *Jafar Imam Naqvi v. Election Commission of India* (May 15, 2014),
[14] *State of Uttaranchal v. Balwant Singh Chaufal and Ors* (2010).

TABLE 3.5 *Topic of explicit PILs, Indian Supreme Court, 2009–2014*

Regulation/commerce	17
Service matters/cooperative societies	17
Criminal/police investigations	15
Corruption	13
Property/land allotment	18
Environment	11
Politics/elections	9
Development/construction	9
Education	6
Preservation of historical monuments and public property	7
Caste (including untouchability)	3
Child rights and trafficking	3
Labor and migration	2
Other (adoption, health and hospitals, animal welfare, euthanasia, right to food, homelessness, right to information, transgender rights, natural disasters, road safety, etc.)	47
TOTAL	177

them (59 percent). Overall, the Court seemed reluctant (perhaps more so than in the past?) to lay down sweeping guidelines or to throw out policies to address broad public problems. Cases in which the Court laid down guidelines, often explicitly seeking to address a gap in legislation, or took on active monitoring of cases to ensure implementation by the executive, as in the famous Right to Food case, were coded as "non-deference." The Court exhibited "non-deference" in 12 policy-oriented PILs (41 percent). For example, it laid down guidelines regarding the rights of transgender individuals,[15] and the investigation of extrajudicial killings by the police.[16]

An example of deference was the following. When asked to strike down the constitutionality of the Juvenile Justice Act on the ground that it prevented the Criminal justice system from prosecuting a juvenile offender, the Court noted: "We refuse to be tempted to enter into the said arena which is primarily for the legislature to consider. Courts must take care not to express opinions on the sufficiency or adequacy of such figures (statistics on juvenile offences)

---

[15] *National Legal Services Authority* v. *Union of India* (UOI) and Ors, MANU/SC/0309/2014.
[16] *Peoples Union for Civil Liberties* v. *State of Maharashtra*, MANU/SC/0882/2014.

and should confine its scrutiny to the legality and not the necessity of the law to be made or continued."[17]

In a case regarding hate-speech, it noted: "The court should not pass any judicially unmanageable order which is incapable of enforcement ... The statutory provisions and particularly the penal law provide sufficient remedy to curb the menace of hate speeches. Thus, person aggrieved must resort to the remedy provided under a particular statute."[18]

In a PIL requesting that the rights to adopt and be adopted by declared Fundamental rights, the Court declined to do so, saying "The legislature which is better equipped to comprehend the mental preparedness of the entire citizenry to think unitedly on the issue has expressed its view ... and the same must receive due respect."[19]

Similarly, in a PIL regarding the allocation of river waters, the Court observed:

> "Candidly speaking, we do not have the expertise to lay down policy for distribution of water within the State. It involves collection of various data, which is variable, and many a times policy formulated will have political overtones. It may require a political decision with which the Court has no concern so long it is within the Constitutional limits. Even if we assume that this Court has the expertise, it will not encroach upon the field earmarked for the executive. If the policy of the Government, in the opinion of the sovereign, is unreasonable, the remedy is to disapprove the same during election. In respect of policy, the Court has very limited jurisdiction."[20]

Finally, in a PIL about criminal records of Ministers, the Court said:

> "we must trust the wisdom of the Prime Minister and Parliament that the elected representative is worthy of being a minister in the Central Government ... While it may be necessary, due to the criminalization of our polity and consequently of our politics, to ensure that certain persons do not become Ministers, this is not possible through guidelines issued by this Court. It is for the electorate to ensure that suitable (not merely eligible) persons are elected to the Legislature and it is for the Legislature to enact or not enact a more restrictive law."[21]

---

[17] *Subramanian Swamy and Ors. v. Raju Thr. Member Juvenile Justice Board and Anr.*, AIR 2014 SC 2140.

[18] *Pravasi Bhalai Sangathan v. Union of India*, AIR 2014 SC 1591.

[19] *Shabnam Hashmi v. Union of India*, AIR 2014 SC 1281.

[20] *Kachchh Jal Sankat Nivaran Samiti and Ors. v. State of Gujarat and Anr.* MANU/SC/0693/2013.

[21] *Manoj Narula v. Union of India*, 2014 (9) SCC 1.

The Court also expressed concern about the misuse of PIL. In order to streamline the use of PIL and prevent abuse, the Court laid down guidelines for the Supreme Court and High Courts to follow, including imposition of exemplary costs on frivolous petitions.[22]

II. CONCLUSIONS

While the stated objective of PILs in the 1980s was to defend the interests of the disadvantaged, the downtrodden, and marginalized populations, it is often argued that this ambition has fallen away. Findings of inequality among the beneficiaries (as measured by access to the courts and win–loss rates) can be used to support this claim.

On beneficiary inequality, we found that a higher number of PILs and fundamental rights claims were brought by litigants from advantaged classes (53 percent) than from disadvantaged classes (13 percent). Some 20 percent of cases were brought on behalf of a diffuse class of litigants, perhaps pointing to the changing nature of the subject matter of PILs towards environmental, corruption, governance, and regulatory issues. The share of cases brought by NGOs or cooperative groups is often correlated with a generalization of benefits to a large population beyond the litigants, but only a small portion of the cases brought by NGOs were brought on behalf of disadvantaged groups. NGOs appear to be using PILs increasingly, but they are using it to tackle newsworthy issues, such as corruption and challenging police investigations.

Win rates amongst litigants from disadvantaged classes were significantly higher (96 percent) than win rates among claimants from advantaged classes (49 percent). The win rate among diffuse classes of litigants was 81 percent. Thus, although the share of litigation brought by disadvantaged classes was smaller, they were more likely to win once they entered the Court. This appears somewhat different from the pattern observed in the 2000–2008 sample, when win rates for advantaged classes were found to be higher than those for disadvantaged classes.

This analysis also revealed that the subject matter of PILs has undergone a change. The large majority of PILs address diffuse public issues, such as corruption and environmental concerns, rather than direct claims by, or on behalf of, the marginalized and underprivileged, such as untouchables or informal sector workers.

---

[22] *State of Uttaranchal v. Balwant Singh Chaufal and Ors* (2010).

There seems to be a favorable disposition towards cases relating to women's issues, particularly violence against women. The Court may have been swayed by public opinion and the media, which paid increasing attention to these concerns in the aftermath of the Delhi gang-rape case in December 2012. That case sparked outrage and demands for stricter punishments for violence against women. The Court also seems to exhibit a more favorable disposition to women and children's cases than to caste-related issues.

What explains these findings? While a systematic inquiry into the reasons for these trends is beyond the scope of this chapter, we can speculate briefly. One possible explanation may be that disadvantaged groups are seeking other routes to advance their claims. With the passing of legislation such as the Right to Education Act (2009), the Right to Information Act (2005), and the National Food Security Act (2013), it may be that claims that were previously brought as PIL can now be pressed through administrative and political channels.

Litigants may also be responding to signals from the Court. Discouraged by low win rates in previous years (2000–2008), or by the relative difficulty of getting a claim for a disadvantaged claimant on the docket, disadvantaged litigants may be more reluctant to expend resources trying to access the Court through PIL and fundamental rights litigation. It is also possible that these patterns of access reflect not only choices on behalf of litigants but also on the part of the Court. For example, having held that PILs in service matters are not maintainable, the Court may be rejecting cases related to caste if they are concerned with reservations in employment or promotion (this may explain the low number of caste-related cases).

Changes in the level of media attention on certain issues and shifts in public opinion may also explain some of the patterns. In a paper examining compliance with right to food orders of the Supreme Court, the authors found that an increase in media coverage, as well as more public concern on the question of economic inequality, were correlated with compliance.[23] Similarly, it may be that public opinion on issues related to women's rights and personal security, and on corruption and environmental pollution, has influenced the Court's disposition towards these issues, leading to higher win rates for women and cases on behalf of diffuse classes.

The findings may also reflect the simple fact that the Court responds to its political environment. PIL emerged in the 1970s when the judiciary was attempting to recapture lost legitimacy and after its complicity in Indira's

---

[23] P. Chitalkar and V. Gauri (2016), "India – Compliance with Orders on the Right to Food" in M. Langford, C. R. Garavito, and J. Rossi (eds.), *Making It Stick: Social Rights Judgments and the Politics of Compliance* (Cambridge University Press), 288–314.

Gandhi's declaration of emergency rule. Many observers think that the Court has lost its post-emergency popularity, perhaps partly because of growing skepticism that PIL no longer serves its original objectives and a sense that the Court is using PIL to engage in judicial "adventurism."[24] The strikingly high win rates in cases by disadvantaged litigants might be interpreted as an attempt to restore the luster of the Court by invoking the original purpose and image of PILs.

Also in response to its political environment, the Court appears to be using the language of deference towards the legislative and executive branches of government. In 59 percent of the policy-relevant PIL cases brought before it, and in which the issue of deference was relevant, the Court noted that the legislature or the executive, rather than the Court, was better equipped or more appropriate to deal with the issue, and refused to take on the role of law-making or policymaking. Although data on deference from the previous era are not available, this may signal a shift in the Court's approach, moving from an activist stance, where the Court laid down guidelines and policies on a wide range of issues, to one with more modest ambitions and a more circumscribed role for the judicial branch.

REFERENCES

Brinks, D. M. and Gauri, V. (2014), "The Law's Majestic Equality? The Distributive Impact of Judicializing Social and Economic Rights." *Perspectives on Politics*, 12(2), 375–393.

Chitalkar, P. and Gauri, V. (2016), "India – Compliance with Orders on the Right to Food" in M. Langford, C. R. Garavito, and J. Rossi (eds.), *Making It Stick: Social Rights Judgments and the Politics of Compliance* (Cambridge: Cambridge University Press), 288–314.

Edwards, S. and Marin, A. G. (2015), "Constitutional Rights and Education: An International Comparative Study." *Journal of Comparative Economics*, 43(4), 938–955.

Gauri, V. (2011), "Fundamental Rights and Public Interest Litigation in India: Overreaching or Underachieving?." *Indian Journal of Law and Economics*, 1(1), 71–93.

Thiruvengadam, A. K. (2009), "Evaluating Contemporary Criticisms of 'Public Interest Litigation': A Progressive Conception of the Role of the Judge," Paper presented at the 2009 Lassnet Conference, New Delhi, India.

---

[24] For example, Mehta, P.B. (2007) "India's Unlikely Democracy: The Rise of Judicial Sovereignty" *Journal of Democracy*, 18 (2) 70–83; Cassels, J. (1989) "Judicial Activism and Public Interest Litigation in India: Attempting the Impossible?" *American Journal of International Law*, 37, 495–512; Thiruvengadam, A. K. (2009) "Evaluating contemporary criticisms of 'Public Interest Litigation': A progressive conception of the role of a Judge," In Paper presented at the 2009 LASSNET Conference, New Delhi.

4

Suo Motu Intervention and the Indian Judiciary

MARC GALANTER AND VASUJITH RAM

I. INTRODUCTION

Proactive judicial intervention has become a familiar if not frequent feature of judging in the higher courts of India since the emergence of public interest litigation (PIL) in the 1980s. We propose to talk about one species of such intervention – the practice of a constitutional court in India taking up a matter *suo motu* (or alternatively *suo moto*) on its own initiative, without being petitioned by a claimant or party, to address a situation that it regards as requiring extraordinary intervention on the part of the court.[1]

Section II of this chapter presents as an example of this phenomenon a recent *suo motu* intervention initiated by the Supreme Court – a case more complex than some *suo motu* interventions but far less complex than others. Section III will trace the emergence of the *suo motu* phenomenon in India, tying its origins to the development of PIL. In Section IV we attempt to measure the incidence of *suo motu* initiatives in the Supreme Court. Section V addresses the idiosyncrasies and perplexities of *suo motu* cases. After underlining the attractions and rewards, we speculatively probe the implications of such intervention.

II. THE BIRBHUM CASE

In this section, we discuss an action initiated on January 24, 2014, by the Supreme Court of India responding to a newspaper article describing the gang-rape of a young woman in a village in Birbhum district in West Bengal.

---

[1] By constitutional courts, we refer to those courts which are empowered to entertain writ petitions under the Indian Constitution. These are the Supreme Court of India and the various High Courts.

The court's *suo motu* intervention led to a judgment delivered two months later,[2] on March 28, by a three-judge bench presided over by Chief Justice P. Sathasivam.[3]

In late January 2014, one of the judges of the Supreme Court, very likely the Chief Justice himself, encountered a news item dated January 23,[4] describing the rape, two days earlier, of a 20-year-old Santhal woman in a remote,[5] West Bengal village.[6] The news item, published in the Business and Financial News section of Reuters.com, presented an account, relying on inputs by the Superintendent of Police, of a gang rape imposed by a "village court,"[7] the news source's term, or a "community panchayat,"[8] the Supreme Court's term, as punishment for having a romantic relationship with "a man from a different community."[9]

---

[2]   *In Re: Indian Woman says gang-raped on orders of Village Court published in Business & Financial News dated 23.01.2014*, Suo Motu Writ Petition (Criminal) No. 24 of 2014, order dated January 24, 2014.

[3]   Id., order dated March 28, 2014, www.sci.gov.in/jonew/judis/41349.pdf, https://perma.cc/ F9MD-MPGQ or (2014) 4 SCC 786. Hereinafter, "Birbhum SC judgment." Page numbers refer to the judgment copy uploaded on the Supreme Court website.

[4]   "Indian woman says gang-raped on orders of village court," Business and Financial News, Reuters.com, January 23, 2014 [Appendix A].

[5]   The locality is described as a "remote village" without "any market place or shop," with only "a few street electric poles … seen at a distance with dim bulb light[s]" in the District Judge's Inspection Report, submitted to the Supreme Court (on file with the authors).

[6]   The members of the village were described as "almost illiterate," and "engaged in agriculture or daily labor" (District Judge's Inspection Report, submitted to the Supreme Court [on file with the authors]). The Santhals are a tribe of some 6 million people living in eastern India, mostly in the states of Jharkhand and West Bengal. For a brief account of their relations to India's legal system, see Vasudha Dhagamwar, *Role and Image of Law in India: The Tribal Experience* (2006). For an extended account of Santhal society, see W. G. Archer, *Tribal Law and Justice: A Report on the Santal* (2014). For a recent survey of their conditions, see Ministry of Tribal Affairs (Xaxa Committee), *Report of the High Level Committee on Socio-Economic, Health and Educational Status of Tribal Communities of India*, May, 2014.

[7]   The West Bengal Chief Secretary's Report to the Supreme Court (on file with the authors) describes it as a "traditional petty dispute redressal mechanism."

[8]   The term "panchayat" (literally a coming together of five) can refer to various indigenous institutions, established or ad hoc, administrative or judicial. Here the Court's reference is to a proceeding that was judicial in the minimal sense of applying and enforcing local norms to a specific "case." That proceeding was locally understood as a salish, an assembly or meeting of a council or assembly. Such bodies are sometimes referred to by newspapers as "kangaroo courts." On the local scene "panchayat" referred to the statutory council that served as an organ of local government.

[9]   Birbhum SC judgment, Page 1. "Community" in contemporary Indian usage refers to a section of the population differentiated by religion, caste, or tribe. In this case, the man was a married Muslim who worked with her. Curiously, the Supreme Court uses the term "community panchayat" although the news account that inspired its intervention does not use the term

Exactly what happened is far from clear. The story centers on a young Santhal woman of unusual initiative and independence, who had gone off to Delhi, 800 miles away, and worked there, returning after a year with savings that enabled her to enjoy consumer goods that were unknown or certainly uncommon among her tribal neighbors.[10] It seems that on Monday, January 20, 2014, she and her paramour, a somewhat older Muslim man with whom she did construction work, were accosted at her home by a group of male villagers, offended by this disapproved liaison. The couple was bound, taken to the local headman, and tied to a tree near his residence. There are conflicting accounts of what ensued. In some accounts a salishi sabha,[11] an assembly of adult males, was convened that evening, and after deliberation there was demand for payment of a large fine by the girl and her family, as well as her paramour, sums far beyond their means. Then the salishi was scheduled for (or postponed or adjourned until) the next morning. According to the young woman in her statement in the First Information Report (FIR), the headman then instructed those in attendance that they may "enjoy the girl in any manner" they wish, as the girl, her family, and her paramour were unable to pay the fine.[12] She described being raped by 13 men in a kitchen shed adjacent to the house of the headman.[13] According to supporters of the accused men, the salishi was to be held in the morning, and the girl and her paramour remained tied up in public view throughout the night.

The next morning on January 21, a salishi convened at 7.00 a.m. and fine amounts were negotiated in the presence of several hundred tribals and a few others, including some local workers of the Trinamool Congress, the ruling party in the State of West Bengal. Thereafter, the girl returned to her home and, after initial reluctance, told family members what had befallen her. The next day (January 22), accompanied by her brothers, she went to the police station at Labhpur (at a distance of 10 kilometers from Subhalpur, the hamlet where the events occurred) and reported that she had been raped. As she was

---

"panchayat" or its Bengali counterpart "shalish" but refers to the body in question as a "village court." See news report in Appendix.

[10] Snehamoy Chakraborty, 'Envy Becomes Savagery', *The Telegraph*, January 24, 2014. See also Sonia Falerio, *13 Men* (2015).

[11] According to H. H. Wilson, *A Glossary of Judicial and Revenue Terms and Useful Words Occurring in Official Documents Relating to the Administration of Government of British India* (1855), "Salis" means an umpire or an arbitrator. The word is derived from "Salas," meaning "three" – here, the arbitrator is supposed to be the third party.

[12] As per the written complaint of January 22 at the Police Station. Copy of the FIR is on file with the authors. ("[A]s they are unable to pay" implies that at least that part of the proceeding concerning the young woman had been completed in the evening.)

[13] Id.

illiterate, one Anirban Mondal – a non-tribal college graduate whose presence and connection remains unexplained – assisted her.[14] The police then rounded up the accused men and sent them to 14-day judicial custody since no police custody was sought.[15]

On the morning of January 23, several newspapers, including the one that inspired the Supreme Court, published accounts reporting the victim and police version of the event. The report that was picked up by the Supreme Court was based on a tip-off from a stringer covering the local police beat.[16] This account resonated because of growing concern about a long series of reports of unpunished rapes in Bengal,[17] and the reverberations of massive public protests about a horrific gang rape in New Delhi (in December 2012) that had led to the death of the victim and the subsequent enhancement of the penalty by Parliament.[18]

The very next day, January 24, in New Delhi, the Chief Justice's bench of the Supreme Court – on its own initiative, without the filing of a case by any party in any court – took the unusual but not unprecedented step of intervening *suo motu*. The Court directed the District Judge of Birbhum District to investigate the matter and report to the Supreme Court within one week. The

---

[14] *State of West Bengal* v. *Jolha Maddi and Ors.*, Sessions Case No. 51 of 2014 at Bolpur, judgment dated September 19, 2014. pp. 20, 81 (on file with the authors).

[15] As per the criminal procedure code, if the investigation is not completed within 24 hours, the police must meet the magistrate with the case diary and the accused. The police can then seek "police custody" of the accused for the next 14 days, which is awarded by the magistrate upon his discretion. After 15 days (1 + 14) as a whole, the accused can only be detained in "judicial custody" (for a total period of 60/90 days, depending on the gravity of the offense – after which bail is the accused's right). Under police custody, the police detain the accused in a lock-up maintained by the police department; whereas under judicial custody, the accused is detained in jail and is technically under the custody of the magistrate. From the perspective of the police, having the accused in police custody is seen as conducive for effective investigation.

[16] Interview, September 3, 2015, with Sujoy Dhar, the journalist who wrote the report that was picked up by the Supreme Court.

[17] As per the latest data compiled by the National Crime Records Bureau, West Bengal has the third lowest conviction rate (after Jammu & Kashmir and Arunachal Pradesh) for crimes under S. 376 of the Indian Penal Code (Rape).

[18] A 23-year-old woman was gang-raped and beaten in a moving private bus with tinted windows. A few days later, the victim died in a Singapore hospital. Large scale protests followed the incident in the capital, Delhi (and other cities) and the government constituted a Committee on Amendments to Criminal Law (Justice Verma Committee). The Committee released its report on January 23, 2013, and recommended significant changes, especially with respect to sex crimes. Soon after, the Criminal Law (Amendment) Ordinance, 2013 was passed, followed by the Criminal Law (Amendment) Act, 2013.

report arrived a week later.[19] However, the Supreme Court found no information with respect to the steps taken by the police and directed the Chief Secretary of West Bengal (that is, the State's chief administrative official, a career civil servant rather than a political appointee) to submit a detailed report within two weeks. The Court also appointed the Additional Solicitor General,[20] Siddharth Luthra, to assist the Court as *amicus curiae* in this matter.[21] Ten days later the Court received a detailed report from the Chief Secretary,[22] on the registration of the FIR, steps taken during the investigation, and other administrative actions, and four days after that the Court directed West Bengal to put on record the legal and medical documentation.

On March 13, some seven weeks after the incident, the Court conducted a hearing at which it heard the *amicus* (the Additional Solicitor General) and counsel for the State, but neither the victim nor those accused in the criminal case were summoned or represented by counsel. The *amicus* pointed to a number of problems in the story: if it was a village salish, how could one account for the presence of outsiders – i.e., the politicians belonging to the ruling party in the state? Was there a salish in session on the evening of January 21, before the alleged rape, as well as in the morning of January 22? How to account for the presence of Anirban Mondal at the police station to serve as the victim's scribe? And, most strikingly, "he pointed out that the aspect as to whether there was a larger conspiracy must also be seen."[23] It appears that he was referring to the discrepancy in the accounts, compounded by the unexplained presence of the ruling party politicians. Counsel for West Bengal assured the court that any deficiencies in the investigation "would be looked into and rectified."[24]

---

[19] Report on the District Judge is on file with the authors. The Chief Judicial Magistrate and two female judges (civil judges of the junior and senior division) accompanied the District Judge for the inspection.

[20] In India the Solicitor-General, the second highest ranking government lawyer (after the Attorney General) and Additional Solicitor-Generals, about 12 in number, are distinguished lawyers who appear on behalf of the Government in the Supreme Court and the High Courts. They are appointed for three-year terms and may also appear on behalf of other clients but not against governmental bodies.

[21] Siddarth Luthra is a Senior Counsel (designated in 2007) with a specialty in the field of criminal law. He is the son of the late K. K. Luthra, an eminent Senior Advocate. He completed his law degree at the Delhi University and studied criminology at Cambridge University. He graciously agreed to be interviewed for his chapter, and we thank him for his help.

[22] Report is on file with the authors.

[23] Birbhum SC judgment, p. 5.

[24] Birbhum SC judgment, p. 6. The Court's judgment contains no further reference to these gaps and discrepancies.

Two weeks later, on March 28, a three-judge bench, with Chief Justice Sathasivam presiding, published its judgment.[25] Proceeding to the merits without any further visible compiling or testing of evidence, it concluded that "[t]he case at hand is the epitome of aggression against a woman."[26] The Court announced that ultimately the question it ought to assess is "whether the State Police Machinery could possibly have prevented the said occurrence. The response is certainly a 'yes.'"[27] Such offenses, declared the Court, result from "the State[']s incapacity or inability to protect the Fundamental Rights of its citizens."[28] Therefore, the state was duty bound to compensate the victim.[29] The Court concluded that "[s]uch crimes can certainly be prevented if the state police machinery work in a more organized and dedicated manner" and that "such crimes are not only in contravention of domestic laws, but also a direct breach of the obligations under international law."[30]

On behalf of the State government, the Chief Secretary had proposed a long list of measures for aiding the victim – including legal aid, allotment of a plot of land, construction of a house, installation of a tube well, and Rs. 50,000 to be paid to the victim within a week. The Court endorsed these arrangements but regarded the Rs. 50,000 compensation as inadequate and directed the State to make a payment of an additional Rs. 500,000 within one month. In addition, the Court asked for details about "the measures taken for security and safety of the family" and for their "long term rehabilitation" as they are "likely to be socially ostracized."[31] The State proposed to build a house for the victim. Alert to possible tensions, the Court insisted that the house, compensation, and other benefits be in her name rather than that of her mother.

The Court opined that "[a]s a long-term measure to curb such crimes, a larger societal change is required via education and awareness" and that there must be policies framed for improving the socioeconomic conditions of women and for the sensitization of the police. The Court closed with a reminder that several parts of the state machinery must work "in harmony with each other to safeguard the rights of women" and that all hospitals,

---

[25] Birbhum SC judgment.
[26] Birbhum SC judgment, p. 13.
[27] Birbhum SC judgment, p. 12.
[28] Birbhum SC judgment, p. 13.
[29] As will be discussed in a later section of this chapter, S. 357B and S. 376D of the Code of Criminal Procedure, 1973 deal with compensation for rape victims.
[30] Birbhum SC judgment, p. 21.
[31] Birbhum SC judgment, p. 20.

public or private, must provide free first aid and treatment to victims of rape or acid attack.[32]

Back in West Bengal, the criminal investigation proceeded, culminating in a trial in the Sessions Court in Birbhum that began, with unusual dispatch, on July 18 and lasted until September 19, and at which all the 13 accused were found guilty and sentenced to 20 years of rigorous imprisonment.[33] As of September 2018, an appeal is pending before the Calcutta High Court.[34]

III. TRACING THE ROOTS

The Supreme Court's action in the Birbhum case appears to discard several expected features of common law litigation, notably the passivity and neutrality of the court to which a case is brought by a claimant or petitioner and the initiative and participation in the proceedings of the parties most directly affected. The absence of these features provoked little surprise.

In the aftermath of the Emergency (in operation from June 25, 1975 to March 21, 1977), the Supreme Court began to eschew common law procedural requirements such as standing, allowing activists or other members of the public to raise constitutional claims on behalf of those deprived of fundamental rights.[35] In an era of populism, the Court sought to bring the impoverished within the fold of the constitutional justice system by innovative and active intervention. An early and paradigmatic instance is the Court's 1979 intervention in the horrific blinding by the Bhagalpur police of 31 under-trial whom they regarded as troublemakers.[36] The Court was impelled to action by the

---

[32] The 226th Report of the Law Commission of India, July 2009 ("Inclusion of Acid Attacks as Specific Offenses in the Indian Penal Code and a Law for Compensation for Victims of Crime") noticed that acid attacks are usually committed against young women, "for spurning suitors, for rejecting proposals of marriage, for denying dowry, etc." As per the affidavit submitted by the Government to the Supreme Court, there were 309 instances of acid attacks in India in 2014. In the case of *Laxmi* v. *Union of India* (W.P. (C) 129 of 2006), the Supreme Court has been periodically issuing orders pertaining to the problem of acid attacks. The Supreme Court has directed strict regulation of the over-the-counter sale of acid and payment of minimum compensation, as well as free treatment of victims even at private hospitals. The Parliament, vide the Criminal Law (Amendment) Act, 2013, made acid attacks a separate criminal offense under the Indian Penal Code (Sections 326A and 326B).

[33] In addition, they were fined Rs. 5,000 with the provision that if the fine were not paid, their sentences would be extended by a year.

[34] CRA 675/2014.

[35] Justice P. N. Bhagwati, "Judicial Activism and Public Interest Litigation," 570–571 (1984–1985). The literature on public interest litigation is vast; see S. P. Sathe, *Judicial Activism in India: Transgressing Borders and Enforcing Limits* (2002); Oliver Mendelsohn, "Life and Struggles in the Stone Quarries of India: A Case Study" in *Law and Social Transformation in India* (2014).

initiative of a lawyer who had no relationship of representation with the victims.[37] For the purpose of evidence, aside from affidavits (a regular feature in writ petition cases), reliance is placed on Court-directed reports of socio-legal commissions, specialists, judges, etc.[38] Typically, in these PILs, the Supreme Court and the High Courts have adopted a collaborative (as opposed to adversarial) approach to procedure, and have ordered injunctive relief or mandated government action. In some instances, the Courts have also awarded substantial amounts of damages to victims— usually without detailed calibration of the victim's injuries.[39]

Suo motu intervention is an offshoot of the development of the PIL system itself. Suo *motu* petitions are a category of PILs and follow a similar system of relaxed rules of procedure. The parallels also extend to the scope of issues tackled and the nature of remedies extended. *Suo motu* petitions differ simply in that the incorporation of cases into the docket of the court is primarily judge-led.

Being born out of the PIL system, the peculiarities of *suo motu* cases are also inextricably wedded to the history of PILs themselves. In many PIL cases, the Court was aided in great part by an active press. In the post emergency era, the press brought to the fore stories of state atrocities and institutional apathy, which deprived vulnerable individuals or groups of their basic rights.[40] Based

---

[36] *Khatri (II)* v. *State of Bihar* (1981) 1 SCC 627 (the first case in which compensatory damages for human rights violations was considered; the compensation was ultimately not granted since the responsibility of the police officers had not been ascertained with finality). The first case in which compensation was granted was that of *Rudul Shah* v. *State of Bihar*, AIR 1983 SC 1086.

[37] Ordinarily, a petitioner invoking the jurisdiction of the Court is expected to be someone who is personally affected by the subject matter of the petition. The only permissible exception to this rule was the writ of Habeas Corpus, where the next friend was allowed to petition the Court since the person in detention would not be able to move the Court. The Supreme Court (and subsequently the High Courts) relaxed these rules of standing in public law adjudication, recognizing that not all sections of the people would be aware of their rights or have the resources to litigate. See S. P. Sathe, "Growth of Public Interest Litigation: Access and Democratization of the Judicial Process," in *Judicial Activism in India: Transgressing Borders and Enforcing Limits* (2002), 201.

[38] Ashok H. Desai and S. Muralidhar, "Public Interest Litigation: Potential and Problems," in B. N. Kirpal et al., eds., *Supreme but Not Infallible: Essays in Honor of the Supreme Court of India* (2002), 151–192.

[39] *See Rudul Shah* v. *State of Bihar*, AIR 1983 SC 1086, *Chairman, Railway Board* v. *Chandrima Das*, AIR 2000 SC 988 and *Bhim Singh* v. *State of J & K*, AIR 1986 SC 494. A detailed list of cases in which courts have granted compensation for violation of the right to life under Article 21 is available in Zia Mody, "Death in Custody: The Breach of Trust and Its Price," in 10 *Judgments that Changed India* (2013), 159.

[40] Upendra Baxi, "Taking Suffering Seriously: Social Action Litigation in the Supreme Court of India," 114 (1985).

on these press stories, social activists wrote letters to judges. The court entertained these letters as PIL petitions. This practice, now labeled "epistolary
jurisdiction," has become a familiar feature of the Indian judicial scene, rare
but highly visible.[41] Most *suo motu* cases, in contrast, arise from judges
themselves taking initiative directly on the basis of reports published in
the press.

Suo motu cases, by definition, allow judges the liberty to direct that particular matters be heard by the court. Although ordinarily allotment of judicial
work to various benches is the prerogative of the Chief Justice, PILs received
in the early years under the epistolary jurisdiction could be admitted and
heard by the judge who received the letter-petition.[42] Soon, this practice
ended, in response to allegations of forum shopping.[43] PIL petitions are now
to be addressed to the Court as a whole. They are screened by a PIL cell,
following which matters are placed before the Chief Justice for assignment. In
essence, this shift in practice took away the power of individual judges or
benches to control issues being brought before the judicial side of the Court
for consideration.[44] In this respect, *suo motu* cases represent an attempt by
judges to claw back this erstwhile power.[45]

Some High Courts have tried to evolve guidelines for initiation of cases suo
motu. While stating that "initiation of writ proceedings suo motu in public
interest is an inalienable part of the constitutional scheme and within the
competence of every Hon'ble Judge," the Karnataka High Court called for
"judicious exercise" of the power in accordance with "administrative instruc-
tion issued and Roster of Sitting prepared by the Chief Justice."[46] The High

---

[41] N. Robinson, "A Quantitative Analysis of the Indian Supreme Court's Workload," 599
[Table 13] (2013).

[42] Baxi, "Taking Suffering Seriously," p. 120.

[43] Justice Pathak remarked, "When the jurisdiction of the Court is invoked, it is the jurisdiction of
the entire Court ... No such communication can be properly addressed to a particular
judge ... Which judge or judges will hear the case is exclusively a matter concerning the
internal regulation of the business of the Court, interference with which by a litigant or a
member of the public constitutes the grossest impropriety." *Bandhua Mukti Morcha* v. *Union
of India*, (1984) 3 SCC 161, 229.

[44] There are reported instances of judges soliciting petitions from journalists. *See* Anuj Bhuwania,
Courting the People: Public Interest Litigation in Post-Emergency India (2017), 35.

[45] Asher Qazi likes *suo motu* actions by the Pakistani Supreme Court to "issue creation," a power
generally reserved for the legislative or executive branch. While one traditional constraint on
judicial power is that judges can only control cases or issues brought before them by litigants,
the practice of *suo motu* petitions eliminates this constraint. Asher A. Qazi, "Suo Motu:
Choosing Not to Legislate Chief Justice Chaudhry's Strategic Agenda," in Mohan Cheema
and Ijaz Gilani, eds., *The Politics and Jurisprudence of the Chaudhry Court* (2015) 284–285.
Since the Indian Supreme Court does not sit *en banc*, even small benches may bring forth
cases for judicial consideration.

Court was of the view that it would be "appreciated" if the matter could be referred the Chief Justice, who in turn would examine the matter and place it before the appropriate bench. The High Court of Madras reiterated these guidelines.[47] The exercise (and misuse) of such powers is of undoubtedly serious importance. In February 2016, a judge of the High Court of Madras stayed his own transfer to the Calcutta High Court by passing a *suo motu* judicial order under Article 226 (which confers writ jurisdiction on the High Courts).[48]

The first identifiable instance of *suo motu* intervention was in 1979 when Judge M. P. Thakkar, then a judge of the Gujarat High Court and later of the Supreme Court, took the initiative of converting "a letter to the editor in a newspaper by a widow mentioning her plight because of the non-payment of the provident fund family pension after her husband's death."[49] Judge Thakkar "ordered a show cause notice to be issued without any further formalities to the Regional Provident Fund Commissioner . . . The arrears were paid just after the first hearing."[50]

In one of the earliest of the few scholarly critiques of *suo motu* intervention, Professor S. K. Agrawala wrote in 1985 that such intervention is dangerous since the veracity of the author and contents of letters to the newspapers' editors are difficult to verify.[51] His stand has been vindicated by the Supreme Court, which has held that anonymous letters must not be entertained by courts as the credentials of the informant and the truth of the allegations would be difficult to verify.[52] Professor Agrawala was also of the opinion that the manner and method of selection of news items would always be inherently arbitrary, and that lack of legal boundaries would mean that petitions could be initiated on any basis (such as information received from a friend).[53]

---

[46] *High Court of Karnataka* v. *State of Karnataka*, AIR 1998 Kant 327.

[47] *The Chief Election Commissioner*, AIR 2011 Mad 103.

[48] Apoorva Mandhani, *Madras HC Judge Justice Karnan stays Supreme Court's order transferring him to Calcutta HC and directs CJI to submit his reply*, LiveLaw.in, available at www.livelaw .in/madras-hc-judge-justice-karnan-stays-supreme-courts-order-transferring-him-to-calcutta-hc-sc-directs-the-cj-not-to-assign-any-works-to-him/. Recently, the same judge passed a *suo motu* order setting aside a contempt case initiated by the Supreme Court against him, and directing withdrawal of judicial and administrative work from those judges. The order also holds that the judges are obliged to pay compensation to the tune of Rs. 14 crore for "mental agony" caused to him.

[49] Special Civil Application 2785/79, High Court of Gujarat. This instance has been recorded in Agrawala, *Public Interest Litigation in India*, p. 20.

[50] Id.

[51] Id.

[52] *Divine Retreat Center* v. *State of Kerala*, AIR 2008 SC 1614.

The rise of the *suo motu* device can be visualized as a concomitant of the PIL process gradually becoming top-down in nature. Arun Thiruvengadam (2013) laments the rising instances of adoption of a "command-and-control" approach by the Supreme Court,[54] identifying its origins in the progressive scholarship in the 1980s, which espoused the application of *personal* value judgment or ideology by judges in their adjudication.[55] He calls this the "deification of activist judges." He highlights the command-and-control approach with the example of *Vineet Narain* v. *Union of India*,[56] where the Court appointed an *amicus curiae*, but shut out intervention in the proceedings by any other party and held proceedings in-camera. He argues that the Supreme Court should instead confine itself to a "facilitative" role in PILs.

Similarly, Anuj Bhuwania (2017) argues that notions of procedure as an "enemy of justice,"[57] and movement towards informalization and indigenization of judicial proceedings, introduced as part of judicial populism in the period following the internal Emergency of 1975–1977,[58] led to early controversies in PIL adjudication. These controversies included instances of judges "choosing the litigants" and allegations of inadequate opportunity to cross-examine and question the evidence. This was followed by what Bhuwania calls the "curious case of the disappearing public interest petitioner." In cases such as *Vineet Narain*, as discussed above, public-spirited petitioners were viewed, in Bhuwania's words, as "impediments to justice." Similarly, in *Sheela Barse's* case,[59] the Supreme Court rejected a petition by Ms. Barse to withdraw her case. Opining that only private litigants may abandon proceedings, the Court installed the Supreme Court Legal Aid Committee as the petitioner and

---

[53] The Report of the International Commission of Jurists Mission to Pakistan reviewed the practice of *suo motu* intervention in Pakistan and provided a similar opinion: "It appears that the Chief Justice sometimes decides to exercise *suo motu* jurisdiction immediately on the basis of reports in the media. This introduces a certain element of chance to the practice which is hardly compatible with the rule of law."

[54] Arun Thiruvengadam, "Swallowing a Bitter PIL? Reflections on Progressive Strategies for Public Interest Litigation in India."

[55] For example, in *Almitra Patel* v. *Union of India* (2000) 8 SCC 19, Justice Kirpal, in a widely criticized judgment, equated encroachers with pickpockets. Thiruvengadam opines that "[Justice Kirpal] was merely incorporating his own value judgments into the task of adjudication – and was thus directly acting on the questionable advice offered by progressive writings in the 1980s."

[56] (1998) 1 SCC 226.

[57] Bhuwania, *Courting the People*, pp. 16–49.

[58] On June 25, 1975, President Fakhruddin Ali Ahmed issued the following order: "In exercise of the powers conferred by clause 1 of Article 352 of the Constitution, I, Fakhruddin Ali Ahmed, President of India, by this Proclamation declare that a grave emergency exists whereby the security of India is threatened by internal disturbance."

[59] *Sheela Barse* v. *Union of India* (1988) 4 SCC 226 at 246.

directed that proceedings be continued. The "logical culmination" of this trend, Bhuwania argues, was to dispense with the need for a petitioner.

It is worthwhile to note that taking *suo motu* cognizance is neither a novel practice nor one confined to the higher courts. Section 23 of the Contempt of Courts Act, 1971 read with the Rules to Regulate Proceedings for Contempt of the Supreme Court, 1975 empowers the Supreme Court to initiate *suo motu* action in contempt cases. Under Section 190(1) of the Criminal Procedure Code, 1973, magistrates of the first class or second class can take cognizance of a criminal offense on their own motion.[60] Many bodies, typically statutorily empowered with the powers of a civil court in the performance of their investigatory functions, are also vested with the authority to take up matters *suo motu*. In the Birbhum case, three such institutions also took *suo motu* cognizance: the National Commission for Women,[61] the West Bengal Commission for Women,[62] and the West Bengal Human Rights Commission.[63] We are concerned here with the distinct practice of the Supreme Court and the High Courts initiating cases *suo motu* under their writ or review jurisdiction. This is an infrequent practice (as we will see in the next section, we have been able to identify just 23 instances in which the Justices of the Supreme Court have invoked this procedure since 1994.).[64] However, the regularization

---

[60] *Abhinandan Jha v. Dinesh Mishra*, 1968 AIR 117. To prevent misuse (or bias) in the exercise of such powers, Section 191 states that if cognizance is taken under clause (c) of Section 190(1), i.e., *suo motu*, the accused is to be informed that he is entitled to have his case inquired/tried by another magistrate (other than the one taking cognizance) and can hence have the case transferred.

[61] Section 10(1)(f) of the National Commission for Women Act, 1990.

[62] Section 11(1)(d) of the West Bengal Commission for Women Act, 1992.

[63] Section 12 of the Protection of Human Rights Act, 1993.

[64] This judicial recourse to *suo motu* initiatives occurs with greater intensity and scope in Pakistan, somewhat less in Bangladesh, and only very occasionally elsewhere in the common law world. By a curious coincidence, at the very time the Indian Supreme Court was taking up the Birbhum case, a three-judge bench headed by the Chief Justice of Pakistan was engaged in a *suo motu* inquiry into two gang rapes in Muzaffargarh district. In one "a panchayat ordered the gang rape of a woman." In the other, a girl died by self-immolation in front of the police station after the accused rapists were released by the police. Reportedly the rape followed the girl's refusal of engagement to one of the culprits. Asham TV News, March 14, 2014, The Nation, 17 March, 2014. A subsequent police report, claiming that the victim was not sexually assaulted and that "the whole incident was a ploy to trap the suspects" was mockingly dismissed by the Supreme Court bench. The Express Tribune, 21 April, 2014. Many of the *suo motu* initiatives in Pakistan engaged with major issues of governance. See Osama Siddique, "The Judicialization of Politics in Pakistan: The Supreme Court after the Lawyers' Movement" (2015); M. H. Cheema and I. S. Gilani, eds., *The Politics and Jurisprudence of the 'Chaudhry Court' 2005–2013* (2014). On Bangladesh, see Ridwanul Hoque, *Judicial Activism in Bangladesh: A Golden Mean Approach* (2011), 152–157.

of *suo motu* initiatives is indicated not only by their increasing frequency but by the recent adoption of Order 38, Rule 12(1)(a) in the Supreme Court Rules, 2013,[65] stating that a PIL may commence following a *suo motu* petition in pursuance of the orders of the Chief Justice or any other Judge.

IV. MEASURING THE INCIDENCE OF *SUO MOTU* INTERVENTION

The Supreme Court's Birbhum intervention is by no means an isolated incident. We have managed to identify 23 cases in the Supreme Court over the period 1994–2018 that fit the *suo motu* prototype. The Supreme Court Registry first applied the label in 2004. Other *suo motu* interventions may have been unreported or escaped our notice.[66]

In our attempt to count *suo motu* initiatives of the Supreme Court, we submitted a request under the Right to Information Act. The Supreme Court responded that "data with respect to 'suo motu' cases is maintained from 2014–15," and gave us a list of four cases, of which two were contempt cases.[67] We then looked at records from the Supreme Court Almanac (SCALE), a comprehensive weekly case reporter that is one of the few reporters that publish the short orders of the Court.[68] For the purpose of this study, we examined all volumes of SCALE from 2000 to 2015. In addition, we searched online databases: Manupatra, Westlaw, and Indian Kanoon. We also supplemented our search by browsing through the chapters on public interest litigation published in the *Annual Survey of Indian Law*. We have collected all those cases which have been either been initiated without any petitioner, usually upon reading a newspaper or press account; or are labeled by the Supreme Court as "*suo motu*." Our search was limited by exclusion of contempt cases and inclusion of only cases which are reported by these sources. Our search revealed only 23 instances of *suo motu* cases initiated by the Supreme Court. A list of these cases, along with the timestamps, is in Table 4.1.

---

[65] The Rules came into force on August 19, 2014, as notified by Circular No. 1/SG./SC Rules/ 2014.

[66] Cf. Bhuwania: "PIL cases did not often end up in any 'judgments' at all but in an endless spiral of 'orders', which are not reported in law journals." Bhuwania, *Courting the People*, p. 10.

[67] Letter No. 232/RTI/15–16/SCI, dated May 27, 2015.

[68] Many lawyers subscribe to SCALE since it reports Supreme Court judgments every week. Most other case reporters are a few weeks, or even months, late. SCALE includes reportable and non-reportable judgments as well as important orders/proceedings. The other case reporters are not similarly comprehensive in their coverage.

TABLE 4.1 Suo motu cases in the Supreme Court according to RTI responses, SCALE and examination of online databases of law reports

No.	Case name	Citation/ case no.	Initiation	Final order	Origin	Subject matter/remarks
1.	In Re: News Item Published in *Hindustan Times* Titles "And Quiet Flows The Maily Yamuna"	Writ Petition (Civil) No. 725 of 1994	Circa July 1994	Pending	Newspaper reports	Pollution in Yamuna river
2.	In Re: Noise Pollution	Writ Petition (C) No. 72 of 1998	Circa January 1998	18/07/2005	An engineer filed a petition after reading newspaper reports that a 13-year-old rape victim's cries for help went unheard owing to noise pollution Court converted it to a *suo motu*-style petition and appointed *amicus curiae*	Regarding high noise pollution levels
3.	In Re: News Item "Power Crisis Paralyses AIIMS"	Writ Petition (C) 333/1998	01/06/1998	10/05/1999	News report in the *Hindustan Times* and *Times of India*	Court learned that medical facilities are being denied to hundreds of patients owing to power cuts

(continued)

TABLE 4.1 (*continued*)

No.	Case name	Citation/ case no.	Initiation	Final order	Origin	Subject matter/remarks
4.	In Re: Death of 25 Chained Inmates In Asylum Fire In Tamil Nadu	Writ Petition (Civil) No.334/ 2001	07/08/2001	Pending	Registrar (Judicial) submitted a note to the bench based on newspaper reports	Chained inmates in Tamil Nadu asylum were burned to death
5.	In Re: Networking of Rivers	Writ Petition (Civil) No. 512 of 2002]	16/09/2002	27/02/2012	Interlocutory Application filed by *amicus curiae* based on President's address on Independence Day	Interlinking of rivers and water management
6.	In Re: News Item "Madhepura in a Tizzy Over Pappu Visit"	*Suo-Motu* Petition No.5410/2004	07/05/2004	14/02/2005	Newspaper report	Politician reported to be roaming in a constituency, despite being in judicial custody in connection with a murder case
7.	In Re: Illegal Detention of Machal Lalung	W. P. (Crl.) 296 of 2005	11/11/2005	03/09/2008 (substantive order on 24/ 10/2007)	Newspaper reports, brought to the notice of the Court by an Advocate	Mentally ill person languishing in judicial custody for 54 years (since 1951)

No.	Case	Petition	Date	Date	Source	Description
8.	In Re: Destruction of Public and Private Properties	Writ Petition (Crl.) Nos. 73 and 77 of 2007	05/06/2007	16/04/2009	TV footage	In the light of the Gujjar violence, Court took *suo motu* cognizance of large-scale destruction of property during agitations/hartals, etc.[a]
9.	In Re: Incident Relating to Crl. Intimidation, Physical Assault & Torture Sustained by Shri B. V. Rao, Member (Judl.), C.A.T.	Writ Petition (Crl.) No. 23 Of 2008	03/03/2008	25/08/2009	Letter written by the CAT (Central Administrative Tribunal) member	Judicial member of a tribunal was threatened/intimidated by the police
10.	In Re: Measures for Prevention of Fatal Accidents of Small Children Due to their Falling into Abandoned Bore Wells and Tube Wells	Writ Petition (Civil) No. 36 of 2009	13/02/2009	06/08/2010	Unclear; likely to be a newspaper report	Children falling into borewells
11.	In Re: Ramlila Maidan Incident	Suo Motu W. P (Crl) 122/ 2011	06/06/2011	23/02/2012	Media reports	Forceful eviction of Baba Ramdev and followers who were protesting against corruption/black money

(continued)

TABLE 4.1 *(continued)*

No.	Case name	Citation/ case no.	Initiation	Final order	Origin	Subject matter/remarks
12.	*Court on its Own Motion v. Union of India* [Amarnath Yatra incident]	*Suo Motu* Writ Petition (Civil) No. 284 of 2012	13/07/2012	13/12/2012	Newspaper reports	Poor arrangements causing deaths during the holy Amarnath Yatra
13.	In Re: Recent Firing Incident, Widely Reported in The Press	*Suo Motu* Writ Petition Civil No. 75/2013	21/11/2012 (case number given later)	Pending	Newspaper reports	Death of two persons, allegedly on account of use of firearms by some private security personnel
14.	In Re: Press Reports Captioning "Punjab Cops Beat up Woman in Public" and "Police Lathi-Charge Protesting Contractual Teachers in Patna"	2013 Indlaw SCO 532	06/03/2013	N/A (no case record available)	Newspaper reports	SC said "Both the incidents have shocked the conscience of the entire nation."
15.	In Re: Indian Woman says gang-raped on orders of Village Court published in Business and Financial News	*Suo Motu* Writ Petition (Criminal) No. 24 of 2014	24/1/2014	28/3/2014	Newspaper report	The Birbhum case discussed in this paper.

	Case	Petition No.	Date	Status	Trigger	Description
16.	In Re: Harassment & Physical Abuse Of Ambika Das, Advocate	*Suo Motu* Writ Petitions Criminal Nos. 92/2014	9/5/2014	Pending	Letter written by Advocate to the SC Registry. But case is listed as 'suo motu.'	Lady Advocate who went to serve copy of judicial order was manhandled at a police station.
17.	In Re: Indiscriminate Misuse of Power by a Minister or Secretary to Allow Certain Individuals to Overstay in Govt Accommodation	*Suo Motu* Writ Petition (Civil) No. 599 of 2014	18/07/2014	24/11/2014	Former CAG Vinod Rai wrote a letter based on media reports, SC takes *suo motu* cognizance of it	Case was dismissed since affidavits showed no misuse and there was no cause for alarm
18.	In Re: Harassment and Physical Abuse of 'M'	*Suo Motu* WP (Crl) 1/2014	22/9/2014	Pending	As Court was rising, Ms 'M' handed a bunch of papers alleging she was gang-raped and that police took no action post-FIR	Police inaction after a woman was allegedly gang-raped
19.	In Re: Outrage as Parents End Life After Child's Dengue Death	*Suo Motu* Writ Petition (Civil) No. 1/2015	16/9/2015	Pending	Newspaper report	Matter taken up by Chief Justice after newspaper report on dengue death; clubbed with a case matter on chikungunya

(continued)

TABLE 4.1 (*continued*)

No.	Case name	Citation/ case no.	Initiation	Final order	Origin	Subject matter/remarks
20.	In Re: Prajwala Letter Dated 18.2.2015 Videos of Sexual Violence and Recommendations	*Suo Motu* Writ Petition (Criminal) No. 3/2015	Unavailable, possibly 13/3/ 2015	Pending	Letter to the Chief Justice	Letter writing to the Chief Justice intimating him about videos of sexual violence being circulated on social networking and instant messaging apps
21.	In Re: Blog Published by Justice Markandey Katju in Facebook	*Suo Motu* Review Petition (Crl.) No. 1/2016	17/10/2016	11/11/2016	Post on Facebook	During the hearing in a criminal review petition, the Court noted a Facebook post by a retired SC judge (Justice Katju) and converted it into a *suo motu* review petition. He was invited to present his view before the Court. The court heard his arguments and decided to dismiss the petition. Alongside, the court issued a separate contempt notice to Justice Katju for

					disparaging remarks made in his posts.
22.	In Re: To Issue Certain Guidelines Regarding Inadequacies and Deficiencies in Criminal Trials	*Suo Motu* Writ (Crl.) No. 1 of 2017.	30/3/2017	Pending	Concern raised by Senior Advocate during the hearings of a separate criminal appeal	During the course of hearing of a criminal appeal, R. Basant, Senior Advocate and former Judge, Kerala High Court raised a concern regarding deficiencies and inconsistent rules of practice before various High Courts. The Supreme Court took suo motu cognizance of this problem and issued notices.
23	In Re: Kathua, Jammu and Kashmir	Suo Motu Writ (Crl.) 1 of 2018.	13/04/2018	30/07/2018	Court informed of developments by a group of lawyers	The Court took suo motu cognizance upon learning that local lawyers sought to prevent the filing of a police report in the case of a rape and murder of an eight-year-old girl.

ᵃ See V. Venkatesan, "SC Intervention in Gujjar Violence: A Few Questions," *Law and Other Things*, June 6, 2007, available at http://lawandotherthings .blogspot.in/2007/06/scs-intervention-in-gujjar-violence-few.html for a full discussion.

The final entry in Table 4.1, involving a gang-rape in a setting of communal conflict, bears some resemblance to the Birbhum case. However, there are many striking differences. In the Kathua case the victim, an eight year old, was kidnapped, raped, and murdered, allegedly as part of a deliberate scheme of communal oppression. Strikingly, unlike Birbhum, there was powerful resistance to the prosecution within local legal circles. The Supreme Court's *suo motu* intervention was in response to the urging of advocates, rather than inspired by victim contact or a news account. That intervention was intermittent and supervisory rather than taking the role of the plenary decision-maker.

Data in Table 4.1 is for cases in the Supreme Court. We are unable to supply comparable data for the High Courts. On the basis of news accounts, we conclude with some confidence that the total number of *suo motu* proceedings in the High Courts is many times larger than the Supreme Court total, but we are unable at this point to present any reliable data on their incidence.

V. BIRBHUM AND BEYOND: *SUO MOTU* AND ITS PERPLEXITIES

In the Birbhum case, we saw a court at the peak of a complex judicial hierarchy reaching, one might say, to the bottom of the system to sort out a matter otherwise unlikely to make its way to this exalted institution.

There are many intriguing aspects to this *suo motu* excursion, with many departures from the Court's regular mode of operation,[69] and from our expectations as observers of courts:[70] the adversarial frame is abandoned; the constraints of passivity are displaced by active outreach and management. Institutional space and time are compressed: instead of being separated by layers of institutional intermediaries and the filters of process, there is an imperative to connect with the immediacy of events. The Court is eager to project itself into the moment of action, to act at the coal face, where the rubber meets the road, liberated from the stylized intermediation of registry,

---

[69] And departure at least in degree from the format of public interest litigation – where the initiative is typically provided by a party or champion. In these *suo motu* actions the Court is not only the ally of would-be "reformers" but the entrepreneurial reformer itself.

[70] Compare the regulatory and enforcement initiatives by judges in American trial courts, departing from the passive and reactive model thought to describe the common law judge, described by Marc Galanter, Frank S. Palen, and John Thomas, "The Crusading Judge: Judicial Activism in Urban Trial Courts" (1979).

clerks and lawyers, pleadings, motions and appeals, that present matters to the Court in standardized digestible packages. We have the Court contending, as directly as it can envision, with the raw facts of the victim's plight. The Supreme Court's aspiration to combine immediacy and effectiveness reveals something important about the Court and about its spectator public. The Court aspires to correct injustice without the constraining forms in which it is enmeshed. This is done publicly, attracts media attention, and is applauded by wide sections of the public that are looking for a champion, an actor that pursues and achieves substantive justice, that can do the right thing, that can get things done – something they don't necessarily see when they look at the ordinary working of legal institutions.

Notably, the Supreme Court in the Birbhum case does not direct the rape accusation into the lower courts, engage the lower court as its agent, or retire to a supervisory or standard-setting role. This may reflect concern about losing momentum or pessimism about the reliability of the lower courts. The result is that the Court retains the starring role, making decisions and issuing orders about various aspects of the investigation and the remedy. We might call this Cinderella law: the Court as good fairy appears, unbidden, to turn the tables on behalf of an obscure and resourceless victim. And, like the beneficiaries of a bountiful fairy, the judges – especially one imagines, the Chief Justice – must be aware that their extraordinary ability to shape events is a wasting asset, one that will evaporate instantaneously on the looming day of their retirement.

We do not mean to denigrate or minimize the Court's genuine concern and its steadfastness and courage. Our question is why its response takes the form of these singular heroic interventions rather than promoting some institutional shake-up,[71] some initiative to empower and equip courts lower in the judicial hierarchy and closer to the matter at hand to engage in this way. The

---

[71] The manner of grant of increased compensation to the victim in the Birbhum case is one such example. As per the latest amendments to criminal law, victims of rape may get compensation under two provisions: S. 357A of the Criminal Procedure Code (Victim Compensation Scheme) and S. 376D of the Indian Penal Code (fine sufficient for medical expenses and rehabilitation to be paid to the victim). As per S. 375B, compensation payable by the government under S. 357A would be in addition to a fine under S. 376D. The procedure for compensation under S. 357A is as follows. If the fine-compensation under S. 376D is insufficient, the trial court recommends compensation to be paid by the government (S. 357A (3)). The matter is referred to the appropriate Legal Services Authority, which determines the quantum of compensation (S. 357A(2)). The government then pays the compensation from its victim compensation scheme. As per S. 357A(6), the appropriate Legal Services Authority can also order for immediate medical facilities and "any other interim relief" as it "deems fit" to "alleviate the suffering of the victim." In unilaterally increasing the compensation amount, the Supreme Court appears to have bypassed the statutory provisions (although it arguably has constitutional powers to do so).

Supreme Court (or these benches at least) seems to envision itself not as a specialized limb of the judicial body with supervisory and standard-setting responsibilities, but as an institution that fully incarnates in its purest and highest form the mission and plenary powers of the judiciary.

The Court's actions mark a departure from the normal operation of the judicial hierarchy. There is an echo here of the disdain with which higher courts in India frequently treat the efforts of the lower judiciary, a hint of the disconnect between the higher judiciary and the ordinary courts.[72] For a moment the Court dramatically invokes and instantiates the presence of a unified and integrated system in which the norms of modern "constitutional" India are realized and embodied. The Court's action registers deviance from these norms, but it announces and dramatizes that there is a remedy that is hierarchically present. For the moment at least the "great pyramid of legal order" is integrated and whole,[73] from the Chief Justice of the Supreme Court at its peak, projecting undiluted remedial justice, to the police constables protecting the victimized villager. The norms of the Indian state are vindicated as the victim is remedied and rehabilitated by the civil law and violators are punished by the criminal law. For a moment the law is whole, effective, benign, and accessible. In the Court's initiative one can hear faint echoes of accounts of the Moghul Emperor Jahangir who reported in his memoirs:

> After my accession, the first order that I gave was for the fastening up of the Chain of Justice, so that if those engaged in the administration of justice should delay or practice hypocrisy in the matter of those seeking justice, the oppressed might come to this chain and shake it so that its noise might attract attention.[74]

As in the Birbhum case, the modern-day judges do not only provide a chain, but they take the initiative, and themselves shake it vigorously on behalf of the

---

[72] Jay Krishnan et al., "Grappling at the Grassroots: Litigant Efforts to Access Economic and Social Rights in India," *Harvard Human Rights Journal* 27, 151 (2014).

[73] Cf. Henry M. Hart and Albert M. Sacks, *The Legal Process: Basic Problems in the Making and Application of Law* (1958), 312.

[74] Henry Beveridge, ed., *The Tuzuk-I-Jehangir,* Memoirs of Jahangir (trans. Alexander Roberts). Jahangir (1569–1627) reigned from 1605 until his death in 1627. His son Shah Jahan (1594–1666), who reigned from 1628 to 1658, substituted "a string that he would let down from the window where he appeared in the mornings. People tied their petitions to this string 'and thus complaints reached the Emperor unhindered.'" Linda T. Darling, "'Do Justice, Do Justice, for That is Paradise': Middle Eastern Advice for Indian Muslim Rulers" (2002). After invoking the comparison to Jahangir, we discovered that a similar comparison was drawn by the late Professor S. K. Agrawala more than 30 years ago. S. K. Agrawala, *Public Interest Litigation in India: A Critique* (1985), 21.

perceived victim. While the Court is free to shake the chain when it is so disposed, the location of the chain, that is, the lever to inspire the court to launch on this infrequent and unpredictable intervention,[75] is, unlike Jahangir's chain, not predictably reachable by the remote suppliant. Its sound is not to summon the caring sovereign, but to proclaim the Court's benign intervention. That intervention is a performance – for the judges themselves, as well as for the wider audience that may be thrilled or at least reassured by the Court's demonstration of the immanence of justice. Apparently, the show is very appealing, at least to some sections of the public and to the judicial actors themselves. As for the officials, the judges of the lower courts, and the police, we may wonder if they are inspired or alienated. In the Birbhum case, the trial was completed in an uncommonly quick span of two months. Records on file with us indicate that the police cited the Supreme Court's intervention to plead against the grant of bail and to urge (unsuccessfully) the Central Forensic Science Laboratory to submit its report in an expedited manner.

The judicial fondness for the *suo motu* strategy suggests several things. First, that the higher courts, that is the Supreme Court and the High Courts, with their extensive original jurisdiction, are not only the hierarchic controllers of the lower courts, but also their rivals for attention, prestige and power – a rivalry that manifests itself in reluctance to accord the lower courts a sphere of autonomy and initiative.[76] Second, it reminds us that India's legal structure is not an orderly unified pyramid radiating legal illumination into unoccupied neutral space.[77] Instead, it is situated in a space populated by a thick tangle of other forms of normative regulation, such as, for example, the rules or standards invoked by the actors in the Bengal village.[78] We make no claim

---

[75] A little more than a year after the Birbhum incident, in March 2015, news erupted about the gang-rape of an elderly nun in Nadia district of West Bengal. The victim, a 71-year-old nun at a convent school, was raped by a group of eight men. A few days later, when an advocate informed the Chief Justice's bench about the incident, the Court refused to take *suo moto* cognizance.

[76] Cf. Krishnan et al., "Grappling at the Grassroots," pp. 183ff. Cf. Bhuwania, who writes that the lower judiciary in India is perceived as corrupt and inefficient, while the higher judiciary apparently transcends such drawbacks. In light of such perceptions, argues Bhuwania, the higher judiciary employs distancing tactics, expressing anguish at the conditions of the lower courts. One consequence of such despair is the search for alternatives, like lok adalats. Bhuwania, *Courting the People*, p. 3.

[77] We do not mean to imply that such an orderly pyramid accurately describes legal institutions in settings outside India that are familiar to us. But the imagery has a powerful hold on the legal imaginary in many places.

[78] A few examples of the many studies of these non-governmental regulatory orders are Maarten Bavinck, *Marine Resource Management: Conflict and Regulation in the Fisheries of the Coromandel Coast* (2001) (regulation among fishermen, boat owners); Julia Eckert, "Urban

that these other forms of regulation are "prior" to the state, that they form a basic substratum of social regulation in contrast to "artificial" or superficial state institutions. These local legalities may come into being together with state institutions or in reaction to the presence, or absence, of state institutions. Local legality may imitate state institutions,[79] and these, conversely, may pretend to embody indigenous forms.[80] But whatever their origin, these non-state regulators are there, and their presence alters the impact and meaning of state law. Like a sandbar formed around the hulk of a sunken vessel, local norms that contradict those embodied in the state's official pronouncements present a challenge to governmental navigation that cannot be ignored or simply overridden by a claim of superior legitimacy. Of course in practice the organs of the state themselves (a conspicuous but not solitary example is the police) frequently exhibit norms and practices that depart from the "higher law" to which they pledge fealty.

Sudden interventions of the higher courts like the one here may take the form of dramatic eruptions of *kadi* justice,[81] in the Weberian sense of responding to individual cases in terms of concrete ethical judgments rather than by routine application of generalized rules. Such intervention has emerged as a prominent instrument of governance and a source of legitimacy for India's system of formal legality, in this case dramatizing the triumph of official law over the familiar but ever surprising and alarming presence of "retrograde" immanent law. So we see the Indian state's institutions of rational bureaucratic legality promoted and defended by adventurous excursions into individualized kadi justice.

Governance and Emergent Forms of Legal Pluralism in Mumbai" (Shiv Sena courts); K. S. Sangwan, "Khap Panchayats in Haryana: Sites of Legal Pluralism" (khap panchayats).

[79] Examples in Nirmal Kumar Bose, ed., *Data on Caste, Orissa*. Calcutta: Anthropological Survey of India, Memoir No. 7 (1960); Maarten Bavinck, *Marine Resource Management: Conflict and Regulation in the Fisheries of the Coromandel Coast* (2001).

[80] For example, the State has established nyaya panchayats, lok adalats, and gram nyayalalas, which try to borrow the charisma of "traditional" institutions. On panchayats, see Upendra Baxi and Marc Galanter, "Panchayat Justice: An Indian Experiment in Legal Access"; Catherine S. Meschievitz and Marc Galanter, "In Search of Nyaya Panchayats: The Politics of a Moribund Institution." On Lok Adalats, see Marc Galanter and Jayanth Krishnan, "Debased Informalism: Lok Adalats and Legal Rights in Modern India" (2003); Marc Galanter and Jayanth Krishnan, "Bread for the Poor: Access to Justice for the Needy in India" (2004). On gram nyayalayas, see Menaka Guruswamy and Aditya Singh, "Accessing Justice: The Gram Nyayalayas Act" (2010). See also Sylvia Vatuk, "The 'Women's Court' in India: An Alternative Dispute Resolution Body for Women in Distress" (2013).

[81] See Max Weber, *Economy and Society*, Vol. 3 (1978), 976. Weber associates *kadi* justice with charismatic adjudication ("the Solomonic award of a charismatic sage, an award based on concrete and individual considerations which demand absolute validity.")

But there are limits on the efficacy of such adventurous judicial initiatives. In the Birbhum case, the Supreme Court seems to abandon some of the cautions and checks institutionalized in the judicial process in the service of broadcasting images of its benign attention. Weber's ideal-typical kadi presumably enjoyed intimate and direct knowledge of the case before him. But inevitably, there are limitations on how much a distant real-world court knows about what actually happened and on how accurately it can ascertain what the consequences of its intervention will be. The clinical and medical notes on the victim in the Birbhum case emphasized her anxiety about social ostracism and excommunication.[82] Despite the Supreme Court's direction to ensure that the victim faced no such setback, local stringers have reported that villagers resisted any aid in support of the victim. Ultimately, she had to be shifted to a government stay home and later to a newly constructed house some distance from her original village. How she will fare remains unknown. We make no claim that she would be better off absent the Supreme Court's intervention. But we wonder if this is an instance of effective use of the scarce resource of judicial attention? What does it do for the judiciary in the eyes of the public? And how does this kind of dramatic and symbolic intervention promote the routine and reliable administration of justice in contemporary India?

We do not claim that the Birbhum case is typical of suo motu interventions of the higher courts. But in its relative simplicity it alerted us to the *suo motu* phenomenon and stimulated many questions about this emergent practice, questions that, we believe, go to the heart of the role, practice, and image of the judiciary in contemporary India.

---

[82] Available on file.

The Newspaper Account that provoked the Supreme Court's Intervention

'Indian woman says gang-raped on orders of village court'
By Sujoy Dhar

KOLKATA, Jan 23 (Thomson Reuters Foundation) – A 20-year-old woman in eastern India was gang-raped by 13 men on the orders of a village court as punishment for having a relationship with a man from a different community, a senior police officer said on Thursday.

The woman, who is now recovering in hospital, told police she was assaulted by the men on the night of January 20 in Birbhum district in West Bengal.

Police said that her male companion was tied up in the village square, while the assault on the woman happened in a mud house.

"We arrested all the 13 men, including the village chief who ordered the gang rape. The accused have been produced in court which remanded them to jail custody," Birbhum's Superintendent of Police, C. Sudhakar, told the Thomson Reuters Foundation.

India toughened laws on sex crimes in March last year following the fatal gang rape of a physiotherapist on a moving bus in Delhi in December 2012. The case led to nationwide protests for better security and has helped sparked a national debate about gender inequalities in India.

The issue was highlighted in local media again last week after a 51-year-old Danish tourist was gang-raped in central Delhi by at least five men whom she had asked for directions.

The West Bengal victim's family told media that she was assaulted because the court believed she had violated the rules of her tribe by falling in love with a man from another community.

The couple were ordered to pay a fine of 25,000 rupees ($400), said the victim's mother, adding that the village head then ordered the rape of her daughter.

Human rights groups say diktats issued by kangaroo courts are not uncommon in rural regions.

In northern parts of India, illegal village councils known as "Khap Panchayats" act as de-facto courts settling rural disputes on everything from land and cattle to matrimony and murder.

But such councils are coming under growing scrutiny as their punitive edicts grow more regressive – ranging from banning women from wearing western clothing and using mobile phones to supporting child marriage and sanctioning the lynching of young couples in so-called honor killings.

The assault comes after a spate of high profile rapes in West Bengal which has brought Chief Minister Mamata Banerjee under fire for not doing enough to stop violence against women.

West Bengal recorded the highest number of gender crimes in the country at 30,942 in 2012 – 12.7 percent of India's total recorded crimes against women. These crimes include rape, kidnapping and sexual harassment and molestation.

Earlier this month, West Bengal's capital, Kolkata, witnessed public protests against police who have been accused of failing to act on the gang rape of a 16-year-old girl who was later murdered.

(The story was refiled to fix date in dateline, no changes to text.)

(Writing and additional reporting by Nita Bhalla; Editing by Sanjeev Miglani and Nick Macfie)

www.reuters.com/article/2014/01/23/us-india-rape-idUS BREA0M0VH20140123, https://perma.cc/QY9P-Q6X9

REFERENCES

Abhinandan Jha v. *Dinesh Mishra*, 1968 AIR 117.

Agrawala, S. K., *Public Interest Litigation in India: A Critique* (New Delhi: Indian Law Institute, 1985).

Almitra Patel v. *Union of India*, (2000) 8 SCC 19.

Archer, W. G., *Tribal Law and Justice: A Report on the Santal* (New Delhi: Concept Publishing Company: 1984).

Bandhua Mukti Morcha v. *Union of India* (1984) 3 SCC 161.

Bavinck, Maarten, *Marine Resource Management: Conflict and Regulation in the Fisheries of the Coromandel Coast* (New Delhi: Sage Publications, 2001).

Baxi, Upendra, "Taking Suffering Seriously: Social Action Litigation in the Supreme Court of India," *Third World Legal Stud.* 107, 114 (1985).

Baxi, Upendra, and Marc Galanter, "Panchayat Justice: An Indian Experiment in Legal Access," in M. Cappelletti and B. Garth (eds.), *Access to Justice: Vol. III:*

Emerging Issues and Perspectives (Milan: Guiffre; Alphen aan den Rijn: Sijthoff and Noordhoff, 1979), 341–386.

Beveridge, Henry, ed., *The Tuzuk-I-Jehangir*; Memoirs of Jahangir (trans. Alexander Roberts), available at http://archive.org/stream/tuzukijahangiriooojahauoft/tuzuki jahangiriooojahauoft_djvu.txt.

Bhagwati, Justice P. N., 'Judicial Activism and Public Interest Litigation', Colum. J. Transnat'l L. 23, 561, 570–571 (1984–1985).

Bhim Singh v. State of J & K, AIR 1986 SC 494.

Bhuwania, Anuj, *Courting the People: Public Interest Litigation in Post-Emergency India* (New Delhi: Cambridge University Press, 2017).

Bose, Nirmal Kumar, ed., *Data on Caste, Orissa*. Calcutta: Anthropological Survey of India, Memoir No. 7 (1960).

Chairman, Railway Board v. Chandrima Das, AIR 2000 SC 988.

Chakraborty, Snehamoy, "Envy Becomes Savagery," *The Telegraph*, Jan. 24, 2014.

Cheema, M. H. and I. S. Gilani, eds., *The Politics and Jurisprudence of the 'Chaudhry Court'* 2005–2013 (Karachi: Oxford University Press, 2014).

Code of Criminal Procedure, 1973.

Criminal Law (Amendment) Act, 2013.

Darling, Linda T., "'Do Justice, Do Justice, for That is Paradise': Middle Eastern Advice for Indian Muslim Rulers," 22 (1&2) *Comparative Studies of South Asia, Africa and the Middle East* (2002).

Desai, Ashok H. and S. Muralidhar, 'Public Interest Litigation: Potential and Problems' in B. N. Kirpal, et al., eds., *Supreme But Not Infallible: Essays in Honor of the Supreme Court of India* (New Delhi: Oxford University Press, 2002) 151–192.

Dhagamwar, Vasudha, *Role and Image of Law in India: The Tribal Experience* (New Delhi: Sage Publications, 2006).

Divine Retreat Center v. State of Kerala, AIR 2008 SC 1614.

Eckert, Julia, "Urban Governance and Emerging Forms of Pluralism in Mumbai," *Journal of Legal Pluralism* 50, 29–60 (2004).

Falerio, Sonia, *13 Men* (Deca Stories, 2015).

Galanter, Marc, Frank S. Palen, and John Thomas, "The Crusading Judge: Judicial Activism in Urban Trial Courts," *Southern California Law Review* 52, 699–741 (1979).

Galanter, Marc and Jayanth Krishnan, "Bread for the Poor: Access to Justice for the Needy in India," *Hastings Law Journal* 55, 789–834 (2004).

"Debased Informalism: Lok Adalats and Legal Rights in Modern India," in Erik G. Jensen & Thomas C. Heller, eds., *Beyond Common Knowledge: Empirical Approaches to the Rule of Law* (Stanford, CA: Stanford University Press, 2003), 76–121.

Guruswamy, Menaka and Aditya Singh, "Accessing Justice: The Gram Nyayalayas Act," *Economic & Political Weekly* 45(43) (Oct. 23, 2010).

Hart, Henry M. and Albert M. Sacks, *The Legal Process: Basic Problems in the Making and Application of Law* (tent. ed., 1958) 312.

High Court of Karnataka v. State of Karnataka, AIR 1998 Kant 327.

Hoque, Ridwanul, *Judicial Activism in Bangladesh: A Golden Mean Approach* (Newcastle upon Tyne: Cambridge Scholars Publishing, 2011).

Indian Penal Code, 1960.

"Indian woman says gang-raped on orders of village court," Business and Financial News, Reuters.com, Jan 23, 2014.

In Re: *Indian Woman says gang-raped on orders of Village Court published in Business & Financial News dated 23.01.2014*, Suo Motu Writ Petition (Criminal) No. 24 of 2014.

In Re: *The Chief Election Commissioner*, AIR 2011 Mad 103.

Kannabiran, Kalpana and Ranbir Singh, *Challenging the Rule(s) of Law: Colonialism, Criminology and Human Rights in India* (New Delhi: Sage Publications, 2008).

Khatri (II) v. State of Bihar (1981) 1 SCC 627.

Krishnan, Jay, et al., "Grappling at the Grassroots: Litigant Efforts to Access Economic and Social Rights in India," *Harvard Human Rights Journal* 27, 151 (2014).

Law Commission of India, 226th Report, July 2009.

Laxmi v. Union of India (W.P. (C) 129 of 2006).

Mandhani, Apoorva, *Madras HC Judge Justice Karnan stays Supreme Court's order transferring him to Calcutta HC and directs CJI to submit his reply*, LiveLaw.in, www.livelaw.in/madras-hc-judge-justice-karnan-stays-supreme-courts-order-transfer ring-him-to-calcutta-hc-sc-directs-the-cj-not-to-assign-any-works-to-him/.

Mendelsohn, Oliver, *Life and Struggles in the Stone Quarries of India: A Case Study in Law and Social Transformation in India* (New Delhi: Oxford University Press, 2014).

Meschievitz, Catherine S. and Marc Galanter, "In Search of Nyaya Panchayats: The Politics of a Moribund Institution," in R. Abel (ed.), *The Politics of Informal Justice: Comparative Studies* (New York: Academic Press, 1982), 47–77.

Ministry of Tribal Affairs (Xaxa Committee), *Report of the High Level Committee on Socio-Economic, Health and Educational Status of Tribal Communities of India*, May, 2014.

Mody, Zia, "Death in Custody: The Breach of Trust and Its Price," in 10 *Judgments that Changed India* (New Delhi: Penguin, 2013), 159.

National Commission for Women Act, 1990.

Protection of Human Rights Act, 1993.

Qazi, Asher A., "Suo Motu: Choosing Not to Legislate Chief Justice Chaudhry's Strategic Agenda," in Mohan Cheema and Ijaz Gilani eds., *The Politics and Jurisprudence of the Chaudhry Court* (Karachi: Oxford University Press, 2015), 281–321, 284–285.

Robinson, N., "A Quantitative Analysis of the Indian Supreme Court's Workload," *Journal of Empirical Legal Studies* 10, 570–601 (2013).

Rudul Shah v. State of Bihar, AIR 1983 SC 1086.

Sangwan, K. S., "*Khap Panchayats in Haryana: Sites of Legal Pluralism*," in Kalpana Kannabiran and Ranbir Singh, Challenging the Rule(s) of Law: Colonialism, Criminology and Human Rights in India (New Delhi: Sage Publications, 2008), pp. 331–353.

Sathe, S. P., *Judicial Activism in India: Transgressing Borders and Enforcing Limits* (New Delhi: Oxford University Press, 2002).

Sheela Barse v. Union of India (1988) 4 SCC 226 at 246.

Siddique, Osama, "The Judicialization of Politics in Pakistan: The Supreme Court after the Lawyers' Movement," in Mark Tushnet and Madhav Khosla, eds., *Unstable Constitutionalism: Law and Politics in South Asia* (New York: Cambridge University Press, 2015).

State of West Bengal v. *Jolha Maddi and Ors.*, Sessions Case No. 51 of 2014 at Bolpur, judgment dated September 19, 2014.

Thiruvengadam, Arun, "Swallowing a Bitter PIL? Reflections on Progressive Strategies for Public Interest Litigation in India," in *The Shifting Scales of Justice: The Supreme Court in Neo-Liberal India* (New Delhi: Orient Blackswan, 2014).

Vatuk, Sylvia, "The 'Women's Court' in India: An Alternative Dispute Resolution Body for Women in Distress," *Journal of Legal Pluralism and Unofficial Law* 45(1), 76–103 (2013).

Venkatesan, V., "SC Intervention in Gujjar Violence: A Few Questions," *Law and Other Things*, June 6, 2007, available at http://lawandotherthings.blogspot.in/2007/06/scs-intervention-in-gujjar-violence-few.html.

Vineet Narain v. *Union of India*, (1998) 1 SCC 226.

Weber, Max, *Economy and Society*, Vol. 3 (Berkeley: University of California Press, 1978).

West Bengal Commission for Women Act, 1992.

Wilson, H. H., *A Glossary of Judicial and Revenue Terms and Useful Words Occurring in Official Documents Relating to the Administration of Government of British India* (London: W. H. Allen, 1855).

5

Public Trust in the Indian Judiciary

The Power to Transform

SUDHIR KRISHNASWAMY AND SIDDHARTH SWAMINATHAN

I. INTRODUCTION

"The politics of the Court – be it the 'purest politics' of constitutional adjudication or the hurly-burly politics of power-sharing at times, power-grabbing at others, represents the best hope for millions of Indians for a new constitutional dawn. If the Court shuns it, it may do so at very grave peril to its own legitimacy and survival in the future" (Baxi, 1980, 248A).

At least since Baxi's stirring endorsement of the Indian Supreme Court's populist turn in 1980, it has become commonplace in Indian constitutional scholarship to assert that the judiciary's immense power rests on its populist legitimacy (Mate, 2015; Robinson, 2009). There have been some attempts to explain why the courts enjoy this legitimacy. Mehta argues that the "legitimacy and power that India's judiciary does enjoy most likely flow not from a clear and consistent constitutional vision," but by giving "enough players enough partial victories to leave them feeling as if they have a stake in keeping the game of political give-and-take going" (P. B. Mehta, 2007, 76–77). Such an attempt to explain the court's legitimacy to be a by-product of an adjudication strategy must be able to demonstrate the relationship between the court's' decision-making and its legitimacy; in other words, that a particular decision of the court generates popular public affirmation. However, there has been no academic effort to empirically confirm that the courts do indeed enjoy such popular legitimacy or explore whether such legitimacy arises from the composition of the court or its approach to adjudication.

Public opinion studies suggest that large numbers of Indian citizens express trust in political institutions such as the legislature, executive and the judiciary. Survey data further reveals that opinions about institutional trust are stable over time. Yet we know very little about what drives institutional trust in the Indian context. Are certain castes and communities more (or less) likely to trust institutions? Do factors such as literacy and the degree of media exposure – factors typically responsible for political socialization – influence institutional trust? Are citizens who express an interest in politics or participate in political activities between elections more likely to trust institutions compared to those who are either uninterested in politics or exhibit low levels of political participation? These sorts of questions focusing on the social and political correlates of institutional trust have been widely debated and examined in cross-national studies but remain unexplored in India.

In this chapter, we undertake the first empirically rigorous investigation of public trust in the Indian judiciary. Legitimacy of political institutions may be assessed and measured in several ways (Gilley, 2006; Weatherford, 1992). While legitimacy invokes a strong normative conclusion of the moral right of the institution to call on a citizen's obedience or allegiance, trust is an indicator that citizens expect fair and positive treatment by a particular political institution. In this way, invariably, trust in institutions is an ingredient of the broader measurement of legitimacy (Bradford, 2015, 18–19). This chapter does not further engage with the methodological debates about the relationship between trust and legitimacy. We investigate the available empirical evidence on the levels of political trust expressed by citizens in Indian institutions – particularly the judiciary.

We first explain variations in the levels of political trust in institutions, especially the courts. Most accounts of Indian politics and public opinion tend to use social and demographic characteristics as the primary framework to explain the nature of political attitudes and outcomes. Drawing on cultural explanations, we ask whether the levels of trust in the judiciary are shaped by class, caste, religious affiliation, literacy or gender. Second, we explore the relationship between citizens' trust in elected and unelected institutions. Is trust in elected institutions such as the central, state, and local governments positively or negatively associated with trust in the judiciary – an unelected institution? Is there evidence for diffuse support for the judiciary? Institutional models of trust suggest that citizens who trust elected institutions have a "reservoir of institutional goodwill" or diffuse institutional support that allows for a higher level of trust in the judiciary. Countermajoritarian models argue the opposite. Unelected institutions are viewed with greater skepticism and distrust relative to elected institutions. Relatedly, we also explore if specific individual political behaviors and institutional attitudes such as political participation, political interest, degree of exposure to media and perceptions of vote efficacy influence trust in the judiciary.

This chapter is structured as follows. Section 2 broadly reviews the theoretical literature on institutional trust to explain how we understand what "trust" means, identifies potential explanations for trust in the judiciary and specifies theoretical expectations for the Indian judiciary. Section 3 focuses on institutional trust in India and measurement, and outlines the data sources. Section 4 develops the multivariate analysis to estimate the relationship between public trust in the judiciary and a set of social, economic and political factors. Section 5 concludes with a discussion.

II. THEORIES OF INSTITUTIONAL TRUST

In this chapter we investigate the nature, extent and reasons for trust in the Indian judiciary. While institutional trust has been studied extensively in other political regimes, less attention has been paid to the origins and extent of political institutional trust in India. Hence, it is essential to begin this section with an overview of theories that briefly explain the concept of trust in general and then more specifically theories of institutional trust. Drawing on extant theorizing on public opinion about institutions in the United States and Europe, especially the US courts, we specify three hypotheses that may be tested with the available evidence on trust in the Indian judiciary.

A. *Social and political trust*

It is commonplace to speak in terms of trust or distrust of particular persons. Here trust is understood as the "belief that others will not deliberately or knowingly do us harm, if they can avoid it, and will look after our interests, if this is possible" (Newton, 2007, 343). This idea of trust explains our intuitions about interpersonal and horizontal relationships between citizens, or social trust, but needs clarification when extended to a citizen's relationship or confidence in public institutions (Giddens, 1990). Political trust may develop through a direct relationship between any person and the institution and be contingent on the performance of the institution or the manner in which it engages with the person (Uslaner, 2017). However, a large number of citizens may not directly engage an institution and instead develop a perception or relationship with the institution based on diffused knowledge gathered from others or the news media. It is also likely that trust or confidence in institutions is shaped through caricatures or stereotypical views that are shared among a wider social group irrespective of significant knowledge about the purposes and functioning of the institution. Political trust in institutions is thus distinct from social trust, and a closer analogue of the broader idea of political legitimacy.

Most of the political science and economics literature in this field explores the relationship between social trust and political trust – often to explain the nebulous idea of social capital (Inglehart, 1997). Others seek to explain if and the extent to which levels of social and political trust in a society affect levels of economic development, rule of law and social order. However, cross-national survey results provide mixed evidence on the relationship between generalized social and political trust (Mattes and Moreno, 2017). Moreover, while social trust seems to have little to do with levels of development, political or institutional trust shows a strong relationship with evaluations of economic and political performance. In this chapter we do not focus on the relationship between social and political trust in India. Instead, we pay close attention to the theoretical understanding of political trust to better understand the nature and extent of trust in the Indian judiciary.

B. *The sources of institutional trust*

The theoretical debate on the origins of institutional trust can be distinguished broadly along two lines (Mishler and Rose, 2001). Cultural or social theories of trust posit that processes of political socialization and interpersonal trust are keys to understanding trust in institutions (Almond and Verba, 1963; Inglehart, 1997; Putnam, 1993). The critical driver for cultural theories is interpersonal trust – or a generalized sense of trust or distrust in individuals that is typically a consequence of early life socialization. Interpersonal trust is shaped through an individual's interactions with family, peers, other kin and community groups, beginning in childhood. Interpersonal trust motivates individuals to engage with others in formal or informal civic organizations (Putnam, 1995). Participation in civic life produces effects that spill over into political life and likely increase trust in political institutions. Scholars subscribing to social theories of trust pay attention to factors such as age, education and gender among others (Dalton, 1996; Inglehart et al., 1998). For instance, younger generations born under consolidated democratic rule are more likely to internalize democratic ideas and exhibit a greater willingness to trust democratic institutions (Catterberg and Moreno, 2006). Higher levels of education, however, could induce more critical attitudes toward political institutions, hence trust declines with levels of education. Thus, according to cultural theories of trust, individual life experiences and early-age socialization create social trust, and this in turn generates trust in political institutions (Newton and Norris, 2000: 6).

Institutional theories, on the other hand, claim that institutional trust is a consequence of institutional performance (Hetherington, 1998; March, 1988;

Newton and Norris, 2000; North, 1990). Mishler and Rose (2001: 31) define institutional trust as the "expected utility of institutions performing satisfactorily." Similarly, Newton (2008: 343) suggests that political trust is a belief that those in power will protect and not harm citizen interests. This perspective suggests that trust in institutions is a product of a rational evaluation of institutional performance by citizens. Individuals develop higher levels of trust in institutions when they are satisfied with policy outcomes and dissatisfaction generates distrust. Policy successes include improved economic performance (Przeworski et al., 2000), an increased liberal political environment particularly in new democracies (Diamond, 1999) or the ability of institutions to resolve conflicts (Hutchison and Johnson, 2011). Therefore, important predictors of political trust include a citizen's satisfaction with government performance, policy outputs and the responsiveness of government institutions to citizen needs.

Institutional explanations of political support for institutions further distinguish between specific and diffuse support. Specific support refers to satisfaction with government outputs and the performance of political authorities, while diffuse support refers to the public's attitude toward regime-level political objects regardless of performance (Hetherington, 1998: 792). Some suggest that trust is associated only with specific support, hence low levels of political trust can be addressed by improved incumbent performance (Citrin, 1974; Citrin and Green, 1986). In contrast, others provide evidence of a link between political trust and certain measures of diffuse support, suggesting that sustained democratic consolidation is pivotal for political trust (Miller and Listhaug, 1990).

The theoretical disagreements on the sources of political trust in institutions carries over into the debates on trust in the judiciary. Studies on trust and confidence in the US Supreme Court focus on this distinction in the source of support, and test to see whether political trust "derives solely from stable factors such as core democratic values, or if citizens alter their evaluations to take into account their views of the Court's ruling" (Grosskopf and Mondak, 1998: 633–634). Diffuse support indicates a broad institutional commitment and consists of a "reservoir of favorable attitudes or goodwill that helps members to accept or tolerate outputs to which they are opposed or the effects of which they see as damaging to their wants" (Easton, 1965: 273). Gibson, Caldeira and Spence (2003: 356) claim that "diffuse support is institutional *loyalty*; it is support that is *not* contingent upon satisfaction with immediate outputs of institutions." While it is likely that both factors, an individual's goodwill for institutions and the impact of court decisions, influence individual political trust, disentangling the effects of the two forms of support has been empirically difficult and the results mixed. Although laboratory experiments show that unpopular decisions lower trust in the US Supreme Court (Mondak, 1991, 1992), i.e. evidence of specific support, survey results indicate the relationship is weak (Caldeira, 1986; Caldeira and Gibson, 1992) and offer stronger evidence that trust and confidence in the US Supreme Court is a function of diffuse support.

C. *Theoretical expectations*

Empirical research on the judiciary in India provides us with little theoretical guidance on what factors are likely to motivate public opinion on the judiciary. However, drawing from extant research on political and social trust and public opinion studies on the US judiciary discussed earlier in this section, we identify three hypotheses that can be empirically tested in the Indian context. A social explanation of trust in the judiciary suggests a focus on individual social, economic and demographic attributes. Factors such as caste identity, religious affiliation, economic class, level of education and gender influence political socialization and social trust, in turn, is likely to shape political trust. Thus we suggest that *Dalit* and *Adivasi* citizens likely view the judiciary differently from other caste identities. Similarly, individuals who identify as Muslim or Christian (i.e., a religious minority) are also likely to perceive the judiciary differently from Hindus. There are also likely differences in perception of the judiciary across economic class groups, levels of education and gender. However, there is less clarity on the direction of the relationship. If the judiciary is perceived as a progressive institution advancing the interests of relatively disadvantaged communities, we would expect to see these same communities express higher levels of trust in the judiciary. We suggest that courts in India generally tend to be seen as allies of the poor and marginalized and are likely to be viewed positively, i.e. engender higher levels of trust. Our first hypothesis thus focuses on social and economic differences likely to influence trust in the judiciary, and is as follows:

H1: [Social/Cultural Trust] Citizens who identify as a caste and religious minority, poor, or non-literates are more likely to trust the judiciary.

Political theories of trust focus on explicitly political factors in order to explain attitudes toward institutions. While not rejecting social explanation, these theories posit that individuals who exhibit a higher engagement with politics are expected to trust institutions more than those who do not engage. For instance, participation in political rallies, campaign events, canvassing and other election-related activities are expected to increase trust in the judiciary. Similarly, an interest in politics is also likely to increase citizen trust in the judiciary. The degree to which an individual is exposed to media sources is also shown to influence public opinion (Zaller, 1992). Finally, citizen attitudes on the value of voting is also likely to induce public institutional trust. Citizens who value their vote, i.e. think of their vote as efficacious, are more likely to trust institutions. Extending this line of thinking to opinions on the Indian judiciary, we specify the second hypothesis that links political factors to trust in the judiciary:

> H2: [Political Trust] Citizens who express an interest in politics between elections, participate in campaign activities during elections, perceive their vote as efficacious or are exposed to media sources are more likely to trust the judiciary.

The third hypothesis relates to diffuse support for the judiciary and is as follows:

> H3: [Diffuse Support] Citizens who trust elected institutions are more likely to trust the judiciary.

Our variant of the diffuse support hypothesis for the judiciary suggests that trust in elected institutions increases the likelihood that an individual trusts the judiciary. We suggest that individuals who trust elected institutions possess a "reservoir of goodwill" that spills over to the judiciary. Citizens who trust elected institutions are said to exhibit a higher level of institutional loyalty, which includes a perception of the judiciary as trustworthy. More generally, we suggest that a favorable disposition toward elected institutions, or institutional loyalty, is positively associated with trust in the judiciary.

III. TRUST IN THE INDIAN JUDICIARY

In this section of the chapter, we move from the theoretical analysis of political trust to sketch out the empirical background to these discussions in India. First, we examine how trust has been measured in India. We review available survey evidence and questionnaires to clarify the scope and extent to which an empirical strategy can help us understand the extent and determinants of trust in the Indian judiciary. Second, we briefly explore variation in patterns of trust across elected and unelected institutions in the data before moving to multivariate tests.

A. Measuring trust in India

We use data from the National Election Studies (NES) post-poll surveys conducted in 1996 and 2009, which we analyze separately for the two years and with pooled models. The NES is a nationally representative post-poll survey conducted in the days following a Lok Sabha election. In addition to standard questions on voting behavior, partisan preferences, campaign exposure and forms of political participation, the surveys also attempt to identify political and social attitudes, and perceptions of institutions, governance and public policy in the Indian electorate. The NES data has been used extensively to study vote choice and the factors that drive voting decisions, but less so to understand attitudes towards political institutions such as the judiciary. The NES 1996 and 2009 datasets contains 9,614 and 6,836 observations respectively. Our exploration into the correlates of trust in the judiciary is among the first systematic analysis of public opinion data on the judiciary in India.

While questions about "trust" and "confidence" in public institutions have been routinely asked in public opinion surveys such as the American NES, the US General Social Surveys, the World Values Surveys and European Barometer studies among others, they have been included infrequently in Indian public opinion surveys. Questions on trust in institutions initially appeared in the 1996 post poll and then again in 2009. The two rounds of State of Democracy in South Asia have included questions on trust in institutions and will likely continue to do so in future rounds. The NES question on trust is as follows: "I would like to seek your opinion about different institutions of India in which you may have great deal of trust, some trust, or no trust at all. How much trust do you have in the (institution)?" The concerned institutions include the national, State and local governments, elected representatives, the judiciary, the Election Commission, the bureaucracy, the police and political parties.

The NES asks the question on political trust in a fairly straightforward manner. As we note earlier, attitudes on trust in the judiciary are likely shaped by an individual's direct interaction with the institution or an assessment based on policy outputs. Respondent views about the judiciary are also influenced by what they think of judges and officers of the Court. However, the formulation itself is free of bias as it does not focus on a specific performative element of the court such as output and efficiency among others, personnel or individual experiences. Instead the question taps into an individual's overall opinion about the judiciary – whether it is thought of it as a legitimate institution. In addition, while the question is a measure of broad institutional trust, we cannot say for certain whether responses are based on systematic and informed evaluations of the judiciary or represent an uninformed view that either over or understates the respondent's true opinion.

Our dependent variable is one that examines trust in the judiciary, and is taken from a question asked in both surveys: "how much trust do you have in the judiciary?" While the question wording is identical in the two surveys, the response categories differ. The 1996 NES uses three response categories for trust in the judiciary: "great deal," "somewhat" and "not at all." In the 2009 NES an additional response category, "not very much," is included. In our analysis, we combine multiple categories of trust into two. For respondents who trust the judiciary a "great deal" or "somewhat," our dependent variable takes a value of 1. Those who report "not very much" or "not at all" are coded as having a value 0 on trust in the judiciary. We use an identical set of variables (dependent and independent) in the analysis for both years. A description of the variables used in the study, coding rules and summary statistics is presented in Appendix 1.

B. *Describing patterns of trust in India*

Before we test the hypotheses specified in the previous section, we describe broad patterns in trust in political institutions in India using the available data. We summarize trust across multiple institutions, both elected and unelected, using National Election Survey 1996 and 2009 data. Elected institutions include the Central (CG), State (SG), and Local governments (LG) and elected representatives, while the unelected institutions include the judiciary, Election Commission of India, government officials, political parties and the police. If respondents answer a "great deal" or "somewhat" when asked the question "how much trust do you have in the (institution)?" we conclude that they have trust in a particular institution.

Figure 5.1 describes the levels of trust across both elected and unelected institutions in India in 1996 and 2009.

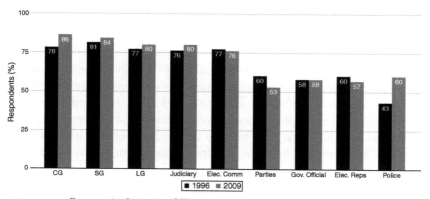

FIGURE 5.1 : Comparative Institutional Trust

We find that more than three out of four respondents put trust in all three elected institutions. However, this level of trust dips alarmingly to nearly 50 percent with elected representatives. Among unelected institutions, nearly three out of four respondents repose trust in the judiciary and the election commission, while trust in political parties, government officials and the police hovers around 50 percent. Hence, the key difference in the level of political trust does not seem to depend on whether an institution is directly elected or not.

Among the unelected institutions, the judiciary and election commission register trust levels comparable to elected institutions, especially the three levels of government. The other unelected institutions fare somewhat worse. However, trust in political parties, government officials and the police are similar to the level of trust expressed in elected representatives. Therefore, at the aggregate level it appears that people express higher levels of diffused trust in institutions, but substantially lower levels of trust in the individuals who populate these institutions and with whom they may have everyday interactions.

When we consider trust in the judiciary for the two years, we find that the proportion of respondents who trust the judiciary is much higher that those who don't. Approximately 76 percent in 1996 and 80 percent in 2009 express some degree of trust in the judiciary. We find that this difference of 4 percent is statistically significant, suggesting that popular trust in the judiciary has increased over time. This increase in the level of trust in the judiciary may be due to the general consolidation of trust in the core public institutions over time in India. While one must explain why some unelected institutions such as the judiciary gain public trust over time while others such as political parties and the bureaucracy lose public trust, this is not the focus of this chapter.

The 1996 and 2009 surveys do not ask respondents to clarify whether their trust resides in a particular level of court – district, High Court or Supreme Court. Hence, no particular conclusion can be reached on whether their responses attach to any particular court. While we are aware that most respondents access the district court and less than 1 percent have any direct engagement with the Supreme Court, this pattern of use is not decisive as we are not concerned in this chapter primarily with a performance based model of trust but rather a diffuse support model of trust in institutions – trust that develops irrespective of direct engagement. Finally, our further research confirms that when respondents are asked to disaggregate the trust they have across the level of courts, they indicate similar levels of trust in the District Court, High Court and the Supreme Court (Azim Premji University, Politics and Society Between Elections, 2017).

The patterns relating to the distribution of trust between institutions we observe in the National Election Studies are consistent with the results published in State of Democracy in South Asia (SDSA 2008, 2017) reports – a cross-country study, including Bangladesh, India, Nepal, Pakistan and Sri Lanka, designed along the lines of the Barometer and World Values surveys. For instance, these reports indicate that non-elected institutions that are distant and removed from everyday citizen interactions, such as the army, the courts and the Election Commission of India, enjoy higher levels of public trust. On the other hand, the bureaucracy, police and political parties generate relatively lower levels of trust among citizens. The reports also suggest that levels of trust vary across minority religious, class and caste divides. Further, these studies find that trust in all institutions in India have increased in the period from 2005 to 2013 by about two percentage points. There are, however, differences in the proportion of respondents who trust elected institutions relative to unelected ones, as well as in proportions of respondents within each set of institutions. About two-thirds of respondents express trust in elected institutions, i.e. the national, state and local government, in 2005. This proportion drops to about 60 percent in 2013. Trust in unelected institutions (with the exception of the army) is relatively lower compared with trust in elected institutions, ranging from about 42 percent (police) to about 66 percent (judiciary). The study also finds a modest increase in the period from 2005 to 2013 in the proportion of respondents who trust unelected institutions. More generally, the series of reports conclude that the unbroken experience of democracy increases levels of trust in South Asia. However, as the sample sizes in the SDSA surveys in India are small we do not integrate this data into this chapter. Though we do not engage in cross-national analysis here, we test some of the SDSA claims for India more extensively in the next section.

IV. SOCIAL, POLITICAL AND DIFFUSED SUPPORT MODELS OF TRUST IN THE JUDICIARY

In this section, we use data from the National Election Studies 1996 and 2009 to test the three hypotheses on trust in courts, namely the social or cultural trust hypothesis, the political trust hypothesis and the diffused support hypothesis. We first present the statistical model we use to test our hypotheses, following it with a discussion of the results.

A. *The model*

In order to estimate a multivariate statistical association between trust in the judiciary and the set of independent variables of interest we employ logistic regression models that take the form:

$$\ln\left[\frac{P(T=1)}{1-P(T=1)}\right] = \beta_0 + \beta_1 X_i + \beta_2 P_i + \beta_3 T\_CG_i + \beta_4 T\_SG_i + \beta_5 T\_LG_i$$

Where P(T=1) is the probability that the respondent trusts the judiciary, and the term $\ln\left[\frac{P(T=1)}{1-P(T=1)}\right]$ is the natural log of the odds ratio. X_i represents the set of social, economic, and demographic characteristics of the respondent. These include key factors such as caste and religious affiliations, education and economic class, gender and location (whether rural or urban) of respondents who are generally expected to be associated with trust in the judiciary, according to social and cultural theories. P_i represents political variables, which are included to test the political trust model. These include political factors such as participation in political activities during elections, interest in political affairs between elections, vote efficacy and the degree of media exposure. Finally, T_CG, T_SG and T_LG are measures of diffuse institutional support and represent respondent trust in central, state and local government respectively. The following sections present the results. Since we do not have data on measures of specific trust, such as citizen opinion on specific Supreme Court rulings in India, we are unable to test hypotheses relating to support for decisions of the judiciary.

B. *Social and cultural sources of trust*

In order to test Hypothesis 1 we statistically examine citizen perceptions of trust in the judiciary through its relationship with a set of explanatory variables that include background characteristics. The first models, 1A and 1B, estimate the association between individual social, economic and demographic characteristics and trust in the judiciary for 1996 and 2009 respectively. The independent variables include caste, religion, economic class, education, gender and location of the respondent. We convert all of the above variables into a set of dummy variables. Consequently, we include three variables for caste group representing *Dalit*, *Adivasi* and other backward classes (OBC), with the General category as the reference group. Similarly, we include three variables for religion – Muslim, Christian and Other (Sikh, Jain, Buddhist), with Hindu as the reference category. We use housing type (*kuccha* –homes built with mud, clay, leaves, bamboo and similar materials – and *pucca* – homes built with cement, bricks, and other durable materials) as our measure of economic class, and make *pucca* housing the reference category. Urban residents and women are coded as equal to 1. We include two dummy variables measuring school level education and college and above, with no schooling as the reference group.

TABLE 5.1 *Logistic regression: social and cultural sources of trust*

	Model 1A: 1996	Model 1B: 2009	Model 1C: Pooled
Dalit	0.05 (0.07)	0.12 (0.10)	0.06 (0.06)
Adivasi	−0.23 (0.09)**	0.06 (0.12)	−0.14 (0.07)
OBC	−0.03 (0.06)	0.12 (0.07)	0.01 (0.04)
Muslim	0.13 (0.08)	0.04 (0.10)	0.09 (0.06)
Christian	0.37** (0.16)	0.11 (0.15)	0.26 (0.11)**
Other religion	0.53** (0.24)	−0.27 (0.14)	−0.01 (0.11)
Women	−0.15** (0.05)	−0.07 (0.06)	−0.12 (0.04)***
Urban	−0.29*** (0.06)	−0.12 (0.07)	−0.21 (0.04)***
Education: school	0.35*** (0.05)	0.24*** (0.08)	0.33 (0.04)***
Education: college	0.55*** (0.12)	0.27** (0.10)	0.41 (0.07)***
Housing: *kuccha*	−0.03 (0.08)	−0.11 (0.09)	−0.05 (0.05)
Housing: mixed	0.01 (0.09)	−0.06 (0.08)	−0.01 (0.05)
Year	-	-	0.15 (0.04)***
Constant	1.11*** (0.09)	1.26*** (0.11)	1.09 (0.07)***
N	9,561	5,833	15,394
Log likelihood	−5,244.02	−2,893.16	−8148.93
Wald X^2	114.66 (12)	24.93 (12)	156.08 (12)

Note: Robust standard errors in parentheses. Significance levels: *** $p < 0.01$; ** $p < 0.05$; * $p < 0.10$.

Beginning with 1A and 1B in Table 5.1, we find that caste identity plays a limited role in explaining differences in perceptions of the judiciary. The coefficients on *Dalit* and OBC respondents are not statistically significant, suggesting that *Dalits* and OBCs do not have a different perception of the judiciary relative to upper castes. This result holds for both years. By contrast, a respondent identifying as Adivasi is less likely to view the judiciary as trustworthy relative to the upper caste in 1996. The coefficient, however, changes sign and loses significance in 2009. In the case of a relationship between religious identity and perceptions of trust in the judiciary, we find that Muslims are not significantly different from Hindus. Similar to *Dalits* and OBCs, Muslims are unlikely to view the judiciary any differently from Hindus. Christians and respondents from other religion groups (Sikh, Jain, Buddhist) are more likely to trust the judiciary than Hindus. The positive relationship for Christians and respondents from other religious groups observed in 1996 is not statistically significant in 2009. Generally, we find that the caste and religious identity variables are not significant in 2009.

Economic class, proxied by housing type, is not statistically significant for explaining variation in trust in the judiciary for either year. Respondents from either mixed or *kuccha* housing types are not different from those from *pucca* housing in their perceptions of judiciary. We find that women are less likely to trust the judiciary. This effect is observed only in 1996 and is not significant in 2009. Urban respondents are less likely to trust the judiciary, but as in the case of women the effect disappears in 2009. However, literacy emerges as a significant variable in both years. Respondents who only attended school and those with an education level of college and above are more likely to trust the judiciary relative to those without any education.

Model 1C is an independently pooled cross-section that includes both years. Pooling the observations from both years increases the number of observations and the generalizability of our results, and lowers error variance. We include an additional variable, Year – a dummy variable that equals 1 in 2009 and 0 in 1996 in order to capture any changes in public opinion in the judiciary that may have occurred over time, i.e. unobserved heterogeneity across time periods. As we noted earlier, caste and identity variables (with the exception of Christian identity) do not play a significant role in explaining the likelihood of trust in the judiciary. Respondents identifying themselves as Christian are more likely to trust the judiciary. Women and urban respondents are less likely to trust the judiciary, and those with schooling and above are more likely to trust the judiciary. We find that the coefficient on Year is significant and positive, suggesting that the passage of time has likely increased trust in the judiciary independent of other factors. We identify two potential sources for this increase in trust. First, the period from 1996 to 2009 witnessed repeated coalition governments at the federal level. It is likely that during this period the courts in India gained in strength to offset the political weakness in the federal government. Relatedly, it is also likely that this generated a greater awareness of the judiciary among citizens. However, the extent to which policy outputs from the courts contribute to an increase in trust over time is less clear.

More generally, these results point to relatively weak support for the cultural model. We find that ethnic identity and economic class, factors that are likely to influence political socialization and interpersonal trust in India, are not systematically associated with trust in the judiciary. *Dalit* and *Adivasi* respondents do not exhibit systematic distrust in the judiciary as social theories of trust would anticipate. Nor do religious minorities such as Muslims and Christians, or relatively poorer respondents. We also find that education does not have the expected relationship with trust in the judiciary. Respondents with higher levels of education are more likely to trust the judiciary. This relationship is consistently strong, casting doubt on a negative relationship between education and trust.

C. *Political correlates of trust in the judiciary*

While the first set of models provide baseline estimates, we expand our empirical analysis to test Hypotheses 2 and 3 by including variables considered as important political correlates of trust in the judiciary. A test of the political model includes four variables: (1) vote efficacy, which measures whether a respondent believes her vote to be efficacious or not; (2) political participation which captures whether a respondent participated in election-related activities such as attending meetings and rallies, and distributing campaign materials; (3) political interest which measures whether a respondent expresses an interest in politics between elections; and (4) the degree to which a respondent is exposed to media sources such as newspaper, television and the radio. With the exception of media exposure, all variables take binary values, and respondents who view their vote as efficacious, who participate in election related activities and express an interest in politics are coded as 1. The degree of media exposure ranges from 3 to 12, i.e. no exposure to any media source to frequent exposure to all three media sources.

In order to test Hypothesis 3 on diffuse support for the court, we include three variables that measure a respondent's trust in three elected institutions of governance: the central, state and local governments (T_CG, T_SG, and T_LG respectively). Similar to the question on trust in the judiciary, these variables ask how much trust a respondent places in these institutions. Responses indicating a "great deal" or "somewhat" are coded as 1 and others as 0. We do this for both years, and include this set of variables in addition to the background variables reported in the previous models. We report the results from a pooled model (Model 2) in Table 5.2.

We find that not all political variables are significantly associated with trust in the judiciary. Respondents who indicate an interest in political affairs are more likely to trust the judiciary, about 3 percent more than respondents who express a lack of interest. Respondents who participate in election-related campaigns are not more likely to trust the judiciary than those who do not. Similarly, perceptions of vote efficacy are not statistically associated with trust in the judiciary. The relationship between trust and media exposure is significant and positive: the higher the degree of media exposure the greater is the likelihood of trust in the judiciary. However, we observe that this relationship is only weakly significant.

TABLE 5.2 *Logistic regression: political and diffuse support sources of trust in judiciary*

	Model 2: Pooled
Dalit	−0.07 (0.05)
Adivasi	−0.001 (0.09)
OBC	0.02 (0.05)
Muslim	0.15 (0.08)
Christian	0.14 (0.13)
Other religion	0.15 (0.15)
Women	0.01 (0.05)
Urban	−0.21*** (0.05)
Education: school	0.10 (0.05)
Education: college	0.22 (0.09)**
Housing: *kuccha*	−0.09 (0.07)
Housing: mixed	−0.07 (0.07)
Political interest	0.16 (0.05)***
Participation	0.05 (0.07)
Vote efficacy	0.01 (0.05)
Media exposure	0.02 (0.01)*
Trust_CG	0.69 (0.06)***
Trust_SG	0.46 (0.07)***
Trust_LG	1.19 (0.05)***
Year	0.02 (0.04)
Constant	−0.67 (0.11)***
N	12,077
Log likelihood	−5,572.71
Wald X^2	1,277.62 (20)

Note: Robust standard errors in parentheses. Significance levels: *** $p < 0.01$; ** $p < 0.05$; * $p < 0.10$.

We find that the variables measuring trust in the central, State and local government have statistically significant correlations with trust in the judiciary. The positive sign on all three coefficients suggests that citizen trust in elected institutions is associated with trust in the judiciary. Holding all variables at mean values and varying the values of trust in elected institutions, we find that respondents who express trust in the local government are about 30 percent more likely to trust the judiciary relative to respondents who do not express trust in local government. Similarly, trust in central government is associated with an 18 percent increase in the likelihood that respondents will trust the judiciary and a 14 percent increase for respondents who trust the State government.

Results from Model 2 suggests that, as with model 1C, caste and religious identity as well as class do not appear to have a significant association with trust in the judiciary. While urban voters are less likely to trust the judiciary, we do not observe a significant difference between men and women. The effect of school education disappears, while the statistical significance of college education and above remains, and the association is positive.

We find strong evidence for the diffuse support hypothesis. Respondents who trust elected institutions are more likely to trust the judiciary. It is commonplace in the political philosophy and political science literature to argue that "the legal system holds a special place among political institutions. Legislative and executive bodies are expected to favor the voters who put them into office. They are partisan, and people's trust in government often is based upon party ties. However, the courts are expected to be fair and nonpartisan" (Uslaner, 2017: 11). However, the results from Model 2 suggest that a counter-majoritarian claim of a negative relationship, i.e. that high levels of trust in elected institutions are associated with low levels of trust in unelected institutions, is not supported in the Indian context. Hence, the trust and legitimacy enjoyed by the Indian judiciary is not competitive with that enjoyed by other political institutions.

To ensure the robustness of the diffuse support hypothesis, we run a series of diagnostics comparing models 1C and 2 to assess the strength of relationship between our variables of interest (cultural, political and diffuse support) and trust in the judiciary. The results are presented in Appendix 2. We show that the evidence that Model 2 presents is consistent across other specifications and diagnostic checks, and hence is the best explanation for the nature of trust in the Indian judiciary.

V. CONCLUSION

In 1980, Rajeev Dhavan proclaimed that the Indian Supreme Court was "the most powerful court in the world" (Dhavan, 1980). Ever since, legal theorists and some political scientists have scrambled to explain how the Supreme Court, and the Indian judiciary more generally have secured and sustained the popular legitimacy to embark on this bold and adventurous path. However, existing accounts do not rest on a sound empirical basis, resulting in inadequate and at times flawed conclusions.

This chapter confirms that the Indian courts enjoy high levels of institutional trust across diverse social and cultural groups. Our first hypothesis that social and cultural identities may result in varied levels of trust in the courts has the least support. So the socially broad based support enjoyed by the courts enables the institution to make bold and strong decisions. We then investigated if political attitudes to elections and democracy, exposure to media or affinity to elected government influenced levels of trust in the courts. We found that while interest in politics and exposure to the media has a positive effect on trust in the courts, voting behavior appears to have little effect.

Our findings on the third diffused support hypothesis significantly alters current understanding of the court's legitimacy. "Court interventions have been widely seen as legitimate, or at least tolerated, because the representative institutions are widely seen as being immobilized, self-serving, corrupt, and incapable of exercising either their basic policy prerogatives or their powers of enforcement" (Mehta, 2004: 186). We find that contrary to this common understanding, the courts receive diffused support, where those who trust in elected institutions also trust in the courts. The counter-majoritarian role of the courts is not the basis for high levels of trust in the judiciary.

The diffused support hypothesis needs to be explored further to examine whether it is a form of "blind trust": a reflexive, unreasoned manifestation of prevailing cultural norms of deference or the result of cognitive deficits (Mattes and Moreno, 2015). We must assess if levels of trust vary with levels of real engagement with, and experience of, the courts. Further, we must explore if trust in the Supreme Court is distinct from that in the lower courts. Finally, it may be useful to carefully assess if the levels of trust in an institution generate a greater confidence and willingness to use the institution. Some preliminary work using trust as the dependent variable has been carried out with respect to the courts and the police (SDSA II, 2017), but this needs to be nuanced to isolate the effect of trust as a dependent variable. A new survey data set created by the Azim Premji University and Lokniti in 2017 will allow for such analysis, and is the focus of our future research in this area.

In this chapter, we have initiated an empirical and analytical enquiry into the nature of political trust in Indian political science. Much more needs to be done. India presents a complex picture of the relationship between low levels of social and interpersonal trust but high levels of institutional and political trust. Unpacking the relationship between these two kinds of trust in India may well explain bigger puzzles in India's politics and development.

Variable Description, Codes and Summary Statistics

		1996		2009	
Variable	Description	N	Mean (SD)	N	Mean (SD)
Trust_Judiciary (Dependent Variable)	How much trust do you have in the judiciary? "A great deal of trust" or "Some trust" = 1; "Not much trust" or "No trust at all" = 0.	9,614	0.67 (0.43)	5,997	0.80 (0.38)
Trust_Central Government (T_CG)	How much trust do you have in the Central Government? "A great deal of trust" or "Some trust" = 1; "Not much trust" or "No trust at all" = 0.	9,614	0.77 (0.42)	5,729	0.87 (0.33)
Trust_State Government (T_SG)	How much trust do you have in the State Government? "A great deal of trust" or "Some trust" = 1; "Not much trust" or "No trust at all" = 0.	9,614	0.80 (0.39)	5,826	0.84 (0.36)
Trust_Local Government (T_LG)	How much trust do you have in the Local Government? "A great deal of trust" or "Some trust" = 1; "Not much trust" or "No trust at all" = 0.	9,614	0.76 (0.42)	5,803	0.80 (0.40)
Political Participation	During the election people do various things like organizing election meetings, joining processions, participating in	9,614	0.09 (0.29)	5,997	0.28 (0.45)

(continued)

(continued)

Variable	Description	1996		2009	
		N	Mean (SD)	N	Mean (SD)
	canvassing, contributing money, etc. to help a party or candidate. Did you do any such thing yourself during the recent election campaign? Yes = 1; No = 0				
Political Interest	Leaving aside the period of elections, how much interest would you say you have in politics and public affairs, a great deal of interest, some interest, or no interest at all? "A great deal of interest" or "some interest" = 1; No interest at all = 0.	9,614	0.35 (0.48)	5,710	0.49 (0.40)
Vote Efficacy	Do you think your vote has effect on how things are run in this country or do you think your vote makes no difference? Yes = 1; No = 0	7,692	0.73 (0.44)	4,955	0.78 (0.41)
Media Exposure		9,614	5.78 (2.71)	5,997	6.61 (2.90)
Caste *Dalit* (SC) *Adivasi* (ST) OBC	Self-classification into official categories of Scheduled Castes (SC), Scheduled Tribes (ST), Other Backward Castes (OBC), and Other Castes (including upper castes)	9,614	0.15 (0.36) 0.08 (0.28) 0.37 (0.48)	5,997	0.16 (0.37) 0.12 (0.32) 0.37 (0.48)
Religion Muslim Christian Other (Sikh, Jain, Buddhist)	Self-classification into official categories of: Hindu, Muslim, Christian, Sikh, Jain, and Buddhist	9,580	0.09 (0.29) 0.03 (0.16) 0.02 (0.13)	5,993	0.12 (0.32) 0.06 (0.24) 0.05 (0.23)
Urban	Urban = 1; Rural = 0	9,614	0.24 (0.43)	5,997	0.31 (0.46)
Women	Women = 1; Men = 0	9,614	0.49 (0.50)	5,997	0.45 (0.50)

Variable	Description	1996		2009	
		N	Mean (SD)	N	Mean (SD)
Education		9,595	0.48	5,929	0.25
No School			(0.50)		(0.43)
School Only			0.46		0.49
College and			(0.50)		(0.50)
Above			0.05		0.25
			(0.23)		(0.43)
Housing/		9,614	0.57	5,900	0.33
Dwelling Type			(0.50)		(0.47)
Kuccha			0.32		0.35
Mixed			(0.47)		(0.48)
Pucca			0.09		0.30
			(0.29)		(0.46)

Model Diagnostics and Robustness Checks

A Hosmer-Lemeshow test of goodness of fit indicates that model 2 (*p-value* = 0.33) fits the data better than model 1C (*p-value* = 0.03). Similarly, the areas under the ROC curve for models 1C and 2 are 0.59 and 0.70 respectively. A test of difference of areas under the ROC curve shows that the area under the ROC curve for model 2 is statistically greater than that under model 1C, indicating that the full specification has higher explanatory power. Finally, we find that likelihood ratio tests comparing the two models indicate that the unconstrained specification is appropriate, and that at least some of the political variables (in model 2) are significantly associated with the likelihood of trust in the judiciary (LR $X_2(7)$ = 5,152.45). The AIC and BIC statistics are lower for model 2 compared to model 1C (AIC (2) = 11,187.43, AIC (1C) =16,325.88; BIC (2) = 11,342.81, BIC (1C) = 16,432.7), indicating that model 2 is an improved fit.

A concern however is the correlation between the three key variables of interest, T_CG, T_SG, T_LG, which indicates that these three variables are likely capturing similar information. For instance the correlation between T_CG and T_SG is 0.53. The correlations between the two other pairs is about 0.38. Given that multicollinearity can produce inaccurate regression estimates, we use principal component analysis to extract the component that captures the largest proportion of variation in T_CG, T_SG, and T_LG – a measure of diffuse support. The variable is standardized with a mean equal to zero and standard deviation equal to 1. Using this measure of generalized institutional trust as the independent variable we rerun Model 2. The results are in Table 5.3.

Note that the results are very similar to Model 2. We find that generalized institutional trust in elected institutions is positively associated with trust in the judiciary. An 0.5 standard deviation increase in generalized institutional trust (GIT) around its mean is associated with a 10 percent increase in trust in the

TABLE 5.3 *Logistic regression: robustness check with alternate trust measure*

	Model 3: pooled
Dalit	0.05 (0.06)
Adivasi	−0.14 (0.08)
OBC	−0.002 (0.05)
Muslim	0.05 (0.07)
Christian	0.23 (0.12)
Other religion	0.13 (0.13)
Women	−0.05 (0.04)
Urban	−0.20*** (0.05)
Literate	0.27*** (0.04)
Housing: mixed	0.01 (0.05)
Housing: *pucca*	0.11 (0.06)
Generalized institutional trust	0.78 (0.01)***
Year	0.02 (0.04)
Constant	1.23*** (0.06)
N	14,996
Log likelihood	−7038.83
Wald χ^2	1,905.12 (14)

Note: Robust standard errors in parentheses. Significance levels: *** $p < 0.01$; ** $p < 0.05$; * $p < 0.10$.

judiciary. While the magnitude of this association is substantively less than the individual effects of T_CG, T_SG and T_LG, the positive and statistically significant association points to diffuse support.

REFERENCES

Almond, G., and S. Verba. (1963). *The Civic Culture.* Princeton, NJ: Princeton University Press.

Baxi, U. (1980). *The Indian Supreme Court and Politics.* New Delhi: Eastern Book Co.

Bradford, B., J. Jackson, and M. Hough. (2015). "Trust in Justice." In E. Uslaner (ed.), *The Oxford Handbook of Social and Political Trust.* New York: Oxford University Press.

Caldeira, G. A. (1986). "Neither the Purse Nor the Sword: Dynamics of Confidence in the U.S. Supreme Court." *American Political Science Review* 80(4): 1209–1226.

Caldeira, G. A., and J. L. Gibson. (1992). "The Etiology of Public Support for the Supreme Court." *American Journal of Political Science* 36(3): 635–664.

Catterberg, G., and A. Moreno. (2005). "The Individual Bases of Political Trust." *International Journal of Public Opinion Research* 18(1): 31–48.

Center for Study of Developing Societies. (2008). *State of Democracy in South Asia (SDSA)*. New Delhi: Oxford University Press.

   (2017). *State of Democracy in South Asia (SDSA), Report II*. New Delhi: Oxford University Press.

Citrin, J. (1974). "Comment: The Political Relevance of Trust in Government." *American Political Science Review* 68(3): 973–988.

Citrin, J., and D. Green. (1986). "Presidential Leadership and the Resurgence of Trust in Government." *British Journal of Political Science* 16(4):431–453.

Dalton, R. J. (1996). *Citizen Politics: Public Opinion and Political Parties in Advanced Western Democracies*. Chatham, NJ: Chatham House.

Dhavan, R. (1980). *Justice on Trial: The Supreme Court Today*. New Delhi: Wheeler.

Diamond, L. (1999). *Developing Democracy: Toward Consolidation*. Baltimore, MD: Johns Hopkins University Press.

Easton, D. (1965). *A Systems Analysis of Political Life*. New York: Wiley.

Gibson, J. L., and G. A. Caldeira. (1992). "Blacks and the United States Supreme Court: Models of Diffuse Support." *Journal of Politics* 54(4): 1120–1145.

Gibson, J. L., G. A. Caldeira, and L. K. Spence. (2005). "Why Do People Accept Public Policies They Oppose? Testing Legitimacy Theory with a Survey-Based Experiment." *Political Research Quarterly* 58(2): 187–201.

Giddens, A. (1990). *The Consequences of Modernity*. Cambridge: Polity Press.

Gilley, B. (2006). "The Meaning and Measure of State Legitimacy: Results for 72 Countries." *European Journal of Political Research* 45: 499–525.

Grosskopf, A., and J. Mondak. (1998). "Do Attitudes Toward Specific Supreme Court Decisions Matter? The Impact of Webster and *Texas v. Johnson* on Public Confidence in the Supreme Court." *Political Research Quarterly* 51(3): 633–654.

Hetherington, M. J. (1998). "The Political Relevance of Political Trust." *American Political Science Review* 92 (4): 791–808.

Hutchison, M. and K. Johnson. (2011). "Capacity to Trust? Institutional Capacity, Conflict, and Political Trust in Africa, 2000–2005." *Journal of Peace Research* 48 (6): 737–752.

Inglehart, R. (1997). *Modernization and Postmodernization: Cultural, Economic and Political Change in 41 Societies*. Princeton, NJ: Princeton University Press.

Inglehart, R., M. Basanez, and A. Moreno. (1998). *Human Values and Beliefs: A Cross-Cultural Sourcebook*. Ann Arbor: University of Michigan Press.

March, J. G. (1988). *Decisions and Organizations*. Oxford: Blackwell.

Mate, M. (2015). "The Rise of Judicial Governance in the Supreme Court of India." *Boston University International Law Journal* 33: 169.

Mattes, R., and A. Moreno. (2018). "Social and Political Trust in Developing Countries: Sub-Saharan Africa and Latin America." In E. Uslaner (ed.), *Oxford Handbook of Social and Political Trust*. New York: Oxford University Press.

Mehta, P. B. 2004. "The Inner Conflict of Constitutionalism: Judicial Review and the Basic Structure." In Z. Hassan, E. Sridharan, and R. Sudarshan (eds.,) *India's Living Constitution: Ideas, Practices, Controversies*. New Delhi: Orient Blackswan.

(2007). "India's Unlikely Democracy: The Rise of Judicial Sovereignty." *Journal of Democracy* 18(2): 70–83.

Miller, A., and O. Listhaug. (1990). "Political Parties and Confidence in Government: A Comparison of Norway, Sweden and the United States." *British Journal of Political Science* 20(3): 357–386.

Mishler, W., and R. Rose. (2001). "What Are the Origins of Political Trust? Testing Institutional and Cultural Theories in Post-communist Societies. *Comparative Political Studies* 34(1): 30–62.

Mondak, J. (1991). "Substantive and Procedural Aspects of Supreme Court Decisions as Determinants of Institutional Approval." *American Politics Quarterly* 19: 174–188.

(1992). "Institutional Legitimacy, Policy Legitimacy, and the Supreme Court." *American Politics Quarterly* 20: 457–477.

Newton, K. (2001). "Trust, Social Capital, Civil Society, and Democracy." *International Political Science Review* 22(2): 201–214.

Newton, K. and P. Norris. (2000). "Confidence in Public Institutions: Faith, Culture, or Performance?" In S. Pharr and R. Putnam (eds.), *Disaffected Democracies*. Princeton, NJ: Princeton University Press.

North, D. C. (1990). *Institutions, Institutional Change and Economic Performance*. New York: Cambridge University Press.

Politics and Society Between Elections. (2017). Azim Premji University and Lokniti, CSDS.

Putnam, R. (1993). *Making Democracy Work: Civic Traditions in Modern Italy*. Princeton, NJ: Princeton University Press.

Przeworski, A., et al. (2000). *Democracy and Development: Political Institutions and Well-Being in the World, 1950–1990*. Cambridge University Press.

Robinson, N. 2009. "Expanding Judiciaries: India and the Rise of the Good Governance Court." 8 *Washington University Global Studies Law Review* 1.

State of Democracy in South Asia (2008, 2017). Lokniti, CSDS.

Uslaner, E. 2017. *Oxford Handbook of Social and Political Trust*. New York: Oxford University Press.

Weatherford, M. S. (1992). "Measuring Political Legitimacy." *American Political Science Review* 86(1): 149–166.

Zaller, J. (1992). *The Nature and Origins of Mass Opinion*. Cambridge: Cambridge University Press.

PART II

The Supreme Court of India, Social and Political Mobilization

6

The Art of Buying Time

Street Vendor Politics and Legal Mobilization in Metropolitan India

KARTHIK RAO-CAVALE

Thank God justice is delayed.

Lawyer for squatter settlers in Racife, Brazil[1]

I. INTRODUCTION

This chapter is concerned with the emergence of legal mobilization as a key element in subaltern politics. While there is a vast scholarship on the judicialization of politics and policymaking in India, there have been relatively fewer studies from the perspective of collective actors representing marginalized social classes in Indian society.[2] And yet, in a growing number of disputes related to dispossession, affected groups (such as small farmers, street vendors, sex workers, and residents of informal settlements) have approached judicial forums for protection.[3] When and under what circumstances did these groups choose to include legal petitioning as a part of their "repertoire of contention" in their struggles against dispossession?[4] And once the judiciary became involved, how did they navigate the challenges of combining litigation with other prevailing forms of contention, such as informal negotiations and street protests aimed at local politicians, bureaucrats, and the police?

In order to address these questions, it is necessary for scholars to turn their attention to social movements and their sociopolitical environment outside the courtroom. As this chapter will show, it also requires us to de-emphasize

---

[1] Quoted in de Sousa Santos 2002, 388.
[2] Indeed, legal innovations introduced by activist judges and lawyers in the 1980s (such as public interest litigation) were premised on the notion that marginalized groups were too poor and disempowered to be able to directly participate in making claims against structural injustice in courts of law. See Baxi 1985.
[3] See Nielsen 2009; Weinstein 2009; and Kotiswaran 2013.
[4] McAdam, Tarrow, and Tilly 2003.

legal *discourse* as observed in the verdicts handed down by courts, and instead pay attention to the *practice* of legal mobilization. In this chapter, I attempt to explore the dynamics of legal mobilization through a study of street vendor politics in two Indian cities – Bombay (Mumbai) and Madras (Chennai.)[5] Street vendors are an important subset of the so-called urban informal sector and account for an estimated 10 million workers countrywide.[6] Like their counterparts in most parts of the world, street vendors in Indian cities are also confronted with a governing framework that consists, in parts, of persecution, tolerance, and regulation.[7] The legal infrastructure typically includes a maze of laws enabling the municipality and the police to exercise control over street vending. However, these laws are often inconsistent with one other, and applied unevenly and selectively in order to maintain an informalized regime for governing street vendors.[8] For the overwhelming majority of vendors who do not have municipal licenses, the threats of forcible eviction and the confiscation of merchandise loom large, along with the routine extraction of rents by a predatory state apparatus.[9]

In this context, the shift to legal mobilization is often explained as an attempt by "new social movements" to surpass the limitations of informal political solutions by using new legal opportunities made available by the Indian judiciary.[10] In an account of the activities of the Self Employed Women's Association (SEWA) – which has played an important role in organizing informal workers in several Indian cities – Renana Jhabvala offers a lucid explanation of the shift to legal mobilization that is worth quoting at length.

> We struggled for many years with the municipal officials and the police until we realized that the problems were deeper than an uncooperative municipality or hostile policemen. We realized that the municipal laws did not have any space for street vendors at all, and that the police laws required that they be "cleared away"; no matter what actions we took, the street vendors were

---

[5] I use the old official names of these cities consistently throughout this chapter as most of the events described in my paper occurred before their names were changed in the mid-1990s. Though I acknowledge that naming and renaming are deeply political acts, I use these names in the interest of historical accuracy and consistency.

[6] Bhowmik 2006.

[7] Bromley 2000.

[8] In Bombay, for instance, the police are legally empowered to penalize any person who obstructs the smooth flow of pedestrian and vehicular traffic, regardless of whether he or she possesses a municipal license for hawking. See Bhowmik 2005 and Anjaria 2006.

[9] Occasional eviction drives assert the authority of political elites over public space, which is necessary for the everyday extraction of rents. See Anjaria 2011.

[10] Bhatt 2006; Bhowmik 2006; and Roever 2016.

always going to be "illegal." We realized that the rallies we took out, the *dharnas* [demonstrations] we held, the negotiations we entered into, would make police actions less brutal for a while, or would save the street vendors their space till the next official in the municipality was appointed, or the next board was elected. The solutions were short term. We also realized that it benefited many to keep street vendors illegal; police and municipality officials could collect bribes and let street vending go on at their discretion, and politicians could get votes as long as vendors remained insecure and dependent on the local politician to negotiate settlements with the authorities. No one was really interested in making the street vendors legal.

Since it was a question of legality, we approached the courts, and in 1984 we got a historical judgment from the Supreme Court of India. After that we went to the Gujarat High Court for various areas in urban Gujarat and from that time on, approached the courts regularly. The relief and solutions from the courts were somewhat longer term, but limited in scope and did not last beyond a few years. So we kept struggling on, feeling that for all our efforts, we were running in place. However, after neoliberal economics gained ascendancy and liberalization policies were implemented in India, we found that the situation had changed. We were no longer running in place, we were being pushed backward. As cities began to aspire to become "world class," as the national agenda became growth of Gross Domestic Product rather than poverty removal, the eviction drives against street vendors become more extensive and longer lasting. We realized that new, higher-level solutions were required. We required new policies and new laws, and we needed them at national rather than local levels. The Self-Employed Women's Association could not do this alone, nor could any other street vendors' association; we needed to get together.[11]

As a veteran activist who has actively participated in street vendor struggles for several decades, Jhabvala is clearly not under the illusion that a favorable court judgment would automatically translate into the protection of street vendor livelihoods. Far from being enamored by what Stuart Scheingold has called the "myth of rights," she is clearly invested in enabling a "politics of rights" for the most marginalized social groups,[12] and has spent much of her career as an activist building up political organizations and coalitions, organizing legal support networks, and inculcating a "legal consciousness" among street vendors who face everyday exploitation at the hands of the police.[13] And yet

---

[11] Jhabvala 2012, xii–xiii.
[12] Scheingold 2010.
[13] For the definitive contributions within the sociolegal scholarship on "legal support structures" and "legal consciousness" as the fundamental elements of a "politics of rights," see Epp 1998; Merry 1990; Ewick and Silbey 1991; and Sarat 1990.

my concern is that her account of the history of street vendor politics in India makes some rather teleological assumptions according to which "progress" necessarily entails specific changes in the repertoire of political claim-making.

To begin with, while she acknowledges that legal recognition of the rights of street vendors is not sufficient to guarantee their livelihoods, she nevertheless implicitly assumes that it is a necessary step. The implication is that "legal" claims produce "longer term" solutions that are more generalizable across both space and time, since they are not affected by change of personnel in government. By extension, Jhabvala assumes that building national or international coalitions and making claims upon "higher level" authorities than the local municipality or police is a necessary step in the political development of street vendors. Finally, while she acknowledges that the security of livelihoods for many vendors may have stagnated or even deteriorated over the past three decades, she ascribes these deteriorating outcomes to exogenous forces (e.g., "neoliberal economics"). These forces need to be countered with even more advanced forms of legal mobilization directed towards "higher level" authorities. In this argument, approaching a court of law acquires significance because it indexes the transformation of street vendors from subjects of local authority to citizens of the national state (with constitutionally guaranteed rights). Clearly her faith in the judiciary and in legal mobilization remains undiminished, despite the fact that street vendors continue to suffer from economic insecurity.[14]

Like the other authors in this volume, I believe that there is a need to eschew such teleological assumptions about the significance of legal petitioning in the repertoires of social movements and instead adopt a more qualified stance towards the potentiality of courts as agents of progressive social change. In this chapter, I draw upon insights from certain strands of the legal mobilization literature to investigate the causes and consequences of legal mobilization from the perspective of the collective actors approaching the court on behalf of marginalized social groups (in this case street vendor associations).[15] The legal mobilization tradition has gainfully demonstrated that we cannot evaluate the consequences of litigation unless we first understand why and under what circumstances certain collective actors decide to approach the judiciary in the first place. Legal mobilization scholars also recognize that those engaged in building and sustaining social movements might approach the

---

[14] For systematic evidence of the continued economic insecurity of street vendors, see Bhowmik and Saha 2012.

[15] For a spirited defense of such "decentered" analysis of legal mobilization see McCann 1992; McCann 2006.

courts because of the cumulative and long-term benefits of the litigation process. Indeed, it is also possible that different political actors within a coalition might have different hopes and expectations from legal mobilization.

Legal mobilization scholars have traced a variety of mechanisms by which social movements might ultimately benefit from litigation. For instance, many social movement organizations might make a strategic choice to approach the judiciary not because they expect a favorable verdict to be immediately implemented, but rather because they expect that it will help shift the public discourse in their favor and therefore be beneficial to their members in the long term.[16] Even "losing" a court case might be a generative process if it helps give a certain issue a lot of public visibility and exposure. Alternatively, a legal petition might constitute a tactical attempt to alter the equilibrium in political negotiation processes outside the courtroom even before a verdict is delivered.[17] Legal mobilization scholars also recognize that much of the litigation by social movements in primarily defensive in character; in other words, movements use the law to consolidate gains made through other means rather than to make entirely new claims on other institutional actors in the political system.[18] However, legal mobilization also has its potential drawbacks, since tactical litigation can be inimical to the interests of movement-building, while the long-term strategies to build political coalitions might entail significant short-term costs.

In this chapter, I make a similar set of heterodox claims about the role of legal petitioning in the political repertoires of street vendor collectives in two Indian cities (Bombay and Madras), which is best understood by juxtaposing it with conventional claims about judicial intervention. In the conventional narrative, it is typically argued that legal mobilization by social movements in India was a response to new legal opportunities made available by the judiciary during its "populist moment" in the 1980s when it actively positioned itself as a protector of marginalized communities through such legal instruments as public interest litigation (PIL).[19] By contrast, the historical case studies in this chapter will demonstrate that the initial shift to legal mobilization by street vendors was a response to serious threats faced by political regimes that had partially shielded them from eviction and exploitation in

---

[16] McCann 1992; Rodriguez-Garavito 2010; Dixon 2007; Sabel and Simon 2004.
[17] McCann 2006; Galanter 1983.
[18] McCann and Lovell 2018.
[19] For the applicability of the concept of "legal opportunity structures" to the PIL movement in India see Mate 2015; Bhuwania 2014; Dhavan 1994. For an elaboration of the concept in US/ international contexts, see Hilson 2002; Vanhala 2012.

previous decades.[20] This becomes evident when one tries to account for the *timing* of legal mobilization: in Bombay, street vendors began approaching the court in the early-1970s owing to the emergence of a new political threat in the form of a nativist movement that targeted migrant street vendors – this was several years prior to the emergence of public interest litigation. By contrast, in Madras, where a stable populist political regime had emerged, street vendors did not consider approaching the court of their own volition until the early 1990s.

These historical case studies suggest that legal mobilization by street vendor collectives has largely functioned as a defensive strategy to buy time, which meant the ultimate verdict of the court did not factor centrally in the calculus of legal mobilization. Even in later years, despite the recognition of certain limited rights of street vendors, the actual remedies granted by courts often involved relocation to areas where the street trade was much less profitable or completely infeasible. Since organized street vendors were wary of such risky relocation and had a strong preference for maintaining the status quo, legal petitioning was primarily used as to forestall the threat of dispossession in the face of a hostile or uncertain political environment. However, my research also suggests that the entrenchment of judicial intervention in the regulation of street vending since the 1990s has hindered the cultivation of horizontal solidarity within and between street vendor collectives at the local level, since legal mobilization neither requires nor rewards efforts by the leadership of street vendor associations to expand membership or the active engagement and participation by the members. This has resulted in the ossification of street vendor associations and a widening gap between permanent street vendors (who are represented in legal cases) and itinerant hawkers (who are typically excluded). These findings call into question the teleological assumptions that color the conventional narrative, since it is by no means evident that legal mobilization is capable of delivering more meaningful and generalized institutional protection for street vending in Indian cities when compared to the populist political regimes of previous decades.

The empirical data for this chapter has been obtained from documentary sources (such as court orders and affidavits) and newspaper archives of the *Times of India* and *The Hindu*. Legal documents were obtained either through public sources or directly from the petitioners and their lawyers. Relevant news reports of the *Times of India* were collected from online databases using

---

[20] My argument bears a certain resemblance to Richard Cortner's "political disadvantage" model, in which interest groups mobilize legal institutions when they find themselves unable to achieve policy goals through lobbying or the electoral process. Cortner 1968; Olson 1990.

search terms related to street vending, and similar data was obtained directly from the librarian of *The Hindu*. Since the historical narrative emerging from documentary and newspaper sources was incomplete in several respects (especially for Madras,) oral histories obtained through interview-based research were used to triangulate and verify factual details. About 15 oral histories were collected from street vendors, leaders of street vendor organizations, and their lawyers in 2012 and 2015. This data was collected as part of a larger study of street vendor politics, which includes detailed study of one centrally located neighborhood (T. Nagar). Oral histories in Bombay were collected from the current leaders of the six main hawker unions in the city.

The rest of the chapter proceeds as follows. In Section 2, I provide brief histories of street vendor politics in Bombay and Madras from 1965 to 1995, and situate these narratives within a broader historical and political canvas. Following the methodological apparatus of the social movements literature, my analysis foregrounds the relationships between political opportunities/ threats, mobilizing structures, and repertoires of contention.[21] In Section 3, I extend this analysis to the present, and offer some brief analytical remarks regarding the consequences of the entrenchment of judicial intervention in the governance of street vending in most Indian cities. I conclude with some theoretical reflections on the relationship between law and subaltern politics, at the levels of both discourse and practice.

II. STREET VENDOR POLITICS IN BOMBAY AND MADRAS: 1965–2000

The method I employ in analyzing the history of street vendor politics consists of drawing out the relationship between urban political regimes and the repertoires of street vendor mobilization from the 1960s onwards.[22] The events described in this section therefore map the shifts in political regimes in Bombay and Madras over a period of three decades, which also broadly reflect the changes in global political economy, as noted by Renana Jhabvala.[23] However, as I will show in the following two subsections, there were significant differences in the manner in which this process unraveled in Bombay and Madras, with important implications for street vendor politics. In other words, the

---

[21] McAdam, Tarrow, and Tilly 2003.
[22] This focus on organizational aspects of street vendor politics has been missing in studies on street vending till very recently. The gap has been filled for the case of postcolonial Calcutta by Ritajyoti Bandyopadhyay in his recent work. My chapter builds on this strand of empirical research on street vending. See Bandyopadhyay 2016.
[23] Jhabvala 2012.

evidence in this section demonstrates that political regimes and the repertoires of contention adopted by subaltern social classes cannot be simply derived from global political economy; there are local particularities that need to be taken into account while understanding these shifts in claim-making practices.

A. *Bombay*

In the early-1960s, political assertion by trade unions affiliated to left-wing parties in Bombay was on the rise. These parties had built around themselves a lively social infrastructure within working-class communities such that cultural activities merged almost seamlessly with labor struggles and electoral politics.[24] In 1960, the Bombay Hawkers' Union was revived by a firebrand young socialist leader named George Fernandes.[25] Fernandes was also engaged in organizing hotel staff, auto-rickshaw, taxicab, and bus transport workers, and workers in the lower levels of municipal services.[26] Hawkers in Bombay served not just as a vote bank, but more importantly as a cadre of dedicated political workers for the various protests and strikes organized by Fernandes and his colleagues.[27] Fernandes became notorious for his ability to bring the city to a halt through his *morchas* (protests) and *bandhs* (general strikes) – not in the least because he controlled unions of workers in several essential services including transportation.[28] While hawkers and other informal workers provided the manpower needed to organize these events,[29] they benefited immensely from the influence Fernandes wielded over municipal policy, not just as a councilor, but also by virtue of his ability to disrupt normal life in the city.[30]

---

[24] See Chandavarkar 2004.

[25] George Fernandes enjoyed a long and successful political career that culminated in his stint as the Union Minister for Defence in the NDA government (1998–2004).

[26] Interview 15 with worker of the Bombay Labour Union, October 9, 2015.

[27] A similar mechanism of political incorporation has been documented in Mexico City. Hawkers were often centrally located in cities and towns, unlike peasants, and enjoyed flexible work schedules, unlike factory workers, which made them ideal for the purpose. See Cross 1998.

[28] See Binoo Nair, "George hops off Taximen's Union, ends ties with the city," *Times of India*, July 24, 2012.

[29] For instance, when George Fernandes led the famous all-India railways strike of 1974, Bombay hawkers were also roped into the protests. *Times of India*, June 15, 1974; "Hawkers protest before newspaper office," June 19, 1974.

[30] For instance, in 1963, the hawkers' union called for a city-wide protest unless the municipal corporation took immediate action to protect the "right to trade" of street vendors. A committee was formed to frame a new licensing scheme, but Fernandes boycotted the committee, terming it an instrument of delay. Soon after, the corporation announced the new scheme, and about 30,000 new licenses were distributed in 1964. *Times of India*, "Current Topics: Hawkers'

But trouble was brewing in Fernandes' backyard. In 1967, a newly established nativist party, the Shiv Sena, unleashed an organized and systematic campaign of ruthless violence against trade unionists in the city.[31] The Shiv Sena embarked on a concerted program to replace the entire array of civic-corporate institutions of the working classes (upon which the trade union movement was based) with those affiliated to the Sena.[32] Unnerved by the rapid pace at which left-wing parties were gaining strength in the city, Bombay's industrialists and political elites covertly extended support to this new political party, while the ruling Congress party ensured that the state machinery turned a blind eye to these acts of violence.[33] Hawkers – especially those who were organized – became a target very early in this process, partly because many of them were Muslims who had migrated from other parts of the country.[34] Anti-hawker rhetoric became a regular feature in the fiery speeches of Shiv Sena leaders,[35] even as the party introduced new hawkers affiliated to itself as market competition, and captured various lucrative sites in downtown areas for them to set up their stalls.[36]

By the mid-1970s, the Congress government began a program of violent curtailment of working-class mobilization through the direct involvement of the state machinery, whose effects were felt by Bombay's hawkers as well.[37]

Agitation, Right to Trade," February 12, 1964; "Liberal Issue of Licenses to Hawkers in the City: Corporation Ratifies 14-Man Body Formation," March 20, 1964; "Permanent squad to curb Hawkers' Nuisance likely," May 31, 1968. The importance of sharing the leadership of the municipal workers' union was corroborated by several independent oral histories. Interviews 12, 13, 15 with hawker union leaders, October 2015.

[31] See Hansen 2001.

[32] Chandavarkar 2004.

[33] Hansen 2001.

[34] On at least four occasions in 1967–1969, south Indian Muslim hawkers on D. N. Road in the downtown area were targeted. On one occasion, as many as 10,000 members of the Shiv Sena participated in a violent demonstration against these hawkers, and their stalls were set on fire. These clashes had spread to other parts of the city by the early 1970s. *Times of India*, "Hawkers' wares looted: Shiv Sena blamed," May 7, 1967; "Agitation against hawkers in city turns violent," May 21, 1968; "Hawkers again at receiving end," May 26, 1968; "Hawkers clash with mob in Kurla, nine hurt," January 9, 1969; "7 hurt in clashes between SS men, hawkers," July 31, 1971; "Stalls set on fire, hawkers assaulted," April 3, 1972.

[35] *Times of India*, "Hawker nuisance: complaint against civic commissioner," November 25, 1967; "Earmarking zones for hawkers urged," January 16, 1970; "Adjournment bid on hawker issue lost," August 6, 1971; "Ending delays, curbing hawkers is SS goal," April 7, 1973.

[36] *Times of India*, "Civic order against hawkers challenged," January 24, 1973.

[37] For example, in 1973, "mobile courts" were introduced to readily prosecute petty offences such as unauthorized hawking, so as to tighten state surveillance and control over street hawking. Hawker unions vigorously and violently protested against the functioning of these mobile courts as they were perceived to be the primary targets of these courts, and they were eventually discontinued. *Times of India*, "Hawkers plan to obstruct mobile courts," February 1, 1973;

In 1974, the police demolished the stalls of nearly 500 hawkers (many of whom possessed valid or expired licenses) in a major downtown market located at D. N. Road.[38] The Bombay Hawkers' Union petitioned the authorities,[39] and organized protest marches,[40] but these efforts were unsuccessful as the Congress strove to clamp down on labor unrest with a firm hand. Such violent repression became even more pronounced during the Emergency (1975–1977),[41] and the municipality restricted hawking to a small number of hawking zones governed by stringent regulations on time and place.[42] The number of hawking licenses had been reduced from a reported 82,000, in the late 1960s,[43] to about 7,000, in 1976.[44]

It was at this time that the Bombay Hawkers' Union first began approaching the judiciary. In the first instance, the union deliberately attempted litigation on behalf of a single member who had been evicted in 1974 despite possessing a valid license (i.e., as a test case).[45] Though the lower court judge was unsympathetic, the High Court on appeal ruled that the police action was "clearly in excess of authority granted by law," and provided an injunction in favor of the evicted hawker, as a result of which nearly 200 evicted hawkers were able to return to work.[46] At this time, the municipality stepped in to prevent these hawkers from returning by choosing not to renew their licenses, thereby necessitating another round of litigation.[47] Early in 1975, the High Court mediated a settlement between the hawkers and the municipality

---

"Hawkers gherao mobile court," February 3, 1973; "Mobile courts gheraoed again by hawkers," February 10, 1973; "Hawkers say mobile court must go," February 13, 1973; "Hawkers want mobile court to be withdrawn," February 23, 1973.

[38] Hawkers at this location had been the targets of the Shiv Sena's ire since the 1960s. *Times of India*, "Police swoop on hawkers' stalls," June 14, 1974.

[39] *Times of India*, "Police to hold talks with the hawkers," June 23, 1974; "Hawkers may be allowed in vehicle-free lanes," June 25, 1974;

[40] *Times of India*, "Hawkers plan morchas," June 15, 1974; "Hawkers protest before newspaper office," June 19, 1974.

[41] During this period, Prime Minister Indira Gandhi exercised her emergency powers to suspend constitutional provisions such as elections, fundamental rights and judicial review, and impose direct presidential rule at all levels of government.

[42] *Times of India*, "Work of shifting hawkers in Dadar begins," January 8, 1977; "Hawkers' zones being set up in city," January 22, 1977.

[43] It is likely that not all of the 82,000 licenses were owned by "genuine" hawkers. But the numbers do suggest that a lot more hawkers enjoyed the security of a license in the late 1960s, when compared with 1976. *Times of India*, "Hawkers' plea: to review licensing policy," January 31, 1970.

[44] *Times of India*, "Plan for hawkers' zone," July 17, 1976.

[45] *Times of India*, "Hawkers' injunction plea turned down," June 20, 1974.

[46] *Times of India*, "Court restrains eviction of Fort hawkers," September 1, 1974.

[47] *Times of India*, "Hawkers file suit against corporation," September 17, 1974.

through which 100 evicted hawkers were to be given fresh licenses.[48] Though the final verdict delivered in this case provided little support for the legal claims made by hawkers,[49] litigation did allow this group of hawkers, who had been targeted both by the government and by the Shiv Sena, to maintain their foothold in the D. N. Road market and survive the harsh political environment of the mid-1970s. When the Emergency was lifted, a united opposition won elections nationally as well as in the state of Maharashtra, and a large number of licenses were renewed by the new government in 1978.[50]

However, the Emergency signified a sharp break in working-class politics in Bombay. The increasing frequency of lockouts and the closure of most of Bombay's textile mills in the wake of a major worker strike in 1982 forced trade unions in the city to take a more conciliatory stance.[51] Moreover, tensions between the hawkers' union and the union for municipal workers had been on the rise, as eviction proceedings against hawkers were often carried out by municipal workers also affiliated to Fernandes's umbrella federation.[52] These emerging contradictions within the political coalition weakened the ability of the union leadership to protect hawkers' interests through the older methods.[53] The difficulties of hawkers had also increased because many textile workers responded to the closure of textile mills in 1982 by joining the informal sector as hawkers.[54] By the 1980s, many hawkers began to quit Fernandes's Bombay Hawker Union to set up splinter groups with the protection of other politicians.[55] These emerging divisions threatened the organizational cohesion of the hawkers' union. Meanwhile, the Congress, which returned to power in the early 1980s, began a vigorous campaign against

---

[48] *Times of India*, "Hawkers issue in court again," April 11, 1975; "Hawkers reach interim accord with civic body," June 24, 1975.

[49] In 1976, the lower court eventually ruled that "hawkers had no right, but only had the liberty to sell their wares on street-pavements." The liberty could be withdrawn at the discretion of the Municipal Commissioner, "as it was not incumbent on him to observe the principles of natural justice." *Times of India*, "Court decision goes against hawkers," September 4, 1976.

[50] Interview 15 with worker of the Bombay Labour Union, October 9, 2015.

[51] See Rajagopal 2011.

[52] Interview 12 with hawker union leader, October 5, 2015.

[53] Hawker union leaders belonging to splinter groups were more critical of the actions of the Bombay Hawkers' Union – they suggested that the union had given up its urgency to fight for hawkers' rights by the early 1980s in order to claim the role of a "responsible" trade union. See Id.

[54] See Bhowmik and More 2001.

[55] These new unions were often organized along religious lines. Hindu hawkers had a tendency to gravitate to the Shiv Sena, whose influence was growing in all parts of the city (Eckert 2004). Hawkers from the Muslim community were organized by Muslim politicians such as Haji Mastan. Interview 13 with hawker union leader, October 7, 2015.

"slums" and street markets in the city, proposing the "voluntary" return of slum-dwellers and hawkers to their "native places" in the countryside.[56] The municipal corporation also declared an absolute moratorium on new hawking licenses,[57] and the challenges faced by the hawkers' union further intensified after the Shiv Sena gained control of the municipal corporation in 1985.[58]

Looking for a way out of a difficult political situation, the new president of the Bombay Hawkers' Union, Sharad Rao,[59] sought the help of Indira Jaising, a lawyer,[60] to file a writ petition to the Supreme Court on behalf of the Bombay Hawkers' Union. Jaising's writ petition, filed in 1982, mounted a constitutional challenge against the sections of the Bombay Municipal Corporation Act that enabled the Municipal Commissioner to make arbitrary decisions regarding distribution and renewal of licenses.[61] However, it became obvious during the hearings that the Supreme Court did not intend to rule in favor of the hawkers' union on this issue, and a separate petition was filed on behalf of the hawkers' union with the less ambitious demand for a comprehensive scheme to accommodate street hawking. The court preferred the latter petition, and sought to adjudicate the dispute using a procedure that was dubbed "non-adversarial," wherein the court sought suggestions for "evolving a satisfactory solution to the problems faced by both the sides."[62] Accordingly, the municipal commissioner drew up a licensing scheme for 49,000 hawkers to be situated in a small number of concentrated hawking zones.

Many activists and legal commentators have cited the *Bombay Hawkers' Union* case as a significant example of the Supreme Court's jurisprudential innovation in the area of socioeconomic rights, which provided new legal opportunities for urban social movements to benefit from.[63] However, these commentators arrive at an exaggerated assessment of the significance of the

---

[56] See Mahadevia and Narayanan 2008.

[57] Rajagopal 2001.

[58] Interview 15 with worker of the Bombay Labour Union, October 9, 2015.

[59] As Fernandes' stature as a national politician grew in the 1970s, the responsibility for several of the unions he led was transferred to Sharad Rao. In 1979, Sharad Rao became a councilor in the Bombay Municipal Corporation. However, the weakening of the socialist movement is reflected in Rao's political career – he never won an election again.

[60] Jaising, a young cause lawyer, had just set up the Lawyers' Collective, a legal aid firm that specialized in public interest litigation.

[61] Refer to Sections 313-A and 314 of the Bombay Municipal Corporation Act, 1888, http://vakinidia.org.

[62] *Bombay Hawkers' Union and others* v. *Bombay Municipal Corporation and others*, 1985 AIR 1206, http://indiankanoon.org/doc/231387/.

[63] As discussed in the introduction, Renana Jhabvala considers it a "historic judgment" that allowed street vendor collectives to doggedly pursue a strategy of legalization in subsequent years. See Jhabvala 2012, xii.

court verdict in the *Bombay Hawkers' Union* case precisely because they fail to situate the case within a broader trajectory of street vendor politics in the city. Examining the case as part of this broader historical and political canvas, I arrive at an entirely different assessment of its significance. First, the evidence suggests that this was not the first instance of street vendors approaching the judiciary as a forum of last resort – the historical record shows that street vendors in Bombay were approaching district- and state-level appellate courts even *during* the emergency, at a time when the fundamental rights had been suspended. While the emergence of public interest litigation in the late 1970s did make the Supreme Court more accessible to these local political groups, this by itself cannot be seen as a significant shift in the "legal opportunity structure" unless one can also demonstrate that litigation at the national level led to more desirable outcomes. As I show in this chapter, there is little basis for such a claim.

Second, I have found little evidence for the claim that there was a significant shift in the "legal consciousness" of street vendors during the early-1980s owing to the arrival of new social movements. In fact, leaders of hawkers' unions in Bombay began framing their demands in the socialist-inspired language of livelihood rights as early as the 1950s, long before the arrival of new social movement organizations such as SEWA.[64] In the 1960s, there were heated debates in Bombay newspapers and in the council of the municipal corporation whether there existed a "right to trade" for street hawkers.[65] Demands for municipal licenses in the 1960s was at least as programmatic (if not more) as the solutions entertained by the judiciary in later years. Hawkers' unions had already become adept at combining programmatic and particularistic claims, and were able to fight policy battles in the municipal council with as much fluency as street battles on behalf of rival political parties over the control of territory. These findings suggest that legal petitioning primarily constituted a change in the forum where claims were made, but did not require any significant change in the language in which claims were articulated.

Finally, there is little evidence that legal mobilization by the Bombay Hawkers' Union was able to achieve anything beyond the maintenance of the status quo in the face of political threats. It is possible that the first petition filed by Jaising, which sought to institutionalize due process in the licensing

---

[64] *Times of India*, "Grant licences to hawkers liberally: appeal to civic authorities," September 26, 1955.

[65] For instance, see *Times of India*, "Current topics: hawkers' agitation, right to trade," February 12, 1964.

process for hawkers, was an attempt to transcend the limits of the existing informal arrangements, but this petition was not successful. Instead, the court offered the hawkers an ad hoc remedy, which entailed confining 49,000 licensed street vendors to "hawking zones" that were to be identified by the municipal corporation. Far from being a satisfactory remedy to their woes, this "solution" was seen by most hawkers as a threat, since they could not be certain that these "hawking zones" would be located such that they attracted a sufficient clientele for such a large number of hawkers to carry out their trade profitably. Indeed, it is instructive that the hawkers' union did not choose to file a follow-up petition to point out the lack of dedicated "hawking zones," as promised by the municipal corporation. Instead, by 1986, the hawkers' union had struck a political agreement with the Shiv Sena-led municipal corporation, leading to a policy which permitted a large number of unlicensed hawkers to continue their trade upon payment of a daily fee as long as the area was not declared as a "no hawking zone."[66]

Conventional accounts of legal mobilization generally tend to emphasize explanatory variables that are internal to the legal field, such as the legal opportunity structures, support networks, and legal consciousness among marginalized social classes. The history of legal mobilization by hawkers in Bombay, however, suggests that the judiciary is more likely to function as a last resort option for marginalized groups, because of which the proximate causes of legal mobilization are likely to lie outside the legal field. In Bombay, for instance, a hostile political climate generated a deep organizational crisis for the Bombay Hawkers' Union, and it was left with few options but to approach the judiciary in an attempt to ward off immediate threats while it tried to strike a political bargain with such political adversaries as the Shiv Sena and the Congress. In the next subsection, I use the case study from Madras to provide further support for the hypothesis that legal mobilization was typically a response to political threats that marginalized groups were unable to resolve through other means.

---

[66] This came to be called the *pauti* system, since municipal officials started giving official receipts (*pautis*) for payments they had been illegally collecting all along (Anjaria 2006). However, the Supreme Court had clarified in *Bombay Hawkers' Union* that the municipal corporation could collect daily fees for hawking "without prejudice to [the] right to remove [the hawkers] should the dynamic situation and the changed circumstances so demand in future." See *Bombay Hawkers' Union and Others* v. *Bombay Municipal Corporation and Others*, 1985 AIR 1206, http://indiankanoon.org/doc/231387/.

B. *Madras*

Whereas left populism and ethnic nationalism emerged as competing political forces in Bombay during the 1960s and 1970s, left populism was subsumed within the ethnic nationalist politics of the Dravidian movement in Madras.[67] After the Dravida Munnetra Kazhagam (DMK) defeated the Congress on a Tamil nationalist platform in the 1967 state elections, economic policies were reoriented towards social welfare.[68] Street vendors also began to benefit from the benevolence of the Dravidian parties in the form of patronage arrangements.[69] In some instances, public markets were constructed by the Corporation of Madras to rehabilitate street vendors,[70] but municipal officials pursued resettlement "not [by] stick, but by persuasion and through sustained campaign."[71] However, in most cases, street vendors were allowed to form associations and use their connections with political leaders to continue operating on the streets in areas where they were most likely to attract a clientele.

When the state government was dismissed during the Emergency and replaced by the direct rule of the centrally appointed governor, there was a concern that patronage arrangements organized by street vendors would not be sustained. However, a group of Congress leaders negotiated a deal such that members of Congress-affiliated associations were allowed to function during off-peak hours.[72] The conciliatory attitude of political and administrative elites was in sharp contrast to the use of Emergency powers to conduct violent clearance drives against street vendors and residents of informal settlements in other cities such as Bombay.[73] Madras was sheltered from the excesses of the Emergency owing to the strong populist impulse that had permeated Tamil politics in general, and elites sought to "approach the problem from a human angle."[74] When the Anna Dravida Munnetra Kazhagam (ADMK) – a splinter

---

[67] Subramanian 1999.

[68] The DMK government introduced a host of populist programs, including subsidized food grains, in situ redevelopment of urban "slums," and increased access for backward caste youths to government jobs. See Subramanian 1999; Raman 2011.

[69] Long time vendors say that there used to be a lot of harassment during the Chief Ministership of M. Bhaktavatsalam of the Congress Party (1963–1967) but that the government became more amenable to political maneuvering after the transfer of power in 1967 to the DMK. Interview 10 with street vendor leaders, September 30, 2015.

[70] *The Hindu*, "Drive against roadside vegetable vendors in city," August 6, 1975.

[71] Id.

[72] Interviews 3, 8, 10 with leaders of various street vendor associations, January 20, 2012, September 29, 2015, September 30, 2015.

[73] See Clibbens 2014.

Dravidian party led by a charismatic cinema star, M. G. Ramachandran – swept into power in 1977, the previous arrangement was continued, with most of the street vendor associations simply shifting their allegiance to ADMK leaders.[75] The leaders of these associations were given contracts from the government to farm out spaces on the pavement to their clients.

The beneficiaries of the elaborate patronage system perfected by the ADMK were typically male stationary vendors who sought to distinguish themselves from itinerant hawkers.[76] In contrast to the hawkers' union in Bombay which, in theory, sought to encompass all street vendors in the city, street vendor associations in Madras were location-specific, gendered, and exclusive in nature. For instance, there were 10 independent street vendor associations in the T. Nagar neighborhood alone, each controlling a particular section of the major thoroughfares in the neighborhood.[77] As Joop de Wit has argued with respect to informal settlements in Madras, the incorporation of their associations into vertical clientelist relations with political parties hindered the horizontal mobilization of the urban poor.[78] The willingness of the state to provide selective benefits to their political clients proved to be extremely divisive, and no broad-based resistance on behalf of street vendors emerged in the 1970s and 1980s.

Indeed, street vendors during this period would have been justified to think that broad-based resistance was not necessary. The stability of the ADMK regime (1977–1987) and the system of patronage it operated resulted in the rapid proliferation of street vendors in Madras, such that street vendor politics in the early 1980s placed more emphasis on the question of party affiliation than on collective mobilization against the threat of eviction.[79] It is worth noting that precisely at the moment when the Bombay Hawkers' Union was

---

[74] *The Hindu*, "Pavement shops on NSC Bose road: panel submits report," July 1, 1978.

[75] One of the ADMK leaders who emerged as a patron for street vendors was Jeppiaar (short for Jesadimai Pangiraj,) then the district secretary of the ADMK party. Some associations affiliated with the communist parties were formed, and they were able to adopt a slightly more confrontational style than their ADMK counterparts, but they were also reliant on their political leadership to make deals with the ruling party on behalf of the members of the association. Interview 9 with leader of street vendor association, September 30, 2015.

[76] Stationary street vendors in Madras do not like to be described as "hawkers," because for them the term refers specifically to itinerant hawkers (*koovi virkum viyabarigal* in Tamil). The Tamil term they use to describe themselves is "*sirukadai viyabarigal*" which translates in English as "petty-shop traders." But official documents continue to refer to both mobile and stationary street vendors as "hawkers," which stationary vendors find demeaning. Interview 4 with two street vendor association leaders, January 23, 2012.

[77] Interview 3 with the leader of a street vendor association, January 20, 2012.

[78] See de Wit 1989.

[79] Interview 3, January 20, 2012.

approaching the court, street vendors in Madras were relatively secure and felt no need to mobilize the law in order to change the status quo. It was left to commercial store-owners in certain areas to make use of public interest litigation in the post-Emergency period to approach the Madras High Court, seeking the eviction of street vendors and the cancellation of contracts to their political patrons.[80] The municipal corporation and the affected vendors' associations argued in favor of the existing system, but the High Court in 1982 struck it down as unconstitutional.[81] Keeping socioeconomic concerns in mind, the Madras High Court brokered a plan to relocate the affected vendors elsewhere.[82] However, with the government supporting the street vendors, the court was able to do little to effectively compel the government to conduct clearance drives in the areas where street vending was now prohibited.[83]

However, by 1985, the populist impulse in Dravidian politics had begun to plateau. The strong control exercised over the party organization by M. G. Ramachandran waned as a result of his illness and eventual death, and the locus of decision-making shifted towards the bureaucracy.[84] Without political pressure to go soft on street vending during this period, the Corporation was able to take decisive action against street vendors in several areas, including outright eviction.[85] Moreover, vendors' associations were not able to influence the policies of the municipal corporation directly, as its deliberative wing had been suspended, and it functioned as an executive arm of the state government during this period.[86] The period after the death of M. G. Ramachandran

---

[80] See *K. Sudarsan & Others v. The Commissioner, Corporation of Madras, & Others*, 1983, AIR 1984 Mad 292, http://indiankanoon.org/doc/73780.

[81] *K. Sudarsan*, AIR 1984 Mad 292.

[82] *M. A. Pal Mohammed & Others v. R. K. Sadarangani & Others*, 1984. AIR 1985 Mad 23, http://indiankanoon.org/doc/125461/.

[83] In some cases, the Corporation did agree to relocate vendors and granted them licenses in the new locations approved by the court. However, in most such instances, the new locations proved to be not as lucrative as the original sites, and the vendors returning to their old spots using their old-fashioned methods of political lobbying. *The Hindu*, "A street paved with problems," May 6, 1992.

[84] One street vendor, in fact, told me that raids on street vendors in the city began almost immediately after the departure of M. G. Ramachandran to the United States for treatment in 1984. Interview 10 with street vendor leaders, September 30, 2015. While the causal connection between the two events suggested here may be more imagined than real, the broader evidence does suggest that there was an overall weakening of the populist impulse in Tamil politics by the mid-1980s. Nithya Raman observes a similar trend in the construction of slum redevelopment tenements in Madras (Raman 2011).

[85] *The Hindu*, "Encroachers cleared in Madras," August 2, 1985; "Encroachment campaign is on," March 2, 1986.

[86] The deliberative wing of the Corporation had been suspended in 1973 after charges of corruption surfaced, and the position of the Mayor was replaced with that of an appointed

was also a period of great political uncertainty, with the control of the state government changing hands several times.[87] In such an environment, the committed party functionary was as much at risk of eviction as a non-political person. Street vendors may not have been as vulnerable to these threats had there been greater horizontal solidarity, but their disorganized state and dependence on political bosses resulted in these challenges becoming insurmountable.

Having observed the costs of relying excessively on political patrons from one party, street vendor associations embraced political versatility,[88] by ensuring that their members and the leadership was drawn from both the Dravidian parties.[89] From the early 1990s onwards, a number of street vendor associations also began filing new petitions in the Madras High Court seeking protection from further clearance drives. By 1994, the vendors' associations were able to secure the services of R. Vaigai, a devoted communist and a prolific labor lawyer.[90] Vaigai filed an appeal in the High Court on behalf of a single vendors' association, and was able to secure a "stay order" which protected vendors from eviction till the appeal process was completed.[91] Following this success, nearly 40 associations obtained stay orders using the help of a legal team that Vaigai put together. In 1997, a Division bench consisting of Justices Kanakaraj and Natarajan ordered the corporation to develop a satisfactory

---

Special Officer. When the ADMK came to power in 1977, it chose to maintain this arrangement as the opposition DMK was considered to be stronger in Madras city, and therefore likely to capture power at the municipal level if elections were to be held. Local self-government for the city was restored only in 1996, after the DMK swept to power at state level.

[87] The death of M. G. Ramachandran caused a split in the ADMK, with neither of the splinter groups being able to hold a majority in the Legislative Assembly. This resulted in the direct rule of the centrally appointed governor for one year, and the DMK won the 1989 elections. However, the DMK government was suspended in 1991 by the central government, and fresh elections were held. The ADMK had reunited and came back to power with a huge majority in 1991 under the leadership of J. Jayalalithaa. Overall, control over the state government changed hands four times in as many years.

[88] Neighborhood associations of the urban poor were also undergoing similar transformations during this period. Joop de Wit was already finding the growing popularity of the "welfare association" during his research on local organizing in the "slums" of Madras in the mid-1980s (de Wit 1989). By the mid-2000s, political neutrality/versatility was the predominant strategy of the local associations in informal neighborhoods. See Coelho and Venkat 2009.

[89] In many associations, the practice was to maintain two groups, and for the leadership of the entire association to be transferred to match any transitions that occurred in the state government. Interview 2 with leader of street vendor association, January 19, 2012.

[90] Vaigai had represented the vendors of NSC Bose Road in the 1980s, and was well regarded by the major communist trade unions in the region as well as the legal fraternity.

[91] This association had received a negative verdict earlier from a single member bench, primarily because they had failed to furnish a list of members and details about the exact locations where they had been conducting their trade.

scheme for regulating street vending throughout the entire city.[92] Vaigai, however, realized that street vendors could not rely on the legal process alone, and therefore mobilized vendors' associations from all parts of the city with the help of communist leaders to establish a federation.[93]

Vaigai's organizing and coordinating efforts turned out to be extremely timely. In the late 1990s, street vendors in many neighborhoods received a rude shock when a different bench of the Madras High Court vacated several stay orders based on petitions filed by adjacent merchants.[94] Sensing an opportunity, the municipal corporation moved to evict street vendors and destroy their stalls and merchandise in 1999. At this time, a large number of people gathered to protest, including Vaigai and her legal team, and the vendors staged a blockade on a major thoroughfare with the help of allies from the communist party.[95] This protest was successful in delaying eviction pending the resolution of the legal dispute. There had been few such public demonstrations organized by street vendor associations in the past, but the existence of the Federation made such collective action possible. The improperly vacated stay orders were restored through an appeal filed in the Supreme Court, and Justice Kanakaraj (who had since retired) was given the task of identifying the existing vendors in each locality and appropriate sites for a licensing scheme to accommodate all of them. But the official censuses were often contested by the street vendors' federation, which carried out enumerations of its own.[96] In 2003, about 5,000 vendors belonging to the associations involved in litigation were identified as part of this scheme.

As in the case of Bombay's street vendor litigation, however, the "solutions" brokered by the court were not considered particularly desirable by the street vendors themselves. For instance, in the neighborhood of Madras where I did most of my fieldwork (T. Nagar), the solution eventually proposed by Kanakaraj was to relocate about 650 vendors spread over two of the busiest thoroughfares in the city to a single multistory municipal market – a proposal unlikely to guarantee the livelihoods of street vendors. Predictably, even after this solution was accepted by all parties in the dispute and affirmed by the Madras High Court, street vendors made no effort to apply pressure on the municipal corporation to implement the scheme by constructing the building

---

[92] Order by Justice Kanakaraj (1997) in W.A. No. 175/230 of 1994.
[93] Interview 6 with R. Vaigai, February 1, 2012. Most of the leaders of the individual associations, however, maintained their connections with the Dravidian parties.
[94] Order by Justice Jagadeesan (2000) in W.P. No. 719 of 1994.
[95] Interview 3 with the leader of a street vendor association, January 20, 2012.
[96] This form of "counter-governmentality" has been observed also among street vendors in Calcutta. See Bandyopadhyay 2011.

where they were to be relocated.[97] Since they were protected by a stay order of the court against evictions until the implementation of the scheme, any delay in its implementation gave them additional time during which they could maintain their street-side stalls, which were typically much more lucrative than the alternative sites proposed.

These observations lead me to the conclusion that the street vendors of Madras who decided to approach the judiciary in the 1990s were, in most respects, driven by the same purpose as the Bombay Hawkers' Union from the 1970s onwards – buying time and maintaining status quo. In both cases, I find little evidence that either the jurisprudential innovations attempted by the judiciary or the final solutions proposed in court verdicts were considered to be of much significance by street vendor collectives. It is true that R. Vaigai provided more than just the necessary legal support for street vendor litigation. She also helped inculcate a legal consciousness among the members of street vendor associations, who had previously been entirely reliant on clientelistic politics. But even in this case, legal support and the inculcation of legal consciousness do not explain the *timing* of legal mobilization very well.[98] Instead, my evidence suggests that litigation was primarily a response to unfavorable changes in the prevailing political regime at the local level, and was an instrument of delay used by vendors to forestall the possibility of eviction or relocation.

Comparative analysis, however, suggests a subtle distinction between threats to street vending in general and threats to the organization of street vendors in particular. In Madras, vendors' associations have traditionally operated as exclusive groups whose control over specific stretches of the street was not contested by other vendors' associations. In this context, though eviction drives caused by regime change posed severe threats to the operation of street markets, they provided opportunities for building organizational cohesion as well. Entrepreneurial leaders such as Vaigai took advantage of these opportunities to promote greater horizontal solidarity among street vendors in the city. In the oppositional culture of Bombay politics, however, wars over territory were common, and many eviction drives by municipal and non-state actors were directed specifically against oppositional unions, even when they were disguised and legitimized using rhetoric against hawkers in

---

[97] Interview 10 with street vendor leaders, September 30, 2015.

[98] Vaigai's services were available even in the 1980s, and street vendors used them when responding to court cases filed by commercial store-owners calling for the eviction of street vendors. However, street vendor organizations did not mobilize the law unless they were compelled to do so by those opposed to them.

general.[99] There is reason to believe, therefore, that for the Bombay Hawkers' Union, litigation was aimed not just at mitigating eviction threats faced by individual hawkers, but also at threats of displacement experienced by the organization as a whole.[100]

However, even if street vendors mobilized the law primarily with the goal of maintaining the status quo, there is still a need to consider the possibility that legal mobilization may have had unintended effects, either to the general benefit or detriment of street vendors. In the following section, I offer some observations on the trajectory of street vendor politics since the 1990s as a result of the growing reliance on legal mobilization by organized street vendors in most Indian cities.

III. IMPACTS OF STREET VENDOR LITIGATION, 1995–PRESENT

As we have seen, the early instances of litigation (i.e., before the 1990s) were driven by political threats caused by regime change, and in most cases were aimed at restoring the status quo. When street vendor collectives attempted to use the law to produce systematic changes in the legal status of street vendors, they generally found the judiciary unwilling to grant recognition to their programmatic claims. Instead, the solutions offered by the judiciary typically involved relocation of street vendors to areas that were unlikely to guarantee a sufficient volume of business, because of which vendors typically tried to delay the implementation of the schemes authorized by the judiciary by using the familiar methods of political negotiation. In other words, street vendor collectives used judicial forums sparingly and often chose to resolve some issues outside the court rather than allowing the judiciary to become the sole forum of grievance redress and dispute resolution. This meant that even though they used judicial forums to buy time and maintain the status quo under otherwise difficult circumstances, their politics was not "status-quoist" in any fundamental sense during this period.

---

[99] During my interviews, old-time hawker union leaders in Bombay were insistent that the Shiv Sena was not against hawkers in general, despite there being no love lost between them and the Sena. When I revisited the newspaper data based on these accounts, I found hints that violence against hawkers was typically politically motivated. For instance, when the police carried out a violent raid in 1974 against hawkers on a major thoroughfare in the downtown area (D. N. Road), only hawkers on one side of the road were targeted. These men had also been targeted by the Shiv Sena in previous years, as they were south Indian Muslims and belonged to Fernandes' union. *Times of India*, "City lights: hawker issue," June 16, 1975.

[100] My argument here mirrors the findings of American legal mobilization scholars who identify "group maintenance" as a distinct, but not necessarily overriding goal of interest group litigation. See Solber and Waltenburg 2006.

However, once the law has been mobilized, it cannot be demobilized very easily; it takes on a life of its own. By the early 2000s, despite street vendors refraining from further litigation, neighborhood activists brought the issue back to the judiciary in both cities. In Bombay, the *pauti* system (which allowed unlicensed hawkers to operate in many areas) was scrapped after an appeal by middle-class residents, and a committee with the representation of hawker unions was formed to identify permanent locations for a much smaller number of hawkers.[101] In Madras, owing to a similar petition by a middle-class neighborhood activist, a retired judge was appointed to coordinate between the government and the street vendor associations, and to oversee the implementation of the Kanakaraj scheme.[102] As a result of this competitive mobilization of the law by street vendors and their opponents, as well as the willingness of the judiciary to maintain oversight over these cases for long periods,[103] courts have, to a large extent, become entrenched sites of dispute resolution and governance on all issues related to street vending. In other words, though legal mobilization was aimed at *temporarily* restoring the status quo, it has altered the very character of the political settlement in the process.

The mobilization of law has also produced what Charles Tilly and Sidney Tarrow have called an "upward scale shift."[104] Legal mobilization as a strategy might have originated as a result of crises in local political regimes, but the entrenchment of judicial intervention lent to the struggles of street vendors in different cities a degree of uniformity. Frustrated by the growing caseload related to petty disputes related to street vending, the higher judiciary directed Parliament to establish a system for street vendor regulation consistent with existing case law.[105] At the same time, street vendor associations began to establish federations at regional, national, and international levels, and built a coalition with civil society organizations, media-persons, academics, and international agencies such as the International Labour Organization.[106]

---

[101] Litigation by neighborhood activists and associations was coordinated by an NGO called CitiSpace. For a critical account of the activities of these middle-class associations, see Anjaria 2009.

[102] Order by Justices A. P. Shah and Prabha Sridevan (2006) in W.P. No. 1049 of 2006, etc. This case was instigated by a middle-class activist with a penchant for filing PILs by the name of "Traffic" Ramaswamy.

[103] The main legal instrument used to maintain direct oversight is the "continuing mandamus," by which the court keeps cases in abeyance while issuing regular orders to the government.

[104] Tilly and Tarrow 2015. Writing specifically about street vendors in Calcutta, Bandyopadhyay describes this process as the "nationalization of the hawker question" (Bandyopadhyay 2016).

[105] *Gainda Ram & Others* v. *Municipal Corporation of Delhi & Others* (2010), http://nidan.in/nidanwp/wp-content/uploads/2014/07/2010-Oct-08Gainda_Ram_vs_MCD.pdf.

[106] te Lintelo 2012.

Their efforts were instrumental in getting the central government to issue policy guidelines for street vendor regulation, which were eventually formalized through Parliamentary legislation.[107] The new Act, passed in 2014, attempts to institutionalize corporatist interest-group mediation by setting up "town vending committees" with mandatory representation for street vendor associations.[108]

While these achievements may appear impressive, they must ultimately be evaluated based on their contribution to securing the livelihoods of street vendors. Most of the research on street vendors suggests that there is no discernible trend of improvement in the protection of their livelihoods.[109] In Bombay, no new licenses have been issued since 1978, when the socialists briefly controlled the state government. The system of collecting daily fees was scrapped in 1998 by the orders of the Bombay High Court and was supposed to be replaced by a licensing scheme, but the proposals approved by the court were never implemented. A town vending committee was constituted in 2014, as per the provisions of the Street Vendors' Act, but the committee is widely accepted to be defunct and has not met since 2014.[110] No steps have been taken to proactively implement the Street Vendors' Act in Madras either. After much delay, the implementation of Justice Kanakaraj's proposal for street vending was finally completed in 2014, but the number of vendors who have benefited through this process is a minuscule fraction of the total number of vendors in Madras. Moreover, most of the multistory municipal markets have proven to be entirely unsuitable for small traders, and many of them have fallen into disuse.[111]

However, even from a realist perspective, judicial intervention must be evaluated based on the counterfactual scenario in which street vendors did not have recourse to the courts. If the livelihoods of a significant number of street vendors would have become even more insecure in the counterfactual case, then judicial intervention must be considered as impactful even when there is no discernible change in the final outcome. Street vendors in both Bombay and Madras took advantage of repeated delays in the legal process to

---

[107] See Street Vendors (Protection of Livelihoods and Regulation of Street Vending) Act (2014), www.indiacode.nic.in/acts2014/7%20of%202014.pdf.

[108] For a strictly lawyerly examination of this new act, see Alva 2014.

[109] Bhowmik, and Saha 2012.

[110] Interview 13 with hawker union leader, October 7, 2015.

[111] For instance, the municipal market constructed for the neighborhood of T. Nagar is a three-storey building with no elevators. Few prospective customers ventured to the second and third floors of the building, where the majority of the vendors were located. Already, a majority of the vendors have downed their shutters, and many have returned to the street illegally.

buy time and prevent hostile political regimes from embarking on sweeping eviction campaigns. When vendors were able to obtain a "stay order" against eviction, the protection guaranteed by the legal process was greatest, and vendors bore none of the costs of judicial delay. For instance, in Madras stay orders obtained by street vendors' associations allowed vendors in many neighborhoods to enjoy a steady livelihood untroubled by threats of eviction and demands for rent for nearly two decades. Even in Bombay, where hawkers' unions found it harder to secure stay orders, the mere fact of a dispute being *sub judice* could induce bureaucratic uncertainty and inertia for significant periods of time, as the municipality waited for clear directives from the court.[112]

Much of this judicial delay was a direct result of the overcrowded dockets of high courts and the Supreme Court, along with the tendency of courts to keep cases in abeyance. To a limited extent, street vendor associations actively contributed to the delay by taking a variety of supplementary disputes to court, rather than resolving them through other means.[113] Boaventura de Sousa Santos has described such practices as attempts by marginalized groups to exploit the plasticity in the "production and distribution of judicial time,"[114] and shift attention from struggles over substantive questions of law to procedural questions (where judges have more flexibility to exercise their individual judgment). Delays can breed further delays, as judges retire or get transferred and new benches have to be constituted and brought to speed. Moreover, because local government bureaucrats are frequently transferred, they tend to lack institutional memory with regard to these repeatedly prolonged cases.[115] This sometimes creates an anomalous circumstance in which street vendor associations begin to show a greater resemblance to "repeat players" (especially when represented by seasoned lawyers such as R. Vaigai) as compared to government lawyers, which gives street vendor associations an advantage in procedural battles.[116]

---

[112] As one neighborhood activist complained, "Often, municipal officials blamed their inaction saying that hawkers had approached the court and the matter is sub judice." See Daily News and Analysis, "BMC seeks HC help to get rid of hawkers," December 17, 2012.

[113] Interview 10, September 30, 2015.

[114] See de Sousa Santos 2002, 388.

[115] Interview 8 with street vendor leader, September 29, 2015. I also observed, during a visit to the municipal corporation in Madras, that the law officer, who was responsible for the corporation's submissions to the judiciary, was largely unaware of (or unconcerned about) the procedural history of the case.

[116] Such a circumstance turns on its head Marc Galanter's prediction that the government is likely to "come out ahead" in litigation because it is an institutional "repeat" player (Galanter 1974).

In addition to the immediate benefits to street vendors threatened by eviction, these procedural battles over judicial time also generate a public perception of legality associated with subsistence livelihoods they seek to defend. As de Sousa Santos has argued, efforts to "seize the law" must necessarily be accompanied by what he calls the "social reconstruction of conflict," which alters the terms in which the dispute is framed and adjudicated.[117] According to Santos, resistance movements can alter the terms of the dispute by generating "interlegal rhetoric" and pitting "one type of law against another" as a means of keeping a dispute alive.[118] For example, by getting courts and the legislature to grant symbolic recognition to street vending as a legitimate occupation, street vendor associations have been able to dispute what would otherwise be uncontroversial actions by the local state. Symbolic recognition at the national level has also helped organizations such as the National Association of the Street Vendors of India organize street vendors in many smaller cities and strengthen the horizontal solidarity among street vendor collectives in different parts of the country. This is indeed an important achievement, which has helped to sustain ongoing political and legal mobilization, even when it has not produced the transformative change that street vendors might have hoped for.

Nevertheless, it is important to emphasize that even the symbolic recognition granted to street vendors is limited, since it relies on a very narrow and limited conception of legality for street vendors as articulated by the Supreme Court of India. For instance, in *Sodan Singh* (1989), a five-member constitutional bench of the Supreme Court of India affirmed the legitimacy of street vending as an "age-old vocation" protected under Article 19(1)(g) of the Indian Constitution (freedom of occupation).[119] However, the court refused to entertain a "right to livelihood" claim based on Article 21 (right to life) and insisted that vendors have neither the right to continue vending at their existing spots, nor the right to reasonable alternative locations being allotted if their existing locations have to be vacated.[120] By signifying traffic as vital to "civic life," and hawking as merely a "private" activity, the Supreme Court reinforced the differentiated and markedly inferior status of street vendors in public space.[121] As a result, the intervention of the judiciary itself functions as an exercise of

---

However, it is important not to under-estimate the overwhelming deference often shown by the judiciary towards the government in many cases.

[117] See de Sousa Santos 2002, 386–388.
[118] See de Sousa Santos 2002, 387.
[119] *Sodan Singh etc. v. New Delhi Municipal Committee and Another etc.* 1989 AIR 1988.
[120] Id.

arbitrary decision-making, rather than contributing towards an institutional framework that would extend meaningful guarantees to street vendors.[122]

It is also possible that the "cunning state" encourages judicialization precisely because this allows it to shirk accountability towards all parties in the conflict.[123] In the medium term, one of the possible consequences of rampant judicialization might be the depoliticization of urban governance. For instance, many leaders of street vendor associations have complained that municipal corporations have become less responsive to their complaints in the past decade, choosing instead to pass on the responsibility of adjudicating even minor claims to the judiciary.[124] Meanwhile, access to judicial forums remains affordable only to a small minority of street vendors who are situated in relatively lucrative street markets; itinerant vendors, women, and vendors located in less desirable areas are typically absent from the litigation process.[125] There is also a growing concern that judicialization has, over the years, been accompanied by a considerably weakening of the organizational cohesion even among the existing street vendor associations.[126] Court battles – unlike street protests – neither require the active participation of affected vendors, nor do they reward efforts to expand the membership base of street vendor associations and federations.

The case of the street vendors' federation in Madras amply illustrates these concerns regarding the effects of judicialization on the organizational cohesion of street vendors. While R. Vaigai's initial efforts to unite street vendor associations were successful, it is telling that the federation made no efforts to incorporate new associations under its banner after it was established, since its leadership feared that incorporating new members and filing court cases on their behalf would weaken the claims of the existing members.[127] Indeed, the court case became the primary glue that held all the existing member associations together. As the court case wound to a close in 2014, many associations began openly expressing their disaffection towards the leadership, and the

---

[121] As Nicholas Blomley has shown, such arguments elevate the seemingly apolitical demands of traffic flow over the political claims of other users of public space, including street vendors. See Blomley 2007.

[122] Schindler 2014; Bhuwania 2016.

[123] See Randeria and Grunder 2011.

[124] Interview 8, September 29, 2015. I also observed this during a meeting between leaders of some street vendor associations and the city Mayor, in which I was allowed to sit in. When the leaders began making competing claims over space, the Mayor stated that he was not at liberty to make any alteration to the allocation of space without the decision being approved by the high court.

[125] Interview 9, September 30, 2015.

[126] Interview 10, September 30, 2015.

[127] Id.

federation splintered into several groups. As a result, the court battles of the 1990s and 2000s have not left a strong organizational legacy for previously unorganized street vendors to rely upon as they attempt to leverage new legal resources (such as the Street Vendors' Act) to their benefit.

IV. CONCLUSION

In this chapter, I have investigated the role of legal institutions in the political repertoires of street vendor associations fighting against displacement and dispossession in urban areas. My findings resonate with those of other scholars who have studied legal mobilization by subaltern groups in India, but also depart from them in certain respects. For instance, in a study of legal mobilization by farmers affected by compulsory land acquisition in Singur, Kenneth Bo Nielsen has argued that "farmers did not consistently attach special importance to their court case. Rather, it was when other avenues of contestation and seeking justice had either narrowed or closed entirely that the court case gained significance for the farmers."[128] Similarly, in a study of legal mobilization by sex workers, Prabha Kotiswaran concludes that during the early phases sex workers did not "use the law as a sword" but rather chose to deploy it "defensively . . . as a shield."[129] Both Nielsen and Kotiswaran argue that subaltern groups continue to pursue "uncivil" forms of political mobilization, including street protests and violent insurgency, in addition to legal mobilization. This chapter similarly suggests that legal mobilization was a useful defensive tool for street vendors facing the risk of eviction. However, my research also points to the risks of such tactical use of the legal process: that when there is competitive legal mobilization by both sides of a dispute, an all-powerful judiciary can fully replace other sites of dispute resolution – an outcome that is somewhat detrimental to subaltern groups since it places them in a permanently defensive stance.

These detailed studies of the relationship between law and subaltern politics clearly contradict any teleological narratives of political and legal modernization one might be tempted to deploy. But they also pose a challenge to popular arguments by postcolonial theorists such as Partha Chatterjee, who maintain a pessimistic stance on the potential of law as a resource for counter-hegemonic politics. Chatterjee's pessimism stems from an effort to trace the distinct trajectories of political institutions and popular political mobilization outside the Western world. Chatterjee argues that the colonial

---

[128] Nielsen 2009, 124.
[129] Kotiswaran 2013, 537.

experience has produced, in countries such as India, a sharp divide between spaces of citizenship (i.e., "civil society") and spaces of governmentality (i.e., "political society"), which map onto the economic circuits of "corporate" and "non-corporate" capital.[130] Chatterjee therefore assumes a strong, almost one-to-one, correspondence between economic logics (accumulation versus subsistence,) grammars of claim-making (universal versus differentiated rights), modes of incorporation (normative citizens versus empirical populations), repertoires of contention (formal petitioning versus informal negotiations/violent insurgency), organizational forms (voluntary and apolitical versus involuntary and partisan), and the favored targets of contentious claims (courts versus politicians).[131]

Since street vendors and other marginalized groups live and work in the shadow of illegality, Chatterjee argues that they are required to organize as empirical populations, and to make exceptional claims based on a framework of differentiated rights. Such claims are unlikely to succeed by mobilizing legal institutions:

> On one side, forces from political society try to use the legal institutions to extend the field of exceptions on the moral ground of securing greater equality. On the other side, those upholding the norms of civil society as the space of equal citizenship resist, also on the grounds of equality, the proliferation of exceptions ... I do not see ... that the advantage lies with those who would like to use the law courts to further extend the recognized space of plural rights.[132]

This pessimism towards the potential of legal mobilization to serve the political projects of marginalized groups stands in contrast to their increasing reliance on legal processes to resist dispossession. And yet, when the discussion is confined to an analysis of legal *discourse*, Chatterjee's pessimism is not unfounded. As the evidence presented in this chapter shows, while courts have often been willing – perhaps even eager – to intervene on behalf of specific groups of vendors, they have been extremely reluctant to recognize any programmatic claims that street vendors and other marginalized groups may make over urban space and the institutions that govern it. At least at the level of discourse, judicial antipathy to the pluralist legal claims advanced by subaltern groups is difficult to deny.

---

[130] Chatterjee 2011, 208–234.
[131] Chatterjee 2004.
[132] Chatterjee 2011, 92.

However, in order to construct "political society" as a category that is simultaneously analytical and empirical, and therefore verifiably different from its constitutive other (i.e., civil society) Chatterjee has to extrapolate his argument from the level of discourse to the level of practice. The paradox of groups in political society mobilizing legal institutions is easily resolved when, following Chatterjee's own suggestion in a recent article, postcolonial legalism is studied as a "field of practice" that is partially autonomous from legal discourse.[133] As Balakrishnan Rajagopal has aptly pointed out, "the higher judiciary [in India] plays its appointed role as an instrument of governance much more often than its traditional role as an institution of justice."[134] If "political society" refers to a social formation in which governmental techniques are given full rein, then it should hardly surprise us that the courts, in their incarnation as forums for pragmatic governance, should engage freely with groups in political society. Under such circumstances, legal discourse can no longer be taken as an accurate barometer for assessing the potentialities of legal mobilization at the level of practice, since marginalized groups might approach the judiciary with a variety of particularistic claims that are not reflected in judgments eventually handed down by appellate courts.

While "competitive electoral mobilization" might have initially provided a fertile environment for groups in "political society" to flourish, these groups are increasingly compelled to employ repertoires of contention which go beyond the electoral arena.[135] Legal mobilization, in particular, has come in handy as a cushion against the vagaries of electoral politics. Marginalized groups have mobilized legal institutions even in the face of hostile legal discourse when they were likely to benefit through indirect mechanisms, such as the operation of judicial time. As Boaventura de Sousa Santos has argued, legal mobilization by subaltern actors leads not to the "formalization" of their livelihoods, but to the "informalization of the official legal system."[136] However, the present challenge for social movements is to refocus their attention on questions of organizational coordination and horizontal solidarity among the subaltern classes, so as to ensure that they are well positioned to take advantage of any new political opportunities that might arise in the future.

---

[133] See Chatterjee 2014. The same argument has also been made by Kotiswaran 2013, 531.
[134] Rajagopal 2007.
[135] See Kotiswaran 2013; Bandyopadhyay 2016; Coelho and Venkat 2009.
[136] See de Sousa Santos 2002, 389.

REFERENCES

Alva, Rohan J. "The Street Vendors (Protection of Livelihood and Regulation of Street Vending) Bill, 2013: Is the Cure Worse Than the Disease?" *Statute Law Review* 35, no. 2 (2014): 181–202.

Anjaria, Jonathan Shapiro. "Street Hawkers and Public Space in Mumbai." *Economic and Political Weekly* 41, no. 21 (2006): 2140–2146.

"Ordinary States: Everyday Corruption and the Politics of Space in Mumbai." *American Ethnologist* 38, no. 1 (2011): 58–72.

"Guardians of the Bourgeois City: Citizenship, Public Space, and Middle-Class Activism in Mumbai." *City & Community* 8, no. 4 (2009): 391–406.

Bandyopadhyay, Ritajyoti. "Politics of Archiving: Hawkers and Pavement Dwellers in Calcutta." *Dialectical Anthropology* 35, no. 3 (2011): 295–316.

"Institutionalizing Informality: The Hawkers' Question in Post-Colonial Calcutta." *Modern Asian Studies* 50, no. 2 (2016): 675–717.

Baxi, Upendra. "Taking Suffering Seriously: Social Action Litigation in the Supreme Court of India." *Third World Legal Studies* (1985): 107–132.

Bhatt, Ela R. *We are Poor but So Many: The Story of Self-Employed Women in India.* New York: Oxford University Press, 2006.

Bhowmik, Sharit K. "Street Vendors in Asia: A Review." *Economic and Political Weekly* (2005): 2256–2264.

"Social Security for Street Vendors." *Seminar* 568 (2006): 49, www.india-seminar .com/2006/568/568_sharit_k_bhowmik.htm.

Bhowmik, Sharit K., and Debdulal Saha. *Street Vending in Ten Cities in India.* National Association of Street Vendors of India, 2012, www.streetnet.org.za/docs/ research/2012/en/NASVIReport-Survey.pdf.

Bhowmik, Sharit K., and Nitin More. "Coping with Urban Poverty: Ex-Textile Mill Workers in Central Mumbai." *Economic and Political Weekly* (2001): 4822–4827.

Bhuwania, Anuj. "Courting the People: The Rise of Public Interest Litigation in Post-Emergency India." *Comparative Studies of South Asia, Africa and the Middle East* 34, no. 2 (2014): 314–335.

"Public Interest Litigation as a Slum Demolition Machine." *Projections: The MIT Journal of Planning* 12 (2016): 67.

Blomley, Nicholas. "Civil Rights meet Civil Engineering: Urban Public Space and Traffic Logic." *Canadian Journal of Law & Society* 22, no. 2 (2007): 55–72.

Bromley, Ray. "Street Vending and Public Policy: A Global Review." *International Journal of Sociology and Social Policy* 20, no. 1/2 (2000): 1–28.

Chandavarkar, Raj. "From Neighbourhood to Nation: The Rise and Fall of the Left in Bombay's Girangaon in the Twentieth Century." In Meena Menon and Neera Adarkar (eds.), *One Hundred Years, One Hundred Voices: The Mill Workers of Girangaon: An Oral History.* Kolkata: Seagull, 2004.

Chatterjee, Partha. *The Politics of the Governed: Reflections on Popular Politics in Most of the World.* New York: Columbia University Press, 2004.

Lineages of Political Society: Studies in Postcolonial Democracy. New York: Columbia University Press, 2011.

"Introduction: Postcolonial Legalism." *Comparative Studies of South Asia, Africa and the Middle East* 34, no. 2 (2014): 224–227.

Clibbens, Patrick. "'The Destiny of this City is to be the Spiritual Workshop of the Nation': Clearing Cities and Making Citizens during the Indian Emergency, 1975–1977." *Contemporary South Asia* 22, no. 1 (2014): 51–66.

Coelho, K., & Venkat, T. The Politics of Civil Society: Neighbourhood Associationism in Chennai. *Economic and Political Weekly* (2009): 358–367.

Cortner, Richard C. "Strategies and Tactics of Litigants in Constitutional Cases." *Journal of Public Law* 17 (1968): 287.

Cross, John Christopher. *Informal Politics: Street Vendors and the State in Mexico City.* Stanford, CA: Stanford University Press, 1998.

Daily News and Analysis, "BMC seeks HC help to get rid of hawkers," December 17, 2012.

de Sousa Santos, Boaventura. *Toward a New Legal Common Sense: Law, Globalization, and Emancipation.* Cambridge, UK: Cambridge University Press, 2002.

de Wit, Joop. "Clientelism, Competition and Poverty: The Ineffectiveness of Local Organizations in a Madras Slum." In Frans Schuurman & Ton Van Naerseen (eds.), *Urban Social Movements in the Third World* (1989): 90.

Dhavan, Rajeev. "Law as Struggle: Public Interest Law in India." *Journal of the Indian Law Institute* 36, no. 3 (1994): 302–338.

Dixon, Rosalind. "Creating Dialogue about Socioeconomic Rights: Strong-Form versus Weak-Form Judicial Review Revisited." *International Journal of Constitutional Law* 5, no. 3 (2007): 391–418.

Eckert, Julia. "Urban Governance and Emergent Forms of Legal Pluralism in Mumbai." *The Journal of Legal Pluralism and Unofficial Law* 36, no. 50 (2004): 29–60.

Epp, Charles R. *The Rights Revolution: Lawyers, Activists, and Supreme Courts in Comparative Perspective.* Chicago: University of Chicago Press, 1998.

Ewick, Patricia, and Susan S. Silbey. "Conformity, Contestation, and Resistance: An Account of Legal Consciousness." *New England Law Review* 26 (1991): 731.

Galanter, Marc. "Why the "Haves" Come Out Ahead: Speculations on the Limits of Legal Change." *Law & Society Review* 9, no. 1 (1974): 95–160.

Galanter, Marc. "The Radiating Effects of Courts." In Keith D. Boyum & Lynn Mather (eds.), *Empirical Theories of Courts* (1983): 117–142.

Hansen, Thomas Blom. *Wages of Violence: Naming and Identity in Postcolonial Bombay.* Princeton, NJ: Princeton University Press, 2018.

Hilson, Chris. "New Social Movements: The Role of Legal Opportunity." *Journal of European Public Policy* 9, no. 2 (2002): 238–255.

Jhabvala, "Foreword" in Sharit K. Bhowmik (ed.). *Street Vendors in the Global Urban Economy.* New Delhi: Routledge, 2012.

Kotiswaran, Prabha. "Sword or Shield? The Role of the Law in the Indian Sex Workers' Movement." *Interventions* 15, no. 4 (2013): 530–548.

Mahadevia, Darshini, and Harini Narayanan. "Shanghaing Mumbai: Politics of Evictions and Resistance in Slum Settlements." In Darshini Mahadevia (ed.), *Inside the Transforming Urban Asia: Processes, Policies and Public Actions.* Concept, 2008: 549–589.

Mate, Manoj. "The Rise of Judicial Governance in the Supreme Court of India." *Boston University International Law Journal* 33 (2015): 169.

McAdam, Doug, Sidney Tarrow, and Charles Tilly. "Dynamics of Contention." *Social Movement Studies* 2, no. 1 (2003): 99–102.

McCann, Michael W. "Reform Litigation on Trial." *Law & Social Inquiry* 17, no. 4 (1992): 715–743.

McCann, Michael. "Law and Social Movements." *Annual Review of Law and Social Science* 2 (2006): 17–38.

McCann, Michael, and George I. Lovell. "Toward a Radical Politics of Rights." In Paul Christopher Gray (ed.), *From the Streets to the State: Changing the World by Taking Power*. Albany, NY: SUNY Press, 2018, 139–159.

Merry, Sally Engle. *Getting Justice and Getting Even: Legal Consciousness among Working-Class Americans*. Chicago: University of Chicago Press, 1990.

Nielsen, Kenneth Bo. "Farmers' Use of the Courts in an Anti-Land Acquisition Movement in India's West Bengal." *The Journal of Legal Pluralism and Unofficial Law* 41, no. 59 (2009): 121–144.

Olson, Susan M. "Interest-Group Litigation in Federal District Court: Beyond the Political Disadvantage Theory." *The Journal of Politics* 52, no. 3 (1990): 854–882.

Rajagopal, Arvind. "The Violence of Commodity Aesthetics: Hawkers, Demolition Raids, and a New Regime of Consumption." *Social Text* 19, no. 3 (2001): 91–113.

"The Emergency as Prehistory of the New Indian Middle Class." *Modern Asian Studies* 45, no. 5 (2011): 1003–1049.

Rajagopal, Balakrishnan. "Pro-Human Rights but Anti-Poor? A Critical Evaluation of the Indian Supreme Court from a Social Movement Perspective." *Human Rights Review* 8, no. 3 (2007): 157–186.

Randeria, Shalini, and Ciara Grunder. "The (Un)Making of Policy in the Shadow of the World Bank: Infrastructure Development, Urban Resettlement and the Cunning State in India." In Chris Shore, Susan Wright, and Davide Pero (eds.), *Policy Worlds: Anthropology and the Analysis of Contemporary Power*. Oxford: Berghahn Books, 2011: 187–204.

Rodriguez-Garavito, Cesar. "Beyond the Courtroom: The Impact of Judicial Activism on Socioeconomic Rights in Latin America." *Texas Law Review* 89 (2010): 1669.

Roever, Sally. "Informal Trade meets Informal Governance: Street Vendors and Legal Reform in India, South Africa, and Peru." *Cityscape* 18, no. 1 (2016): 27–46.

Sabel, Charles F., and William H. Simon. "Destabilization Rights: How Public Law Litigation Succeeds." *Harvard Law Review* (2004): 1015–1101.

Sarat, Austin. "The Law is All Over: Power, Resistance and the Legal Consciousness of the Welfare Poor." *Yale Journal of Law & Humanities* 2 (1990): 343.

Scheingold, Stuart A. *The Politics of Rights: Lawyers, Public Policy, and Political Change*. Ann Arbor: University of Michigan Press, 2010.

Schindler, Seth. "Producing and Contesting the Formal/Informal Divide: Regulating Street Hawking in Delhi, India." *Urban Studies* 51, no. 12 (2014): 2596–2612.

Solberg, Rorie Spill, and Eric N. Waltenburg. "Why do Interest Groups Engage the Judiciary? Policy Wishes and Structural Needs." *Social Science Quarterly* 87, no. 3 (2006): 558–572.

Subramanian, Narendra. *Ethnicity and Populist Mobilization: Political Parties, Citizens and Democracy in South India*. New Delhi: Oxford University Press, 1999.

Te Lintelo, Dolf J. H. "Advocacy Coalitions Influencing Informal Sector Policy: The Case of India's National Urban Street Vendors Policy." In Sharit K. Bhowmik (ed.), *Street Vendors and the Global Urban Economy*. New Delhi: Routledge, 2012.

Tilly, Charles, and Sidney G. Tarrow. *Contentious Politics*. New York: Oxford University Press, 2015.

Vanhala, Lisa. "Legal Opportunity Structures and the Paradox of Legal Mobilization by the Environmental Movement in the UK." *Law & Society Review* 46, no. 3 (2012): 523–556.

Weinstein, Liza. "Democracy in the Globalizing Indian City: Engagements of Political Society and the State in Globalizing Mumbai." *Politics & Society* 37, no. 3 (2009): 397–427.

7

Court as a Symbolic Resource

Indra Sawhney *Case and the* Dalit *Muslim Mobilization*

M. MOHSIN ALAM BHAT

I. INTRODUCTION

While scholars have studied the social and political impact of courts for decades, growing number of studies have started to focus on the symbolic dimension of law in social movement mobilization. In particular, scholars have pointed out how courts' decisions provide movement actors with symbolic resources to conceptualize and articulate their grievances.[1] Law provides valuable discursive tools to mobilizations for generating support among their constituents and political elite, as much as reorienting and "channeling" their claims.[2]

Engaging with this scholarship on the role of courts in social movement mobilization, this chapter will study the impact of the Indian Supreme Court's decision in the 1992 case of *Indra Sawhney*.[3] *Indra Sawhney* came at the end of a long political and constitutional controversy over the contours of legitimate affirmative action in India, in particular the role of caste identity in the determination of potential beneficiaries. In the watershed decision, the Supreme Court endorsed the Central Government's implementation of the

---

[1] *See, e.g.,* Michael W. McCann, *Rights at Work: Pay Equity Reform and the Politics of Legal Mobilization* (University of Chicago Press, 1994); Michael W McCann, "How Does Law Matter for Social Movements?," *How Does Law Matter* 76 (1998): 88; Stuart A. Scheingold, *The Politics of Rights: Lawyers, Public Policy, and Political Change,* 2nd ed. (University of Michigan Press, 2004); Helena Silverstein, *Unleashing Rights: Law, Meaning, and the Animal Rights Movement* (University of Michigan Press, 1996).

[2] William N Eskridge, "Channeling: Identity-Based Social Movements and Public Law," *University of Pennsylvania Law Review* 150, no. 1 (2001): 419–525.

[3] *Indra Sawhney v. Union of India, Supp* (3) SCC 217 (1992) [hereinafter *Indra Sawhney*].

Mandal Commission Report that had recommended an ambitious public employment quota scheme or reservations for low castes.[4]

One way to evaluate the impact of *Indra Sawhney* is to study the implementation of the Indian reservations regime shaped by the Supreme Court. I take a different route to understand the decision's consequences. I look at the impact of the decision – in symbolic and strategic terms – on social groups engaged in mobilization for inclusion.

I focus on the mobilization of *Dalit* Muslims – a unique social group lying at the intersection of religious and caste-based subordination. The word *Dalit* refers to the erstwhile Untouchables castes. India is a deeply "compartmental" society, marked by entrenched social hierarchies and economic inequality.[5] Central to this compartmentalization is *caste* – a notion that escapes easy definitions. Caste is as much an institution of social stratification as it is an identity, a religious doctrine and a group marker. Perhaps the best way to approach caste would be to define it as a hierarchical arrangement of social classes, mostly occupational, based on the *Brahmanical* (upper caste Hindu) doctrine of "purity and pollution." The caste system (or the *varna* system) is often said to constitute four distinct caste groups;[6] but in reality, it constitutes thousands of discrete, and sometimes hazy, groups marked by endogamy and hereditary occupations. At the bottom of the caste hierarchy are the *Sudras* or the low castes. And those outside the system altogether are the untouchable castes or *Dalits*. The latter have historically been the most marginalized class of people, suffering from exclusion from temples and public spaces.[7] Adopted in 1950, the Indian Constitution – which used the category of "Scheduled

---

[4] For a discussion on the law and politics of the case, *see* Rajeev Dhavan, "The Supreme Court as Problem Solver: The Mandal Controversy," in *The Politics of Backwardness – Reservation Policy in India*, ed. V. A. Pai Panandiker (Centre for Policy Research, 1997), 262; Marc Galanter, "The Long Half-Life of Reservations," in *India's Living Constitution: Ideas, Practices, Controversies*, ed. Zoya Hasan, E. Sridharan, and R. Sudarshan (Anthem Press, 2005), 306.

[5] Marc Galanter, in his magisterial work on the Indian "compensatory discrimination" scheme notes that "Indian society has been described as a "compartmental" society; within it a vast number of groups maintain distinct and diverse styles of life. The system by which these groups are related and mutually accommodated is so complex as to defy general description." Marc Galanter, *Competing Equalities: Law and the Backward Classes in India* (University of California Press, 1984), 5.

[6] These four *varnas* are the *Brahmins* (priestly class), the *Kshtriya* (warrior class), the *Vaishya* (mercantile class), and the *Sudra* (low castes).

[7] For an overview of the subject, *see* Sidney G. Tarrow, *The Untouchables: Subordination, Poverty and the State in Modern India* (Cambridge University Press, 1998); Hidden Apartheid: Caste Discrimination against India's "Untouchables" (Human Rights Watch, 2007), www.hrw .org/report/2007/02/12/hidden-apartheid/caste-discrimination-against-indias-untouchables.

Castes" (SCs) for this class of people – abolished the practice of untouchability and instituted a robust regime of affirmative action for *Dalits*.

But this regime excluded those *Dalits* who convert – or have historically converted – out of Hinduism. While the Constitution did not provide any concrete definitional criteria for the determination of SCs, institutional and political practices confirm that caste-groups suffering from "extreme socio-economic backwardness linked with the historical practice of untouchability" would be given the SC status. In place of a textual criterion, the Constitution provided a procedure for SC enumeration. Article 341 empowered the Central Government (through the President) to enlist the SCs via an executive order. And subsequent alterations required a parliamentary statute. The first enumeration order in 1950 ("1950 Order") via paragraph 3 excluded anyone who did not profess the Hindu religion. While Sikhs and Buddhist converts were included in 1956 and 1990 respectively, the *Dalit* Muslim and *Dalit* Christian converts continue to remain disqualified from SC status. And this is despite mounting evidence that *Dalit* Muslims continue to be extremely socially and educationally marginalized – or, as a national study noted, "unquestionably the worst off among all *Dalits*."[8]

The *Dalit* Muslims started organizing in the early 1990s to get greater political and governmental representation, and eventually coalesced around the demand for the removal of the religious bar under the 1950 Order.[9] This chapter argues that *Indra Sawhney* provided valuable symbolic resources to the *Dalit* Muslim mobilization, enabling them to expand its support among the political elites as well as its constituents. The decision also facilitated opening up new arenas of contesting *Dalit* Muslim exclusion in the form of class litigation in the Supreme Court.

In Section II, I describe the legal outcome in *Indra Sawhney* in the background of its politics, and underline the explicit and implicit components that made it a relevant resource for the *Dalit* Muslim mobilization. *Indra Sawhney* came to authoritatively sanction the centrality of caste-identity in the Indian affirmative action regime. Equally important to this interpretation of constitutional equality was its jettisoning of religious doctrine as the sole definitional criterion for "caste." Consequently, the Supreme Court majority

---

[8] Dalits in the Muslim and Christian Communities: A Status Report on Current Social Scientific Knowledge 13, http://ncm.nic.in/pdf/report%20Dalit%20%20reservation.pdf.

[9] *See* Mohammad Sajjad, *Muslim Politics in Bihar: Changing Contours* (Routledge, 2014); Zoya Hasan, *Politics of Inclusion: Castes, Minorities, and Affirmative Action* (Oxford University Press, 2011); Yoginder Sikand, *Islam, Caste, and Dalit-Muslim Relations in India* (Global Media Publications, 2004).

came to recognize the existence of caste-like social stratification among Muslims.

These elements in the text of the decision were soon utilized by the young *Dalit* Muslim mobilization. But as I point out, *Indra Sawhney* did not speak to the *Dalit* Muslim claims – or even the SC issue – in any obvious manner. The decision becoming a symbolic resource for the mobilization was what Mertz has called the "unintended" consequences of court decisions.[10] These flowed from the *mediating* role that the movement political infrastructure – the *Dalit* Muslim movement in this case – plays in mobilizing legal meaning in pursuit of their political aims.

I focus on this in Section III, by studying the movement politics of my protagonist, the United Muslim Morcha (hereinafter Morcha) – the organization that first started to espouse *Dalit* Muslim claims and continues to be the most prominent voice for the cause. Created as a platform for many small Muslim groups, Morcha started to aggressively appropriate *Indra Sawhney* – and the allied understanding of constitutional equality – in its representations and public pronouncements by the end of the 1990s. I show that approaching *Indra Sawhney* as having a static meaning misses the most crucial component of the evaluation of its symbolic potential for movement actors. The decision became a symbolic resource for the mobilization through a construction of its meaning in the throngs of *Dalit* Muslim politics. Elements in the decision were creatively interpreted by Morcha to activate its symbolic potential. Morcha came to interpret the decision in light of their context, while adopting it in pursuance of its politics – reflecting the dialectical nature of law and politics.[11] This *mediating* role of political infrastructure that I elaborate can only be fully appreciated by decentering the study of judicial impact by giving due regard to the pronounced role of beliefs and strategies of movement actors.

Discussing the outcomes of Morcha's appropriation of *Indra Sawhney* and constitutional equality – which I do in Section IV – presents a dilemma. The *Dalit* Muslim mobilization has still not succeeded in removing the religious bar. While the absence of a resolution makes the final assessment of their strategies difficult, it also makes for an opportunity to understand the role that the decision has played – and continues to play – in Morcha's mobilization. I argue that the most noticeable impact of Morcha's legal discursive shift was

---

[10] Elizabeth Mertz, "A New Social Constructionism for Sociolegal Studies," *Law & Society Review* 28 (1994): 1243.

[11] Elizabeth M. Schneider, "The Dialectic of Rights and Politics: Perspectives from the Women's Movement," *New York University Law Review* 61 (1986): 589.

the generation of support among Muslim elites. I also show that the legal framing contributes to the continuing expansion of the *Dalit* Muslim mobilization among its constituents. I finally discuss the role of legal discourse in the opening up of new institutional strategies in the form of litigation in the Supreme Court.

While I evaluate the impact of *Indra Sawhney* on the activities of the *Dalit* Muslim mobilization, I do not claim that its eventual successes are purely – or even primarily – the result of the decision. Rather than isolating the role of the decision, I attempt to place it as part of a dynamic political process. Numerous factors played a role in the eventual achievements of Morcha. And *Indra Sawhney* – or the *Dalit* Muslim appropriation of it – was one among many. Through this chapter, I emphasize the importance of a motivated movement infrastructure, its ability to harness electoral incentives, and its ability to reach out to constituents and political elites. But all these factors dynamically interacted with Morcha's ability in interpreting legal decisions – and *Indra Sawhney* in particular – in their favor.

II. THE SAID AND UNSAID IN *INDRA SAWHNEY*

Indra Sawhney is part of a long and contested history of caste-based affirmative action in India. As I mention above, the Indian Constitution provided an affirmative action regime for the erstwhile Untouchables or SCs. It also included the indigenous people – or the "Scheduled Tribes" – in this regime. In contrast to these categories that were explicitly based on caste or community identity, the Constitution enabled the State to provide for affirmative action for a third category: the ambiguously labeled "other socially and educationally backward classes" or "other backward classes" (OBCs). The only test for the identification of the OBCs forthcoming in the constitutional text was their social and educational backwardness. It was not only unclear what would amount to this "backwardness"; but also more contentiously, as time would tell, what role caste-identity was to play in this identification.

Till *Indra Sawhney*, the controversy around the role of caste-identity was tangled in conflicting judicial opinions. The legal question was whether it was constitutionally permissible to recognize caste-groups – which were found to be socially and educationally marginalized – as beneficiaries of quota policies? Or should caste-identity – and its place in the *Brahminical* order – be one of the many criteria for the determination of social and educational "backwardness"?

By the 1980s, this question had reached national-political proportions. Many political parties, espousing the claims of their OBC constituents, started vehemently demanding reservations for non-SC low-caste communities in public employment and education. This "quota politics" found a rallying cry in the non-implementation of the 1981 Mandal Commission Report,[12] which had recommended an ambitious affirmative action scheme for 3,743 caste-groups. In 1989, Mandal mobilization succeeded to find a prominent space in the Central Government – leading to the implementation of the bulk of Mandal's recommendations, especially the quota in public employment.

The nine-judge bench of the Supreme Court in *Indra Sawhney* was called to determine the constitutionality of the Mandal-inspired OBC quota policy. Mostly upholding the quota policy, the majority endorsed the centrality of caste-identity in the identification of affirmative action beneficiaries. The Supreme Court accepted that within certain quantitative limits, caste-based quotas were constitutionally sustainable provided the caste-groups in question were transparently shown to be "backward." The majority also endorsed the Mandal Commission's empirical test for "backwardness." This included not just the position of the group in the caste hierarchy, but also their relative social and educational marginalization.

The Court's approval of OBC quota – especially after the vehement mobilization of the "backward class" movement – understandably had a potentially signaling effect on Indian politics.[13] Another aspect within the pages of the decision that came to have a deep impact on the *Dalit* Muslim mobilization was its treatment of the institution of caste itself.

The Indian courts in their jurisprudence have operated with contrasting conceptions of the institution of caste. Marc Galanter has noted that these conceptions have included treating caste as a *sacral* or purely religious demarcation, associational ties within social groups without a necessary connection with social hierarchy, and as a mark of access to the "level of resources and attainments relative to other groups in the society."[14] I call the last understanding the *subordinated* conception of caste, as it conceives caste as encoding forms of social and political power. *Subordinated* caste eschews the narrowly religious definitions of the institution. Rather, it reflects a secularized definition where being low caste carries with it the condition of exclusion from

---

[12] Christophe Jaffrelot, *Religion, Caste, and Politics in India* (Primus Books, 2010), 254.
[13] Yogendra Yadav, "Reconfiguration in Indian Politics: State Assembly Elections, 1993–95," *Economic and Political Weekly* 31 (1996): 102.
[14] Marc Galanter, "Changing Legal Conceptions of Caste," in *Law and Society in Modern India*, ed. Rajeev Dhavan, Reprint (Oxford University Press, 1993), 143.

social and political goods, and thus entails entrenched and historical marginalization.[15]

The *Indra Sawhney* majority came to operate with – even explicitly approve – this secularized conception of *subordinated* caste. The sociological conception of caste was based on a factual premise. As one of the majority opinions noted, there was an "integral connection between caste, occupation, poverty and social backwardness."[16] It was also based on an understanding of the Indian social condition – that "a caste can be and quite often is a social class in India."[17] The secularized sociological conception of caste was a crucial endorsement of the Mandal Commission as well as the larger Mandal movement.[18] It was also the strongest repudiation of the influential strands of the Court's previous jurisprudence that had understood caste as "artificial" and poverty as the only constitutionally legitimate target of affirmative action policies.[19]

An important manifestation of *subordinated* caste in *Indra Sawhney* was the recognition of Muslim social stratification. In his concurring opinion, Justice Sawant noted:

> Distinct religions like Buddhism, Jainism and Sikhism were born as revolts against casteism. When, therefore, first Islam and then Christianity made their entries here. . .many from the lower castes embraced them. . . However, the change of religion did not always succeed in eliminating castes. The converts carried with them their castes and occupations to the new religion. The result has been that even among Sikhs, Muslims and Christians casteism prevails in varying degrees in practice, their preachings [*sic*] notwithstanding . . . Casteism has thus been the bane of the entire Indian society.[20]

---

[15] Another way to conceive of this conception of caste is to contrast it with what I have called "horizontal" caste, which is caste conceived as denoting horizontally placed social groups. *Subordinated* caste, in contrast, is a "vertical" conception of caste, denoting power relations and hierarchy among these social groups. Courts have interpreted caste, including caste among Muslims, in both these horizontal and vertical variants. See M. Mohsin Alam Bhat, "Muslim Caste under Indian Law: Between Uniformity, Autonomy and Equality," *Quaderni Di Diritto e Politica Ecclesiastica* 20, Special Issue (2017): 165.

[16] *Indra Sawhney*, 765 (*per* Justice Reddy).

[17] Id., 859(3) (*per* Justice Reddy).

[18] See *Mandal Commission Report* 30, 57. See, *also*, Rammanohar Lohia, "Towards the Destruction of Castes and Classes", in *The Caste System* 79; Yogendra Yadav, "What Is Living and What Is Dead in Rammanohar Lohia?," *Economic & Political Weekly* 45, no. 40 (2010): 97.

[19] *M.R. Balaji v. State of Mysore*, AIR 1963 SC 649. For a longer discussion on the changing conceptions of caste and its impact on the evolving Indian affirmative action jurisprudence, see M. Mohsin Alam Bhat, "Conflict, Integration and Constitutional Culture: Affirmative Action and Muslims in India" (JSD Dissertation, Yale Law School, 2017).

[20] *Indra Sawhney* 399 (*per* Justice Sawant). See, *also*, idem, 83, 94 (*per* Justice Pandian).

This recognition of Muslim social stratification was the continuation of the Court's endorsement of the Mandal Commission Report. The Report had relied on growing sociological literature on Indian Muslims,[21] and accepted that "[t]hough caste system is peculiar to Hindu society yet, in actual practice, it also pervades the non-Hindu communities in India in varying degrees," including the Muslims.[22] In fact, the Report included 82 Muslim groups among its proposed list of OBCs.

Despite these references to Muslim social stratification, *Indra Sawhney*'s recognition remained only partial. The reason for this was the ambivalence of the Mandal Report itself toward Muslim caste. While it had been clear in understanding caste among Hindus as a sociological category, it continued to privilege religious doctrine in the case of Muslims. In an awkward non sequitur, especially in the light of its recognition of caste social stratification among Muslims, the Report asserted that

> despite the prevalence of caste system among non-Hindu communities in varying degrees ... [these religions] are totally egalitarian in their outlook ... and any social differentiation based on caste is anathema to them. In view of this, caste cannot be made the basis for identifying socially and educationally backward classes among non-Hindus.[23]

Finally, the Report proposed the inclusion of Muslim (or other non-Hindu) groups that were Untouchable converts, and those occupational communities that were still known with their traditional names and whose analogous Hindu castes had been included among the OBCs.[24] This left "Muslim caste" in the Mandal Report – and in *Indra Sawhney* – vaguely parasitic on "Hindu" caste and troublingly underdeveloped. It also did not categorically articulate Muslim *subordinated* caste as it did in the Hindu case.

The significance of all this, in the context of the *Dalit* Muslim mobilization, is worth stressing. *Indra Sawhney* was not about the SC category at all. But what made it potentially useful for the *Dalit* Muslim mobilization was its enthusiastic adoption of *subordinated* caste that treated caste as a secular, sociological, and transreligious phenomenon. The decision also noted the

---

[21] For example, a prominent sociologist, Imtiaz Ahmad had famously argued that "as a basis of social relations amongst [Muslims], but its form has been greatly weakened and modified and differs from the Hindu caste model in certain details." Imtiaz Ahmad, "Introduction," in *Caste and Social Stratification among Muslims in India*, ed. Imtiaz Ahmad (South Asia Books, 1978), xxviii.

[22] *Mandal Commission Report* §§12.11–16.

[23] *Mandal Commission Report* §12.16.

[24] *Mandal Commission Report* §12.18.

existence of Muslim social stratification. But where *Indra Sawhney* remained ambivalent was how caste-like Muslim stratification really was. Muslim caste – despite caste's secularization – remained an outlier in the pages of *Indra Sawhney*.

III. LAW-TALK IN THE *DALIT* MUSLIM MOBILIZATION

By the time the *Indra Sawhney* decision was pronounced, Morcha had started to lay the seeds of a young *Dalit* Muslim movement. Under the leadership of Ejaz Ali, a practicing surgeon in Patna (State of Bihar), Morcha was created as a platform joining 26 poor Muslim occupational groups in 1994. It operated, in the words of Lloyd and Susanne Rudolph, as a "caste association,"[25] which represented the material and political interests of the member caste-based occupational groups. Morcha espoused a catena of demands – including quotas for "backward class" Muslim groups, their greater political and governmental representation, and increased State funding in their activities.

Caste was the central idiom of Morcha's political activities. While Ejaz Ali had not been an active participant in the Mandal mobilization, there is little doubt that the role of social stratification in his politics was a reflection of the growing political salience of caste in India, especially Bihari politics. The challenge for Morcha, though, was to make "Muslim caste" a visible motif around which *Dalit* Muslims could make their claims. Consequently, it spent considerable energy – through protests and propaganda – claiming that Muslim society was as caste ridden, even *"Brahminical,"* as the Hindu one.[26] Morcha's strategies were oriented toward their primary audience at this time – the political parties in Bihar. Its members approached prominent leaders of political parties for the acceptance of their demands. They also started building a popular constituency during elections in order to further influence these political parties.[27]

---

[25] Lloyd I. Rudolph and Susanne Hoeber Rudolph, *The Modernity of Tradition: Political Development in India* (University of Chicago Press, 1984).

[26] "Muslim 'Pariahs' Warn of Quitting Islam," *Times of India*, Patna, Tuesday, July 19, 1994. *See* Ejaz 'Ali, Kyon Chaahiye Musalmano Ko Aarakshan?, *Veer Arjun*, New Delhi, October 13, 1996; Ejaz 'Ali, Anti-Islamic Elite Muslims Opposed to Reservations for the Oppressed, *Dalit Voice*, Bangalore, January 16, 1996; Ali Anwar, *Bihar Ke Musalmanon Ki Rajniti Ke Rang Badalne Lage*.

[27] See Interview with Kamal Ashraf, dated January 6, 2014 (on file with author).

It was only by the late 1990s that Morcha's demands coalesced around a "one-point programme,"[28] that of getting SC status for *Dalit* Muslims, or what Ejaz Ali called "Mission 341." This centrality of the SC status was not the result of Morcha's members conceiving their exclusion as a legal anomaly. In fact, there is no evidence that legal language was either used in the Morcha discourse until that point, or that its members had paid any meaningful attention to their exclusion's legal dimension. The importance of the SC exclusion was more immediate. What struck the Morcha leadership, as one member recalled, was the complete absence of government support to Muslims even as the "Hindu" *Dalits* from the same occupations were provided "immense benefits."[29] Moreover, caste-like social stratification was patently visible in the everyday life for the *Dalit* Muslims. Residents of the *Dalit* Muslim localities – many of whom were associated with Morcha – told me that the "Muslim caste" articulation of the organization resonated with their experiences of exclusion. There was, and continues to be, an upper-caste Muslim taboo for intermarriage. They also reported incidents of separation in dining. Each of these features – ranging from endogamy to social exclusion – represented the caste-like features of Hinduism. These experiences have been extensively recorded in the sociological literature on Muslim social stratification.[30]

Understandably, Morcha members, like their other *Dalit* Muslim neighbors, came to understand caste as a transcommunity phenomenon, based on hereditary occupations rather than religious faith. This version of the secularized and sociological *subordinated* caste seeped into the Morcha discourse. They argued that conversion out of Hinduism did not remove caste since all the historical and social disabilities continued in the new religion. *Dalit* Muslims continued in their professions that were considered to be unclean by the upper-caste – whether Hindu or not. While Morcha did not discover *subordinated* caste from *Indra Sawhney*, it did come to construe the decision – and constitutional equality – in light of these experiences.

The appropriation of the constitutional discourse happened through multiple encounters with the bureaucratic state. By the mid-1990s, Morcha expanded its audience from primarily Bihar-based political parties to Delhi. It started to individually approach politicians of national prominence and

---

[28] M. Ejaz Ali, "On Muslim Reservation" (excerpted from the *Dalit Voice*), in *Muslim India* 202 (October 1999): 472.

[29] Interview with Riasuddin Bakhho, dated January 8, 2014 (on file with author).

[30] Dalits in the Muslim and Christian Communities: A Status Report on Current Social Scientific Knowledge 13, http://ncm.nic.in/pdf/report%20Dalit%20%20reservation.pdf.

organize marches.[31] What it discovered were deeply entrenched understandings of religious and caste identity – in political and bureaucratic circles – that
legitimized their exclusion from the SC status. The strongest theme of opposition was the refusal to recognize the existence of caste among Muslims.
Political actors continued to argue that since there was no caste in the Islamic
doctrine, it would be a contradiction to extend it to Muslims. For them,
"[r]eligion cannot ... be lost sight of in regard to Scheduled Castes."[32] As a
"secret" cabinet note circulated in 1996 stated: Scheduled Caste converts to
Christianity (and Islam) "do not constitute a caste but a religious group."[33]

The resistance to the *Dalit* Muslim inclusion was also expressly interpreted
as pandering to minorities. The cabinet note implicitly referred to this by
stating that the inclusion of *Dalit* Christians would lead to similar demands
among the Muslims. An editorial of a prominent national daily expressed
similar fears:

> The largesse extended to Dalit Christians ... is certain to spur more sections
> to demand similar privileges. Some populists are bound to ask, if Dalit
> Christians can get it, why not Dalit Muslims? The overzealous may even
> revive the claim for reservations for the entire Muslim community.[34]

Thus, Morcha's demands were barricaded by a perception of a "casteless"
Muslim faith, the centrality of religious doctrine to the SC category, and the
view that their demand's acceptance was unprincipled political opportunism.

In the face of this opposition, the Morcha leadership started to invest their
limited material and human resources to understanding the legal underpin-
nings of their exclusion. One of the prominent members of Morcha told me:

> We purchased many law textbooks for the first time in 1996 after a protest
> march in Delhi. We studied them carefully...getting many portions and

---

[31] *See* Interview with Ejaz Ali, dated January 15, 2014 (on file with author). National dailies started
reporting Morcha's national activities of persuading individual leaders around this time. See,
e.g., Rao, PV for "Dalit Muslim Quota?," *The Pioneer*, November 12, 1999, quoted in *Muslim
India* 205 (January 2000): 24.

[32] *See Rajya Sabha Debates*, September 3, 1976, statement of K. Brahmananda Reddi, id. at col.
48–49; *Lok Sabha Debates*, May 28, 1990, statement of Uma Bharati, col. 55; *Rajya Sabha
Debates*, May 8, 1990, statement of P. Shiv Shankar, col. 299; id., statement of Sangh Priya
Gautam, col. 305.

[33] Ministry of Welfare, Government of India, Note for the Cabinet (Secret) regarding
Recognition of Scheduled Caste converts to Christianity as Scheduled Castes, No. 12016/30/90-
SCD (R. Cell), ¶18. This note was filed in the Kerala High Court in the case C.M.P.
No. 35569 of 1996 in O.P. No. 16330 of 1995, dated December 20, 1996.

[34] "Divide, Sub-Divide, Rule," Editorial, *The Pioneer*, March 9, 1996, extracted in *Muslim India*
161 (May 1996): 227.

judgments translated. We spoke with lawyers who could explain to us the constitutional position. We realized that our exclusion was constitutionally unjust.[35]

This was the beginning of law-talk in the Morcha discourse. Morcha prepared a memorandum that it presented to numerous political leaders, including Prime Minister Manmohan Singh in 2005, which framed its opposition to the *Dalit* Muslim exclusion as a violation of constitutional equality.[36] It noted that:

> Dalits among Muslims ... are still denied of it [*sic*, the Scheduled Caste status], although there are many socio-professional groups in Muslim community ... which are socially, educationally and professionally similar to those found in Dalit of Hindu community [*sic*].

According to the Morcha, this exclusion was "contradictory ... [i]n a secular country like India." The memorandum carefully annotated extracts of the *Indra Sawhney* decision, highlighting the portions where the Supreme Court had recognized the existence of Muslim social stratification and had defined caste as "occupational."

Explaining *Morcha's* use of the constitutional discourse, Ejaz Ali told me:

> We looked at this [legal sources] later, but realized that this was exactly what we had been arguing. Just look at the judgment [*Indra Sawhney*]. The Court has accepted that caste is socio-professional, and exists among Muslims. The exclusion of *Dalit* Muslims is unconstitutional and discriminatory. Either you say you are secular and believe in equality, and remove the religious bar; or accept that this country is not secular and keep the exclusion. You cannot have it both ways.[37]

While the explicit endorsement of *subordinated* caste and references to Muslim social stratification made *Indra Sawhney* a relevant symbolic resource for Morcha, this process must be understood in a more complex fashion. As I point out above, the decision did not mandate the extension of the SC status to Muslims; and its recognition of Muslim caste was ambivalent at best. What made the decision symbolically resourceful was the ability of the Morcha to mobilize and activate legal meaning in a strategic fashion: the Court's decision was constructed by the *Dalit* Muslims in a resourceful manner.

---

[35] Interview with Kamal Ashraf, dated January 6, 2014 (on file with author).

[36] All India United Muslim Morcha, Memorandum to the Prime Minister, "For Inclusion of Dalit Muslims in Scheduled Caste Reservation under Article 341," dated April 19, 2005.

[37] Interview with Ejaz Ali, January 4, 2014 (on file with author).

This "dialectic" quality of the law-talk in Morcha is captured by what social movement literature calls "interpretive framing." This is related to how social movement actors make sense of their world through a process of meaning-making.[38] This perspective, as Snow notes, "is rooted in the symbolic inter-actionist and constructionist principle that meanings do not automatically or naturally attach themselves to the objects, events, or experiences we encounter, but often arise, instead, through interactively based interpretive processes."[39] Social movement actors are "signifying agents" that engage in meaning construction.[40] Transformed into mobilizing tools, interpretive framing results in a "collective frame" that interprets the state of affairs in order to "activate adherents, transform bystanders into supporters, exact concessions from targets, and demobilize antagonists."[41]

For Morcha, constitutional equality became the collective mobilizing frame through its construction and interpretation of *Indra Sawhney*. It mobilized the decision's acceptance of *subordinated* caste and the recognition – albeit partial – of Muslim caste as a legal endorsement of its claims. The legal framing allowed Morcha to position its claims against its opposition. As Ejaz Ali recalled: "We told them [unsympathetic political actors and state bodies] that this was not a political issue. It was a constitutional issue. Our Constitution gives us these rights, and you are taking them away from us."[42]

This framing soon started to reflect in Morcha's interventions and the public discourse around *Dalit* Muslim exclusion. Morcha spent years persuading the political party elites in the State of Bihar, and increasingly came to deploy the legal framing. In 1999, as they stood outside, the State Assembly passed a resolution asking the Central Government to remove the religious bar. One of the members of the Bihar Council argued – reflecting constitutional equality and *subordinated* caste – that the "Constitution [was] not on the basis of religion ... But how is this just if a *dhobi* [washerman caste] is an SC and a Muslim *dhobi* is not."[43] In the 2000 Insaaf (Justice) Conference in New Delhi, Ejaz Ali demanded *Dalit* Muslim inclusion and argued that "the

---

[38] David A. Snow, Robert D. Benford, et al., "Ideology, Frame Resonance, and Participant Mobilization," *International Social Movement Research* 1, no. 1 (1988): 197–217; David A. Snow and Robert D. Benford, "Master Frames and Cycles of Protest," *Frontiers in Social Movement Theory*, 1992, 137; Sidney G. Tarrow, *Power in Movement: Social Movements and Contentious Politics*, 3rd ed. (Cambridge University Press, 2011), 144.

[39] David A. Snow, Sarah A. Soule, and Hanspeter Kriesi, eds., *The Blackwell Companion to Social Movements*, 1 ed. (Wiley-Blackwell, 2007), 384 (reference removed).

[40] Id.

[41] Id. at 385. See also Snow, Benford, et al., "Ideology, Frame Resonance, and Participant Mobilization."

[42] Interview with Ejaz Ali, January 4, 2014 (on file with author).

religious bar [was] against the letter and spirit of secularism" under the Constitution.[44] This argument was reflected in the parliamentary bill backed by Morcha in 2000. While the bill failed, its "Objects and Purposes" stated that their exclusion was "against the Fundamental Rights" and hence "an unconstitutional act." In its pamphlets, Morcha called their "paradoxical" exclusion a "fraud on constitution [*sic*],"[45] and a "blot on the face of our secular constitution."[46] And *Indra Sawhney* was a useful resource to make this claim. Quoting the decision, Ejaz Ali argued that "the presence of caste systems [*sic*] among non-Hindu religion has been proved several times in this historic Mandal's judgment ... [The] Apex court has already given [the] verdict which is by now universal for all type of reservation."[47]

Before moving on to the evaluation of the outcomes that the legal framing may have achieved, it would be worthwhile to further underline the context in which *Indra Sawhney* and constitutional equality became symbolically relevant for Morcha. Situating this context helps us understand how and why court decisions become attractive symbolic resources for social movement mobilization.

The legal framing and appropriation of *Indra Sawhney* in Morcha happened because of the resistance it faced – from the bureaucracy, and unsympathetic members of the media and political parties. While none of these actors could be easily influenced through Morcha's political-electoral mobilization, law-talk was particularly well suited to address them. Through the framing in terms of the Constitution, Morcha was seeking legitimacy for its demands. Specifically, it could articulate its demands not as *merely political* but as *constitutional and legal*. Of course, what this required was a broader political context in which the Indian constitutional discourse has the cultural traction to legitimize political action – or what many law and-social movement scholars have called the "legitimating effects of legal discourse."[48]

---

[43] See Bihar Legislative Council – April 17, 1999 (Session 133), speech of Shakil Ahmed Khan, p. 3. See also Speech of Tulsi Singh, p. 9; Proceedings of Bihar Assembly, July 21, 2000, speech of Shashikumar Rai.

[44] Andalib Akhter, "Muslim Dalits Demand Parity with other Dalits," *The Milli Gazette*, www.milligazette.com/Archives/15102002/1510200258.htm (last visited March 20, 2015).

[45] Ejaz Ali, Mandal's Judgements & Dalit Muslim Reservation, undated.

[46] Ejaz Ali, Jihad, All India Backward Muslim Morcha, undated, p. 6.

[47] Ejaz Ali, Mandal's Judgements & Dalit Muslim Reservation, undated.

[48] Amy Kapczynski, "The Access to Knowledge Mobilization and the New Politics of Intellectual Property," *The Yale Law Journal* 117 (2008): 865–866. See also Nicholas Pedriana, "From Protective to Equal Treatment: Legal Framing Processes and Transformation of the Women's Movement in the 1960s," *American Journal of Sociology* 111, no. 6 (2006): 1718–1761; Scheingold, *The Politics of Rights: Lawyers, Public Policy, and Political Change*.

I cannot fully develop this claim here, but the bare fact that the constitutional discourse appeared to Morcha as an attractive "collective frame" points to this cultural background. *Indra Sawhney* became an important symbolic resource in the context of the barriers that other methods – in particular electoral methods – could not remove, and in the cultural background of constitutional legitimacy.

Moreover, the symbolic relevance of *Indra Sawhney* was also contingent on an existing and highly motivated social movement infrastructure. Scholars such as Charles Epp have noted the crucial role of grassroots mobilization by advocacy groups – or what he calls the "support structure of legal mobilization" – for the creation of the growing centrality of rights for courts.[49] I point to the "support structure" for a different reason. As our case study shows, court decisions became pertinent only when Morcha was able to expend its resources to generate legal literacy among its members and to mobilize legal meaning.

IV. CONSEQUENCES OF FRAME ALIGNMENT

In this section, I delineate four ways in which Morcha's adoption of the legal collective framing – through the appropriation of *Indra Sawhney* – affected their mobilization. First, the legal framing allowed them to reach out to the political elites within the Muslim community. Secondly, Morcha's network deployed its legal framing in the outreach toward its potential constituents and the creation of the *Dalit* Muslim identity. Thirdly, the collective framing in terms of constitutional equality contributed to it reaching out to political elites and the State machinery. And fourthly, the legal framing laid the possibilities of a new strategy toward reform in the shape of class litigation in the Supreme Court.

None of these were the consequences *only* of Morcha's legal framing. In this section, I point out the role of the other factors. Nevertheless, I also note how these factors dynamically interacted to produce the changes I discuss.

A. *Reaching out to intra-community elites*

The challenge for Morcha since the time of its inception was to reach out and persuade its political audience: the political parties – at the State and Central level – as well as the bureaucrats and government bodies in charge of shaping

---

[49] Charles R. Epp, *The Rights Revolution: Lawyers, Activists, and Supreme Courts in Comparative Perspective*, 1st ed. (University of Chicago Press, 1998).

policy. But interestingly, apart from these two sets of players, the biggest opposition to Morcha's demands came from within the Muslim community.

While this is still the case to a major extent, Muslim electoral and civil society politics was primarily dominated by upper-caste Muslims at the time of Morcha's inception.[50] This leadership consistently refused to acknowledge the *Dalit* Muslim claims. One source of their suspicion was the fear that an acceptance of Muslim social stratification – which was the basis of Morcha's demands – would fracture their electoral constituency. For example, an influential Muslim leader blamed organizations such as *Morcha* for "dividing a cohesive" community,[51] and reducing its "political weight and . . . bargaining power."[52] Religious clerics in particular interpreted claims of Muslim social stratification as both divisive and un-Islamic. For them, *Morcha* represented the agenda of introducing "caste" – a notion fundamentally contrary to Islam's proclaimed egalitarian principle – in the Muslim community.

The initial strategy of Morcha was antagonism. In its early politics, Morcha leadership attacked the upper-caste Muslim leadership for ignoring the everyday issues of Muslims. They also insisted that while Islam was against the caste system, the Muslim society reflected casteism. In a 2002 interview, Ejaz Ali argued that:

> The idea of setting up [Morcha] stemmed partially from a recognition of the complete failure of the traditional Muslim leadership . . . In this the Hindutva [Hindu right wing] forces . . . and the traditional Muslim leadership, which wants to maintain its hegemony and control over the community, seem to be acting in tandem with each other, playing on emotional issues and diverting the attention of the Muslim masses from issues of vital importance . . . a new Muslim leadership should emerge, championing the issues that concern the survival and progress of the poorest Muslims.[53]

---

[50]   Irfan Ahmad, "A Different Jihad: Dalit Muslims' Challenge to Ashraf Hegemony," *Economic and Political Weekly* 38, no. 46 (November. 15–21, 2003): 4886–4891. Mohammad Sajjad, *Muslim Politics in Bihar: Changing Contours* 274, 1st ed. (2014); Khalid Anis Ansari, "Rethinking the Pasmanda Movement," *Economic & Political Weekly* 44, no. 13 (2009): 8–10; Khalid Anis Ansari, "Pluralism, Civil Society and Subaltern Counterpublics," Plur. Work. Pap. Ser. Pap. No 92011 (2011), www.hivos.nl/knowledge/content/download/65367/541333/file/PWP %20no%209%20Pluralism,%20Civil%20Society%20and%20Subaltern%20Counterpublics% 20online.pdf (last visited October 1, 2013); for a famous critique based on a study of Muslim presence in political parties and civil society, see Ali Anwar Ansari, *Masawaat Ki Jung - Pasemanzar: Bihar Ke Pasmaanda Musalman* (Freedom Books, 2007).

[51]   *See* Shahabuddin Demands Separate Quota for Muslims, September 28, 1991, *Muslim India* 107 (November 1991): 509.

[52]   See also Inclusion of Muslims in SC List Harmful- Shahabuddin's Reply to Ejaz Ali, 16 June, 1999, in *Muslim India* 199 (July 1999): 318.

By the time its demands started to coalesce around "Agenda 341," Morcha's aggressive posturing started to reflect discrete – and significant – changes. Ejaz Ali and his comrades started approaching and persuading the upper-caste Muslim leadership, and the religious leadership in particular. And their articulation in terms of constitutional categories played an important role in this process. Speaking about his strategy, Ejaz Ali told me:

> We met all the major Muslim leaders. We met Ali Miya [Maulana Nadwi, an influential North Indian Muslim religious cleric], who had been our critic. We told him that nothing in our demands was unconstitutional. He thought we were saying that Islam had caste. We explained to him the constitutional position: how various occupational groups were getting affirmative action benefits under the law. We told him that it was unjust, morally and legally, that Muslim occupations are bereft of these constitutional benefits when the same occupations from other communities are getting it. This is not a religious issue. It is a constitutional issue.[54]

Continuing with this strategy, Morcha diluted its trenchant political critique of the Muslim leadership.[55] Rather than posing itself as a political – and potentially electoral – opponent, it came to foreshadow its *legal* demand.

By 2009, the previous objections from Muslim religious and political leaders became rare. Prominent organization representing Muslims, which were dominated by what Morcha had called upper-caste Muslims, endorsed the *Dalit* Muslim demand.[56] This was also reflected in the positions of prominent religious organizations.[57] Morcha's legal framing was not the only reason for this transformation. In part, it was the result of the failure of the Muslim leadership to get affirmative action for all Muslims. Nevertheless, the

---

[53] Yoginder Sikand, "Dalit Muslims," accessed February 23, 2015, www.outlookindia.com/article/Dalit-Muslims/216144.

[54] Interview with Ejaz Ali, January 6, 2014 (on file with author).

[55] This perceptible shift – toward amity with the dominant Muslim leadership – resulted in a split in Morcha in 1998 and the creation of a new "backward class" Muslim organization, the Pasmanda Mahaz. See Interview with Usman Halalkhor, dated January 8, 2014 (on file with author).

[56] Social Justice Movement: National Conference, New Delhi October 7, 1998 Resolution (Extracts), *Muslim India* 191 (November 1998): 510; Convention on Reservation in Education, New Delhi, August 29, 2006 – Resolution, *Muslim India* 267 (September 2005): 88, 85; Declaration of Muslims as Backward Class- Shahabuddin's Letter to PM's High Level Committee, August 30, 2005; Resolution of the Muslim Convention for Reservation, February 2, 2009, Delhi; National Workshop of Muslim NGOs, New Delhi, December 22–24, 2006: Brief Report & Resolutions, *Muslim India* 272 (February 2007): 20–1.

[57] "Muslim and Christian Leaders Meet Home Minister on Reservation for Dalit Muslims and Christians," *The Milli Gazette*, January 22, 2010, www.milligazette.com/dailyupdate/2010/20100122_002_Reservation_Dalit_Muslims_Christians.htm.

importance of legal framing lay in neutralizing this leadership's reservations. The ubiquity of the constitutional discourse in their supporting statements makes this apparent. For example, a prominent religious cleric supported the *Dalit* Muslim demand on the ground that their exclusion was "against the spirit of the Constitution."[58] Similarly, observers of deliberations within the Muslim community have noted the "forceful" and ubiquitous theme of the exclusion's illegality.[59] The demand was neither perceived to be un-Islamic nor politically divisive.

B. *Building a* Dalit *Muslim constituency*

Scholars of legal mobilization have noted the catalytic role of law in social movement politics: law's role in generating consciousness among constituents by providing a "normative language for identifying, interpreting, and challenging" the unjust state of affairs.[60] Since legal framing appeared in the Morcha discourse years after its inception, there is little evidence that constitutional equality and *Indra Sawhney's* catalytic function for the organization. Morcha's early successes with its constituents are better understood as the politicization of their everyday caste-based exclusion during and after the Mandal mobilization.

Nevertheless, the more recent mobilizations through the larger *Dalit* Muslim network of Morcha that I was able to observe a specific catalytic function of legal framing. The legal framing has played an *inscribing* function among the *Dalit* Muslim constituents, who come to see their identity in a positive and assertive light rather than as a form of stigmatization.

The biggest challenge for *Dalit* Muslim leaders in building their constituency was their early caste framing. The potential constituents were reluctant to accept the stigmatized *Dalit* or SC label because of its association with untouchability and "pollution." As a prominent Muslim "backward class" leader told me, "Even those Muslims who were suffering in their dire conditions, and who knew that they would get benefits did not want to associate with our cause. They did not want to be called Untouchables."[61]

---

[58] "Muslim Groups Back SC Status for Muslim, Christian Dalits," Rediffwww.rediff.com/news/report/muslim-groups-back-sc-status-for-muslim-christian-dalits/20120131.htm, accessed October 1, 2016.

[59] Mumtaz Alam Falahi, "Table Misra Report, Include Dalit Muslims in SCs: Muslim MPs, Intellectuals," *The Milli Gazette*, July 18, 2009, http://twocircles.net/2009jul18/table_misra_report_include_dalit_muslims_scs_muslim_mps_intellectuals.html#.V-_E45N95E5.

[60] McCann, *Rights at Work*, 48–91.

[61] Interview with Shabbir Ahmad Ansari, September 26, 2013 (on file with author).

Dalit Muslim leaders came to deploy a similar strategy that they used in persuading the Muslim elite. They told their constituents that the category of SC was not a stigmatized category, but a "secular and constitutional" category.[62] Morcha leaders told me that this strategy convinced *Dalit* Muslims that demanding SC status was a matter of getting State benefits through their constitutional rights.

Since Morcha leaders made these claims, it is difficult to verify the success of this strategy among the *Dalit* Muslims that the organization first mobilized in Bihar. Therefore, I base my arguments on the activities of the Khatik Samaj in the State of Maharashtra. Khatik Samaj – an organization representing the Muslim butcher caste – became actively involved in *Dalit* Muslim activism as a part of Morcha's larger national network. In 2014 and 2015, it organized a series of outreach rallies among Khatiks and other *Dalit* Muslims to generate awareness, especially for their Supreme Court petition that I discuss in Part IV.D. From September to December 2014, I followed these outreach rallies and observed their tactics and strategies.

One of the most striking features of the outreach rallies and strategies was the appropriation and deployment of the constitutional rights discourse by the movement leaders. Most of the speeches usually started with framing the demand for the *Dalit* Muslim inclusion as a claim for "joining the national mainstream" and gaining recognition of constitutional rights. For example, Javed Pasha, one of the lead speakers, told a crowd of 300 people on September 19, 2013 in Bandra (Mumbai) that:

> The preamble of the Constitution says that there shall be no discrimination on the basis of religion. This has been written in the Constitution. Isn't the Constitution secular? Our fight is for the Constitution. We are not throwing darts in the dark. Had that been the case, then we would not have received any support in the Parliament and in the Legislative Assemblies ... The Presidential Order us anti-national – it kills the spirit of the Constitution, it's secular principle ... This is a nationalistic movement ... It is a movement for the Constitution, to protect its soul.

This was consistently the framing for all the speakers. The movement leaders often repeated that the 1950 Order had "strangled the Constitution,"[63] and had "defrauded" not just the Muslims but the Constitution as well.[64] Apart from the speeches, the outreach materials and posters also had a conspicuous

---

[62] See Interview with Shabbir Ahmad Ansari, September 26, 2013 (on file with author); Interview with Riasuddin Bakhho, dated January 8, 2014 (on file with author).

[63] Speech by Shamsher Khan Pathan, Bandra (Mumbai), September 19, 2013.

[64] Speech of Meeraj Siddiqui, Aurangabad, September 29, 2013.

presence of the Constitution and its specific provisions. The posters that called for a larger participation among *Dalit* placed the constitutional provisions of against discrimination right at the center of its framing.

The foregrounding of the Constitution resonated with the audience of these outreach rallies – mostly daily wage *Dalit* Muslims. In particular, they widely shared two themes. The first was a feeling of constitutional betrayal. One member of the audience told me after the rally:

> We were given this Constitution by Ambedkar [Dr. B. R. Ambedkar, the Chairperson of the Constitution's Drafting Committee and an iconic *Dalit* leader]. And he ensured that everyone would get their rights. But these political parties have conspired against his wishes and against his Constitution.[65]

A strong association with the SC category accompanied this widely shared perception of political deceit. I was told:

> Being Scheduled Caste is not a bad thing. They [Muslim religious leaders] tell us this, but they are wrong. This is just the word the Constitution uses for people from our occupations, and those who are very poor like us. We will not become Hindus or untouchables. We will get the rights that the Constitution promises us.[66]

All the constituents I met extensively shared the centrality of the "constitutional" – and thus the non-religious character – of the SC category. In these discursive practices, the legal framing was contributing to the creation of the political identity of *Dalit* Muslims. As scholars have noted, collective framing does this by articulating "specific claims ... about a group's strategic, moral, and cathectic or relational character."[67] The legal framing in the case I discuss allowed the *Dalit* Muslims to distance their identity from the stigmatized practices of dehumanization, and adopt a positive rights-based relationship through the Constitution.

---

[65] Field notes, September 19, 2013, Bandra (Mumbai).
[66] Field notes, September 21, 2013, Kurla (Mumbai).
[67] Scott A. Hunt, Robert D. Benford, and David A. Snow, "Identity Fields: Framing Processes and the Social Construction of Movement Identities," *New Social Movements: From Ideology to Identity* edi. Enrique Laraña, Hank Johnston, and Joseph R. Gusfield (Temple University Press, 1994): 185–208. See also Francesca Polletta and James M. Jasper, "Collective Identity and Social Movements," *Annual Review of Sociology* 27 (2000): 283–305; Alberto Melucci, "Getting Involved: Identity and Mobilization in Social Movements," *International Social Movement Research* 1, no. 4 (1988): 329–348.

C. Reaching out to the state and political elites

By 2007, the *Dalit* Muslim demands had gained national attention. This was in part the contribution of two government-sanctioned studies that recommended their inclusion in the SC category: the 2006 Report of the Prime Minister's High Level Committee headed by Justice R. Sachar, and the 2007 Report of the National Commission for Religious and Linguistic Minorities headed by Justice R. Misra.[68] The Misra Commission, in particular, endorsed the conception of *subordinated Dalit* caste that *Morcha* had been advocating. It noted that caste was "a social phenomenon . . . shared by almost all Indian communities irrespective of their religious persuasions." The *Dalit* Muslim exclusion "conflict[ed] with the letter and spirit of the constitutional provisions," and recommended the Government to "de-link the Scheduled Caste status from religion and make the Scheduled Castes net fully religion-neutral."[69]

Unlike the cases of intra-Muslim elites and constituency building, legal framing – or even Morcha – may not have played the central role in these endorsements. The slow process of setting up an institutional inquiry into the *Dalit* Muslim and *Dalit* Christian demands had started as early as 1980, when the Minorities Commission of India received numerous individual petitions against the Muslim exclusion.[70] The Commission appears to have shown an inclination toward the removal of the bar, but expressed the need for a thorough empirical investigation that did not happen for another two decades. It was only in 1995 – around the time of a heightened *Dalit* Muslim activism under Morcha – that the Commission, now called the National Commission for Minorities, strongly recommended the removal of the bar.[71] Further, in 2005, the Commission set up another extensive study on the conditions of *Dalit* Muslims that – after reporting extreme socioeconomic marginalization – finally recommended their inclusion in the SC category.

Therefore, by the time the two inquiries were constituted, the inclusion of *Dalit* Muslims already had an institutional past. But what made them different

---

[68] Prime Minister's High Level Committee, Social, Economic and Educational Status of the Muslim Community in India: A Report (2006), www.minorityaffairs.gov.in/sites/upload_files/moma/files/pdfs/sachar_comm.pdf [hereinafter *Sachar Committee Report*]; 1 & 2 Ministry of Minority Affairs, Report of the National Commission for Religious and Linguistic Minorities (2007), www.minorityaffairs.gov.in/sites/upload_files/moma/files/pdfs/volume-1.pdf [hereinafter *Misra Commission Report*].

[69] *Misra Commission Report* §16.3.3.

[70] *See Third Annual Report of the Minorities Commission* 31–2 (December 31, 1980).

[71] *See* Letter to the Secretary of the Government of India, dated August 3, 1995, IO-45/95-NCM.

from the previous cases was an unprecedented involvement of Muslim groups – *Dalit* Muslims and others – in the consultative process.[72] Members and affiliates of Morcha made numerous representations to the evidence-collection teams.[73] Moreover, with the emergent consensus among all sections of the Muslim community, these interventions were united in their disavowal of the religious bar. During these interventions, the legal framing became one of the central modes of opposition.[74] Each of these elements was at least partly influenced by Morcha's legal framing strategies.

D. *New strategies*

In 2008, the Khatik Samaj decided to file a class petition – or a public interest petition – in the Supreme Court, challenging the constitutionality of the 1950 Order.[75] This was not the first time *Dalit* Muslims had approached the courts. For example, numerous petitions had been filed in the Bombay High Court since the 1980s. These petitions arose from public service conflicts and had been filed by individuals.[76] But it was only in 2008 that a *Dalit* Muslim organization had filed a petition – that too in the Supreme Court.

Not all the affiliates of the broader *Dalit* Muslim movement agreed with this strategy. In particular, Morcha had consistently maintained that the litigation strategy was ill suited for the movement. This was not because of the organizations suspicion of the legal discourse. On the contrary, by this time, Morcha had started to lay extensive claim to constitutional equality. The reason was Ejaz Ali's suspicion of the judicial institutions. He told me:

The courts do not decide based on law. They decide based on media, newspapers. There should be enough *baichaini* [restlessness] on the ground,

---

[72] The Sachar Report noted that during the consultative process "[a]ctivists made a strong case for the inclusion of Muslim groups with similar occupation as that of Hindu SCs in the SC list." See *Sachar Committee Report* 194.

[73] Interview of Ali Anwar Ansari, July 23, 2013 (on file with author); Interview with Salahuddin Shibu, June 23, 2013 (on file with author).

[74] See *Sachar Committee Report* 202.

[75] *Akhil Maharastra Khatik Samaj* v. *Union of India*, Writ Petition (C) No. 13 of 2008.

[76] See, e.g., *Shamsul Haque Qureshi* v. *MPSC/State of Maharashtra*, W.P. No. 839/89 (hereinafter *S.H. Qureshi*); *Bahana Samaj Kalyan Mandal*, W.P. No. 3342/97; *Nasir Khan* v. *Caste Scrutiny Committee*, W.P. No. 3385/97; *Dr. Qayyum Khan* v. *Returning Officer, Gondia*, W.P. No. 814/99; *Abdul Aqueel s/o Sk. Ismail* v. *Nagar Parishad Achalpur*, W.P. No. 4154/2000. Three other cases were filed but their details are unknown. These include *Niyaz Ahmad* v. *Nagar Parishad* (represented by Advocate Kasat), *Abdul Mannan* v. *Nagar Parishad, Umerkhed* (represented by Advocate Gilda) and a case represented by Advocate M. Z. Haque.

among our people. Otherwise we will not win the case. And once we lose, we
cannot even fight politically.[77]

Consequently, Morcha decided to pursue the strategic course of grassroots
mobilization, while creating political pressure on and persuading political
elites.[78]

But behind the variation in the perception of the judiciary, there is potentially another reason for the differing reform strategies. Morcha was well
placed in the highly electorally competitive states (or provinces), such as
Bihar, to garner political mileage. The state had five key political parties,
out of which four were eyeing the Muslim vote.[79] In this electorally competitive space, Morcha was able to position itself as an influential Muslim player.
During the election cycle, Morcha often threatened to support one party over
the other.[80] This political influence contributed to one of the main parties
nominating Ejaz Ali to the upper house of the Parliament in 2008. As opposed
to Bihar, the State of Maharashtra is far less electorally competitive – being
essentially a bipolar competition between the Hindu right-wing parties and
the "secular" ones. This drastically reduces the maneuvering space for *Dalit*
Muslim organizations to influence political decisions. In this context of
limited political opportunities, litigation appears as a stronger strategy for
reform.

Beyond these two reasons, the normalization of the *Dalit* Muslim legal
claims played an important role in the choice to litigation as strategy. Mahmood Nawaz, one of the prominent members of Khatik Samaj and the funder
of the litigation campaign was aware of the religious bar since the 1980s
through the individual petitions that had been filed in the Bombay High
Court. But it was only by 2007, when legal framing has familiarized him and
his comrades with the potential veracity of the legal case, that he decided to
invest in an expensive litigation. His confidence in his case was also reinforced
by the endorsements of the Sachar and Misra reports.[81]

---

[77] Interview with Ejaz Ali, January 5, 2014 (on file with author).
[78] *An Interview with Ejaz Ali* (twocirclesTV, 2011), 22, www.youtube.com/watch?v=K53Zc6Otei8.
[79] These political parties include the Congress, Janata Dal (United), Rashtriya Janata Dal, Lok
    Jan Shakti Party, and the BJP. Except for the BJP, the other parties compete for the
    Muslim vote.
[80] *See* Sajjad, *Muslim Politics in Bihar*, 301–302.
[81] Interviews of Mahmood Nawaz, September 19–25, 2013, Bandra (Mumbai).

V. CONCLUSION

In this chapter, I have made two separate but related claims about the impact of *Indra Sawhney*. The first is the impact of the decision on the activities of Morcha itself. *Indra Sawhney* endorsed *subordinated* caste – which conceptualized caste as a transreligious, sociological, and secular institution – and referred to Muslim social stratification. Nevertheless, the decision was neither about the SC category, nor could it fully overcome the ambivalence toward "Muslim caste." What made it a relevant symbolic resource for Morcha was the dialectical process of legal framing. Morcha constructed the intonations and the silences of the decision as an endorsement of its claims.

The second impact of the decision was indirect, though equally unintended. Morcha's legal framing facilitated it to reach out to its critics among the Muslim elite and construct a positive collective identity for its constituents. Morcha and its affiliates also managed to get institutional endorsements, which came to voice their constitutional positions; and they also built new strategies in terms of litigation. The latter two did not result purely from the legal framing. But the larger political consequences of *Indra Sawhney* – which had strengthened the mobilization – came to aid these developments.

Some of the most profound facets of this *Dalit* Muslim story are worthy of generalization, both in terms of our assessment of the impact of court decisions or litigation, as well as our assessment of how to approach this inquiry in the Indian context. The *Dalit* Muslim mobilization teaches us that we should be open to appreciating the unintended and indirect, yet significant consequences of court decisions. In the case of *Indra Sawhney*, what mattered for the *Dalit* Muslim mobilization were those textual fragments of the judgment that were legally marginal. But soon they were both politically – and legally – salient. These textual fragments, which lawyers will describe as mere *obiter dicta*, became resources for symbolic legitimation, political opportunity, and court litigation for the *Dalit* Muslim mobilization.

The *Dalit* Muslim mobilization was able to appropriate the Supreme Court's decision, and with it the Indian Constitution's promise of the right to equality, in the most creative of ways. This reflects an extension of what historian Rohit De has called the "multiple lives of law" – where litigants before the courts come to use laws in ways that go far beyond the historically pedigreed boundaries.[82] The "multiple lives of law" traverse multiple spaces – parliaments, courts, and in our case the unruly domain of political

---

[82] Rohit De, "Mumtaz Bibi's Broken Heart: The Many Lives of the Dissolution of Muslim Marriages Act," *The Indian Economic & Social History Review* 46, no. 1 (2009): 105–130.

mobilizations. They also traverse the multiple forms that the law takes – statutes, constitutions, and in our case court decisions. They invite officials as much as actors such as our legally illiterate "low caste" Muslims. The assessment of judicial impact has to consider the slipperiness of legal meaning and authoritative interpretation.

The *Dalit* Muslim story also cautions us about the specific context in India that should be taken seriously while assessing judicial impact. Enforcement of law – rights, court decisions, or the Constitution – is very much about political negotiation in India.[83] This places both the political electoral context and the existence of partisan support on an important footing. Politics matters for the impact of court decisions in India. So does the existence of political infrastructure. My account of Morcha hasbrought out one dimension of this facet. The existence of social movement infrastructure allowed for the activation of *Indra Sawhney*. This infrastructure was the creative force in the appropriation and interpretation of the Court's decision. At the same time, the strategies adopted by this infrastructure were contingent on the political-electoral possibilities. More specifically, while law-talk in its various forms was viable and useful in some electoral contexts, litigation was attractive in the others. If we are to fully appreciate the impact of courts, we need to relate the political and institutional constraints that may push political actors to adopt diverse utilizations of court decisions.

REFERENCES

Ahmad, Imtiaz. "Introduction." In *Caste and Social Stratification among Muslims in India*, edited by Imtiaz Ahmad, xvii. South Asia Books (Manohar, 1978).
Akhter, Andalib. "Muslim Dalits Demand Parity with Other Dalits." *The Milli Gazette.* www.milligazette.com/Archives/15102002/1510200258.htm (accessed March 20, 2015).
Ali, Ejaz. "Anti-Islamic Elite Muslims Opposed to Reservations for the Oppressed." *Dalit Voice*, January 16, 1996.
"Jihad." Undated manuscript.
"Kyon Chaahiye Musalmano Ko Aarakshan?" *Veer Arjun*, October 13, 1996.
"Mandal's Judgements & Dalit Muslim Reservation." Undated manuscript.
"Mandal's Judgements & Dalit Muslim Reservation." N.d. *An Interview with Ejaz Ali*. twocirclesTV, 2011. www.youtube.com/watch?v=K53Zc6Otei8 (accessed September 1, 2018).

[83] For a discussion on law enforcement and the Indian state, *see* Upendra Baxi, *The Crisis of the Indian Legal System* (Vikas, 1982), 24–25.

Ansari, Ali Anwar. "Bihar Ke Musalmanon Ki Rajniti Ke Rang Badalne Lage." N.d. *Masawaat Ki Jung - Pasemanzar: Bihar Ke Pasmaanda Musalman.* Freedom Books, 2007.

Ansari, Khalid Anis. "Pluralism, Civil Society and Subaltern Counterpublics." Plur. Work. Pap. Ser. Pap. No 92011 (2011), www.hivos.nl/knowledge/content/down load/65367/541333/file/PWP%20no%209%20Pluralism,%20Civil%20Society% 20and%20Subaltern%20Counterpublics%20online.pdf (accessed October 1, 2013).

"Rethinking the Pasmanda Movement." *Economic & Political Weekly* 8–10 (2009).

Baxi, Upendra. *The Crisis of the Indian Legal System.* Vikas, 1982.

Bhat, M. Mohsin Alam. "Conflict, Integration and Constitutional Culture: Affirmative Action and Muslims in India." JSD Dissertation, Yale Law School, 2017.

"Convention on Reservation in Education, New Delhi, 29 August, 2006 – Resolution." *Muslim India* 267 (September 2005): 88, 85.

"Muslim Caste under Indian Law: Between Uniformity, Autonomy and Equality." *Quaderni Di Diritto e Politica Ecclesiastica* 20, Special Issue (2017): 165.

De, Rohit. "Mumtaz Bibi's Broken Heart: The Many Lives of the Dissolution of Muslim Marriages Act." *The Indian Economic & Social History Review* 46, no. 1 (2009): 105–130.

Deshpande, Satish. "Dalits in the Muslim and Christian Communities: A Status Report on Current Social Scientific Knowledge." National Commission for Minorities, Government of India, January 17, 2008. http://ncm.nic.in/pdf/report %20dalit%20%20reservation.pdf.

Dhavan, Rajeev. "Divide, Sub-Divide, Rule, Editorial, the Pioneer, 9 March, 1996." Extracted in *Muslim India* 161 (May 1996): 227.

"The Supreme Court as Problem Solver: The Mandal Controversy." In *The Politics of Backwardness - Reservation Policy in India*, edited by V. A. Pai Panandiker, 262. Centre for Policy Research, 1997.

Epp, Charles R. *The Rights Revolution: Lawyers, Activists, and Supreme Courts in Comparative Perspective.* 1st edition. University of Chicago Press, 1998.

Eskridge, William N. "Channeling: Identity-Based Social Movements and Public Law." *University of Pennsylvania Law Review* 150, no. 1 (2001): 419–525.

Falahi, Mumtaz Alam. "Table Misra Report, Include Dalit Muslims in SCs: Muslim MPs, Intellectuals." *The Milli Gazette*, July 18, 2009. http://twocircles.net/ 2009jul18/table_misra_report_include_dalit_muslims_scs_muslim_mps_intellec tuals.html#.V-_E45N95E5.

Galanter, Marc. "Changing Legal Conceptions of Caste." In *Law and Society in Modern India*, edited by Rajeev Dhavan, Reprint, 141. Oxford University Press, 1993.

Competing Equalities: Law and the Backward Classes in India. University of California Press, 1984.

Government of India. Report of the Backward Classes Commission. 1980.

"The Long Half-Life of Reservations." In *India's Living Constitution: Ideas, Practices, Controversies*, edited by Zoya Hasan, E. Sridharan, and R. Sudarshan, 306. Anthem Press, 2005.

Hasan, Zoya. *Politics of Inclusion: Castes, Minorities, and Affirmative Action.* Oxford University Press, 2011.

Human Rights Watch. Hidden Apartheid: Caste Discrimination against India's "Untouchables." 2007. www.hrw.org/report/2007/02/12/hidden-apartheid/caste-dis crimination-against-indias-untouchables (accessed August 25, 2018).

Hunt, Scott A., Robert D. Benford, and David A. Snow. "Identity Fields: Framing Processes and the Social Construction of Movement Identities." In *New Social Movements: From Ideology to Identity*, edited by Enrique Laraña, Hank Johnston, and Joseph R. Gusfield, 185–208, Temple University Press, 1994.

"Inclusion of Muslims in SC List Harmful- Shahabuddin's Reply to Ejaz Ali, 16 June, 1999." *Muslim India* 199 (July 1999): 318.

Indra Sawhney v. Union of India, Supp. (3) SCC 217 (1992).

Jaffrelot, Christophe. *Religion, Caste, and Politics in India*. Primus Books, 2010.

Kapczynski, Amy. "The Access to Knowledge Mobilization and the New Politics of Intellectual Property." *The Yale Law Journal* (2008): 804–885.

Lohia, Rammanohar. "Towards the Destruction of Castes and Classes." In *The Caste System*, Rammanohar Lohia, 79.

McCann, Michael W. "How Does Law Matter for Social Movements?" In *How Does Law Matter* 76, edited by B.G. Garth and A. Sarat, 88, Northwestern University Press, 1998.

"M. Ejaz Ali On Muslim Reservation (excerpted from the *Dalit Voice*)." Extracted from *Muslim India* 22 (October 1999): 472.

Rights at Work: Pay Equity Reform and the Politics of Legal Mobilization. University of Chicago Press, 1994.

Melucci, Alberto. "Getting Involved: Identity and Mobilization in Social Movements." *International Social Movement Research* 1, no. 4 (1988): 329–348.

Mertz, Elizabeth. "A New Social Constructionism for Sociolegal Studies," *Law & Society Review* 28 (1994): 1243–1265.

Ministry of Minority Affairs. "Muslim and Christian Leaders Meet Home Minister on Reservation for Dalit Muslims and Christians." *The Milli Gazette*, January 22, 2010. www.milligazette.com/dailyupdate/2010/20100122_002_Reservation_Dalit_Muslims_Christians.htm.

"Muslim Groups Back SC Status for Muslim, Christian Dalits." Rediff. www.rediff.com/news/report/muslim-groups-back-sc-status-for-muslim-christian-dalits/20120131.htm (accessed October 1, 2016).

"Muslim 'Pariahs' Warn of Quitting Islam." *Times of India*, Patna, July 19, 1994.

"Report of the National Commission for Religious and Linguistic Minorities," May 10, 2007. www.minorityaffairs.gov.in/sites/upload_files/moma/files/pdfs/volume-1.pdf.

Pedriana, Nicholas. "From Protective to Equal Treatment: Legal Framing Processes and Transformation of the Women's Movement in the 1960s." *American Journal of Sociology* 111, no. 6 (2006): 1718–1761.

Polletta, Francesca, and James M. Jasper. "Collective Identity and Social Movements." *Annual Review of Sociology* (2001): 283–305.

Prime Minister's High Level Committee. "Rao, PV for "Dalit Muslim Quota?," *The Pioneer* November 12, 1999." Extracted in *Muslim India* 205 (January 2000): 24.

"Resolution of the Muslim Convention for Reservation, February 2, 2009, Delhi; National Workshop of Muslim NGOs, New Delhi, December 22–24, 2006: Brief Report & Resolutions." *Muslim India* 272 (February 2007): 20.

"Social, Economic and Educational Status of the Muslim Community in India: A Report." Cabinet Secretariat, Government of India, November 17, 2006. www.minorityaffairs.gov.in/sites/upload_files/moma/files/pdfs/sachar_comm.pdf.

Rudolph, Lloyd I., and Susanne Hoeber Rudolph. *The Modernity of Tradition: Political Development in India*. University of Chicago Press, 1984.

Sajjad, Mohammad. *Muslim Politics in Bihar: Changing Contours*. Routledge, 2014.

Scheingold, Stuart A. *The Politics of Rights: Lawyers, Public Policy, and Political Change*. 2nd edition. University of Michigan Press, 2004.

Schneider, Elizabeth M. "The Dialectic of Rights and Politics: Perspectives from the Women's Movement." *New York University Law Review* 61 (1986): 589.

Sikand, Yoginder. "Dalit Muslims." www.outlookindia.com/article/Dalit-Muslims/ 216144 (accessed February 23, 2015)

Islam, Caste, and Dalit-Muslim Relations in India. Global Media Publications, 2004.

Silverstein, Helena. *Unleashing Rights Law, Meaning, and the Animal Rights Movement*. University of Michigan Press, 1996.

Snow, David A., and Robert D. Benford. "Master Frames and Cycles of Protest." *Frontiers in Social Movement Theory* (1992): 133–155.

Snow, David A., Robert D. Benford, et al. "Ideology, Frame Resonance, and Participant Mobilization." *International Social Movement Research* 1, no. 1 (1988): 197–217.

Snow, David A., Sarah A. Soule, and Hanspeter Kriesi, eds. *The Blackwell Companion to Social Movements*. 1st edition. Wiley-Blackwell, 2007.

Snow, David A., Sarah A. Soule, and Hanspeter Kriesi, "Social Justice Movement: National Conference, New Delhi 7 Oct., 98 Resolution." Extracted in *Muslim India* 191 (November 1998): 510.

Tarrow, Sidney G. *Power in Movement: Social Movements and Contentious Politics*. 3rd edition. Cambridge University Press, 2011.

The Untouchables: Subordination, Poverty and the State in Modern India. Cambridge University Press, 1998.

Yadav, Yogendra. "Reconfiguration in Indian Politics: State Assembly Elections, 1993–95." *Economic and Political Weekly* 31 (1996): 95.

"What Is Living and What Is Dead in Rammanohar Lohia?" *Economic & Political Weekly* 45, no. 40 (2010): 93.

8

PUCL v. Union of India
Political Mobilization and the Right to Food

ALYSSA BRIERLEY

I. INTRODUCTION AND THEORETICAL FRAMEWORK

India has struggled with addressing hunger and malnutrition for a substantial part of its history.[1] Famines were not unusual in colonial India,[2] with some so severe that they resulted in the death of a third of the local population, as was the case in 1770 in Lower Bengal and Bihar.[3] In the late nineteenth century, a Famine Commission was established and Famine Codes were developed to support rural livelihoods when drought occurred. This was done by providing relief works in recognition of the fact that the primary cause of famine was a failure of entitlements owing to the reduction of agricultural labor during times of drought.[4] Over time, this intervention proved successful – famines continued in the early twentieth century but eventually ceased, the last having occurred in 1943 in pre-independence Bengal.[5]

While the post-colonial period in India saw marked improvements in famine prevention, the nutritional situation of Indians has persistently lagged behind global norms. As Jean Drèze and Amartya Sen have observed, "India's success in famine prevention seems to have done little to help it prevent

---

[1]   Colin Gonsalves. 2009. *Right to Food.* (4th ed.). New Delhi: Human Rights Law Network. At viii. [*Gonsalves*]; Dan Banik. 2007. *Starvation and India's Democracy.* London and New York: Routledge. At 2–3.

[2]   Jean Drèze. 1991. "Famine Prevention in India." In *The Political Economy of Hunger: Volume 2: Famine Prevention,* edited by Jean Drèze and Amartya Sen, 13–122. Oxford: Clarendon Press. At 20. [*Drèze, 1991.*]

[3]   Government of India. 1880. *Report of the Indian Famine Commission.* London: Her Majesty's Stationary Office. https://archive.org/details/FamineCommission at para. 42.

[4]   Drèze, 1991, *supra* note 2 at 17.

[5]   Jean Drèze and Amartya Sen. 1989. *Hunger and Public Action.* Oxford, Oxford University Press. At 209. [*Drèze and Sen.*]

chronic hunger."[6] India has continued to experience high levels of malnutrition in the general population and staggering rates of malnutrition in children. These indicators stand in stark contrast to the lofty language in the Indian Constitution and a number of Supreme Court judgments that have recognized the right to food as a part of the right to life.

In 2001, a small group of activists decided to file a petition at the Supreme Court following yet another drought that resulted in a number of starvation deaths.[7] The human rights organization, People's Union for Civil Liberties (PUCL), requested that the government provide the massive amounts of food it was storing as a result of its national food procurement and distribution program to those who were starving. This seemingly modest request initiated what became a 16-year court battle to hold the government accountable for the right to food. Coinciding with this court case has been a vibrant civil society movement advocating for the right to food, demonstrating a tremendous amount of political mobilization from the village level to the highest institutions in the country.

Literature that has studied the impact of strategic, public interest or social purpose litigation has long highlighted the important link between litigation and social mobilization. Some scholars have noted the limited nature of court orders in the absence of sustained social mobilization. Gerald Rosenberg's groundbreaking study *The Hollow Hope* looked beyond victories in court to assess the impact of those judgments on the issues they were intended to address.[8] Rosenberg found – much like the activists and organizers who were interviewed for this study – that victories in court on their own do not necessarily result in the changes hoped for by those who were motivated to turn to the court. Rather, it was only after sustained periods of political mobilization by civil society actors that the results intended by the judgments outlined in *The Hollow Hope* were realized in practice.

Michael McCann's *Rights at Work* serves as an important follow up to Rosenberg,[9] and highlights the many ways in which litigation can be helpful in achieving the goals of social movements and activists, irrespective of whether they have been successful in court. McCann identified that this can happen in one of several ways: by contributing to building the social movement; by providing an opportunity for the movement to push for changes

---

[6]   *Id.* at 8.

[7]   *PUCL* v. *Union of India & Ors.* W.P. (C) 196/2001. [*PUCL* v. *Union of India*]

[8]   Gerald Rosenberg. 1991. *The Hollow Hope: Can Courts Bring about Social Change?* Chicago: Chicago University Press. [*Rosenberg.*]

[9]   Michael McCann. 1994. *Rights at Work: Pay Equity Reform and the Politics of Legal Mobilization.* Chicago: Chicago University Press. [*McCann.*]

to policy in a way that corresponds to the movement's demands; by allowing for the social movement to have some degree of control over the reform of policy and its implementation; and by having a transformative impact on issues beyond those that were the subject of the litigation.

This chapter focuses on the first element of McCann's analysis as it applies to the Right to Food litigation in India, namely the impact of the litigation on the formation of the Right to Food campaign. Rosenberg observed in *The Hollow Hope* that "court action may invigorate and encourage groups to mobilize and take political action."[10] Similarly, in *Rights at Work*, McCann found that litigation had an important impact on the subsequent social mobilization and indeed that this may have been one of the most important impacts of such litigation. For McCann, legal advocacy – both in and out of the courts – can catalyze a social movement. In the case of the subject of his inquiry, the pay equity movement in the United States, litigation was used to publicize the issue, which helped to generate "rights consciousness" among aggrieved individuals and communities. However, McCann also found that the resulting mobilization was not consistent throughout the country; therefore, various contextual factors in the form of both "opportunity structures" and "resource distributions" helped to explain the development of mobilization and account for its variability across time and place.

Some scholars have looked at the use of litigation as a deliberate strategy or tactic employed by an already existing social movement. Alan Hunt, for example, argues that litigation must be understood as a tactic "to be deployed within a much broader conception of an essentially political, rather than legal strategy."[11] Similarly, Siri Gloppen has observed that litigation is often one aspect of a larger social mobilization campaign that can include a wide variety of public action.[12] Litigation can help create rights awareness and encourage advocacy by helping marginalized people understand their complaints as rights violations, and it can also bring issues of rights into the social and political discourse, impacting public deliberation of those issues. Simply put, rights claims can help to activate and mobilize people.

---

[10] *Rosenberg, supra* note 8 at 26. Rosenberg referenced Scheingold (1974, 131), who found in his review of the literature on the civil rights struggle in the United States that the victories in court did not have their intended impact, and the failure of court victories to translate to broader social change led movement actors to seek other avenues of political mobilization instead.

[11] Alan Hunt. 1990. "Rights and Social Movements: Counter-Hegemonic Strategies." *Journal of Law and Society* 17(3): 309–328.

[12] Siri Gloppen. 2008. "Litigation as a Strategy to Hold Governments Accountable for Implementing the Right to Health." *Health and Human Rights* 10(2): 21–36.

All of these dynamics are crucial to generating an understanding of the utility and potential impact of court decisions – it is clear, and it is the starting point of this chapter, that court cases can have positive impacts on the social movements themselves, regardless of whether success in court is achieved. However, many questions remain about the nature of the relationship between litigation and social activism, both in terms of the causal dynamics (in what context does social activism lead to litigation, and in what context is the causal relationship reversed) and the explanatory factors (why and how does social mobilization happen), and few studies exist that examine these dynamics in detail using empirical data.

One of the greatest legacies of the *PUCL* case has been the development of the Right to Food campaign ("the Campaign"). Until the case was filed, there was no such campaign;[13] indeed, the Campaign emerged from and became organized around the case.[14] Taking Rosenberg and McCann's findings with respect to the role of courts in catalyzing social movements, this chapter will explore the role of the Indian Supreme Court in creating what has become one of the most significant contemporary social movements in India.

II. STRUCTURE AND METHODOLOGY

Rights at Work serves as a useful starting point for this endeavor. McCann's broad analysis provides a comprehensive review of how and why mobilization occurred in the context of pay equity litigation in the United States as well as the ways in which litigation contributed to the goals of the social movement outside the courtroom in the four specific areas of movement building, policy development, policy implementation and broader transformative change in related areas. While there is evidence that the *PUCL* case contributed to the goals of the Right to Food activists ("the RTF activists") in all four of these areas, the focus of this chapter is limited to the impact of the case on the first: movement building.

Not all litigation results in social mobilization. Indeed, a very similar case on a near identical issue to what was litigated in the *PUCL* case was filed a number of years earlier,[15] raising a similar legal issue and seeking similar relief

---

[13] Interview with Right to Food activist 1. New Delhi. June 20, 2013 [*Activist 1*]; Interview with Right to Food activist 2. New Delhi. July 1, 2013 [*Activist 2*]; Interview with Right to Food activist 3. New Delhi. June 28, 2013 [*Activist 3*]; Interview with Right to Food activist 4. New Delhi. July 2, 2013 [*Activist 4*].

[14] *Id*, *Activist 4*; Mander, Harsh. 2012. "Food from the Courts: The Indian Experience." *IDS Bulletin* 43(S1): 15–24.

[15] *Kishen Pattnayak And Anr. v. State Of Orissa* AIR 1989 SC 677.

in the context of starvation deaths in the Kalahandi district in the state of Odisha.[16] That case did not serve as a catalyst for a widespread national movement for the right to food. McCann's analysis of the changing structures of opportunity and changing organizational resources serves as a way to explain how and why differences were observed between various groups or branches of the movement on pay equity. This serves as the theoretical and analytical starting point for this chapter, which will seek to explain why the *PUCL* case resulted in mobilization but the Odisha matter did not.

Like McCann, this chapter uses a multidimensional methodological approach that includes qualitative data gathering in the form of in-depth personal interviews, on-site data collection, participant observation and secondary academic research. In order to conduct interviews, engage in participant observation and complete on-site data collection, I travelled to India on three occasions between May 2013 and January 2015, spending over five months researching this subject in Delhi, Mumbai, Bangalore, Kolkata, rural West Bengal and rural Chhattisgarh. During that time, I conducted over 100 interviews with lawyers, activists, government officials and individuals on whose behalf the petitioners and activists were working. These interviews were largely unstructured, although attempts were made to cover many of the questions that McCann used in *Rights at Work*, where applicable.[17] Participant observation was conducted by attending various campaign events, attending in person at the Commissioner's office and campaign office, and accompanying campaign and Commissioner's office members in their advocacy work with government officials and in court. On one occasion, I accompanied a team of community-based monitors on an audit of the Mid-Day Meal Scheme (MDMS) in the north of West Bengal, and on several occasions I was able to hear directly from vulnerable and marginalized communities,[18] in Delhi and Mumbai, about the difficulties they faced in accessing the food schemes that the Court in the *PUCL* case ordered as mandatory. While much of this research does not appear directly here, my writing is informed by all of these experiences.

---

[16] The current official name of the state referenced is Odisha; however, at the time of the litigation discussed below, the state's official name was Orissa. I use the previous name of the state in the case citation and the current official name of the state in all other contexts.

[17] My approach to covering similar topics to McCann differed in one key respect: rather than conducting interviews with a goal of generating a statistically significant trend to represent how movement activists felt about a particular issue, the interviews conducted as part of this study were key informant interviews.

[18] This includes the homeless, slum dwellers, those living in shanties, railway stations and those who are socially marginalized, including Dalits and women.

This chapter begins with brief overviews of each of the cases and then turns to an analysis of the variations in the opportunities for reform, followed by the variations in the organizational resources available to the petitioners in each case. The analysis of contextual factors here differs substantially from that of McCann in an important way. In *Rights at Work*, McCann conducted a comparison of various local manifestations of the pay equity movement in different cities throughout the United States during the same time period. Here, the contextual factors differ between the *PUCL* case and the earlier matter in Odisha, in that the comparison crosses not only geography but also time.

III. *PUCL V. UNION OF INDIA*

In the context of a massive drought in Rajasthan, in which media reports highlighted instances of people dying of starvation,[19] local activists under the banner of the PUCL turned to the court for a remedy. In its petition, PUCL asked several questions: whether the right to life included the right to food, and whether the right to life created an obligation on the state to provide food, either to those who could not afford it, or in the event that surplus grains under the control of the State were rotting.[20]

In one of the first orders of the case, the Court extended the application of the petition beyond the Government of India and Food Corporation of India, who were the initial respondents, and included every State and Union Territory government as respondents.[21] The Court also requested that the Government of India respond to the claims of the petitioners by indicating what it was doing to ensure the right to food. In an affidavit to the Court, the government

---

[19] Neelabh Mishra. 2001. "Post-Mortem of Hunger." *Hindustan Times*, April 4, 2001. [*Neelabh Mishra*, 2001.]. Neelabh Mishra. 2001 "Anatomy of Hunger." *Hindustan Times*, May 2001. *Neelabh Mishra*. 2001 "Drought and Deaths." *Frontline*, April 14, 2001. P. Sainath. 2001. "Rajasthan's Drought: Abundance of Food, Scarcity of Vision." *The Hindu*, March 18, 2001.

[20] The specific questions raised in the petition were: "A. Starvation death is a natural phenomenon while there is a surplus stock of food grains in the Government godown. Does the right to life mean that people who are starving and who are too poor to buy food grains ought to be given food grains free of cost by the State from the surplus stock lying with the State, particularly when it is reported that a large part of it is lying unused and rotting? B. Does not the right to life under Article 21 of the Constitution of India include the right to food? C. Does not the right to food, which has been upheld by the Hon'ble Court, imply that the State has a duty to provide food especially in situations of drought, to people who are drought affected and are not in a position to purchase food? See petition at: www.righttofoodindia.org/ case/petition.html at para. 2".

[21] *PUCL v. Union of India*, supra note 7. Order of November 28, 2001.

listed eight different schemes that in some way provided for the food security
of Indians, including the Public Distribution System (PDS) which provides
subsidized foodgrain to those who qualify, the MDMS for school children, the
Integrated Child Development Scheme (ICDS), which provides food for
pregnant and lactating mothers and children under 6, a number of pension
schemes aimed at widows (National Family Benefit Scheme), people with
disabilities and the elderly (National Old Age Pension Scheme), an additional
supplemental foodgrain entitlement for the desperately poor (Annapoorna),
maternity benefits (National Maternity Benefit Scheme) and, at the time,
work for food schemes, which have since been converted by legislation into
a rural employment program that guarantees up to 100 days of work for rural
labourers (National Rural Employment Guarantee Scheme or NREGA).

On November 28, 2001, the Supreme Court of India made a sweeping order
that had a number of impacts, including recognizing these schemes as legal
entitlements. The Court also universalized the two schemes aimed at child
malnutrition – MDMS and ICDS – that were only being offered on a limited
basis at that time. The Court remained seized of the matter for over 16 years,
issuing over 100 orders. In 2002, the Court established a Commissioners office,
which served the function of monitoring the implementation of the court
orders at the aggregate level and advocating for change directly to the state and
central governments. In 2004, the Court ordered a number of changes to the
MDMS, including expanding the entitlements that beneficiaries were to
receive, ordering the government to create infrastructure to support the
program, provide funds, change its policies on some aspects of the administration of its program, and monitor and generally improve the quality of the
program.[22] In 2006, the Court made a similar order regarding the ICDS,
expanding entitlements of beneficiaries and ordering that 1.4 million Angan-
wadi Centres be opened to deliver the program.[23]

The Court spent a great deal of time in the latter half of the 2000s
considering the PDS and struck a committee to look at this issue in great
detail. Former Justice Wadhwa led and remained seized of this inquiry for
several years, investigating state by state the problems plaguing the PDS and
reporting his findings to the Court. Finally, starting in 2009, the Court turned
its mind to the issue of homelessness as a result of one of the approximately
100 interlocutory applications that had been filed in the case, and ordered the
establishment of homeless shelters across the country. In between all of
this, the Court received regular updates on the implementation status of its

---

[22] *Id.*, Order of April 20, 2004.
[23] *Id.* Order of December 13, 2006.

various orders, which were overseen on a day-to-day level by the appointed Commissioner's office.

Activism on the right to food began shortly after the case was filed, with grassroots activists from around the country coming together to form a national campaign for the right to food. This campaign has representation in many states throughout India, and a significant presence in Delhi, where it frequently advocates directly to government, organizes national protests and, until the case was dismissed in February 2017, supported the needs of the case by supplying information to the Court by way of the Commissioner's office. The Campaign is well organized and structured, holding regular and at times annual national conventions attended by hundreds or thousands of activists, during which campaign policy is developed. The Campaign publishes a great deal of information, both for use at the local and grassroots level, as well as for publication in mainstream media and academic sources. It has also engaged strategically with the media to ensure its message is widely disseminated. In sum, the *PUCL* case generated a well-organized and structured mass social movement on the right to food with the capacity to mobilize people at the grassroots level as well as make its persuasive pitch to those at the highest levels of power in the country.

IV. *KISHEN PATNAYAK* V. *STATE OF ORISSA*

In 1988, Kishen Patnayak, a former parliamentarian who had been very active in filing public interest litigations, filed a petition at the Supreme Court. The petition was filed on the basis that starvation deaths had occurred in the district of Kalahandi in Odisha, which has long been known as the "starvation capital of India."[24] Petitioners were able to demonstrate not only that starvation deaths were taking place, but also that it was primarily caused not by the drought experienced by the community, but rather because the system of relief works that was in place to alleviate the impact of the drought was simply not reaching the people of the community.[25] Another petition was filed around the same time by the India People's Front, highlighting the persistent issues of starvation in the Kalahandi and Koraput districts of Odisha, requesting intervention by the Supreme Court. The Court appointed a judge to conduct an inquiry, resulting in the Panda Commission Report of 1988, which

---

[24] Dan Banik. 2010. "Governing a Giant: The Limits of Judicial Activism on Hunger in India." *Journal of Asian Public Policy* 3(3): 263–280. At 269 [*Banik*, 2010.]

[25] Interview with lawyer familiar with the case. New Delhi. August 13, 2013. [*Lawyer 1.*]

concluded that no starvation deaths had occurred.[26] Although the Court took no further judicial action, it remained unconvinced by the Panda report and directed the Odisha government to be more active in responding to the needs of the community in the context of hunger and starvation.[27] At that time, the state government assured the court that it would address the situation and, while the Court effectively dismissed the petition, left open the possibility that the petitioner could reopen the case at a later time should the situation not improve.[28]

When the situation had not improved,[29] the Indian Council of Legal Aid filed a follow-up petition at the High Court in Odisha in 1996.[30] That case was transferred to the Supreme Court, which opined on the matter and transferred the case to the National Human Rights Commission (NHRC) to monitor.[31] The result was that the case was removed from the adversarial process and the parties agreed to interim measures for a period of two years.[32]

When the NHRC took hold of the case, the mandate over which it presided was quite broad. The case became more broadly focused on social welfare and gradually expanded from food to many other aspects of social well-being.[33] Measures ordered by the NHRC included providing a tubewell suitable for 250 people in order to further rural water supply and sanitation, opening primary health care centers including mobile health units, the removal of the ceiling on the number of pensions available to the people of the region, and appointing a committee to study land reforms. The MDMS, which had been offered to children since 1998–1999, was monitored, as was the Employment Assurance Scheme, with soil conservation and forestation identified as appropriate areas for job creation.[34] Temporary feeding centers were converted into permanent feeding centers, as the NHRC recognized that the food for work schemes that would typically be initiated in such circumstances would not be appropriate – some people of Kalahandi were so weak that they could not walk for half a kilometer and others were so desperate for food they

---

[26] *Banik*, 2010, *supra* note 24 at 269.

[27] *Id.*, at 270.

[28] *Supra* note 25, *Lawyer 1.*

[29] *Gonsalves*, *supra* note 1 at v.

[30] Chaman Lal. 2007. "NHRC and Right to Food." In *Food Security and Judicial Activism in India*, ed. Human Rights Law Network, 113–116. New Delhi, Socio-Legal Information Centre. at 113. [*Lal.*]

[31] *Supra* note 25, *Lawyer 1.*

[32] *Lal*, *supra* note 30.

[33] *Supra* note 25, *Lawyer 1.*

[34] *Lal*, *supra* note 30 at 114.

were eating leaves.[35] Deaths due to malaria, diarrhea and cholera as a result of mosquitos and poor nutrition were also addressed, and the NHRC ordered that a medicine kit should be supplied to assist with malaria and diarrhea.[36]

In its entirety, the Orissa matter ultimately presided over a much broader range of issues than the *PUCL* case, including rural water supply and sanitation, primary health care, disease prevention and land reform. The opportunity therefore for activists to engage in a wide variety of social issues by virtue of the fact that they had been placed on the agenda by the judicial system was significant. Moreover, the circumstances of the Kalahandi districts of Odisha were subject not just to the petitions outlined above, but also to earlier litigation related to bonded labour and the exploitation of tribal groups by moneylenders in 1988, as well as a petition on starvation and the sale of children in 1990, both of which resulted in another inquiry that confirmed that starvation deaths did occur.[37] All of this resulted in a significant amount of media attention, and the subsequent voting out of office of the then-Congress government. Yet despite all this, large-scale mobilization on the right to food did not happen. The following sections will examine a number of factors that help to explain why that may have been the case.

V. OPPORTUNITIES FOR REFORM

Social movements develop when a need faced by a disadvantaged group must be filled. However, the simple existence of that need does not mean that a social movement will emerge. According to McCann, the degree and form of deprivation matter less than the nature and sources of the hardship.[38] Citing Piven and Cloward, McCann explains that this amounts to the fact that the issue must be seen as wrong and subject to redress, or that people must understand their hardship as a product of social conditions, that it wrongfully deprives them of their rights, and that realistic options exist for addressing and remedying the deprivation.[39]

McCann details two related aspects of opportunities for reform: hardships experienced by individuals and changes to political culture and state institutions. On the first point, McCann observes that the subjective

---

[35] *Supra* note 25, *Lawyer 1.*
[36] *Id.*
[37] *Banik,* 2010, *supra* note 24 at 270.
[38] *McCann, supra* note 9 at 93.
[39] *Id.*

understandings of opportunities are often related to increased hardships that accrue to marginalized individuals during the time of social change or crisis.[40] He notes that these types of transformations "typically create new systemic vulnerabilities, new alignments of group power, new spaces for creative citizen action, or growing tensions between emerging social power relations and residual justifications for power that can be exploited by oppressed or marginalized groups."[41] Similarly, in her study of the impact of the constitutional entrenchment of equality rights on LGBTQ activism in Canada, Miriam Smith emphasizes the importance of structures on social movement activism, finding that the choices of activists and movement actors are framed and influenced by the broader political environment in which they operate.[42] On the latter point, McCann highlights the importance of changing political structures on mobilization, including rights-based activism and legal reform, and the institutional factors among both the bureaucracy and elected officials that make it more or less likely for mobilization to occur.

The context in which the *PUCL* case was filed differed significantly from that of the matter in Odisha. The following section details the most relevant contextual differences.

VI. UNDERSTANDING HARDSHIPS IN THE CONTEXT OF A NEOLIBERAL STATE

When the cases were filed is germane to understanding why a social movement catalyzed in the *PUCL* case but not in *Kishen Patnayak*. Activism as a phenomenon is predicated on a subjective understanding of activists and movement participants that they are experiencing a hardship, and it requires that the subjective understanding of that hardship in turn be linked with the historical context in which it is experienced. Starvation has occurred in India for centuries.[43] However, the particular circumstances of starvation are context-specific and, as a result, potential activists interpret these events differently based on their subjective understanding of their current environment and circumstances.

---

[40] *Id.*, at 94.
[41] Id. Here, McCann references Peter K. Eisinger. 1973. "The Conditions of Protest Behavior in American Cities." *American Political Science Review* 67: II–28 and Frances Fox Piven and Richard A. Cloward. 1979. *Poor People's Movements: Why They Succeed, How They Fail.* New York: Vintage.
[42] Miriam Smith. 1999. *Lesbian and Gay Rights in Canada: Social Movements and Equality-Seeking, 1971–1995.* Toronto: University of Toronto Press.
[43] *Supra* notes 1, 2 and 3.

In 1988, when Kishen Patnayak filed his case, Kalahandi was indeed in dire straits. However, India had long suffered from inept and corrupt bureaucracies, as well as from starvation and hunger. No major changes in broad economic or food policy had occurred and the state was providing universal access to the PDS which, notwithstanding its terrible track record in delivering what was meant to be a universal service, at least made it appear to people that the government was doing something about hunger.

The context in 2001 was quite different. By 2001, neoliberalism had entered into Indian economic policymaking, through India's New Economic Policy (NEP). India sought assistance from the International Monetary Fund (IMF) following a substantial balance of payments crisis, which prompted the NEP, starting in 1991.[44] The NEP, like many of the well-documented cases of IMF assistance elsewhere in the world, resulted in the widespread application of principles of liberalization, privatization and globalization to virtually all economic and industrial policy in India.[45] This was a marked difference from the approach previously taken by India, and had material impacts on equality and social justice, two principles which were enshrined in the Indian constitution. Relevant changes to food policy following India's turn to the NEP include a removal of government controls on many aspects of the economy, the removal of regulation of food stuffs and, following India's accession to the World Trade Organization, the targeting of programs that had previously been universal. This had implications on both the production and consumption sides of the food system in India.

With respect to consumption, the targeting of the PDS began in 1997, and almost immediately reports began to appear of corruption and cronyism in the composition of the lists that designated those who qualify for subsidized foodgrains.[46] The result in many cases was the omission of those who were below the poverty line and the inclusion of those who weren't. Reports of starvation deaths began appearing shortly thereafter.[47] Impacts on production were equally significant given the role that agriculture plays in the rural labor market. Many rural farmers relied for their livelihoods on the state

---

[44] World Bank. 2012. "Structural Adjustment in India." Accessed August 31, 2018. http://lnweb90 .worldbank.org/oed/oeddoclib.nsf/b57456d58aba40e585256ad400736404/ 0586cc45a28a2749852567f5005d8c89.

[45] Montek Ahluwalia. 1994. "India's Quiet Economic Revolution." *Columbia Journal of World Business* 29 (1): 6–12. Montek Ahluwalia. 2002. "Economic Reforms in India since 1991: Has Gradualism Worked?" *The Journal of Economic Perspectives* 16(3): 67–88.

[46] Interview with journalist familiar with the case. New Delhi. July , 2013. [*Journalist 1.*]

[47] See, e.g., Neelabh Mishra. 2002. "Hunger Deaths in Baran." *Frontline* 19(24), December 6, 2002.

to purchase their food, through the state-run system of procurement that supplies the foodgrain that the PDS distributes. Therefore, when government policies related to supporting farmers changed, the situation became quite dire for farmers. Around this time, reports of farmer suicides also became commonplace.[48]

By the time the *PUCL* case was filed, India had experienced 10 years of neoliberal economic policies that had caused a great deal of strain on the poor and pushed them and those who worked on their behalf beyond their limits.[49] Notwithstanding the fact that India's food security apparatus, in particular the PDS, prior to neoliberalism was inefficient and failed in many ways to assist those who needed it the most, there was not a sense that this was due to anything other than bureaucratic ineptitude or the same general level of corruption that existed in the delivery of government programs elsewhere in the country. India's adoption of neoliberalism provided future movement activists with a narrative and understanding of India as a state in retreat, no longer capable or willing to provide for its citizenry or uphold the promises of social justice upon which it was founded.

VII. THE CHANGING POLITICAL ENVIRONMENT

A. *Expansion of the rights agenda and rights consciousness*

According to McCann, the legacy of rights-based legal reform in America not only benefited the specific populations at which they were aimed, but it also created space for subsequent activism around pay equity.[50] Earlier rights-based struggles around civil rights, for example, laid the normative framework for rights-based entitlements and the legal framework for subsequent legal challenges. At the same time, affirmative action programs developed during that time to address gender disparities proved to be disappointing. This combination of the failure of government attempts to address the problem and a rich history of rights-based activism to solve analogous problems in the past led women to seek redressal of their grievances through organizing.

Likewise, activism on the right to food benefited from the legacy of rights-based activism in India. Following the state of emergency called by Indira Gandhi during 1975–1977, the role of courts fundamentally changed. Many

---

[48] The reasons for this are complex but many have attributed this phenomenon, at least in part, to the more precarious situation farmers found themselves in following the reforms of the NEP.

[49] See, e.g., P. Sainath. 1996. *Everybody Loves a Good Drought*. New Delhi: Penguin.

[50] *McCann, supra* note 9 at 101.

theories abound as to reason for the change, the exploration of which is beyond the scope of this chapter. Regardless of the reason why, from this moment onwards, courts in India became concerned with a wider subject matter and relaxed a number of procedural rules, which resulted in a veritable explosion of rights litigation. In particular the Court removed form requirements, allowing for petitions to be received in non-traditional formats (i.e., letters and postcards), and it also relaxed the requirement of standing, which allowed people to file petitions on behalf of aggrieved individuals in place of the aggrieved individuals themselves.[51] The combination of these two procedural changes allowed for the creation of public interest litigation (PIL).

As a result of the political context and the opportunities provided by these procedural changes, a significant legal opportunity emerged, in which it was particularly advantageous for activists to turn to courts to solve their grievances. As a result, a tremendous number of human rights cases were filed during this time, which can be understood as falling into three distinct waves. In the first wave during the late 1970s, the Supreme Court concerned itself with the protection of civil liberties, including police brutality and torture, custodial rape and inhuman treatment in jails. The second wave consisted of the recognition of socioeconomic rights of those on the margins of society: hawkers, pavement dwellers, rickshaw pullers, construction workers, Adivasis and Dalits. The third wave, which began in the 1990s, can be understood broadly as cases concerning environmental rights, including air and water pollution and drinking water quality.[52]

At the time of Kishen Patnayak's case, a number of significant human rights victories had occurred in court, including rulings that had abolished bonded labor,[53] and protected unorganized labor from exploitation.[54] All of these provided a context within which Kishen Patnayak's decision to turn to the court to address a grievance framed as a human rights issue was logical.

However, a number of crucial victories on human rights issues occurred in the period around 1988 when Kishen Patnayak filed the original PIL on the Orissa matter and 2001 when PUCL filed their case. These included the very well known and widely cited *Olga Tellis* v. *Bombay Municipal Corporation*,[55] which recognized the right to shelter, *Mohini Jain*

---

[51] S. P. Sathe. 2002. *Judicial Activism in India*. New Delhi: Oxford University Press. At 107.

[52] Sanjay Ruparelia. 2013. "A Progressive Juristocracy? The Unexpected Social Activism of India's Supreme Court." Working Paper 391. The Helen Kellogg Institute for International Studies. At 16–17. [*Ruparelia.*]

[53] *Bandhua Mukti Morcha* v. *Union of India & Others* 1984 AIR 802.

[54] *P.U.D.R.* v. *Union of India* 1982 AIR 1473.

[55] 1986 AIR 180.

v. *State of Karnataka*,[56] which recognized the right to education, and *Subhash Kumar* v. *State of Bihar & Ors*,[57] which recognized the right to clean air and water.

In addition to the general rights consciousness that had been developing throughout the period leading up to the filing of the *PUCL* case, the growth of rights-based approaches to development also contributed to the subjective understanding of the activists who ultimately turned to the Court. Rights-based approaches to development, both at the level of discourse and with respect to on-the-ground work, were gaining substantial traction in the development community by the time the *PUCL* case was filed.[58] The notion of a rights-based approach to development was located within the capability approach to development articulated in the writings of Nobel Prize-winning Indian economist Amartya Sen.[59] The most significant and influential work in this realm was the Nobel Prize-winning *Development as Freedom*, which was published in 1999 – just two years before the *PUCL* case. Indeed, one of the people among the group that came together to file the *PUCL* case was economist Jean Drèze, a longtime collaborator of Amartya Sen.

India experienced a substantial amount of rights-based activism around development issues in the immediate lead-up to the filing of the *PUCL* case, including the campaigns for the Right to Education,[60] and the Right to Information (RTI).[61] RTI in particular was seen as instrumental in bringing the rights perspective into the development discourse,[62] and was also very clearly tied to the right to food, as RTI was often used to obtain information in the context of inadequately implemented food entitlements or programs related to livelihoods, such as the food for work schemes.[63] Prior to RTI, the development discourse in India was premised on the idea of welfare or charity, as it was in many parts of the world.[64]

---

[56] 1992 AIR 1858.

[57] 1991 AIR 420.

[58] Varun Gauri and Siri Gloppen. 2012. "Human Rights-Based Approaches to Development: Concepts, Evidence and Policy." *Polity* 44(4): 485–503.

[59] See, e.g., Amartya Sen. 1981. *Poverty and Famines: An Essay on Entitlement and Deprivation.* Oxford: Oxford University Press; Amartya Sen. 1999. *Development as Freedom.* Oxford: Oxford University Press.

[60] Varun Gauri and Daniel Brinks. 2008. *Courting Social Justice: Judicial Enforcement of Social and Economic Rights in the Developing World.* New York: Cambridge University Press.

[61] Interview with Right to Food Activist 5. New Delhi. July 9, 2013. [*Activist 5.*]

[62] *Supra* note 46, *Journalist 1.*

[63] The SGRY was created shortly after the case was initially filed, which was later phased out for the more comprehensive NREGA program.

[64] *Supra* note 61, *Activist 5.*

RTI activists framed development in the context of rights, and located the concept within the right to life, understanding that, if development or livelihood schemes were withheld from the poor, their life chances would be reduced and their right to life denied.[65] In the context of food, the concept of a right to information helped highlight not only the corruption in food programs but also the structural problems, such as the fact that India was exporting foodgrain out of the country at a time when people were starving.

Finally, the movement towards understanding these grievances as rights served as a way to mobilize people. One activist interviewed described a "consensus" that began to emerge at that time around using the rights-based framework as a mobilizing tool.[66] From a practical standpoint, a rights-based framework was advantageous and very useful for mobilization, because it allowed people to: "mobilize around fairly concrete ends ... and at least to a limited extent, [hold] elected governments at all levels accountable to certain promises that they've made [and] certain things that are enshrined in various laws."[67]

The idea of a right to food was therefore one that was gaining traction within this context of increased rights consciousness, increased rights-based litigation and a general concern over issues related to food production and consumption arising at the time the *PUCL* case was filed. The right to food was described in 2013 by those involved in the *PUCL* case as "an idea whose time had come."[68] However, while this may be true for the later years of the *PUCL* case, the same cannot be said of the time when Kishen Patnayak filed his case. Much of the theoretical, legal and practical underpinning of the right to food occurred in the 1990s, in the years leading up to the filing of the case. While significant human rights cases were indeed being filed prior to *Kishen Patnayak*, they tended to focus on civil and political rights. It wasn't until the mid-1990s that major judicial victories related to social and economic rights occurred. *Kishen Patnayak* simply did not have the benefit of that context.

---

[65] *Id.*

[66] Interview with Activist 6. New Delhi., July 9, 2013. [*Activist 6.*] With one important proviso: "This does not mean that we look at the rights framework as the only framework or the only way in which you would try to bring about transformation."

[67] *Id. Activist 6.*

[68] Jean Drèze. 2004. "Democracy and the Right to Food." *Economic and Political Weekly* 39(17): 1723–1731.

B. *Institutional factors*

Another relevant consideration are institutional factors that affect state behavior and, in particular, the response of the state to the issue.[69] In this respect, several aspects of the *PUCL* case differed in important ways from the *Kishen Patnayak* case and encouraged mobilization in a way that wasn't generated in Odisha: the orientation of the case around several specific food schemes, the continuing mandamus of the court, the expansion of the case from Rajasthan to apply throughout the country, and the creation of the Commissioner's office monitoring mechanism.

When the government responded to PUCL's petition, it did not contest the order,[70] and instead listed all of the programs that existed to provide for the food security of Indians, including maternity benefits, supplemental feeding programs for children under the age of six and pregnant and lactating mothers (ICDS), mid-day meal programs for children (MDMS), a national program of subsidized foodgrain and employment guarantee programs that supported livelihoods, pensions, and other support schemes in the event of disability or death of breadwinners. The government's strategy was to demonstrate that it was already taking the action necessary to address the concerns of the petitioner. However, this resulted in the Court issuing its groundbreaking order of November 28, 2001, which universalized two of the programs that the government was providing on a limited basis – MDMS and ICDS. More importantly from the standpoint of mobilization, it also opened space for contestation as to the extent to which the government was living up to its promises and complying with its own schemes, which would become the central theme of the mobilization carried out by the Campaign and the subject of most of the interventions of the parties to the court case over the subsequent decade. The responses of the Court to the interventions in Odisha were markedly different – dismissing it when Kishen Patnayak filed it in the first instance and transferring it to the NHRC in the second.

---

[69] In the case of pay equity, McCann identified four relevant institutional factors, all of which were specific to the issue of pay equity in the United States and do not apply here: the relatively high number of female public sector employees that made the sector vulnerable to reform, the fact that the issue of pay equity became an electoral issue and came to influence voting patterns and therefore affected the political response to the issue, the development of standards for evaluation and remuneration of employees based on merit during a period of civil service reform, and the state-specific political organizational and cultural differences that could account for differences in mobilization activity across geographies.

[70] Interview with Right to Food Activist 7. New Delhi. August 7, 2013. [*Activist 7.*]

The second institutional factor that encouraged mobilization in the *PUCL* case was the fact that the case was under a continuing mandamus at the Supreme Court, which had the effect of keeping the matter pending before the Court for 16 years between 2001 and 2017. This kept the issue live before the highest court of the land, which resulted in the periodic issuing of orders that clarified government obligations and kept the issue in the public eye during that period. In the Odisha matter, the NHRC reviewed the matter for several years in a similar manner, but the NHRC simply did not generate the same amount of publicity as the Supreme Court.

The third aspect of *PUCL* that led to mobilization was the fact that the Supreme Court expanded the case from the state of Rajasthan to the entire country.[71] This created a perceived need for a national network to develop to support the case through research, information gathering and public education. Since there wasn't one at the time, the network that began in Rajasthan quickly expanded throughout the country, primarily through the individual connections and personal networks of those who were involved at the outset.[72] In contrast, the Odisha matter applied only to two small districts in Odisha, far away from the attention of very active civil society groups in Delhi and Rajasthan; it simply did not capture the imagination of activists in other areas of the country. Moreover, since it was not extended to the rest of the country, a national network was not necessary, and therefore did not emerge.

C. *Monitoring mechanisms*

When the Odisha matter was filed for the second time, the Supreme Court transferred the matter to the NHRC for it to monitor. The Commission didn't impose orders on the State; rather, the state determined what it would do and under what timelines, and a Special Rapporteur monitored to make sure that the commitments of the state were implemented.[73]

This is not dissimilar to the *PUCL* case where, in one of its first major orders, the Court appointed two individuals to serve as Commissioners on the court case,[74] initially with a view to providing grievance redressal for those who remained unable to access their entitlements under the various food schemes.[75] However, their role evolved into a threefold strategy of monitoring

---

[71] *Id.*
[72] *Supra* note 46, *Journalist 1.*
[73] *Supra* note 25, *Lawyer 1.*
[74] PUCL v. Union of India, *supra* note 7. Order of May 8, 2002.
[75] Interview with Right to Food Activist 8. New Delhi. June 10, 2013. [*Activist 8.*]

implementation of the court orders at a high level, advising the Court in an *amicus curae* role and doing a substantial amount of mediation and advocacy with the state and central governments.[76] In large part because of the broader mandate of the Commissioners in the *PUCL* case and the fact that the case was extended to apply to all of India, the existence of the Commissioners mechanism also had a significant impact on mobilization around the right to food in a way that was simply not possible in the Odisha case.

Much of the attention on the Commissioner's office focused on its role in reporting to the Court on the progress made on implementation;[77] however, more than half of the work of the Commissioner's office involved interfacing with state officials, state governments, the government of India and the Planning Commission.[78] The Commissioners did, for example, make a point of meeting officials in the state governments once or twice a year during their busiest periods,[79] and were invited to advise and assist individuals at the highest level of government, including Central Government Ministers and State Chief Ministers, and a number of government bodies in the policy-making process, including bodies tasked with identification of those below the poverty line,[80] and the Planning Commission in the formulation of the government's Five Year Plan as it related to women, children and nutrition.[81]

The Commissioners office was given the latitude to consult with whomever it chose and it deliberately sought out advice and input from activists working on the ground who had begun to rally around the case in its early years. They met frequently with members of the Campaign, both at the national and state level. As the Commissioners were engaged in a great deal of direct government advocacy, they often travelled to the states to meet Chief Secretaries. Prior to meeting them, they would often meet the state-level campaign members, because they would provide independent advice to the Commissioners based on what was happening on the ground.[82] Moreover, the Commissioners expected the Campaign to play a role in ensuring the implementation of the commitments they gained through meetings with the

---

[76] Id., *Supra* note 13, *Activist 2*.

[77] Lauren Birchfield and Jessica Corsi. 2010. "Between Starvation and Globalization: Realizing the Right to food in India." *Michigan Journal of International Law* 31: 691–764. At 729. [*Birchfield and Corsi.*]

[78] *Supra* note 75, *Activist 8*. Interview with N. C. Saxena, Commissioner appointed by the Supreme Court of India in Writ Petition (Civil) 196/2001. New Delhi. January 2015. [*Saxena.*]

[79] *Id.*

[80] *Id.*

[81] Interview with Government official 1, January 2015.

[82] Interview with Harsh Mander, Commissioner appointed by the Supreme Court of India in Writ Petition (Civil) 196/2001. New Delhi. January 2015. [*Mander.*]

state level governments.[83] The Commissioners therefore had strong working relationships with civil society actors at the state level and shared a common understanding of what should be accomplished by the case. Indeed, many of the Commissioners' state advisors, who gathered data and conducted research for inclusion in the Commissioners' reports to the Court and submissions to government, were also the state-level leaders of the Campaign.

Additionally, many of the individuals who worked at the Commissioners' office as staff support, researchers or advisors were also representative of civil society and associated with the Campaign.[84] The Commissioners viewed themselves and their office as independent from the Campaign[85] and neither of them were officially part of the Campaign. However, many of their staff played active and official roles in the Campaign, and one of the Commissioners openly supported the Campaign.[86] That being said, the Commissioner's office officially took a neutral view, recognizing that both the Campaign as a whole and individuals in the Campaign could take a more adversarial view on the issues,[87] as could individuals who worked in the Commissioners' office who were also part of the Campaign. Finally, some of the Commissioners' office staff were part of the Case Advisory Committee, which worked with the petitioner, PUCL, and the petitioner's lawyer, Colin Gonsalves, to advise on the direction and the strategy of the case.

This unique arrangement was born partly out of necessity and partly out of desire. It was necessary because the Commissioner's office needed reliable data about what was happening on the ground to use in their discussions with the state and national governments about how the programs could be improved, to share best practices, and help state level officials improve the program through advocacy on these issues; and in many cases those closest to the issues were those who were active in the Campaign.[88] It was also necessary because the Commissioners' office was quite small, with only four or five staff,[89] so it relied on the inputs from other advisors elsewhere in the country out of necessity—it simply could not cover the ground it needed to cover in order to become an effective advocate for these issues on its own. This arrangement also allowed the Campaign to have a de facto seat at the

---

[83] *Id.*

[84] While this is true of the staff of the Commissioners' Office, the Commissioners themselves were not part of the RTF campaign.

[85] *Supra* note 82, *Mander.*

[86] *Id.*

[87] *Supra* note 78, *Saxena.*

[88] *Supra* note 82, *Mander.*

[89] *Supra* note 13, *Activist 1.*

policy-making table and allowed people in the Campaign to use the Commissioner's office as a means to access the Supreme Court directly.[90]

The relationship between the Campaign and the Commissioner's office was strong and collaborative, and this was a significant contributing factor to the success of the *PUCL* case and the Campaign. The Commissioner's work, in turn, has been described as "flowing out of the Campaign" because "[i]t's always the people's movement that creates any kind of body like the food commissioners . . . One was very much connected with the other."[91] Indeed, it was the Campaign that proposed the specific individuals who would ultimately be appointed by the Court to serve as Commissioners.[92]

Therefore, the unique relationship between the Commissioners and the Campaign has provided the Campaign with the ability to access the Court and influence the case through official channels, complementing and supporting their mobilization efforts in other areas. In contrast, in the Odisha matter, there simply was no comparable institution to the Commissioner's office. The NHRC served a similar role in theory – monitoring the progress of the food schemes in the KBK district of Odisha – but given the relatively small mandate and ground to cover, there was neither a need nor a place for a widespread network of researchers and activists to contribute to that process.

VIII. ORGANIZATIONAL RESOURCES

McCann highlights the importance of organizational resources in taking advantage of the political opportunities that present themselves to potential movement activists. The first category of resources available to activists comprises instrumental resources, such as money and professional and technical expertise, which have a very direct impact on mobilization. The other category of resources relates to internal social movement culture and includes associational bonds and interdependent relations.[93] Looking at the different organizational resources available to Kishen Patnayak and PUCL, two crucial elements stand out: the existence of networks within which activists were already organized and engaging in related human rights advocacy and activism, and the leaders who were involved at the helm of the Campaign.

---

[90] *Supra* note 61, *Activist* 5.

[91] Interview with Government Official 1, January 2015.

[92] *Supra* note 61, *Activist* 5.

[93] *McCann, supra* note 9 at 109.

IX. ACCESS TO LOCAL AND NATIONAL ACTIVIST NETWORKS

It is well understood that the *PUCL* case was filed in the context of a drought in Rajasthan.[94] What is often not highlighted in third party accounts of the case is that, by the time the case was filed, activists and community groups, organized under the umbrella group Akal Sangharsh Samiti,[95] had been working for many months mobilizing for relief for those affected by the drought.[96] Activists first gathered people together on this issue in 2000,[97] their primary concern being that the *Famine Code*, which governed the obligations of the state in the context of a drought, wasn't being implemented.[98] In particular, it mandated a work guarantee that provides relief in the form of food and/or wages to those who avail of it; however, in late 2000 and early 2001, not enough people affected by the drought were able to access that relief. Activists continued to agitate and journalists came to Rajasthan to report on the starvation deaths that were happening at the time. Well-known economist and academic Jean Drèze met with the group and calculated, based on publicly available information, that there were 40 million metric tonnes of food in government storage facilities (godowns). A campaign emerged in Rajasthan to highlight this absurdity of "hunger amidst plenty,"[99] which included public action, such as large public dharnas (large sit-ins),[100] protesting outside the godowns and a "media blitz" on the hunger deaths that had occurred. A total of 52 organizations participated in that campaign.[101]

After that, activists agitating for the implementation of work for food schemes and implementation of the *Famine Code* and human rights lawyers discussed the idea of filing a PIL on the issue of food. The case was filed in March of 2001 with PUCL as the petitioner and was subsequently scheduled for its first appearance in July of that year. The activists who filed the case were not particularly hopeful that much would come of it,[102] and, in the meantime, continued with their public action.[103] Therefore, by the time the case came

---

[94] *Birchfield and Corsi, supra* note 77 at 694; *Gonsalves, supra* note 1 at 3; George Kent. 2005. *Freedom from Want.* Washington, DC: Georgetown University Press.
[95] A rough translation of this is "Famine Struggle Committee."
[96] *Gonsalves, supra* note 1 at v; *supra* note 61, Activist 5; *supra* note 75, Activist 8; *supra* note 46, Journalist 1; *supra* note 13, Activist 1.
[97] *Supra* note 70, Activist 7.
[98] *Gonsalves, supra* note 1 at 3.
[99] *Supra* note 61, Activist 5.
[100] *Supra* note 46, Journalist 1.
[101] *Supra* note 70, Activist 7.
[102] *Id.*
[103] *Id.*

up for a hearing on July 26, 2001, a tremendous amount of activism, public attention and parliamentary attention had occurred on this issue.[104]

Activists and community organizers throughout India were capable of being mobilized when *PUCL* was filed, largely because of other activism that was happening around the country leading up to that time. By the time the *PUCL* case was filed, activist networks and connections already existed, as well as well-established strategies for mobilization and public action,[105] through, for example, the campaigns for the Right to Education (RTE) and the Right to Information (RTI). The RTI campaign, for example, began long before the RTF campaign and many of the same activists involved in the former became active with the right to food. Activists were therefore effectively primed both for similar tactics of public action and for a rights-based approach to the issue of food.

Groups engaged in community organization and activism elsewhere in the country were able to be moblized by the RTF campaign for a number of reasons. First, the work that they were already doing was related to right to food, albeit not under a common theme. The case served to galvanize the activists already working on these and other related issues and brought them under the broader cause of the right to food.[106] Those involved in the Campaign at the time, as well as those who became involved subsequently, describe the situation as one in which "people [were] working on food and malnutrition issues but they were dormant in terms of social mobilization and networking,"[107] but because "litigation ignites what is dormant,"[108] "the case and the media attention gave them courage, morale and ignited the move-ment,"[109] mobilizing people to come together in a campaign,[110] and united those already working on food and malnutrition under the "right to food" banner.[111]

Second, activists had been working on issues related to land, forests, women's issues and displacement, all of which are large complex issues and very difficult to make progress on given the entrenched interests involved. The RTF case allowed these groups to win small victories by getting something for

---

[104] *Id; supra* note 61, *Activist 5.*
[105] *Supra* note 75, *Activist 8.*
[106] *Supra* note 13, *Activist 3.*
[107] Interview with lawyer familiar with the case. New Delhi. August 15, 2013 [Lawyer 2]. See also *supra* note 13, *Activist 3.*
[108] *Id, Lawyer 2.*
[109] *Id.*
[110] *Supra* note 13, *Activist 1, Activist 3, Activist 4.*
[111] *Supra* note 13, *Activist 3.*

the community, even though the main struggle may have initially been something else altogether.[112] Effectively the RTF case diverted existing activism and efforts to small, winnable victories that were possible at that time for communities that badly needed relief in some form.

In contrast, Kishen Patnayak was an individual working on his own, without an organization or a network of like-minded activists within which he was embedded. Moreover, the activists that may have been available to him at the time were simply not working on related issues, nor were they organized into a robust network that was already engaged in related rights-based activism. In the mid- to late 1980s, many of the activists who were active in the lead up to the *PUCL* case simply were not active on these issues and the struggles for the RTE and RTI had not yet happened. Much social activism in the late 1970s and 1980s focused on civil and political rights arising from the imposition of the emergency, and early instances of legal activism on human rights issues focused on the same, as well as housing and environmental rights.[113]

X. LEADERSHIP

The individuals involved from the outset of the *PUCL* case were also crucial in generating political mobilization on the issue. When the possibility of filing a case to try to force the government to distribute rotting foodgrains was first considered, eventually culminating in the *PUCL* case, the individuals involved at the outset all had a tremendous amount of legitimacy and experience in social activism and public interest litigation, and were capable of mobilizing large numbers of people through their networks and organizations.

Those involved in the early discussions that would ultimately result in the filing of the *PUCL* case included the General-Secretary of one of India's leading human rights organizations and a well-known human rights defender, two of India's most prominent human rights lawyers, a well-known journalist who had been reporting on rural poverty and starvation in Rajasthan, one of India's most well-respected development economists and several other prominent social activists with deep roots in struggles for rural poverty, the right to information, social inclusion and experience in grassroots mobilization. These individuals had the skills, legitimacy, gravitas and energy to facilitate mobilization around these issues.

When the Court extended the case throughout the country, a national network had to be created. Here, the petitioners and activists looked to

---

[112] *Supra* note 75, *Activist 8.*
[113] *Ruparelia, supra* note 52.

like-minded NGOs and civil society allies to assist them in expanding their network and provide research and administrative support. Grassroots activists with significant expertise in mobilization and public action also joined, expanding the presence of the Campaign in West Bengal, Madhya Pradesh, Chhattisgarh, Jharkhand, Gujarat and other states. Finally, leaders of the National Campaign for the People's Right to Information also became supporters of the RTF Campaign, as did Nobel Prize-winning economist Amartya Sen and Man Booker Prize winner Arundhati Roy, lending substantial credibility to this important issue.

When the case was filed in the Supreme Court by PUCL, key members of the Campaign engaged in a great deal of "hard work and planning" to build linkages across different states and to bring people together.[114] Members of the Campaign organized events that were attended by notable members of civil society and leading intellectuals, including Amartya Sen.[115] Leaders of the Campaign were well connected through activist networks throughout the country and were able to draw upon those connections to build a national movement around the right to food. The approach was deliberately multifaceted, as one activist recalled, and this was a function of the Campaign's leadership:

> in terms of shared vision [between the leaders of the Campaign], I think there's some basic understanding of how we must use every democratic space available to us. So whether it's the media, whether it's a court, whether it's street action or even research that we must use all these different means to increase the profile of these issues. So I think that this group coming together and having a good working relationship and being able to sit together and plan these relatively big events and then to bring in the media and to make sure that it got space . . . I think that . . . these three or four people who shared similar concerns and who had the energy and the vision to make it happen were working together at that point of time.[116]

Other activists have recognized the specific individuals involved as having played a key role in the success of the Campaign and its ability to mobilize and inspire others to join it, as well as the superior skills of the legal team involved.[117] These individuals were able to bring people together, foster links

[114] *Supra* note 13, *Activist* 3.
[115] See, for example, Harsh Mander. [undated] "The Struggle for the Right to Food." www.sccommissioners.org/Starvation/Articles/strugglertf.pdf.
[116] *Supra* note 13, *Activist* 3.
[117] *Supra* note 13, *Activist* 4.

across different states and use whatever democratic space was available to them including the media, the court, street action, research and lobbying.

In the *Kishen Patnayak* case, however, activist "bench strength" simply was not there. Kishen Patnayak was a former parliamentarian and teacher who, while very active in filing public interest litigations, did not connect his litigation with a broader campaign of social activism. He brought cases without the intent to engage in public action in order to enforce court orders. There wasn't a network of people engaged with him on the starvation issues in Odisha prior to filing the case, nor were any steps taken to build a broad base of support following the filing of the petition as there was in the *PUCL* case. The result was that the mobilization that existed throughout the time of the *PUCL* case simply wasn't there in Odisha.[118] As one RTF activist pointed out, "we could have gotten an order and sat back ... but we pursued, pursued, pursued, we still pursue ... Kishen Patnayak was on his own."[119]

XI. CONCLUSION

The RTF Campaign that arose out of the *PUCL* case played an instrumental role in organizing people around the right to food and placing this issue squarely on the public agenda in a way that had never been done before,[120] notwithstanding the fact that an almost identical issue was put before the Indian courts previously. According to one RTF activist:

> [The case] led to expansion of food schemes and many landmark orders. But if I was to say what did all that lead to? It led to the construction of a societal argument on the right to food, which has now led to legislation in the Food Security [Act]. That's the journey we have made – to convince this nation of close to 1 billion and a quarter people that there is something that we must do about it.[121]

The *PUCL* case created a space for activism on the issue that wasn't there previously – a space with room for direct advocacy, research and data gathering, and a space to challenge neoliberal economic policies that had previously dominated the Indian policy landscape in the decade leading up to the case. This policy discourse was so powerful that many activists involved in the case believe it would have resulted in the winding down of food programs,

---

[118] Interview with Right to Food Activist 9. New Delhi. June 22, 2013 [*Activist 9.*]
[119] *Supra* note 70, *Activist 7.*
[120] *Supra* note 118, *Activist 9.*
[121] *Supra* note 75, *Activist 8.*

such as the PDS. Not only was the PDS not wound down, but as a result of the interventions of the Court and civil society, the PDS and all other food security schemes considered by the Court were expanded, strengthened and implemented more effectively and comprehensively than they were prior to the case.

How and why this occurred is an important part of this story. In sum, the *PUCL* case was able to generate political mobilization for a number of reasons related to the structural opportunities that emerged in the time period leading up to the filing of the case, including the broader political economy and the specific mobilization happening at the time and place the case was filed. Changes in the broader political opportunities including particularities related to the case itself, the creation of the Commissioner's office which created an official channel for the views of civil society to feed into the court process, as well as increased rights consciousness that had built up over time all helped by creating the motivation to mobilize. Organizational resources in the form of activists being organized into preexisting networks who were available to be mobilized, as well as specific individuals who could lead the movement, also helped make mobilization possible.

All of this contrasts to the *Kishen Patnayak* case in Odisha, which generated no such activism. In many respects, the two cases were very similar in that they dealt with a similar issue within a similar context, yet the impact on social mobilization couldn't be more different. The *PUCL* case demonstrates that social activism can be generated from litigation when a well-connected group of social activists pursues litigation that is well received by the Court, in the context of an existing degree of rights consciousness within civil society, a genuine sense that citizens have been wronged and that the wrong they have experienced is capable of being redressed. Kishen Patnayak's experience demonstrates that when a single individual pursues litigation without being part of an activist network and without the intention to generate social mobilization, social mobilization may not occur even when that litigation is well received by the Court. This finding holds true even when the results are strong for the litigants: arguably the results of the second Odisha case were more positive than *PUCL*, with a broader scope of issues the Court was willing to consider (not just food but water, land, sanitation and health), and a stronger and more institutionalized monitoring and implementation mechanism in the form of the NHRC and a Special Rapporteur with investigatory powers. The contrasting experiences of these two cases demonstrates that social mobilization doesn't happen simply because a court provides the opportunity. Rather, the context is important and those involved must take advantage of the opportunity.

REFERENCES

Ahluwalia, Montek. 1994. "India's Quiet Economic Revolution." *Columbia Journal of World Business* 29(1): 6–12.

2002. "Economic Reforms in India since 1991: Has Gradualism Worked?" *The Journal of Economic Perspectives* 16(3): 67–88.

Banik, Dan. 2007. *Starvation and India's Democracy.* London and New York: Routledge.

2010. "Governing a Giant: The Limits of Judicial Activism on Hunger in India." *Journal of Asian Public Policy* 3(3): 263–280.

Birchfield, Lauren, and Jessica Corsi. 2010. "Between Starvation and Globalization: Realizing the Right to Food in India." *Michigan Journal of International Law* 31: 691–764.

Drèze, Jean. 1991. "Famine Prevention in India." In *The Political Economy of Hunger: Volume 2: Famine Prevention,* edited by Jean Drèze and Amartya Sen, 13–122. Oxford: Clarendon Press.

2004. "Democracy and the Right to Food." *Economic and Political Weekly* 39(17): 1723–1731.

Drèze, Jean, and Amartya Sen. 1989. *Hunger and Public Action.* Oxford: Oxford University Press.

Gauri, Varun, and Daniel Brinks. 2008. *Courting Social Justice: Judicial Enforcement of Social and Economic Rights in the Developing World.* New York: Cambridge University Press.

Gauri, Varun, and Siri Gloppen. 2012. "Human Rights-Based Approaches to Development: Concepts, Evidence and Policy." *Polity* 44(4): 485–503.

Gloppen, Siri. 2008. "Litigation as a Strategy to Hold Governments Accountable for Implementing the Right to Health." *Health and Human Rights* 10(2) 21–36.

Gonsalves, Colin. 2009. *Right to Food.* (4th ed.). New Delhi: Human Rights Law Network.

Government of India. 1880. *Report of the Indian Famine Commission.* London: Her Majesty's Stationary Office. https://archive.org/details/FamineCommission.

Hunt, Alan. 1990. "Rights and Social Movements: Counter-Hegemonic Strategies." *Journal of Law and Society* 17(3): 309–328.

Kent, George. 2005. *Freedom fom Want.* Washington, DC: Georgetown University Press.

Lal, Chaman. 2007. "NHRC and Right to Food." In *Food Security and Judicial Activism in India,* edited by Human Rights Law Network, 113–116. New Delhi, Socio-Legal Information Centre.

Mander, Harsh. 2012. "Food from the Courts: The Indian Experience" *IDS Bulletin* 43 (S1): 15–24.

[undated] "The Struggle for the Right to Food." www.sccommissioners.org/Starva tion/Articles/strugglertf.pdf.

McCann, Michael. 1994. *Rights at Work: Pay Equity Reform and the Politics of Legal Mobilization.* Chicago: Chicago University Press.

Mishra, Neelabh. 2001. "Anatomy of Hunger." *Hindustan Times,* May 2001.

2001 "Drought and Deaths." *Frontline,* April 14, 2001.

2001. "Post-Mortem of Hunger." *Hindustan Times,* April 4, 2001.

2002. "Hunger Deaths in Baran." *Frontline* 19(24), December 6, 2002.

Rosenberg, Gerald. 1991. *The Hollow Hope: Can Courts Bring about Social Change?* Chicago: Chicago University Press.

Ruparelia, Sanjay. 2013. "A Progressive Juristocracy? The Unexpected Social Activism of India's Supreme Court." Working Paper 391. The Helen Kellogg Institute for International Studies.

Sainath, P. 1996. *Everybody Loves a Good Drought*. New Delhi, Penguin.

2001. "Rajasthan's Drought: Abundance of Food, Scarcity of Vision" The Hindu, March 18, 2001.

Sathe, S. P. 2002. *Judicial Activism in India*. New Delhi: Oxford University Press.

Sen, Amartya. 1981. *Poverty and Famines: An Essay on Entitlement and Deprivation*. Oxford: Oxford University Press.

1999. *Development as Freedom*. Oxford: Oxford University Press.

Smith, Miriam. 1999. *Lesbian and Gay Rights in Canada: Social Movements and Equality-Seeking, 1971–1995*. Toronto, University of Toronto Press.

World Bank. 2012. "Structural Adjustment in India." http://lnweb90.worldbank.org/oed/oeddoclib.nsf/b57456d58aba40e585256ad400736404/0586cc45a28a274985256 7f5005d8c89. Accessed August 31, 2018.

CASES

Bandhua Mukti Morcha v. Union of India & Others 1984 AIR 802.

Kishen Pattnayak And Anr. v. State of Orissa AIR 1989 SC 677.

M. C. Mehta v. Union of India Writ Petition (Civil) No. 13029 of 1985.

Mohini Jain v. State of Karnataka, 1992 AIR 1858.

Olga Tellis v. Bombay Municipal Corporation 1986 AIR 180.

P.U.C.L. v. Union of India & Ors. W.P (Civil) 96/2001.

P.U.D.R. v. Union of India 1982 AIR 1473.

Subhash Kumar v. State of Bihar & Ors, 1991 AIR 420.

PART III

Welfare Rights and the Environment

9

A Case for Qualified Hope?

The Supreme Court of India and the Midday Meal Decision

ROSALIND DIXON AND RISHAD CHOWDHURY

On November 28, 2001, the Supreme Court of India (SCI) directed State governments to mandatorily provide every child attending a government or government-aided primary school with a free-of-cost, cooked midday meal.[1] Today, what is popularly known as the 'Midday Meal Scheme' covers an estimated 120 million schoolchildren across India, and is the largest school nutritional program in the world.[2] Whether or not the Bench was at the time fully cognizant of the reach of the Order, or its potential consequences, it might be thought to be one of the most ambitious judicial interventions in the realm of socioeconomic rights in any jurisdiction in the world.

This chapter surveys the existing social science evidence on the "implementation" of the Midday Meal Decision,[3] and suggests that, despite notable gaps and flaws, the evidence seems strongly to support a finding that the scheme has in fact dramatically expanded since 2001, and in ways that meet the goals of its proponents. This is especially striking when one considers the sheer scope of the Court's order. This was not simply a minor decision, which affected a marginal area of public policy. It was one of the most

---

[1] Order dated November 28, 2001, *Peoples Union for Civil Liberties* v. *Union of India & Others*, *Writ Petition (Civil)* No. 196 of 2001, available at www.righttofoodindia.org/orders/nov28.html.
[2] Basic information about the Scheme, and the Court orders relating to the same, is available on the website of the Right to Food Campaign. See *School Mid-Day Meals*, RIGHT TO FOOD CAMPAIGN, at www.righttofoodcampaign.in/school-meals.
[3] Throughout this chapter, we use the term "Midday Meal Decision" or variants of the same. There has been, in fact, no final decision or judgment, in that sense, in the Writ Petition before the SCI. The Writ Petition remains pending in the SCI, and interlocutory orders have been passed in the same from time to time. We use the term "decision" for convenience, but it also helps illustrate the larger point that there is perhaps no universal pattern to judicial intervention in such social rights litigation, and that different Courts employ different means (or techniques) to accomplish their objectives.

ambitious decisions ever rendered by the Court, and sought to radically transform both educational and nutritional policy in India.

A more difficult question is whether the Court can claim credit for this expansion in the funding and reach of the scheme. One possibility is that the expansion of the Midday Meal Program simply reflected a growing political commitment to addressing childhood malnutrition, and using school meals as a means of achieving this goal. This view reflects the *"Hollow Hope"* thesis of Gerald Rosenberg, which argues that in a US context, the Supreme Court has largely been ineffective in creating – rather than reflecting – broader social change.[4]

This chapter, however, suggests that there is at least some evidence pointing to a more active role for the Court: the Court seems effectively to have helped counter "burdens of inertia" in the roll-out of the scheme in certain parts of India; and to have expanded the scope and ambition of the scheme in other parts of the country.[5] It did so, we suggest, both by increasing public attention to government performance in delivering the scheme, and the potential sanctions facing local government actors if they failed to take active measures to support the roll-out of the scheme in various states.

The experience of judicial intervention, in this context, thus arguably gives support for a thesis of qualified hope in relation to the capacity of courts to achieve important forms of social change – i.e. to help counter "burdens of inertia" in the realization of rights, albeit under quite special social and political conditions. We do not explore, in this short space, the extent to which this thesis applies to other cases within India, let alone comparatively. We simply suggest it is one possible reading of the Midday Meal experience in India, and as such, that there is some evidence to support the *plausibility* of a theory of qualified hope.[6]

The remainder of the chapter is divided into five parts. Part I provides a brief explanation of the Midday Meal Decision, and its broader constitutional

---

[4] GERALD ROSENBERG, THE HOLLOW HOPE (2nd ed., 2008).

[5] Rosalind Dixon, *Creating Dialogue about Socioeconomic Rights: Strong-Form versus Weak-Form Judicial Review Revisited*, 5 INT'L J. CONST. L. 391 (2007); Rosalind Dixon, *The Supreme Court of Canada, Charter Dialogue, and Deference*, 47 OSGOODE HALL L.J. 235 (2009); Rosalind Dixon, A *Democratic Theory of Constitutional Comparison*, 56 AM. J. COMP. L. 947 (2008); Rosalind Dixon, *The Core Case for Weak-Form Judicial Review*, 38 CARDOZO L. REV. 2193 (2017).

[6] In this sense, we suggest that our method might be regarded as following something like Ran Hirschl's "most difficult cases" principle: if the SCI can achieve change of this scale and difficulty, it suggests that it might also be able to do something similar for less ambitious or large-scale forms of change. See RAN HIRSCHL, COMPARATIVE MATTERS: THE RENAISSANCE OF COMPARATIVE CONSTITUTIONAL LAW (2014).

context. Part II considers evidence as to the expansion of the Midday Meal Program across India in the years following the Court's interim orders, and its consequential impact on nutritional and educational outcomes. Part III considers the degree to which the seeming success of the decision may be attributable to factors other than the Court decision itself, or the degree to which the Court itself may have contributed to the realization of the right to food. Part IV considers the extent to which, even if successful in contributing to social change in this context, the Court's role might have depended on a quite specific set of social and political preconditions. Part V offers a brief conclusion about the broader lessons to be drawn from this experience.

I. THE DECISION

Self-described as "socialist" in character,[7] the Indian Constitution places on the State – in the Directive Principles of State Policy in Part IV of the Constitution – the mandate of "striv[ing] to minimize the inequalities in income, and endeavour[ing] to eliminate inequalities in status, facilities and opportunities."[8] The Directive Principles further mandate the State to "regard the raising of the level of nutrition and the standard of living of its people and the improvement of public health as among its primary duties."[9] Further, while the fundamental rights in Part III of the Constitution (which are enforceable by the High Courts and the SCI) generally focus on civil and political liberties and are couched in negative terms, these have been expansively interpreted by the SCI to impose positive obligations on the State to secure to its citizens a dignified life. More particularly, the right to life enshrined in Article 21 of the Constitution has been interpreted to include the right to a dignified life with the basic necessities essential for the same. In *Maneka Gandhi* v. *Union of India*,[10] the SCI read the right to life expansively, and also concluded that the State could not abrogate the right without resort to a "just, fair and reasonable" procedure. In the landmark case of *Olga Tellis* v. *Bombay Municipal Corporation*,[11] the SCI held the right to shelter to be an integral part of the right to life, and hence injuncted the State from evicting homeless persons without adhering to due process.

---

[7] The Preamble to the Constitution of India commences with these words: "We the People of India, having solemnly resolved to constitute India into a sovereign, socialist, secular, democratic Republic..."

[8] Article 38(2), Constitution of India.

[9] Article 47, Constitution of India.

[10] AIR 1978 SC 597.

[11] (1985) 3 SCC 545.

More directly relevant to this chapter, the SCI also read in the right to education within the broader right to life. While the Constitution mandated – albeit in the non-binding Directive Principles – that the State should provide free and compulsory education for all children between the ages of 6 and 14 years within a period of 10 years,[12] it is self-evident that the State failed miserably on this count.[13] In the landmark *Unnikrishnan* judgment, the SCI held that the right to life enshrined in Article 21 of the Constitution encompassed within itself the right to education.[14] The *Unnikrishnan* judgment itself attracted mixed reactions from various stakeholders, and appears to have remained substantially unenforced. While it is therefore not clear that the *Unnikrishnan* judgment had a tangible impact on governmental education policy in and of itself, it arguably gave some prominence to the right in public discourse, and may have given the Government an additional impetus in proposing and finally enacting the Constitution (Eighty-Sixth) Amendment Act, 2002, incorporating the right to free and compulsory education as a fundamental right in the Constitution.[15] Simultaneously with the coming into force of Article 21A, Parliament enacted The Right to Free and Compulsory Education Act, 2009 [Right to Education Act], with the stated objective of setting out a statutory framework for the achievement of the (now fundamental) right to free and compulsory primary education.[16]

The Midday Meal Scheme itself has a long and checkered history. In pre-independence India, a scheme for providing midday meals to school children was initiated in the State of Tamil Nadu in the year 1925. Subsequent to independence in 1947, schemes were initiated by certain State Governments in the 1950s and 1960s. The concept is generally believed to have been initiated by the State of Tamil Nadu in 1956. Nonetheless, it is fairly clear that the schemes remained at a local or State level, and coverage was limited. In 1995, the Central Government adopted the program, but the pace of implementation was slow. It is in this context that the

---

[12] See Article 45, Constitution of India (prior to the enactment of the Constitution (Eighty-Sixth) Amendment Act, 2002).

[13] See generally Rishad Chowdhury, *The Road Less Travelled": Article 21A and the Fundamental Right to Primary Education in India, Indian Journal of Constitutional Law,* 4 IND. J. CONST. L. 24 (2010).

[14] (1993) 1 SCC 645.

[15] Article 21A, Constitution of India: "The State shall provide free and compulsory education to all children of the age of six to fourteen years in such manner as the State may, by law, determine." See also Vijayashri Sripati & Arun K. Thiruvengadam, *Constitutional Amendment Making the Right to Education a Fundamental Right,* 2 INT. J. CONST. L. 148 (2004).

[16] See *id.*

Supreme Court came to pass directions inter alia concerning implementation of the Midday Meal Program.

Interestingly, and as is fairly common in the context of India's public interest litigation (PIL) jurisprudence, the original relief sought in the Right to Food case was rather different, though the broader animating concerns were the same. The People's Union for Civil Liberties – one of India's largest and best-reputed human rights organizations – approached the Supreme Court with a Petition that was both simple and intuitively appealing. Impleading both the State and the Food Corporation of India (FCI) as parties, the Petitioner said that it was constitutionally impermissible for the State to permit starvation deaths to occur in India, when close to 50 million tons of food grain was stored (in some cases rotting) in governmental warehouses (belonging to the FCI).[17] The relief sought focused on revitalization of the Public Distribution System (hereafter PDS, mandated to provide basic quantities of essential food materials to the public at subsidized rates), as well as the inadequacy of relief work in draught-affected areas of the country.[18] The availability of food grain made a defense founded on the lack of resources implausible, and the Court issued wide-ranging directions along the lines sought. The Petition stayed with the Court, and the relief sought (and granted) evolved over the course of time. It is in this context that the Petitioner came to raise the issue of the Midday Meal Program, and the Court's order dated November 28, 2001 came to be passed.

The operative portion of this order reads:

(i) It is the case of the Union of India that there has been full compliance with regard to the Mid-Day Meal Scheme (MDMS). However, if any of the States gives a specific instance of non-compliance, the Union of India will do the needful within the framework of the Scheme.

(ii) We direct the State Governments/Union Territories to implement the Mid-Day Meal Scheme by providing every child in every Government and Government assisted Primary Schools with a prepared mid day meal with a minimum content of 300 calories and 8–12 grams of protein each day of school for a minimum of 200 days. Those Governments providing dry rations instead of cooked meals must within three months start providing cooked meals in all Govt. and Govt. aided Primary Schools in all half the Districts of

[17] See Writ Petition (C) No. 196 of 2001, www.righttofoodindia.org/case/petition.html.
[18] The relief sought in the original Writ Petition is summarized on the website of the Right to Food Campaign. See *The "Right to Food" Case*, RIGHT TO FOOD CAMPAIGN, at www.righttofoodcampaign.in/legal-action/-right-to-food-case.

the State (in order of poverty) and must within a further period of three months extend the provision of cooked meals to the remaining parts of the State.

(iii) We direct the Union of India and the FCI to ensure provision of fair average quality grain for the Scheme on time. The States/Union Territories and the FCI are directed to do joint inspection of food grains. If the food grain is found, on joint inspection, not to be of fair average quality, it will be replaced by the FCI prior to lifting.[19]

Certain features of the order stand out prominently. First of all, the order dealt with many social welfare programs of the Government, of which the Midday Meal Program is merely one. It appears that the Midday Meal Program is likely the component of the order which has the widest impact. In any case, the Midday Meal Program is the aspect of the order that the present chapter focuses on. As with many important orders passed by the SCI in the realm of social welfare rights, the order proceeds without explicitly stating the reasons supporting it. Nonetheless, the order reflects the arguments by various stakeholders, including the Union and State Governments (as well as the FCI), in the prior hearings before the Court. Furthermore, the order is only an interim one: the Court monitored the matter from time to time, and continues to do so until the present time of writing. In fact, this Writ Petition (along with other similar matters) was subsequently assigned by the Chief Justice to a specially-constituted Bench of the Court, designated as the Social Justice Bench, to assemble every working Friday at 2.00 p.m.[20]

II. ASSESSING "COMPLIANCE"

What has been the record of compliance with the Court's decision in the 15 or so years since it was handed down? One important indicator of compliance with the decision is the degree to which it has been endorsed, and entrenched, by subsequent national legislation. In 2013, the principle laid down in the decision was explicitly endorsed in the National Food Security Act, 2013.[21] Passed after extensive debate, the Act enshrines both a range of other statutory entitlements to a minimum quantity of rations and a statutory right to a midday meal for schoolchildren between the ages of 6 and 14 years.[22]

---

[19] *Supra* note 1.
[20] See Social Justice Bench (Listing Notice), http://sci.nic.in/FileServer/2014–12-17_1418816381 .pdf.
[21] Section 5(1)(b), National Food Security Act, 2013.
[22] *Id.*

Even prior to the 2013 legislation, but subsequent to the SCI's Order, the scheme undoubtedly expanded significantly in its scope and reach. In October 2007, the program was extended to cover children studying in the upper primary classes (i.e., classes VI–VIII) in 3,479 Educationally Backwards Blocks. The nutritional norm for the upper primary stage was fixed at a higher level, i.e., 700 calories and 20 grams of protein. The scheme was further extended to all parts of the country from April 1, 2008. The broader point remains that the Midday Meal Program, as well as the larger mandate of the universalization of primary education, has undeniably been energized in the years following the SCI's intervention in 2001 and soon thereafter.

Expenditure incurred is a straightforward metric; the number of school children covered by the program is another. Examined on these parameters, it is undeniably the case that the program has expanded rapidly in the years following the SCI's landmark order in November 2001. Expenditure by the Government of India on the Midday Meal Program expanded, though gradually so, in the years following the SCI's initial orders – from 1,031.24 crores in 2001–2002 to 1,237 crores in 2002–2003 and 1,375 crores the following year.[23] The expenditure rose more rapidly from the year 2005–2006 onwards and almost doubled in the two years between 2005–2006 and 2007–2008.[24] While some of the increase in expenditure might have been limited to countering inflation, the rapid increase in outlays (such as between 2005 and 2008), clearly outpaced inflation. Furthermore, the improvement in reach and coverage of the program also makes clear that the increased expenditure went far beyond merely countering inflation, and did in fact meaningfully expand the program. Thus, in its survey for the year 2013–2014, the National University of Educational Planning and Administration [NUEPA] reported that 88.6 percent of schools (government or government-aided) provided midday meals and 74.9 percent of such schools had a kitchen shed.[25] In 2006–2007, the percentage of schools with such a kitchen shed stood at 29 percent.[26]

Another measure of impact would be the degree to which it has achieved the more concrete goals underlying such a program. At a practical level, Jean

---

[23] The budget figures for the relevant years are helpfully summarized in *The School Feeding Program in India*, MS SWAMINATHAN RESEARCH FOUNDATION, Aug. 2011, at 29, www.mssrf.org/sites/default/files/School-Feeding-Programmes-in-India.pdf.

[24] *Id.*

[25] NATIONAL UNIVERSITY OF EDUCATIONAL PLANNING AND ADMINISTRATION, ELEMENTARY EDUCATION IN INDIA: TRENDS (2005–06 – 2013–14) 1 (Jan. 2015).

[26] NATIONAL UNIVERSITY OF EDUCATIONAL PLANNING AND ADMINISTRATION, ELEMENTARY EDUCATION IN INDIA – WHERE DO WE STAND? STATE REPORT CARDS (2006–07) XIV (Nov. 2008).

Drèze argues that the Midday Meal Program could be seen to have three broad objectives: educational advancement, improving child nutrition and increasing social equity, or reducing caste based distinctions.[27] The most obvious beneficial outcome expected is with respect to attendance rates in school; it is hoped that the regular provision of midday meals incentivizes greater enrolment (and, more significantly, attendance) by all students, but particularly those who might otherwise face social or practical barriers to attendance.

Furthermore, it is thought that improvement in classroom participation is not merely quantitative but also qualitative. Preventing hunger obviously has immense intrinsic value, but is also thought to enhance learning outcomes by enabling poor children to focus on what is being taught.[28] Faced with a choice of allocation of resources to counter hunger and malnutrition, the State might plausibly prefer the Midday Meal Program since it enables targeted delivery in a relatively controlled environment. There might be a concern that alternatives (such as the PDS system or direct cash transfers to impoverished families) might not meet the objective as well, either because the money is diverted to other needs or because all vulnerable sections are not equally served. These alternative modes might fail either on account of leakages and inefficiencies within the governmental structure or because of other social and cultural obstacles such as discrimination against female children.

The objective of promoting social equality gains salience in the context of India's history of stratification and division along caste lines, where eating together would be taboo (particularly for *Dalit* and upper-caste students). The Supreme Court has tried to actively promote this objective by mandating that, in the appointment of cooks and helpers, preference would be given to persons who are from the Scheduled Castes or Scheduled Tribes.[29]

The available social science evidence also suggests that there have been important gains since 2001 in all three of these contexts. It is, of course, difficult to show that the Court's decision itself has caused improvements in any of these. One of the complicating factors in assessing the success (or lack thereof) of the SCI's intervention in a case of this kind is that there is activity at multiple levels (and by multiple wings of government) around the time of,

---

[27] Jean Drèze & Aparajita Goel, *Future of Mid-Day Meals*, 38 Ec. Pol. Weekly 4673 (2003).

[28] See, e.g., Diana F. Jyoti, Edward A. Frongillo & Sonya J. Jones, *Food Insecurity Affects School Children's Academic Performance, Weight Gain, and Social Skills*, 135 J. Nutrition 2831 (2005).

[29] See Order dated April 20, 2004, *Peoples Union for Civil Liberties v. Union of India & Others*, Writ Petition (Civil) No. 196 of 2001, www.righttofoodindia.org/orders/apr2004.html.

and subsequent to, the judicial intervention by the SCI, and the Court's decision itself reflects an ongoing trend toward increased support for school meal programs. But that is also inevitable. Court interventions do not take place in a vacuum, but in the midst of a complex mix of political and social circumstances. Indeed, the central theme of *The Hollow Hope* is precisely this – that various factors so constrained the US Supreme Court that its directives in the realm of school integration and abortion rights could not really be effective.[30] We therefore think it is fair to regard this evidence, of improvement in various educational and nutritional outcomes in India post 2001, as at least prima facie evidence of a certain degree of "success" on the part of the SCI in creating social change with regard to approaches to education and child nutrition. In some cases, there is also additional social science evidence to suggest that the relationship is causal.

In general, there has clearly been significant progress in the realm of primary education in India in recent years. Enrolment in primary classes increased from 101.16 million in 2002–2003 to 131.85 million in 2006–2007 and further to 137.1 million in 2011–2012, before showing a declining trend.[31] With respect to retention of students, the ratio of Grade V to Grade I stood at 93 percent in 2013–2014, compared with 70 percent in 2005–2006.[32] In primary grades, the annual dropout rate estimated in 2013–2014 stands at 4.7 percent, compared with 10 percent in 2005–2006.[33] Another factor that is generally regarded as important to attain the objective of universal elementary education is a high level of transition from the primary to the upper primary level.[34] This indicator has improved significantly from 64.48 percent in 2002–2003 to 89.58 percent in 2012–2013.[35]

Some studies have also found a direct causal relationship between the Midday Meal Program and increases in school attendance, post-2011. One study, which used propensity score matching to analyze the effect of midday meal provision on school attendance, found that attendance rates

---

[30] See ROSENBERG, *supra* note 4, at ch. 2, 6, 7.

[31] NATIONAL UNIVERSITY OF EDUCATIONAL PLANNING AND ADMINISTRATION, ELEMENTARY EDUCATION IN INDIA: PROGRESS TOWARDS UEE at para. 5.1 (Aug. 2014).

[32] NATIONAL UNIVERSITY OF EDUCATIONAL PLANNING & ADMINISTRATION, ELEMENTARY EDUCATION IN INDIA: TRENDS (2005–06–2013–14), *supra* note 25, at 2.

[33] *Id.*

[34] NATIONAL UNIVERSITY OF EDUCATIONAL PLANNING AND ADMINISTRATION, ELEMENTARY EDUCATION IN INDIA: PROGRESS TOWARDS UEE *supra* note 32, at para. 5.9.

[35] *Id.*

were 29 percent higher for beneficiaries of the program in government schools, and 22 percent overall, compared to non-beneficiaries.[36]

Assessing the impact of the program, and its expansion, on the nutritional status of children is more complicated, but several studies have attempted to examine the relationship between the Midday Meal Decision and nutritional outcomes for children. For instance, a study carried out by researchers from the Department of Community Health, St. John's Medical College, Bangalore, compared the nutritional status of children in corresponding age groups before and after the introduction of the scheme in Karnataka in 2003 (and the earlier intervention by the Supreme Court in 2001).[37] The children studied were those enrolled in four government lower primary schools.[38] Health records of 634 children were assessed (340 records for the year 2001 and 294 for the year 2005).[39] The study generally found an improvement in the nutritional status of children subsequent to the introduction of the scheme.[40] This was evidenced by a reduction in stunting among both boys and girls, and also by a reduction in the proportion of children with Grade 3 and Grade 4 under-nourishment.[41]

Similarly, a non-governmental organization active in the realm of education – *Pratichi* – published, in February 2010, a qualitative assessment of the impact of the Midday Meal Program in West Bengal.[42] The Report offers a nuanced (but overall positive) view of the impact of the Midday Meal Scheme on the nutritional status and educational experience of rural and urban primary school students in West Bengal. This follows up on an earlier report of the same organization finding clear evidence of a positive impact of the program on school attendance rates.[43] The 2004 Report found as follows:

---

[36] Stephanie Bonds, "Food for Thought: Evaluating the Impact of India's Midday Meal Program on Educational Attainment" (Unpublished manuscript) (May 2012), http://econ.berkeley.edu/sites/default/files/Bonds.pdf.

[37] Christie Minj et al., *Impact of School Mid Day Meal Program on the Nutritional Status of Children in a Rural Area of South Karnataka, India*, 2 INT'L J. CURRENT RESEARCH ACADEMIC REV. 78 (2014).

[38] *Id.*

[39] *Id.*

[40] *Id.*

[41] *Id.*

[42] PATICHI (INDIA) TRUST, THE PRATICHI REPORT ON MID-DAY MEAL: THE MID-DAY MEAL PROGRAMME IN URBAN PRIMARY AND RURAL UPPER PRIMARY SCHOOLS IN WEST BENGAL (2010), www.righttofoodindia.org/data/pratichi_report_on_mid_day_meal.pdf.

[43] See Kumar Rana, "The Possibilities of Midday Meal Programme in West Bengal," Paper presented at the Workshop on West Bengal: Challenges and Choices, Centre for Social Sciences, Calcutta, July 27–28, 2004, www.righttofoodindia.org/data/mdms_kumarRana_WB.doc.

A comparative analysis of the average attendance records of the children (for the month prior to the launching of the programme and for the month preceding the study) shows a 10.1 percentage point of increase in the rate of attendance. A comparison between the records of the schools with and without the MDM programme also substantiates the difference – while the non-MDM schools had a rate of attendance of 60.6 percent in the month preceding the study, it was 71.9 percent in the case of the schools with MDM programme.[44]

Some critics argue that the program may not contribute significantly towards the nutritional well-being of children if parents account for the program by reducing the food provided to the children at home. Several studies, however, directly refute this concern: a 2007 study by Alfridi concluded that the program significantly increased the daily intake of calories, iron and protein for recipient children. In other contexts, social scientists have found that while there is some tendency for poor parents to substitute between school feeding programs and home meals, the substitution effect is far from complete, so that school feeding programs do tend to increase the nutritional allocation of recipient children.[45]

For caste-based norms, and equality, the evidence is more limited. Given the supposedly universal nature of the scheme, there is little effective way of identifying the causal effects of the scheme, even in the context of any observed changes in social norms regarding caste. And if parents seek to avoid this aspect of the decision, by sending children a packed lunch or having them return home to eat, there would often be limited reporting of this fact. But the evidence that exists does point to the Court's decision being implemented, as intended: the general evidence is that children are being required to sit together to eat, regardless of caste. If the Court's decision is implemented in this way, it also seems extremely likely that there would be some positive change in caste-based norms. The experience for children of eating together at school might not always translate into a willingness to mix in other contexts, but it would clearly break down at least some of the strongest taboos surrounding caste-based differences.

[44] *Id.*

[45] Hanan G. Jacoby, *Is There an Intrahousehold Flypaper Effect? Evidence from a School Feeding Program*, 112 Econ. J. 196 (2002).

Admittedly, progress with respect to implementation of the Court's orders was mixed, even in the Court's own estimation.[46] In April 2004, the Supreme Court observed as follows:

> It is a matter of anguish that despite lapse of nearly three and half years, the order dated 28th November, 2001 has not been fully implemented by all the States and Union Territories. As already stated earlier, many of the States have given only half-baked information and figures. Further, we wish to make it clear that the fact that some of the States were permitted to at least make a start in some of the districts in terms of the order dated 2nd May, 2003 does not mean that this Court has modified or varied the earlier order dated 28th November, 2001. It is a constitutional duty of every State and Union Territory to implement in letter and spirit the directions contained in the order dated 28th November, 2001.[47]

The social science literature also clearly reveals a range of gaps in the implementation of the program. Even scholars generally supportive of the program concede the existence of significant flaws, and point to poor infrastructure (such as the lack of running water, toilets and staff to run the program) and administrative lacunae.[48] Some gaps are geographical in nature, and certain States perform significantly worse than others. A Performance Audit of the Program covered 130 villages spread over 12 districts of Orissa and Uttar Pradesh.[49] The study results revealed that the performance of the Midday Meal Scheme was better in Orissa than in Uttar Pradesh:[50] 86.7 percent of Orissa's children were getting the second best category of midday meals (i.e., regular but inadequate and unsatisfactory meal), whereas only 51.8 percent of the children in Uttar Pradesh were in this category.[51]

The uncertain quality of the food served is often relatable to corruption and inefficiencies in the procurement and distribution processes.[52] Unsurprisingly, poorer and rural districts are the worst affected. There have been several

---

[46] See, e.g., the discussion in Nick Robinson, *Expanding Judiciaries: India and the Rise of the Good Governance Court*, 8 WASH. U. GLOBAL STUD. L. REV. 1, 56 (2009).

[47] See *supra* note 29.

[48] Rama V. Baru et al., *Full Meal or Package Deal?*, 43 ECON. POL. WEEKLY 20 (2008).

[49] PARSHURAM RAI, PERFORMANCE AUDIT OF FOOD SECURITY SCHEMES IN ORISSA AND UP (Centre for Environment and Food Security, New Delhi, 2011), www.indiaenvironmentportal .org.in/files/performance%20audit%20of%20food%20security.pdf.

[50] *Id.*

[51] *Id.*

[52] See, e.g., *Lessons Learned from India's Midday Meal Scheme for Schoolchildren*, THE GUARDIAN, Aug. 11, 2014, at www.theguardian.com/global-development/2014/aug/11/india-midday-meal-scheme-schoolchildren.

reports in recent years of children falling ill after consumption of the midday meal, clearly raising serious concerns about the quality control mechanisms in place.[53]

To an important degree, however, both the Court and the government have responded to these gaps and flaws, by refining their orders and the design of the program. In an order dated May 8, 2002 and in subsequent orders, the Court appointed certain experts (as Commissioners) to monitor implementation of the orders of the Court in the matter. These Commissioners are mandated to monitor the implementation of the interim orders passed by the SCI in the Writ Petition, to review the performance of the Union and States Governments in implementing the concerned programs, to investigate complaints and failures, and to make recommendations to the State Governments and the Supreme Court with respect to the enforcement of the right to food.[54] A number of the individuals appointed to perform this role have also been quite prominent. An expert in the relevant area – Dr. Naresh Chandra Saxena, former Secretary to the Planning Commission and former Secretary in the Ministry of Rural Development – is currently Supreme Court appointed Commissioner.[55] Mr. Harsh Mander – a former Indian Administrative Service Officer but today better known as a social activist – has been appointed as Special Commissioner.[56]

These Commissioners have submitted detailed reports and recommendations to the SCI over the years, incorporating among other things their views of the progress made by different States in complying with the Court's orders. The assistance derived by the Court from these reports is evident; for example, the Court's order of April 20, 2004 refers to the Commissioners' analysis of the

---

[53] See, e.g., *Bihar Midday Meal Horror: 22 Children Die in Saran, 50 Students Fall Ill in Madhubani*, THE TIMES OF INDIA, July 17, 2013, https://timesofindia.indiatimes.com/india/Bihar-midday-meal-horror-22-children-die-in-Saran-50-students-fall-ill-in-Madhubani/articleshow/21121325.cms; *Mid-Day Meal Horror Continues; Over 100 Fall Sick in TN*, BUSINESS STANDARD, July 18, 2013, www.business-standard.com/article/current-affairs/mid-day-meal-horror-continues-over-100-fall-sick-in-tn-113071800702_1.html; *Centre Seeks Report from Bihar on Mid-Day Meal Tragedy*, BUSINESS STANDARD, July 17, 2013, www.business-standard.com/article/economy-policy/centre-seeks-report-from-bihar-on-mid-day-meal-tragedy-113071700793_1.html.

[54] See Order dated May 8, 2002, *Peoples Union for Civil Liberties* v. Union *of India & Others*, Writ Petition (Civil) No. 196 of 2001, www.righttofoodindia.org/orders/may8.html; Order dated October 29, 2002, *Peoples Union for Civil Liberties* v. *Union of India & Others*, Writ Petition (Civil) No. 196 of 2001, www.righttofoodindia.org/orders/oct29.html.

[55] Information about the Commissioners, and their functioning, is available on a dedicated website established to make accessible their work. See *About Us*, SUPREME SCCOMMISSIONERS, at www.sccommissioners.org/about-us/.

[56] *Id.*

progress made by different States.[57] In the same order, the Court also issued directions, in terms of the recommendation made by the Commissioners, to the effect that the Midday Meal Program should be extended even during vacation time in drought-affected areas of the country.[58]

There is also extensive correspondence between the Commissioners and various State Governments regarding the implementation of the food security schemes being monitored by the SCI (including though not limited to the Midday Meal Program).[59] The pattern appears to be that the Commissioners, in discharge of their functions, seek information – either generally or in response to some particular situation presenting an immediate challenge (such as floods, draught or other natural calamities) – regarding the State's actions to implement the existing governmental programs and thereby progressively realize the right to food. At least in certain cases, the Commissioners' intervention by itself appears to prompt corrective action on the part of the concerned authorities.

III. AN EXPANDING PROGRAM AND THE COURT'S ROLE

The evidence is thus quite clear that the Midday Meal Program did in fact expand significantly from both a quantitative and qualitative standpoint in the years immediately following the Supreme Court's orders in this case. The harder question is whether this expansion in the scope and goals of the program was "caused" by the Court's intervention, or was merely a consequence of the changed political environment and the ideological leanings of the newly elected government. We consider these alternative possibilities in the next two sections.

A. Hollow Hope *Revisited?*

One possibility is that the Court played an extremely marginal role in actually promoting the expansion of the Midday Meal Program in this context, and thus in achieving the educational and nutritional benefits outlined above.[60] The program had been formally adopted by the Central Government in 1995, and subsequent to that the battle was largely about the size of the

---

[57] See Order dated April 20, 2004, *supra* note 29.
[58] *Id.*
[59] Much of this correspondence is available at *Public Distribution System: Commissioners' Interventions*, RIGHT TO FOOD CAMPAIGN, www.righttofoodindia.org/pds/pds_commissioners_interventions.html.
[60] See generally ROSENBERG, *supra* note 4.

budget allocation, or quantity of resources, that would be made available to ensure that the program was realized on a truly national basis. While budgetary allocation for the program from the Central Government rose steadily in the years following the SCI's intervention, this occurred without any explicit reference to the Court's order.[61]

Indeed, in his budget speech in July 2004 (just months after the SCI's follow-up order of April 20, 2004), persuading Parliament to pass a new tax designed in large part to fund expansion of the Midday Meal Program, Finance Minister Chidambaram said this:

> In my scheme of things, no issue enjoys a higher priority than providing basic education to all children. The NCMP [National Common Minimum Program] mandates Government to levy an education cess. I propose to levy a cess of 2 per cent. The new cess will yield about Rs.4000–5000 crore in a full year. The whole of the amount collected as cess will be earmarked for education, which will naturally include providing a nutritious cooked midday meal. If primary education and the nutritious cooked meal scheme can work hand in hand, I believe there will be a new dawn for the poor children of India.[62]

The broader political context was itself both to explain the Court's order, and the expansion of the program. The United Progressive Alliance (UPA), a Congress-led coalition, government came to power in May 2004 on an election manifesto strongly advocating what it described as equitable growth, including greater government support in the sectors of public education and healthcare.[63] The loss of the National Democratic Alliance (NDA), BJP-led coalition, government, was understood by observers, with the benefit of hindsight at least, as being attributable to an out-of-touch electoral campaign it headlined as "India Shining."[64] The idea underpinning this campaign was that India was experiencing a rising middle class, and enhanced opportunities for business growth and foreign investment – but this contrasted starkly with

---

[61] For a very helpful analysis of the budgetary allocations (and processes) concerning the program, *see* ACCOUNTABILITY INITIATIVE, PAISA DISTRICT SURVEYS MID-DAY MEAL SCHEME (June 2013), http://mdm.nic.in/Files/OrderCirculars/Final_PAISA_MDM_Report_18july_2013 .pdf.

[62] P. Chidambaram, Minister of Finance, Union Budget 2004–2005 Speech, July 8, 2004, http://indiabudget.nic.in/ub2004–05/bs/speecha.htm.

[63] MANIFESTO OF THE INDIAN NATIONAL CONGRESS: 2004 GENERAL ELECTIONS (2004).

[64] See, e.g., *Shock Defeat for India's Hindu nationalists*, THE GUARDIAN, May 14, 2004, at www.theguardian.com/world/2004/may/14/india.randeepramesh.

the reality of widespread poverty and malnutrition.[65] In contrast, the Congress Party's focus on rural and marginalized communities was thought to have struck a chord with the electorate.[66]

This might also itself have been a factor supporting the willingness of the SCI to adopt the orders it did in the case: a bare reading of the orders of the SCI suggests that the Government did not oppose most of the relevant orders, with the result that these were not passed in a particularly adversarial setting.[67] It also meant that the implementation of the Court's orders took place within a supportive political context. The program had been initiated, in certain parts of the country at least, well before the Court's intervention and adopted by the Central Government in 1995 (several years before the SCI's Orders), and there was independent legislative activity in furtherance of some of these concerns that cannot really be traced to these orders of the Court. For instance, Parliament recognized the right to primary education as a fundamental right, by way of a constitutional amendment, in 2002 (although this was formally notified into force only in 2010).

B. A Role for the Court?

We suggest, however, that the evidence does in fact point to the Court playing some role in broadening access to the Midday Meal Program across India, and a program with more ambitious goals – i.e., goals that included cooked meals, with higher nutritional value, and the effective incorporation of an anti-caste principle. Prior to the Court's orders in 2001, there were vast disparities geographically in the extent and manner of implementation of the program. No legislation governing the field had yet been enacted, and therefore the approach of different States varied widely. There was also little pressure for poorly governed States to adopt the Program, much less maintain an acceptable level of quality, whereas after 2001 there was a progressive expansion in the Program across various States.

The Court also directed that the meal must necessarily be a cooked midday meal; previously, most States were providing dry rations to the children. The Court further specified certain simple, minimal standards with respect to the nutritional content of the meals, directing that the meals should have at least

---

[65] See, e.g., Poorvi Chitalkar & Varun Gauri, *India: Compliance with Orders on the Right to Food, in* SOCIAL RIGHTS JUDGMENTS AND THE POLITICS OF COMPLIANCE: MAKING IT STICK 288 (Malcom Langford ed., 2017) (noting a newspaper headline at the time that asked "If India is booming, why are its children starving?").

[66] See *id.*

[67] See HUMAN RIGHTS LAW NETWORK, RIGHT TO FOOD (4th ed., 2009).

300 calories and 8–12 grams of protein. While, as Part II notes, deviations and lapses of course continued, there were also fairly high levels of compliance with this directive.

How and why might the Court's intervention have helped achieve this form of expansion in the program? One explanation, we suggest, lies in the capacity for the implementation of complex social programs of this kind to be subject to persistent "burdens of inertia" – or political and bureaucratic dynamics that dramatically slow the adoption and implementation of some or all aspects of the program.[68] Inertia of this kind, as one of us has suggested elsewhere, can affect the enjoyment of a range of fundamental constitutional and human rights; and is thus an important reason for constitutional democracies to give courts powers of constitutional judicial review: courts have a range of both communicative and coercive tools available to them, which can effectively help counter or reverse inertia of this kind.[69] They can bring increased attention to certain issues or arguments for legal and constitutional change; and use "strong" or coercive remedial tools to force executive officials to pay attention to issues of implementation.[70]

The approach of the SCI in the *Midday Meal* Case also closely followed this pattern: The Court's decision itself brought significant and sustained attention to the issue; and its willingness to retain jurisdiction over a number of years, and pass coercive orders, increased the pressure on State and local officials to take active steps to roll-out the program in their area. The Court's intervention thus arguably both increased pressure on the Central government to fund the program, and on State and local government officials to devote the time and resources necessary to implement it, in a way that had an important capacity to overcome "burdens of inertia" in the roll-out of the program, in various States.[71]

---

[68] Dixon, *Creating Dialogue, supra* note 5; Dixon, *A Democratic Theory, supra* note 5; Dixon, *The Supreme Court of Canada, supra* note 5; Dixon, *The Core Case, supra* note 5. For an exploration of these arguments in the Indian context, see also Rishad Chowdhury, *"The Road Less Travelled": Article 21A and the Fundamental Right to Primary Education in India*, 4 INDIAN J. CONST. L. 24 (2010).

[69] Dixon, *The Core Case, supra* note 5.

[70] *Id.*

[71] There is a rich literature concerning "dialogue" between the judiciary and other organs of the State in furtherance of the enforcement of socioeconomic rights. In this chapter, we focus on the back-and-forth between the Court and the executive in the aftermath of the Court's directions, and the exchange of information and perspectives incidental to the implementation of those directions. Our account is quite plausibly consistent with the fuller understanding of "dialogue" developed in this body of literature, but the constraints of this chapter do not permit us to develop this account fully. See generally Dixon, *Creating Dialogue, supra* note 5.

i. Communicative effects and media attention

Apart from direct compliance with the Court's directions, the evidence suggests that one clear effect of the decision was to increase media attention to the issue of malnutrition, and the right to food in India. In the United States, a number of political scientists have shown that court decisions can directly increase the attention given to certain issues by the media. In the context of the right to food campaign, this seems to have been a clear consequence of both the Court's 2001 order and subsequent enforcement orders. In a 2004 study, Jean Drèze found that in the six months between January and June 2000, *The Hindu* (one of India's leading English-language newspapers) published 300 op-eds, but not a single opinion piece on the right to food or malnutrition. Between 2001 and 2012, in contrast, Poorvi Chitalkar and Varun Gauri found that there were 118 articles related to the right to food.[72] They also found a similar increase in coverage of the issue in an English-language weekly magazine, *Outlook*.[73]

In interviews with members of the Right to Food Campaign, Brierley also found that this reflected a distinct change in the ability of members of the Campaign to persuade the mainstream media to address issues of malnutrition and food security.[74] The Campaign worked actively throughout the period to ensure that the media did in fact cover issues around the right to food. It also worked to encourage the media to publicize the success of the program in increasing school attendance, in a way that gradually helped build popular support for the program.[75]

Coverage of this kind had an important capacity to prompt more critical reflection on the part of the middle class about the "India shining" narrative of the BJP, and the degree to which it obscured pressing issues of inequality and poverty.[76] Arguably, it also helped promote competition between various political representatives and parties over issues of inequality and human rights. For individual legislators, or elected officials, it meant that it often became politically advantageous to take action demonstrating their commitment to the program.[77] And for political parties, "the fact that food security . . . bec[ame] a political issue" meant that in many states, political parties and candidates

---

[72] Chitalkar & Gauri, *supra* note 65.
[73] *Id.*
[74] Alyssa Brierley, "PULC and Political Mobilization 20" (Unpublished manuscript) (2018).
[75] See *id.* at 14.
[76] Chitalkar & Gauri, *supra* note 65.
[77] See Brierley, *supra* note 74, at 18.

actively competed to show their commitment to the program.[78] It is instructive, for example, that the present NDA Government recently emphatically denied suggestions and criticisms by various opposition parties that it had diluted the Central Government's commitment to the Midday Meal Program.[79]

ii. Coercive effects and pressure on state and local officials

The Court in the Midday Meal Decision further deployed a complex set of tools for monitoring implementation of the decision, which have arguably played an important role in ensuring the effectiveness of the Court's intervention. These orders involved intensive ongoing monitoring by the Court itself, and were inherently coercive in nature: The SCI retained the case on its docket, and passed follow-up orders from time to time. The Court also appointed Commissioners who proactively monitored State Governments in their implementation of the program.

This complex form of judicial monitoring had a number of effects. One was to create a ready source of information and expertise as to best practices regarding the implementation of the program.[80] Another was to ensure that, if state officials did not take action to implement the program, they faced a number of potential adverse consequences. By issuing a writ of continuing mandamus, or maintaining ongoing supervisory jurisdiction in the case, the SCI effectively retained power to impose a variety of sanctions for noncompliance with its orders. This included specific orders relating to the mode and timing of delivery of the program, and the power to impose sanctions for contempt of court. For individual State and local officials, this meant that any deliberate or flagrant decision not to comply with the Court's orders could attract both financial and criminal penalties, including imprisonment.

Actual orders for contempt were rarely issued in the case: only two orders for contempt were issued in the 14 years in which the Court has monitored implementation of the case. But, as one of us suggested elsewhere in the context of a power of legislative override, sanctions need not ultimately be used in order to exert an indirect influence on behavior: if sanctions for contempt were seen as a credible possibility, in the event of deliberate noncompliance with the Court's orders, in equilibrium one would expect far

---

[78] See *id.* at 15.
[79] *Ministry of HRD Committed to Flagship Schemes of School Education Including Mid Day Meal Scheme*, Press Information Bureau, Government of India, May 29, 2015.
[80] Brierley, *supra* note 74, at 10.

fewer instances of deliberate non-compliance.[81] Moreover, in parallel litigation involving the Right to Food, sanctions for contempt were applied far
more frequently, thereby meaning that there was in fact a quite credible signal
from the Court that it would be willing to use its powers to punish for
contempt, in appropriate cases.[82] Another important sanction available to
the Court, at least indirectly, was more administrative in nature: as Robinson
found in interviews in Bihar, many State and local executive officials were
concerned that if they did not diligently implement the Court's orders, they
would get "negative remarks in their record," which in turn would adversely
affect their chances of promotion.[83]

The Court's ability to impose sanctions of this kind was also greatly aided by
an effective monitoring apparatus: in part, this depended on favorable background political conditions, this time in the form of the passage of The Right
to Information Act, 2005, which allowed individuals (for a small fee) to access
a wide variety of information about local government performance. But it also
depended on the work of the Commissioners as part of the Court's formal
mechanism for monitoring implementation of its orders: the Commissioners
were extremely effective in obtaining information from State and local officials about the actual implementation of the program in various areas, and
thus in creating the necessary factual record for further enforcement or
sanctions by the Court.[84]

IV. BEYOND THE MIDDAY MEAL CASE

Even if one views the Court's intervention as "successful" in this way, one
might question the degree to which this success is generalizable, even within
the Indian context. On one reading, the facts of the case were quite unique:
they involved an attempt by the petitioner to persuade the government to
distribute surplus grain in the midst of a serious drought, which was causing
widespread hunger and malnutrition.[85] In one sense, it is thus unsurprising
that the government chose not to oppose the order sought by the petitioner,

---

[81] Dixon, The Supreme Court of Canada, supra note 5. But see Nick Robinson, Closing the
Implementation Gap: Grievance Redress and India's Social Welfare Programs, 53 COLUM.
J. TRANSNAT'L L. 321, 343 (2013) (noting that some officials suggested there was no credible
threat of sanctions for contempt).

[82] See Brierley, supra note 74.

[83] Robinson, supra note 81, at 343.

[84] See id. at 342–343; Brierley, supra note 74.

[85] Compare Brierley, supra note 74.

and instead worked with the Right to Food Campaign to ensure the successful implementation of the Court's order.

Put differently, even seeing the case in a broader perspective, as implicating an attempt by the petitioner to entrench and expand the coverage of an existing school feeding program, the "success" of the Court's intervention may have depended on a range of relatively demanding preconditions – including strong monitoring by experts, strong social movement activism and favorable political conditions.[86] The Court's success in this context also cannot be understood without attention to the role played by the Right to Food Campaign.[87] When the Campaign first began, it was largely focused on constitutional litigation itself. But over time, as the litigation was successful, leaders of the Campaign came to see the litigation not so much as an end, but as a natural focus for coordinating a broader set of political efforts to change government policy regarding food security. There was also an important triangular relationship between the Court, the government and civil society in this context: the Commissioners' Office, as Brierley has pointed out, was given wide discretion to engage with a range of civil society actors, and in exercising that discretion chose to meet regularly with members of the Campaign at the national and state level. Many members of the Commissioners' staff were also current or former members of the Campaign, and the Commissioners have appointed various State advisors drawn directly from the Campaign.[88]

The success of the Court's intervention should also be seen in light of background political conditions, and in particular the degree of political competition over the issue in various states. In Orissa in the 1990s, the High Court issued orders in relation to the right to food which highlighted large numbers of deaths from starvation, and this led to increased media coverage of the issue. But this also led to little ultimate change in the government's response.[89] We suggest that this was in part because, despite the appearance of strong political competition between the Janata Party and the Congress in the State, the reality was that the State government was controlled by a single family (the Patnaiks), which had little real electoral incentive to respond to the decision.[90] At Central level, in contrast, political pressure existed even within the UPA government that came to power in 2004, in the form of the large and

---

[86] *Id.* at 17.
[87] *Id.*
[88] *Id.* at 9.
[89] Chitalkar & Gauri, *supra* note 65, at 6–8.
[90] For a general overview, see N. R. Mohanty, *Orissa Politics: An Overview*, SANGHARSH INDIA, May 3, 2009, at https://sangharshindia.wordpress.com/2009/05/03/orissa-politics-an-overview/.

influential block of "Left" parties, which had refused to join the Government but extended support from the outside and were critical to the UPA maintaining a parliamentary majority.[91] This itself created an important source of political pressure for the government to respond to public demands for broader roll-out of the program, following the publicity created by the Court's decision.

Whether all of these factors were critical to the success of the Court's order is impossible to know: clearly not all of these preconditions will be met in every case in which a constitutional court attempts to exert social change by the enforcement of constitutional rights. Focusing on the potential preconditions for successful constitutional change by courts, however, need not be read as a source of constitutional pessimism: it may also be understood as the basis for a theory of "qualified hope" about the capacity of courts to create social change, in partnership with other actors.

V. CONCLUSION: A CASE FOR QUALIFIED VERSUS HOLLOW HOPE?

What, then, do we make the Indian experience in the context of the Midday Meal Decision from a broader comparative perspective? On one level, the decision involved a highly ambitious form of judicial intervention: a decision by a court to order the universal delivery of a highly specific and ambitious school meal program, designed to deliver educational, nutritional and broader anti-discrimination goals, against the backdrop of clear existing limits on state capacity to deliver these goals. The program has also had notable success in achieving almost all these goals. Briefly, outlays in monetary terms increased significantly in the years following the Court's orders. Further, the reach and expansion of the program in terms of schools and children covered has also increased steadily in recent years. The Midday Meal Program has now received statutory recognition after the enactment of the National Food Security Act, 2013.

But equally, the Midday Meal Decision did not arise in a vacuum, but in the context of momentum towards both the universalization of primary school education, and the expansion of the Midday Meal Program by the Union Government, as well as the paradoxical (and morally troubling) situation of significant malnutrition despite overflowing governmental food stocks.

---

[91] In the 2004 Elections, the Communist Party of India (Marxist) won 43 parliamentary seats and the Communist Party of India won 10 seats. Along with some smaller parties, this block of "Left" parties enabled the UPA Government to cross the halfway mark in the Lok Sabha (the lower house of Parliament).

The question this raises is whether it is fair to attribute any of the subsequent expansion in the reach and funding of the program, to the Court itself. On one reading, the most significant reason for the expansion of the Midday Meal Program was the broadly supportive environment for expansion of the program, enhanced by the backlash to the previous Government's "India Shining" electoral campaign and the consequent election of the UPA government in 2004. On this account, given the tentative steps taken towards the adoption of the program by the Central Government in 1995 and its (slow) expansion since that time, the election of the UPA government would have brought about the same momentum, regardless of whether the interim orders of the SCI in the Right to Food case had been passed or not.

Another reading, however, is that the Court's intervention played an important role in several ways. It brought significant and sustained public attention to the issue, in ways that made it harder for governments to refuse to fund, and it increased pressure on local and state executive officials to take steps to roll-out the program, in ways that helped counter significant local inertia in the roll-out of the program in certain parts of India.

We suggest in this chapter that this is the better way of interpreting the available evidence on the implementation of the decision. Even if we accept this interpretation, however, there remain a range of unanswered questions about the broader lessons this experience offers for comparative scholars: to what extent do the conditions that helped support implementation of the Midday Meal Decision apply in other cases, even in India, let alone in other constitutional democracies? And if they don't, does this imply that comparably ambitious forms of judicial intervention are likely to fail? We also do not attempt to answer these questions in this chapter. Rather, we aim to point to the *Midday Meal Decision* as an example of the *potential* for courts to achieve significant social change, albeit under quite special social and political conditions – or as providing the empirical basis for the *plausibility* of a theory of "qualified hope" about the capacity of courts to create meaningful social change, in partnership with other actors.

There is clear value to scholarship that reminds us of the limits to courts as a vehicle for advancing the interests of the poor or otherwise disadvantaged. Scholarship of this kind helps remind us of the need to engage popular and legislative politics, as well as judicial institutions, if we are to create meaningful social change; and by most accounts, there is very limited scholarship of this kind in India.[92]

---

[92] See e.g. Arun Thiruvengadam, "Assessing the Social Rights Jurisprudence of India: Perspectives from Constitutional Theory and Comparative Law," Paper presented at the

But too great a focus on the limits of constitutional litigation as a tool for social change can also obscure the degree to which constitutional litigation and social action, when done right, can reinforce each other, in ways that enhance the value and efficacy of both as mechanisms of democratic self-government.

REFERENCES

About Us, SUPREME SCCOMMISSIONERS, at www.sccommissioners.org/about-us/.
ACCOUNTABILITY INITIATIVE, PAISA DISTRICT SURVEYS MID-DAY MEAL SCHEME (June 2013), http://mdm.nic.in/Files/OrderCirculars/Final_PAISA_MDM_Report_18july_2013.pdf.
Baru, Rama V. et al., *Full Meal or Package Deal?*, 43 ECON. POL. WEEKLY (2008).
Bihar Midday Meal Horror: 22 Children Die in Saran, 50 Students Fall Ill in Madhubani, THE TIMES OF INDIA, July 17, 2013, https://timesofindia.indiatimes.com/india/Bihar-midday-meal-horror-22-children-die-in-Saran-50-students-fall-ill-in-Madhubani/articleshow/21121325.cms.
Bonds, Stephanie, "Food for Thought: Evaluating the Impact of India's Midday Meal Program on Educational Attainment" (Unpublished manuscript) (May 2012), http://econ.berkeley.edu/sites/default/files/Bonds.pdf.
Brierley, Alyssa, *PULC and Political Mobilization* 20 (Unpublished manuscript) (2018).
Centre Seeks Report from Bihar on Mid-Day Meal Tragedy BUSINESS STANDARD, July 17, 2013, www.business-standard.com/article/economy-policy/centre-seeks-report-from-bihar-on-mid-day-meal-tragedy-113071700793_1.html.
Chidambaram, P., Minister of Finance, Union Budget 2004–2005 Speech, July 8, 2004, http://indiabudget.nic.in/ub2004–05/bs/speecha.htm.
Chitalkar, Poorvi & Varun Gauri, *India: Compliance with Orders on the Right to Food*, in SOCIAL RIGHTS JUDGMENTS AND THE POLITICS OF COMPLIANCE: MAKING IT STICK (Malcolm Langford ed., 2017).
Chowdhury, Rishad, *The Road Less Travelled: Article 21A and the Fundamental Right to Primary Education in India*, 4 INJLCONLAW 24 (2010).
Dixon, Rosalind, *A Democratic Theory of Constitutional Comparison*, 56 AM. J. COMP. L. 947 (2008).
Creating Dialogue about Socioeconomic Rights: Strong-Form versus Weak-Form Judicial Review Revisited, 5 INT'L J. CONST. L. 391 (2007).
The Core Case for Weak-Form Judicial Review, 38 CARDOZO L. REV. 2193 (2017).
The Supreme Court of Canada, Charter Dialogue, and Deference, 47 OSGOODE HALL L.J. 235 (2009).
Drèze, Jean & Aparajita Goel, *Future of Mid-Day Meals*, 38 ECON. POL. WEEKLY 4673 (2003).
HIRSCHL, RAN, COMPARATIVE MATTERS: THE RENAISSANCE OF COMPARATIVE CONSTITUTIONAL LAW (2014).

Constitutional Reform Lecture Series, University of Zurich, May 7, 2015, www.asienundeuropa.uzh.ch/events/lectureseries/reform/thiruvengadam_en.html.

HUMAN RIGHTS LAW NETWORK, *RIGHT TO FOOD* (4th ed., 2009).

Jacoby, Hanan G., *Is There an Intrahousehold Flypaper Effect? Evidence from a School Feeding Program*, 112 ECON. J. 196 (2002).

Jyoti, Diana F., Edward A. Frongillo & Sonya J. Jones, *Food Insecurity Affects School Children's Academic Performance, Weight Gain, and Social Skills*, 135 J. NUTRITION 2831 (2005).

Lessons Learned from India's Midday Meal Scheme for Schoolchildren, THE GUARDIAN, Aug. 11, 2014, www.theguardian.com/global-development/2014/aug/11/india-midday-meal-scheme-schoolchildren.

Mid-Day Meal Horror Continues; Over 100 Fall Sick in TN, BUSINESS STANDARD, July 18, 2013, www.business-standard.com/article/current-affairs/mid-day-meal-horror-continues-over-100-fall-sick-in-tn-113071800702_1.html.

MANIFESTO OF THE INDIAN NATIONAL CONGRESS: 2004 GENERAL ELECTIONS (2004).

Minj, Christie et al., *Impact of School Mid Day Meal Program on the Nutritional status of Children in a Rural Area of South Karnataka, India*, 2 INT'L J. CURRENT RESEARCH ACADEMIC REV. 78 (2014).

Ministry of HRD Committed to Flagship Schemes of School Education Including Mid Day Meal Scheme, Press Information Bureau, Government of India, May 29, 2015.

Mohanty, N. R. *Orissa Politics: An Overview* SANGHARSH INDIA, May 3, 2009, https://sangharshindia.wordpress.com/2009/05/03/orissa-politics-an-overview/.

National Food Security Act, Section 5(1)(b), 2013.

NATIONAL UNIVERSITY OF EDUCATIONAL PLANNING AND ADMINISTRATION, ELEMENTARY EDUCATION IN INDIA: TRENDS (2005–06 – 2013–14) 1 (Jan. 2015). PROGRESS TOWARDS UEE.

WHERE DO WE STAND? STATE REPORT CARDS (2006–07) (Nov. 2008).

Order dated November 28, 2001, *Peoples Union for Civil Liberties* v. *Union of India & Others*, Writ Petition (Civil) No. 196 of 2001, www.righttofoodindia.org/orders/nov28.html.

Order dated April 20, 2004, *Peoples Union for Civil Liberties* v. *Union of India & Others*, Writ Petition (Civil) No. 196 of 2001, www.righttofoodindia.org/orders/apr2004.html.

Order dated May 8, 2002, *Peoples Union for Civil Liberties* v. *Union of India & Others*, Writ Petition (Civil) No. 196 of 2001, www.righttofoodindia.org/orders/may8.html.

Order dated October 29, 2002, *Peoples Union for Civil Liberties* v. *Union of India & Others*, Writ Petition (Civil) No. 196 of 2001, www.righttofoodindia.org/orders/oct29.html.

PATICHI (INDIA) TRUST, "THE PRATICHI REPORT ON MID-DAY MEAL: THE MID-DAY MEAL PROGRAMME IN URBAN PRIMARY AND RURAL UPPER PRIMARY SCHOOLS IN WEST BENGAL" (2010), www.righttofoodindia.org/data/pratichi_report_on_mid_day_meal.pdf.

Public Distribution System: Commissioners' Interventions, RIGHT TO FOOD CAMPAIGN, www.righttofoodindia.org/pds/pds_commissioners_interventions.html.

RAI, PARSHURAM, PERFORMANCE AUDIT OF FOOD SECURITY SCHEMES IN ORISSA AND UP (Centre for Environment and Food Security, New Delhi, 2011),

www.indiaenvironmentportal.org.in/files/performance%20audit%20of%20food%
20security.pdf.

Rana, Kumar, "The Possibilities of Midday Meal Programme in West Bengal," Paper
presented at the Workshop on West Bengal: Challenges and Choices, Centre for
Social Sciences, Calcutta, July 27–28, 2004, www.righttofoodindia.org/data/
mdms_kumarRana_WB.doc.

Robinson, Nick, *Closing the Implementation Gap: Grievance Redress and India's
Social Welfare Programs*, 53 COLUM. J. TRANSNAT'L L. 321 (2013)

Expanding Judiciaries: India and the Rise of the Good Governance Court, 8 WASH.
U. GLOBAL STUD. L. REV. 1 (2009).

ROSENBERG, GERALD N., THE HOLLOW HOPE: CAN COURTS BRING ABOUT
SOCIAL CHANGE (2nd ed.) 2008.

School Mid-Day Meals, RIGHT TO FOOD CAMPAIGN, www.righttofoodcampaign.in/
school-meals.

Shock Defeat for India's Hindu nationalists, THE GUARDIAN, May 14, 2004, www
.theguardian.com/world/2004/may/14/india.randeepramesh.

Social Justice Bench (Listing Notice), http://sci.nic.in/FileServer/2014–12-17_1418816381
.pdf.

Sripati, Vijayashri & Arun K. Thiruvengadam, *Constitutional Amendment Making the
Right to Education a Fundamental Right*, 2 INT. J. CONST. L. 148 (2004).

Thiruvengadam, Arun, "Assessing the Social Rights Jurisprudence of India: Perspectives from Constitutional Theory and Comparative Law," Paper presented at the
Constitutional Reform Lecture Series, University of Zurich, May 7, 2015, www
.asienundeuropa.uzh.ch/events/lectureseries/reform/thiruvengadam_en.html.

The Right to Food Case, RIGHT TO FOOD CAMPAIGN, www.righttofoodcampaign.in/
legal-action/-right-to-food-case.

The School Feeding Program in India, MS SWAMINATHAN RESEARCH FOUNDATION,
Aug. 2011, at 29, www.mssrf.org/sites/default/files/School-Feeding-Programmes-in-
India.pdf.

Writ Petition (C) No. 196 of 2001, www.righttofoodindia.org/case/petition.html.

10

Implementation in the Delhi Pollution Case

Lessons for the Future

ROBERT MOOG

I. INTRODUCTION

It has been well over 30 years since M. C. Mehta filed writ petition 13029 in 1985 with the Indian Supreme Court. Generally referred to as the Delhi Pollution Case (DPC), this public interest litigation (PIL) has generated an enormous amount of publicity and controversy. Perhaps because of the tremendous complexity involved in shifting the public transport system (all buses, taxis and auto rickshaws) of a rapidly modernizing city of some 15–16 million people from petrol and diesel to compressed natural gas (CNG), the case has captured the fascination of the public, academics, and policymakers in India, as well as academics elsewhere. It encompasses sociological, economic, engineering, climate science, and public health issues in addition to the legal questions confronted and for some the very troubling matter of institutional relations and boundaries crossed. Depending on one's perspective, it is either a stunning example of the Court's determination and persistence to get a cumbersome and resistant executive to simply carry out its constitutional and statutory responsibilities, or an undemocratic overreach by an institution ill equipped to design detailed environmental policy, but doing just that.

The objective of this chapter, however, is not to relitigate the case for and against democracy. Rather, well over a decade after the last of the major orders pertaining to the switch to CNG was issued in the case, this chapter seeks an answer to the question of how a court conspicuous for the problems it confronts in implementing many of its decisions, particularly those involving policymaking, successfully oversaw the implementation of such a controversial order;[1] one

---

[1] Nick Robinson has described the Court's difficulties in enforcement of many PILs, as "systematic." He notes the policies handed down by the Court "are overseen by a bureaucracy that is understaffed, under-trained, under-resourced, and, not surprisingly, often corrupt." See

that many court observers almost certainly considered the Court ill-equipped to handle. The argument put forward is that the DPC was unusual in bringing together a confluence of factors that favored the eventual success of the Court, and wore down those forces, both public and private, opposed to it. It is not that these are all essential to implementation in this case or any other, and certainly some are far more important than others. The factors are organized into two tiers. The first, which it is argued is crucial when the Court adopts a policy-making role and therefore is inherently prospective in nature, consists of three modes of monitoring orders: by the court itself; by a court appointed authority; and by a stakeholder. Depending on the peculiarities of a given case, one, two, or all three of these may come into play. The second tier consists of what can be considered facilitators or inhibitors depending on their presence or absence or the shape they take. These are: localness; specificity of the order; urgency; credibility of the court; publicity; market forces; and stability of the benches.

The first section of the chapter looks at some of the commonly cited weaknesses of courts as policymakers and then focuses on the Indian case and doctrinal and structural variations that are relevant to understanding the level of success achieved in the DPC. After that a history of the case is provided, followed by an overview of what the Court did and did not achieve, and lastly an analysis covering the variables more closely and how they interacted with the implementation of the CNG portion of the case.

II. PROBLEMS WITH COURTS AS POLICYMAKERS AND THE INDIAN CASE

As far back as 1977, Donald Horowitz argued that courts make very poor policymakers. The weaknesses listed combined to make it extremely difficult to produce coherent policy, or so Horowitz argued. It is, however, his final issue which goes to the heart of this chapter. Horowitz notes, "(c)ourts have no inspectors who move out into the field to ascertain what has happened. They receive no regular reports on the implementation of their policies."[2] Ordinarily, the feedback loop for courts to know if their decisions are implemented entirely, partially, not at all, correctly or incorrectly, and any

Nick Robinson, "Expanding Judiciaries: India and the Rise of the Good Governance Court," 8 *Washington University Global Studies Law Review* 1, 55 (2009).

[2]   Donald Horowitz, *The Courts and Social Policy* (Washington, D.C.: Brookings Institution, 1977), 55. Gerald Rosenberg also points to the limited enforcement powers of United States courts' as a significant constraint on their ability to produce social reform. See Gerald N. Rosenberg, *The Hollow Hope: Can Courts Bring about Social Change?* (Chicago: University of Chicago Press, 2008, 2nd ed.), 15–21.

unintended consequences is through an interested party bringing the case back into court. Agree or disagree, Horowitz was describing courts in the United States. This chapter concerns itself with a very different institution, the Indian Supreme Court, operating in very different political, social, and legal settings. There are significant doctrinal and structural variations that, at least at face value, appear to give the Indian Supreme Court significant advantages in producing appropriate policies and seeing them implemented.

The key doctrinal addition in India is the highly expansive version of PIL developed by the Court itself. The DPC was a very early example of an environmental PIL. The process associated with PILs is important in understanding not only how the case got to the Supreme Court in the first place, but the road it has traveled over its 30-plus years of existence and its ultimate outcomes.[3] PILs were originally designed to facilitate access to the upper courts (Supreme Court and High Courts), particularly for the disadvantaged, through adaptations such as the relaxed standing requirements under which any member of the public deemed to have sufficient interest can file a case in the public interest.[4] (This has been understood to include Supreme Court advocates, academics and others who it is determined have a sincere interest in pursuing the cause of justice in the public interest.)[5] Through a constitutionally based writ petition these cases can proceed directly to the Supreme Court, if involving a fundamental right,[6] or to a High Court, for a fundamental right or "any other purpose."[7] A Justice can even initiate the process himself or herself through *suo motu* ("on its own motion") jurisdiction after hearing about some injustice that he or she feels warrants the Court's attention.[8] In addition to the relaxed standing requirements, the proceedings allow for a good deal of flexibility with few hard and fast rules attached. Ideally the process is supposed to be non-adversarial, leading to a collaborative effort

---

[3] The case is still ongoing. The most recent order found was issued on May 1, 2018 and pertained to the availability of BS VI fuel throughout the districts comprising the National Capital Region (NCR). BS standards are based on the European emission standards.

[4] *S.P. Gupta and Ors.* v. *President of India and Ors.*, AIR 1982 SC 149.

[5] This explains why M. C. Mehta's name appears in the title of the case in question. Mehta, a Supreme Court lawyer, is a frequent petitioner before the Supreme Court in environmental as well as other public interest matters and is the named petitioner in many of them.

[6] Constitution of India, Article 32.

[7] *Id.* Article 226.

[8] Justice Kuldeep Singh used this authority in an order issued on November 18, 1996 to require the Delhi Administration to produce a plan to reduce air pollution in Delhi. See Urvashi Narain and Ruth Greenspan Bell, "Who Changed Delhi's Air: The Roles of the Court and the Executive in Environmental Policymaking," Resources for the Future, Discussion Paper, 10 (2005). This order was made independent of the DPC. Although well known for his environmental decision-making, Justice Singh was not part of the DPC.

to solve the problem at hand. This allows for an extremely broad information-gathering process that can go far beyond the facts of any given case and make use of specialized investigative committees to report back to the Court, often with recommendations. It also allows for continuous oversight by the court, often through the use of interim orders, while the process can drag on for years, if not decades. Lastly, remedies available to the court are almost boundless.[9]

There are also structural features of India's Supreme Court that factor into any analysis of the implementation of orders issued in the DPC. The Court currently has an authorized strength of 30 Associate Justices and the Chief Justice, although as of August 10, 2018 there were six vacancies.[10] The Justices sit alone or in benches ranging from two to "constitution benches" consisting of five or more.[11] Benches are chosen by the Chief Justice, which makes the position potentially quite powerful, although the mandatory retirement age of 65, combined with an informal system of seniority for appointment to the position, generally translates into short tenures for the Chief's position.[12] Of the 39 orders found relating directly to the DPC, 34 had three justice benches and the remaining 5 had two justice benches.[13] There was also remarkable

---

[9] PIL has its critics. A mini-industry has developed around the criticism of what many argue is the Court's undemocratic actions. See, e.g., Pratap Bhanu Mehta, "The Rise of Judicial Sovereignty," 18 *Journal of Democracy* 70 (2007); Surya Deva, "Public Interest Litigation in India: A Quest to Achieve the Impossible," in Po Jen Yap and Holning Lau (eds.), *Public Interest Litigation in Asia* (New York: Routledge, 2011), 57; and Anuj Bhuwania, "Courting the People: The Rise of Public Interest Litigation in Post-Emergency India," 34 *Comparative Studies of South Asia, Africa and the Middle East* 314 (2014). While not a broad attack on PIL, Armin Rosencranz and Michael Jackson did warn of the dangers present in the Court exercising such expansive powers in the DPC. See Armin Rosencranz and Michael Jackson, "The Delhi Pollution Case: The Supreme Court of India and the Limits of Power," 28 *Columbia Journal of Environmental Law* 223 (2003).

[10] Supreme Court of India, http://supremecourtofindia.nic.in/).

[11] Constitution of India, Article 145(3).

[12] Dipak Misra, the current Chief Justice, took over the position on August 28, 2017 and will be retiring on October 2, 2018. The preceding Chief Justice, Jagdish Singh Khehar, served just under eight months in the position (Supreme Court of India, *supra* note 10).

[13] One author gave the total number of orders issued in the case as of 2007 to be over 100, although it is unclear how she arrived at that number (Lavanya Rajamani, "Public Interest Environmental Litigation in India: Exploring Issues of Access, Participation, Equity, Effectiveness and Sustainability," 19 *Journal of Environmental Law* 293, 315 (2007). The Manupatra database was used to search the orders issued in the case. Although initially filed in 1985, the first order from the Court that could be found came in 1990. One of the frustrations in researching the Indian Supreme Court is that reporting services do not report all orders and decisions of the Court. With regard to this problem, see Nick Robinson, "A Quantitative Analysis of the Indian Supreme Court's Workload," 10 *Journal of Empirical Legal Studies* 570, 597–598 (2013).

stability on the benches with Justices B. N. Kirpal and V. N. Khare each participating in 21 of the orders, 20 of them together. All of the hearings they participated in together came during the height of CNG activity in the case, between 1997 and 2002. Combining small benches with stable participation allows for two or three committed justices to drive policy. This, of course, depends on the acquiescence of the current Chief Justice in the exercise of his or her appointment powers. Significantly, in 32 of the 39 orders found up to August 12, 2016 and used for this study, the then Chief Justice was part of the bench, suggesting approval on their part of the direction in which the case was moving.

III. HISTORY OF THE CASE

As already noted, the DPC was not a single dramatic event. Rather it was a slow, at times tortuous, decades-long issuing of orders, expressions of frustration, and give and take with those responsible, while much of the time Delhi's air continued to worsen. The CNG order under consideration here was just one aspect of it, which came to a head during the 1997–2002 period.

It began in 1985 with the filing of a PIL before the Supreme Court grounded in the government's non-compliance with the Air (Pollution and Control Act) 1981, the government's first attempt at regulating air pollution.[14] From the beginning, the case was linked to health concerns surrounding Delhi's pollution problems.[15] The 1985–1996 period was characterized by the Court providing the Delhi and central government authorities with ample opportunity to take action regarding the mounting air pollution problems confronting Delhi. As Narain and Bell observed, starting in about 1990 the court became more active, but primarily by trying to prod the authorities to implement the relevant law and the policies they themselves (the authorities) had developed.[16] This period can also be seen as a time when certain Justices on the Court began to educate themselves on the issues. Of course, while all of this was happening the air quality in Delhi was continuing to deteriorate, largely because of the rapid increase in the number of vehicles from 841,000 in 1985 to 2,629,000 in 1996.[17] The 1985–1996 period also experienced a dramatic change in the legal landscape of environmental law beginning with the

---

[14] Seven years earlier the government had passed The Water (Prevention and Control of Pollution) Act, 1974.

[15] See, e.g., Rosencranz and Jackson, *supra* note 9, 232 and Rajamani, *supra* note 13, 298.

[16] Narain and Bell, *supra* note 8, 3–10.

[17] MoEF (Ministry of Environment and Forests), Government of India, *The White Paper on Pollution in Delhi with an Action Plan*, (1997), chapters 2–3.

passage of the Environmental Protection Act in 1986, which provided the central government with broad rule-making authority over not just air pollution but all environmental issues. Significantly, §3(3) of the Act also granted the central government the power to establish authorities to assist in the implementation of its pollution control responsibilities. The Supreme Court itself has used this power on occasion to create authorities to assist in the implementation and oversight of their orders.[18] It is of particular significance here because it was used by the Court to force the government's hand in the creation of the Bhure Lal Committee, which was to play an essential role in the DPC. Other relevant legislation and rules passed or issued during this period include an amendment to the Air Act in 1987 designed to facilitate implementation of the original Act, the Motor Vehicles Act of 1988, and the Central Motor Vehicle Rules of 1989. The latter two were used by the Court in orders pertaining to permits necessary to operate buses (see, e.g., March 26, 2001) and taxis (see, e.g., May 10, 2016), and also certain orders pertaining to issues of traffic safety (see, e.g., November 20, 1997). In addition to the statutory changes, the court took matters into its own hands when in 1991 Justice Kuldeep Singh expanded the right to life in Article 21 of the constitution to incorporate a right to clean air and water.[19]

The tools were now in place if and when the Court's frustration with inaction and delaying tactics of the local and central authorities boiled over and it felt the need to take matters into its own hands. Ironically, in the DPC the Court does make extensive use of all of these, except the original basis for the case, the Air Act.

The period 1997–2002 marks the time when the justices' patience with excuses and delays runs out. It is also the period that corresponds to the time on the bench of the two justices who dominate the case, at least in terms of the number of orders in which they are involved and the significance of those orders, Justices B. N. Kirpal and V. N Khare.[20] In the first order issued with these two justices sitting together with then Chief Justice J. S. Verma (the first

[18] Examples of when this was employed by the Court include two major water pollution cases, *Vellore Citizens Welfare Forum* v. *Union of India*, AIR 1996 SC 2715, which involved pollution from leather tanneries in Tamil Nadu, and S. *Jagganath* v. *Union of India*, AIR 1997 SC 811, which involved shrimp farming and its resulting pollution. See G. Baskaran, *Pollution Control Acts*, (Chennai: C. Sitaram & Co., 1998), 7.

[19] *Subhash Kumar* v. *State of Bihar & Ors.*, AIR 1991 SC 420. Justice Singh was very active in the development and constitutionalization of environmental rights during the early and mid-1990s. Among his major decisions during that period are the previously cited *Vellore Citizens Welfare Forum* and S. *Jagganath* cases (*id.*).

[20] Justice Kirpal was appointed to the Court on September 11, 1995 and served as Chief Justice from May 6, 2002 until his retirement on November 7, 2002. Justice Khare was appointed to the

of seven he joined) the groundwork is laid for the remainder of time that Kirpal and Khare remain on the bench.[21] In the order dated November 18, 1997 the Court relies on the EPA and Articles 21 (right to life), 47 (duty to improve public health), and 48A (duty to protect and improve the environment) of the Constitution. The former as a Fundamental Right is justiciable, but the latter two are listed in the Directive Principles of State Policy and therefore should be non-justiciable. However, the Court held that these rights are so crucial to the well-being of the citizenry that they should be subsumed under the right to life in Article 21. The themes of urgency surrounding deteriorating environmental conditions, concern over the public health ramifications of these conditions, and frustration with the authorities' failure to take appropriate actions to improve the air quality and protect the public health are ones that are repeated constantly during this period. Setting the bar quite high, the order asked the government to lay out in a national plan the steps it intended to take to "restore the quality of the environment at least to the level at which it existed in 1977." It also strongly advised the central government to create an authority under §3(3) of the EPA to ensure the government carried out its constitutional and statutory environmental responsibilities relevant to this case. In the end, however, the justices in this order gave the central government "one more opportunity" to discharge those responsibilities.

During this period there are three major orders handed down by the Court in which specific guidelines regarding types and ages of vehicles that can be used in Delhi along with strict timelines were detailed. The first of these was issued on July 28, 1998 at which time the Court, showing its impatience with the Delhi administration, noted that "precious little" had been done by the state administration regarding vehicular pollution. It then proceeded to issue a series of four instructions of its own and adopt wholesale 13 additional measures included in a Bhure Lal Committee report that had been prepared for the Court.[22] Among the more controversial of these measures along with their completion dates were: the implementation of limits on the use of commercial vehicles over 15 years old (October 2, 1998); limitations on the driving of

Court on March 21, 1997 and served as Chief Justice from December 19, 2002 until his retirement on May 1, 2004 (Supreme Court of India, *supra* note 10).
[21] This was the first order retrieved using Manupatra with those justices together on the bench.
[22] Officially titled the Environment Pollution (Prevention and Control) Authority for the National Capital Region (EPCA) and authorized under the EPA §3(3), the committee had been constituted on January 29, 1998 by the Ministry of Environment and Forests (MoEF), but only after considerable badgering by the Court. It is commonly referred to as the Bhure Law Committee for the early period during which he held the chairmanship.

"goods vehicles" in the city during the day (August 15, 1998); financial incentives for the replacement of all post-1990 autos and taxis with new clean fuel vehicles (March 31, 2001); conversion of the entire city bus fleet to burn CNG (March 31, 2001); and the expansion of CNG supply outlets from 9 to 80 throughout the city (March 31, 2000). At the end of the order, the court issued a "strong caution" to the parties that the time frame "shall be adhered to." The second major order was delivered on April 29, 1999, and again was based upon a report written by the Bhure Lal Committee. This dealt with the 90 percent of vehicles in Delhi which were private (non-commercial) and gave dates by which no new registrations for these would be allowed unless the vehicle conformed to Euro I and then Euro II standards regardless of the fuel burned.

The last of the major orders was dated April 5, 2002 and was the longest and most detailed of all the orders considered here. Since the July 28, 1998 order both the Delhi authorities and the central government had been delaying implementation and requesting extensions, and they tried again with this filing. The justices demonstrated particular contempt for the Union of India's actions up to this point, when they let it be known that there was "no doubt that its intention, clearly, is to frustrate the orders passed by the Court."[23] The Court then goes on to dismantle all of the current arguments presented by the central authorities. They began by thoroughly discrediting the Mashelkar Committee and its report, a committee formed in 2001 by the central government to report on vehicular pollution in Delhi. As the justices observed:

> In 2001, the Union of India hurriedly set up a committee headed by Mr. R.A. Mashelkar to give a report with regard to vehicular pollution. It was surprising that since 1986, the Union of India had not thought of setting up such a Committee until after 31st January, 2001, when an order was passed in which the apathy on the part of the Government in carrying out the orders of this Court was taken note of, and the authorities were ordered to comply with the orders passed. The composition of the Mashelkar Committee was such that none of its members was either a doctor or an expert in public health. The said Committee submitted its report, which does not show any serious concern in protecting the health of the people.[24]

The Court then proceeded to rebut all of the arguments presented for delaying implementation and/or altering the July 28, 1998 order including: that there was a shortage of CNG and that the government was unable to supply enough for the transportation sector in Delhi (the Court observed that

---

[23] *M. C. Mehta v. Union of India* AIR 2002 SC 1696, §7.
[24] *Id.* §8.

there was no CNG shortage, and priority in the delivery of CNG was to go to the transport sector over industry, the public health taking precedence over "the health of a balance sheet of a private company");[25] rather than an entire fleet of CNG buses, a mix of CNG and diesel buses would produce only a minimal difference in the reduction of pollution levels (the Court found this "patently untenable");[26] a breakdown in the CNG pipeline could paralyze the transport system (the court found this possibility remote and commented that the pipeline stored up to three months' supply); and no more than 200 diesel buses could be phased out per month (the Court found that 800 was the correct number). The Court affirmed the timeline as specified in the earlier order and among other things added to it by specifying the amount of CNG to be delivered to Delhi daily, the imposition of daily fines for the continued use of diesel buses, and the phasing out of 800 diesel buses per month.

IV. HOW WELL HAS THE COURT DONE?

Over the years, as this case matured, both the justices and the parties involved had to educate and reeducate themselves on the constantly changing realities of vehicular pollution in Delhi and the improving knowledge base from which to find solutions. Delhi's pollution problem became a target that was moving extraordinarily rapidly. Indicative of this are the pollution indices from 1989 to the first half of 1997 shortly before the Court handed down its order adopting the Bhure Lal Committee's recommendations.[27] There is also a shifting and sometimes confusing set of goals which the Court identifies at various times and which is not necessarily by the Court's design. Partially this is because of the occasional merging of various petitions before the Court, and partially the inevitability of broadening the scope of considerations when dealing with a subject such as vehicular pollution (merely one piece of the larger air pollution problem) impacted by local, regional, and national policies. While it starts out as a case concerned with the air pollution in Delhi, out of necessity at times the Court extends that to the NCR (involving parts of

---

[25] *Id.* §16.

[26] *Id.* §33.

[27] See MoEF, *supra* note 17, which provides pollution data from 1989 to 1997. Levels of carbon monoxide, sulfur dioxide, and nitrogen dioxide were all up significantly. The change in suspended particulate matter was reported as negligible owing to a change in the thermal power plants in Delhi. The one area that showed progress by 1997 was in lead pollution levels, which had stabilized thanks in part to the start of the phasing out of leaded petrol. See S. A. Rizwan, Baridalyne Nongkynrih, and Sanjeev Kumar Gupta, "Air Pollution in Delhi: Its Magnitude and Effects on Health," 38 *Indian Journal of Community Medicine* 4 (2013).

the neighboring states of Haryana, Rajasthan, and Uttar Pradesh). There are also orders in which the Court references the four "metros" (Delhi, Mumbai, Kolkata, and Chennai) (February 14, 1996), a set of nine other polluted cities where the air quality is "critical" (April 5, 2002), and, lastly, some of its orders have a national reach, such as the phasing out of leaded petrol (February 14, 1996). There are also orders where the Court becomes involved with the minutiae of motor vehicle regulations and safety issues. Included among these are seating limits on school buses (December 16, 1997), the use of bus lanes and the removal of "hoardings" or billboards (November 20, 1997), and requirements to be met before someone can drive a school bus (December 1, 1998). However, for the purposes of this chapter, all of this is largely extraneous to what became the core of the case for many, the shift to clean fuels, and in particular CNG in Delhi, designed to improve the air quality which in turn should positively impact public health.

How well has the Court done? Looking at a sampling of the headlines and stories that have come out of Delhi beginning in 2014 is anything but encouraging – "New Delhi, the World's Most Polluted City, Is Even More Polluted than We Realized,"[28] "Breathing Poison in the World's Most Polluted City,"[29] "Holding Your Breath in Delhi,"[30] "80 People Die in Delhi Every Day from Air Pollution: Parliament Is Told,"[31] and "How Delhi Became the Most Polluted City on Earth."[32]

Despite such headlines, it is important to note the Court's success with regard to the conversion to CNG and other cleaner fuels. However, the results are mixed at best in the area of air quality, with little to show in terms of health benefits. Regarding the Court-ordered shift to cleaner fuels, the Court in an October 1994 ruling initially ordered the central government to phase in low leaded petrol first to the four metros by December 1994 and then throughout the country by December 1996. This was to be followed by a move to unleaded petrol in the metros by April 1995 and in the rest of the country by

[28] Rishi Iyengar, "New Delhi, the World's Most Polluted City, Is Even More Polluted than We Realized," *Time* November 27, 2014.

[29] Anu Anand, "Breathing Poison in the World's Most Polluted City," BBC News April 19, 2015, www.bbc.com/news/magazine-32352722.

[30] Harris Gardiner, "Holding Your Breath in Delhi," *New York Times* May 29, 2015.

[31] NDTV, "80 People Die in Delhi Every Day from Air Pollution: Parliament Is Told," July 23, 2015, www.ndtv.com/delhi-news/80-people-die-in-delhi-everyday-from-air-pollution-parliament-is-told-784541.

[32] Umair Irfan, "How Delhi Became the Most Polluted City on Earth," *Vox* November 25, 2017, www.vox.com/energy-and-environment/2017/11/22/16666808/india-air-pollution-new-delhi.

April 2000. This was all successfully instituted with relative ease.[33] As already mentioned, the move to CNG for public transport vehicles in Delhi was a far more complex and drawn-out process with a more determined resistance displayed by both the Delhi and central authorities. Still, the process of converting auto rickshaws, taxis, and buses to CNG was successfully completed by 2003. With the court paying particular attention to the buses in its April 5, 2002 order, they were entirely CNG powered by December 2002.[34] By the end of 2003 it was reported that a total of 90,000 buses, taxis, and auto rickshaws were using CNG.[35] Some were new vehicles that burned CNG, while others were older ones that were retrofitted with CNG kits to enable them to use the fuel. By 2008–2009 the Centre for Science and Environment (CSE), a major environmental NGO based in Delhi, reported that the total of CNG vehicles in Delhi (commercial and non-commercial) had risen to nearly 290,000.[36] The infrastructure to support the increase in CNG vehicles also grew rapidly, with the number of stations dispensing CNG increasing from 30 in 2000 to 150 in 2009 to more than 300 by 2013.[37]

While the Court met with significant success in having its orders ultimately followed regarding the use of CNG and other clean fuels, questions surrounding improvement in the quality of the air in Delhi are more contested. In the early days after the switch to CNG the reviews were generally positive. Narain's and Bell's 2005 paper, optimistically entitled "Who Changed Delhi's Air," commented on "Delhi's dramatic evolution from the world's fourth-most polluted city," and referenced a 2003 survey that indicated the public viewed the improvement in air quality as one of the main achievements of the Delhi government.[38] The next year an article posted on the United Nations Environment Program (UNEP) website spoke of Delhi's pollution level having been checked, and a decline in the level of four different pollutants (carbon monoxide, nitrogen dioxide, lead and sulfur dioxide).[39] Whatever good news

---

[33] Rajamani, *supra* note 13, 298.

[34] Ruth Greenspan Bell, Kuldeep Mathur, Urvaishi Narain, and David Simpson, "Clearing the Air: How Delhi Broke the Logjam on Air Quality Reforms," 46 *Environment* , 22, 30 (2004).

[35] "Clean Fuel Worsens Climate Impacts for Some Vehicle Engines," *Science Daily* March 5, 2011, http://forhumanliberation.blogspot.com/2011/03/222-clean-fuel-worsens-climate-impacts.html.

[36] Anumita Roychowdury, CNG *Programme in India: The Future Challenges* (New Delhi: Centre for Science and Environment, 2010), appendix 2.

[37] Rahul Goel and Sarath Guttikunda, "Role of Urban Growth, Technology, and Judicial Interventions on Vehicle Exhaust Emissions in Delhi for 1991–2014 and 2014–2030 Periods," 14 *Environmental Development* 6, 12 (2015).

[38] Narain and Bell, *supra* note 8, 1.

[39] UNEP, "CNG Conversion: Learning from New Delhi" (2006), 7. There were others however who raised questions over what role if any the switch to CNG played in reductions for specific

there was early on, pollution levels began to rise again within five or six years of the switch to CNG. There were primarily two factors at work that drove air pollution back to its highly dangerous levels. The first was the exponential increase in the number of vehicles in Delhi and the surrounding area, most of which occurred in the areas of two-wheelers and private cars, which were never part of the CNG mandate. (In 2012 it was estimated that the public transport sector accounted for no more than 20 percent of Delhi's pollution.)[40] Between 1990–1991 and 2011–2012 the former increased from 1.2 to 4.6 million and the latter from 0.4 to 2.3 million.[41] The second cause of the increased air pollution is from sources other than vehicles. These can include manufacturing industries; power plants; brick kilns; private generators; burning of waste; and road dust.[42] Most of these have to do with levels of particulate matter, although not exclusively. For example, Kandlikar notes power generation can be a factor in sulfate emissions as well.[43] In its February 2014 Report, EPCA confirmed the early improvement in air quality and then the sharp reversal. It noted a 16 percent decrease in PM_{10} from 2002 to 2007, but then followed by a 75 percent increase between 2007 and 2012.[44] The report also cited a 30 percent increase between 2002 and 2011 in nitrogen oxide levels.[45] The major reason they cite for the reversal is the previously mentioned increase in private vehicles. Among other causes listed is a sharp decrease in the price differential between CNG and diesel, which makes the purchase of diesel vehicles more attractive, a decrease in bus ridership and too few buses, and the lack of a region-wide inter-city transport plan.[46]

pollutants. See, e.g., Milind Kandlikar, "Air Pollution at a Hotspot Location in Delhi: Detecting Trends, Seasonal Cycles and Oscillations," 41 *Atmospheric Environment* 5934 (2007).

[40] Sarath Guttikunda, "Air Pollution in Delhi," XLV11 *Economic & Political Weekly* 24, 24 (June 30, 2012).

[41] Goel and Guttikunda, *supra* note 37, 10.

[42] See *id.* 7 and Guttikunda, *supra* note 40.

[43] Kandlikar, *supra* note 39.

[44] Airborne particulate matter is generally measured as PM_{10} or $PM_{2.5}$, which refers to the size of the particles. These are the standard measurements used by the World Health Organization. See WHO, *WHO Air Quality Guidelines for Particulate Matter, Ozone, Nitrogen Dioxide and Sulfur Dioxide: Global Update 2005*, (2006), 9.

[45] EPCA, *Report on Priority Measures to Reduce Air Pollution and protect Public Health*, (2014), 5. This was the latest incarnation of the Bhure Lal Committee, which by 2014 was commonly referred to simply as the EPCA. The EPCA continues to issue reports when requested to do so by the Supreme Court. See the EPCA website for a complete listing of its reports (www.epca .org.in/).

[46] *Id.* 3–4.

Despite the switch to CNG and a short-term decrease in particulate matter, by 2007 the numbers were increasing again and the health benefits that were so important to the Court in justifying its involvement in the case had not come to fruition. In the same 2014 report the EPCA cited several studies of the health effects of air pollution in Delhi. The most disturbing was a 2012 study conducted by the Central Pollution Control Board and the Chittaranjan National Cancer Institute of Kolkata, which looked at over 11,628 school children in Delhi. Among its conclusions was a finding that one out of every three children had reduced lung function.[47] More recently, a 2014–2015 study of respiratory cases at two of Delhi's top hospitals showed a dramatic increase in such cases in conjunction with the rise in particulate matter, after the number of such cases had dropped in the immediate aftermath of the implementation of the CNG orders. It was reported that the All India Institute of Medical Sciences had approximately a 300 percent increase in admissions to its outpatient respiratory ward between 2007–2008 and 2014–2015, and the Vallabhai Patel Chest Institute showed a 36 percent increase in admissions to its outpatient ward between 2006–2007 and 2013–2014.[48] If there is any solace to be taken in this regard, it is in Goel and Guttikunda's finding that the level of $PM_{2.5}$ has been significantly reduced below what it would have been had the CNG order not been implemented.[49] However, demonstrating the potential range of variables to be considered and the complexities that can arise when broadening vehicular pollution policy to public health results, one of the authors of a University of British Columbia study focusing on the pollution produced by different types of engines in auto rickshaws concluded that if policymakers want to optimize health benefits then clean fuels might be more effectively used in cooking stoves than in transportation.[50]

V. ANALYSIS

An important point of comparison is the successful implementation of the comparatively simple phasing out of leaded gasoline (and the accompanying move to premixed fuels for certain vehicles). These were put into practice with

---

[47] *Id.* 6.

[48] Pritha Chatterjee, "Leave Delhi: That's What Doctors Are Prescribing to Patients with Serious Respiratory Ailments," *Indian Express* April 2, 2015.

[49] Goel and Guttikunda, *supra* note 37, 14–15.

[50] See "Clean Fuel Worsens Climate Impacts for Some Vehicle Engines," *supra* note 35 in which Milind Kandlikar, one of the authors of the University of British Columbia study, is quoted as saying the use of clean fuels for cooking rather than transportation "could save many more lives."

little resistance, and certainly far less than the move to CNG encountered.[51] Both were earlier recommendations that originated with the government, but about which little or nothing had been done. The Court was simply pushing the authorities to implement plans they had devised. Still, that alone was probably not the only reason for the ease with which these were implemented. As opposed to the switch to CNG, the order did not involve either the purchase of new vehicles or the retrofitting of older ones to handle a new fuel, nor was there any new infrastructure that had to be put in place to make these changes.

The case of the shift to CNG is far more complex. It required close to 100,000 vehicles either to be converted to run on CNG if possible, and if not then simply replaced with new vehicles. Additionally, the infrastructure to deliver the new fuel had to be put into place. The requirements surrounding both the infrastructure necessary for distribution and that needed to ensure the security and storage of the CNG supply were covered in the Bhure Lal Committee's July 2001 Report.[52] It was certainly not as simple as one high-ranking Delhi official suggested in a 2003 interview that once the government realized the Court was serious and not going to change the order it decided to comply.[53]

Any case involving policymaking is going to require monitoring of some sort unless the party(ies) which is the subject of the order opts to comply of their own volition. Even in those cases in which implementation takes place with little or no resistance, monitoring may be necessary to ensure correct and full implementation, as well as a check on any unintended consequences.[54] Such monitoring can come from three sources: the Court itself, a Court-appointed authority, and stakeholders. These are not mutually exclusive, and in many cases more than one can be involved. How these interact begins with the Court itself. Depending upon the interest of the justices involved, and their available time and resources, a court-appointed monitor might not be necessary, and the role of stakeholders in monitoring may be minimized. The DPC case is unusual in this regard. While all three were present, it was the Court itself which was the primary monitor with its insistence on a constant flow of

---

[51] Bell et al., *supra* note 34 27.
[52] EPCA, *Report on Clean Fuels*, (2001), 14–16.
[53] Bell et al., *supra* note 34, 30.
[54] One other possibility would be that market forces align to drive the implementation. Again, this would probably still require some minimal monitoring for accuracy, thoroughness, and unintended consequences. Rosenberg has raised the issue of market forces and their potential influence on courts' ability to produce social change in the United States context. See Rosenberg, *supra* note 2, 33–35.

Court appearances and continuous reporting on progress made.[55] Its use of timelines provided the justices themselves with a set of simple metrics by which to measure progress made or lack thereof.[56] As earlier noted, from 1997 through 2002, which was the crucial period for the CNG portion of the case, 21 individual orders were found. There were certainly others, although how many is unclear.[57] What added to the intensity of the Court's monitoring was that this was a local issue and all of the key actors were local, which lessened the need for a "middle man" to monitor implementation. Still, this second level of monitoring was not totally absent. This sometimes took the form of applications filed with the Court regarding problems with details of the implementation of their orders.[58] What was largely absent from this case was a court-appointed authority charged with overseeing implementation. The Bhure Lal Committee, although it has been referred to as a "monitoring committee," functioned almost exclusively in an advisory capacity for the Court.[59] Rosencranz and Jackson referred to the Bhure Lal Committee as an "advisory research board" and noted that the justices "relied almost exclusively" on the committee's findings when arriving at decisions in the DPC.[60]

---

[55] In a November 6, 2000 interview with the author, retired Justice Kuldeep Singh emphasized the importance of continuous monitoring by him as an essential element to implementation of his environmental orders. In particular he referenced the so-called Taj Trapezium Case (*M. C. Mehta* v. *Union of India* AIR 1997 SC 734), which involved reducing pollution in Agra near the Taj Mahal by having industries switch to gas from coal and, if not, either move or close.

[56] Shankar and Mehta, in their article on Indian upper courts' decision making in public health and education, noted that even when timelines were used courts still often required monitoring of them by stakeholders. See Shylashri Shankar and Pratap Bhanu Mehta, "Courts and Socioeconomic Rights in India," in Varun Gauri and Daniel M. Brinks (eds.), *Courting Social Justice: Judicial Enforcement of Social and Economic Rights in the Developing World,* (Cambridge: Cambridge University Press, 2008), 176. The difference in the DPC case was that much of the time the Supreme Court was the initial monitor, the one insisting that the parties report directly to them.

[57] Some of these were referenced in publications (see, e.g., UNEP 2006), and the Court itself referenced earlier orders not found in the Manupatra database. For example, the Court in its major order of April 5, 2002 referenced CNG related orders from April 27, 2001 and September 17, 2001, neither of which was found.

[58] For example, the Court's order of April 4, 2001 was in response to an application by a friend of the court concerning delays by the Delhi administration in issuing bus permits.

[59] Geetanjoy Sahu does include the Bhure Lal Committee as one example of a Court appointed monitoring committee, although the DPC is not a case he uses in his study and it seems an ill-fitting label based on its actual function in the case. See Geetanjoy Sahu, *Environmental Jurisprudence and the Supreme Court,* (Hyderabad: Orient Black Swan, 2014), 136. The two cases he looks at in his study both had monitoring committees appointed, but neither case was in Delhi. The Dahanu power plant case was from Maharashtra and the Vellore Citizens Welfare case from Tamil Nadu.

[60] Rosencranz and Jackson, *supra* note 9, 235–236.

While the monitoring function, whether performed by one, two, or all three of the above, is crucial in most if not all orders involving policymaking, the DPC case incorporated the seven following variables that can either facilitate or inhibit implementation and may influence the form it takes: localness; specificity of the order; urgency; publicity; credibility of the court; market forces; and stability of the benches. All of the seven worked in favor of implementation in the case, except for one, market forces. However, even there it was not a simple case of aligning against implementation, but elements cut both ways.

As mentioned above, localness and specificity of the order were both factors in the Court's ability to perform much of the monitoring itself. One author suggested a possible Delhi bias that may come into play with some justices. That is an inclination to first clean up where they live.[61] Whether that was the fact here or not, there is another aspect to localness, which is the inevitable daily reminder of the severity of the problem when living in the midst of it. Bhure Lal commented on this aspect of the case in a 2004 interview, when noting that "[c)itizens will no longer accept 'billowing black smoke',"[62] and the justices living in Delhi were part of that citizenry. What compounded such daily reminders was the publicity surrounding the case (as I mention later).

The specificity or narrowness of the DPC decision also facilitated its implementation. Undoubtedly the shift to CNG for vehicles was complex, but it was limited to those involved in public transportation and to Delhi. This allowed the court to delve into the complexities of CNG availability, cost, and comparative emissions among other issues, many of which were peculiar to Delhi. Rosencranz and Jackson argued that the specificity was a weakness because it would affect only Delhi, and the issues would have to be relitigated for other cities.[63] It is this limitation, however, that makes its implementation more likely. Broad orders lacking specificity (substantive or geographic) potentially invite far greater implementation problems.[64]

While there was always a health component to the case, the urgency of the health issues driven by air pollution as the 1990s progressed was captured by

---

[61] Rajamani, *supra* note 13, 303.

[62] *Id.* 316.

[63] Rosencranz and Jackson, *supra* note 9, 251.

[64] An example of this type of order involves the midday meal scheme by which the Court ordered that every government and government assisted primary school had to provide students with a midday meal meeting particular caloric and protein requirements (*Peoples Union for Civil Liberties* v. *Union of India and Others*, Writ Petition (C) No. 196 of 2001). See, e.g., Shankar and Mehta, *supra* note 56, 176 concerning implementation issues confronted in the case.

the 1996 CSE report *Slow Murder: the Deadly Story of Vehicular Pollution in India*, which documented the severity of air pollution in Delhi and other major metropolitan areas. It was reportedly Justice Kuldeep Singh's reading of this report that inspired him to issue the earlier noted *suo motu* notice to the Delhi government ordering it to submit an action plan to deal with the city's air pollution.[65] Although Justice Singh was not part of the DPC, this highlights the increasing urgency of the health issues relating to the quality of Delhi's air. There are expressions of anxiety spread throughout the orders issued in the DPC concerning increasing levels of air pollution and public health. It was the April 5, 2002 order, however, when the Court cited a series of studies from India and the United States linking air pollution to respiratory ailments, lung cancer, and heart disease. The justices in that order also cited World Bank data on the health costs associated with air pollution in Delhi.

Lacking an enforcement arm, courts at times may need to leverage their credibility or legitimacy in order to assist in having some of their more controversial decisions implemented. The Supreme Court, since it rehabilitated its image in the post-Emergency period,[66] has been considered by many to be one of the few institutions in India that works.[67] With regard to the role of the Court's credibility in the DPC case, one set of authors suggested that a relatively weak central government may have simply calculated that it did not want to continue its confrontation with a popular Supreme Court, one that "enjoyed a unique status in Indian society."[68] It certainly helped that a popular Court was seen as being on the public's side in this struggle with the government and private companies.

External actors also played key roles in securing implementation, particularly by highlighting the public health dangers associated with air pollution, and by publicizing the case itself and the Court's role in it. As mentioned previously, the CSE played a crucial role early in the process by accentuating the health hazards and attracting the Court's attention with its 1996 report *Slow Murder*. As the case progressed, the CSE, by publicizing the proceedings, continued in its effort to keep the case in the public eye.[69] Just as

---

[65] Narain and Bell, *supra* note 8, 10.

[66] The Emergency, which suspended civil liberties and placed enormous power in the hands of the Prime Minister, lasted from June 1975 to March 1977. It was declared by the President Fakhruddin Ali Ahmed at the request of Prime Minister Indira Gandhi.

[67] See, e.g., Avani Mehta Sood, "Gender Justice through Public Interest Litigation: Case Studies from India," 41 *Vanderbilt Journal of Transnational Law* 833, 845–847 (2008) and Robert Moog, "Activism on the Indian Supreme Court," 82 *Judicature* 124 (1998).

[68] Bell et al., *supra* note 34, 37.

[69] *Id.* 30–31.

important, or more so, for publicity purposes in the DPC was the extensive press coverage it received. This both raised the level of public awareness of the issues, and also the role of the Supreme Court as defender of the public's interests. One study directly links this press coverage to the implementation of the CNG order. Using newspaper articles that contained public interest litigation + air pollution + New Delhi as a proxy for the level of information available on the problem of air pollution in Delhi, Rathinam and Raja found a significant increase in such articles beginning in the late 1990s.[70] They found a statistically significant relationship between the publicity generated and the reduction in certain pollution levels through 2004, and argue that this "spillover effect" from the publicity surrounding PILs and air pollution in Delhi functions as an "informal regulatory mechanism," pressuring state actors to conform to the Court's orders.[71] Rathinam and Raja are not the only ones to recognize the importance of the role played by the press in this PIL.[72] Rajamani finds a similar effect when she notes the media attention given the case, and its effect on lowering the level of the public's tolerance towards the air pollution problem.[73]

Market forces were an inevitable part of the implementation question in a case requiring new infrastructure and the purchase of new vehicles or retrofitting of old ones. In the end, their effects seemed to be mixed. Some of those worried about costs advocated for a multiple clean fuel policy which would have left the market to operate by allowing the consumers to choose among the available fuels. Then there were the obvious questions about the costs associated with any new infrastructure required. The World Bank in a 2001 Briefing Note raised these as well as other potential costs, albeit not restricted to the Delhi case, but in an international context. In order to compensate for the higher costs, among the recommendations was one to institute a taxation policy that would make the cost of CNG to the consumer approximately half that of the fuel to be replaced.[74] Others expressed concern over the relatively high cost of new CNG buses compared to new diesel buses, the former costing 1.6 times more.[75] Offsetting some of these concerns were countervailing factors that made the switch more economically palatable.

---

[70] Francis Xavier Rathinam, and A. V. Raja, "Courts as Regulators: Public Interest Litigation in India," 16 *Environment and Development Economics* 199, 211 (2011).

[71] *Id.* 204.

[72] See, e.g., Bell et al., *supra* note 34, 31.

[73] Rajamani, *supra* note 13, 316.

[74] World Bank, "International Experience with CNG Vehicles," *World Bank South Asia Urban Air Quality Management Note No. 2*, (2001), http://documents.worldbank.org/curated/en/748641468337184646/pdf/multiopage.pdf.

Goel and Guttikunda cited a series of factors that served to bring the scales more into balance. These include the fact that by 2002 CNG was the cheapest fuel when compared with petrol (50+ percent cheaper) and diesel (20 percent cheaper). In addition, there were cheaper operating costs with CNG vehicles. The cost of retrofitting older non-CNG vehicles had dropped and, as mentioned earlier, the availability of CNG at stations in Delhi was increasing rapidly.[76] Regarding the high cost of new CNG buses, Rosencranz and Jackson cited a study from the United States which argued that owing to lower fuel costs and less engine wear a CNG bus would pay for itself in about three years.[77] On balance, market forces did not make CNG implementation a certainty, but neither did they present an insurmountable barrier to the Court's plans.

A final factor, albeit difficult to show empirically, is the stability of the composition of benches handling an issue. Here, during the crucial period of 1997–2002 when the CNG part of the case took shape and had to be implemented, Justices Kirpal and Khare participated in 21 and 20 of the 21 orders found, with Kirpal as the Chief Justice for two of them. Additionally there was little turnover among the third justices during that period. Justice Verma, then the Chief Justice, sat on 8 of the benches, after which Justice Anand sat on 10 for which he was Chief Justice in 6, and finally Justice Bhan sat on 4 benches at the very end of the period. On an institution with comparatively short terms on the bench to have such continuity and demonstrate such persistence, particularly when the issue is so complex and the learning curve so steep, can be a significant boost in not just arriving at a reasonable solution to the problem, but to its implementation as well.[78]

Owing to intensive Court monitoring and the convergence of a rich collection of facilitators, the Supreme Court was able to ultimately achieve the conversion of Delhi's public transport vehicles to CNG even though initial deadlines were missed. Through its own persistence and the expertise of the Bhure Lal Committee, in the end it produced a detailed set of objectives that proved defensible, doable, and at an acceptable cost.

---

[75] Magali Dreyfus, "The Judiciary's Role in Environmental Governance," 43 *Environmental Policy and Law* 167, 172 (2013).

[76] Goel and Guttikunda, *supra* note 37, 12–13.

[77] Rosencraz and Jackson, *supra* note 9, 240–241.

[78] Horowitz argues that because judges are generalists, the processing of specialized information "is one of the jobs that many judges do with the least skill and the greatest impatience" (Horowitz, *supra* note 2, 25). This is the learning curve that stable benches in PIL matters with the assistance of expert advisory committees can at least partially overcome.

VI. CONCLUSION

As suggested in the introduction, the DPC is unusual in the confluence of this particular set of factors favoring implementation. Most other cases in which the Court designs new or reformed policy will not be able to match what was present in this case, beginning with the justices devoting so much time and effort to their ongoing monitoring. Effective oversight will have to come from one or both of the other two sources. Of course, if no authority is appointed by the Court the burden falls upon the stakeholders in the case. Even when the Court appoints a monitoring commission, the work of stakeholders may involve monitoring the commission's work itself, in addition to that of any government agencies and private parties involved. This often requires resources and persistence from non-governmental organizations or other peti- tioners who may have little of one or both. Sahu, focusing on the petitioners in his two case studies, concludes that differences in their relative resource capacities was a key factor in the far more effective implementation of the orders of the Court in the Dahanu power plant case then those in the Vellore Citizens' Welfare Forum case.[79] These problems are heightened when the subject of the case is situated far from Delhi, as in Sahu's case studies, and may be exponentially worsened when a decision has national ramifications, such as the midday meal case. In such a situation it may be a network of NGOs that must be established, absent a preexisting network, to oversee implementation.

The DPC did not confront such problems owing to the intensity of the Court's own oversight. Shankar and Mehta, whose focus was on health and education cases, argued that environmental cases comprise a peculiar subset of policymaking by the Court owing to greater NGO activity and the high level of interest in the subject matter by a subset of justices.[80] That may well be the case, but whether that is reflected in a higher success rate of implementa- tion requires much greater study.[81] Here there was far more at work assisting the Court in its struggles toward implementation of its orders beyond any monitoring involved. The localness element was a major factor in simplifying monitoring, but Delhi, as the national capital, also likely heightened the perception of urgency and level of publicity. When the other facilitators are factored into the equation, (specificity, credibility, stability on the bench, and

---

[79] Sahu, *supra* note 59, 139–143. Also see Shankar and Mehta, *supra* note 56, 176, regarding the necessity of NGO monitoring in some cases.

[80] *Id.* 177.

[81] See Sahu, *supra* note 59, 120–152, for a more thorough discussion of implementation in environmental cases.

comparatively balanced market forces) the case had significant advantages over what most others are likely to have. What mix is necessary in any given situation, or whether additional ones may be present, will differ, but regardless of such case specific peculiarities, monitoring remains critical.

It is always dangerous drawing generalizations from a particular case. Still, the DPC provides an interesting twist to the perspectives on courts and their limitations as policymakers. With the structural and doctrinal advantages built into the Indian Supreme Court, the case demonstrates how significant policy shifts, albeit generally narrow ones, can be directed and ultimately implemented from a committed bench in the face of resistance from government and private actors. However, stepping back from the highly focused view on implementation of the CNG portion of the case, one gets a different perspective on the relative success of the Court in achieving its more aspirational objectives of reducing air pollution and improving public health outcomes. Less than a decade after the implementation of the CNG mandate, Delhi's air pollution and its attendant health problems were, in many respects, as bad, or worse, than in 2003. (In defense of the Court, one can make the case, as Goel and Guttikunda did, that the situation would have been even worse without the shift to CNG.)

The DPC serves to underline the reality that even the Indian Supreme Court with its built-in advantages fell prey to weaknesses inherent in most if not all courts attempting to design comprehensive policies, particularly in an area as complex as air pollution.[82] Any such attempt as that into which the Court found itself drawn in the DPC would stretch its reasoning beyond merely public transport vehicles to private ones, which constitute the vast majority in Delhi. Since many of these travel from other states into the city, this then converts the issue into one of regional if not national proportions, as does the fact that some of the pollution itself may originate from sources outside the city and then flow into it. It also found itself pulled into tangential areas, such as motor vehicle registration, traffic regulation, and expressway construction.[83] A truly comprehensive policy would also bring into play all

---

[82] These built-in advantages allowed the Court to very nearly overcome Rosenberg's three constraints on courts producing social reform which he outlined in his work on US courts. The limited nature of constitutional rights and issues of judicial independence presented comparatively little resistance. Still, while the Court was able to implement the CNG portion of the case, limitations on the Court's ability to develop the comprehensive policies needed left the justices a good deal short when it came to their more ambitious goals. See Rosenberg, *supra* note 2, 10 and more generally 9–32.

[83] As the case has continued into its fourth decade, the Court has found itself handing down orders dealing with such issues as diesel burning taxis from the NCR outside Delhi proper and

sources of pollution, not merely vehicular, and perhaps even consideration of possible alternative uses for clean fuels other than for vehicles in order to optimize health benefits through the reduction of indoor pollution.[84] As the concentric rings around its original detailed policy continue to expand, it becomes obvious that even this Court lacks the capacity to produce a sufficiently comprehensive set of policies to deal effectively with Delhi's air pollution and the health problems that arise from it. In the end, the Court cannot do it itself. It requires the lead to be taken by the political leadership with administrators following, and in many cases with the cooperation of stakeholders, to shape and institute shifts in policy sufficiently comprehensive to produce results as broad as those sought by the Supreme Court in this case.

REFERENCES

Agarwal, Anil, Anju Sharma Sharma, and Anumita Roychowdhury, *Slow Murder: The Deadly Story of Vehicular Pollution in India*, New Delhi: Centre for Science and Environment 1996.

Anand, Anu, "Breathing Poison in the World's Most Polluted City," BBC News April 19, 2015, www.bbc.com/news/magazine-32352722, last accessed August 23, 2018.

Baskaran, G., *Pollution Control Acts*, Chennai: C. Sitaram & Co. 1998.

Bell, Ruth Greenspan, Kuldeep Mathur, Urvaishi Narain, and David Simpson, "Clearing the Air: How Delhi Broke the Logjam on Air Quality Reforms," 46 *Environment* 22, 2004.

Bhuwania, Anuj, "Courting the People: The Rise of Public Interest Litigation in Post-Emergency India," 34 *Comparative Studies of South Asia, Africa and the Middle East* 314, 2014.

Chatterjee, Pritha, "Leave Delhi: That's What Doctors Are Prescribing to Patients with Serious Respiratory Ailments," *Indian Express* April 2, 2015.

"Clean Fuel Worsens Climate Impacts for Some Vehicle Engines," *Science Daily* March 5, 2011, http://forhumanliberation.blogspot.com/2011/03/222-clean-fuel-worsens-climate-impacts.html, last accessed August 23, 2018.

how to deal with new business models for taxis such as Uber (May 10, 2016), as well as expressway construction in the neighboring state of Haryana (July 15, 2016).

[84] There is also the question of how concerned the Court should be with any possible unintended effects its policies may give rise to, for example on the emission of greenhouse gases. Although the Court apparently did not take into consideration any potential effects on such emissions of different fuels, with different engines in different vehicles, by raising such concerns Reynolds and Kandlikar further highlight the complexity of the task confronting not just the justices, but any other policymakers that become involved as well. See Conor C. O. Reynolds, and Milind Kandlikar, "Climate Impacts of Air Quality Policy: Switching to a Gas-Fueled Public Transportation System in New Delhi," 42 *Environmental Science & Technology* 5860 (2009).

Deva, Surya, "Public Interest Litigation in India: A Quest to Achieve the Impossible," in *Public Interest Litigation in Asia*, PoJen Yap and Holning Lau (eds.), New York: Routledge, 2011, 57.

Dreyfus, Magali, "The Judiciary's Role in Environmental Governance," 43 *Environmental Policy and Law* 167, 2013.

EPCA (Environment Protection [Pollution and Control] Authority for the National Capital Region), *Report on Clean Fuels*, 2001.

Report on Priority Measures to Reduce Air Pollution and protect Public Health, February 2014. www.epca.org.in/#, last accessed August 18, 2018.

Gardiner, Harris, "Holding Your Breath in Delhi," *New York Times* May 29, 2015.

Goel, Rahul and Sarath Guttikunda, "Role of Urban Growth, Technology, and Judicial Interventions on Vehicle Exhaust Emissions in Delhi for 1991–2014 and 2014–2030 Periods," 14 *Environmental Development* 6, 2015.

Guttikunda, Sarath, "Air Pollution in Delhi," XLVII *Economic & Political Weekly* 24, June 30, 2012.

Horowitz, Donald, *The Courts and Social Policy*, Washington, D.C.: Brookings Institution 1977.

Irfan, Umair, "How Delhi Became the Most Polluted City on Earth," *Vox* November 25, 2017, www.vox.com/energy-and-environment/2017/11/22/16666808/india-air-pollution-new-delhi, last accessed August 23, 2018.

Iyengar, Rishi, "New Delhi, the World's Most Polluted City, Is Even More Polluted than We Realized," *Time* November 27, 2014.

Kandlikar, Milind, "Air Pollution at a Hotspot Location in Delhi: Detecting Trends, Seasonal Cycles and Oscillations," 41 *Atmospheric Environment* 5934, 2007.

Mehta, Pratap Bhanu, "The Rise of Judicial Sovereignty," 18 *Journal of Democracy* 70, 2007.

MoEF (Ministry of Environment and Forests), Government of India, *The White Paper on Pollution in Delhi with an Action Plan*, 1997.

Moog, Robert, "Activism on the Indian Supreme Court," 82 *Judicature* 124, 1998.

Narain, Urvashi and Ruth Greenspan Bell, "Who Changed Delhi's Air: The Roles of the Court and the Executive in Environmental Policymaking," Resources for the Future, Discussion Paper 2005.

NDTV, "80 People Die in Delhi Every Day from Air Pollution: Parliament Is Told," July 23, 2015, www.ndtv.com/delhi-news/80-people-die-in-delhi-everyday-from-air-pollution-parliament-is-told-784541, last accessed August 23, 2018.

Rajamani, Lavanya, "Public Interest Environmental Litigation in India: Exploring Issues of Access, Participation, Equity, Effectiveness and Sustainability," 19 *Journal of Environmental Law* 293, 2007.

Rathinam, Francis Xavier and A. V. Raja, "Courts as Regulators: Public Interest Litigation in India," 16 *Environment and Development Economics* 199, 2011.

Reynolds, Conor C. O. and Milind Kandlikar, "Climate Impacts of Air Quality Policy: Switching to a Gas-Fueled Public Transportation System in New Delhi," 42 *Environmental Science & Technology* 5860, 2009.

Rizwan, S. A., Baridalyne Nongkynrih and Sanjeev Kumar Gupta, "Air Pollution in Delhi: Its magnitude and Effects on Health," 38 *Indian Journal of Community Medicine* 4, 2013.

Robinson, Nick, "Expanding Judiciaries: India and the Rise of the Good Governance Court," 8 *Washington University Global Studies Law Review* 1, 2009.

"A Quantitative Analysis of the Indian Supreme Court's Workload," 10 *Journal of Empirical Legal Studies* 570, 2012.

Rosenberg, Gerald N., *The Hollow Hope: Can Courts Bring about Social Change?* Chicago: University of Chicago Press 2008 (2nd ed.).

Rosencranz, Armin and Michael Jackson, "The Delhi Pollution Case: The Supreme Court of India and the Limits of Power," 28 *Columbia Journal of Environmental Law* 223, 2003.

Roychowdury, Anumita, *CNG Programme in India: The Future Challenges*, New Delhi: Centre for Science and Environment 2010.

Sahu, Geetanjoy, *Environmental Jurisprudence and the Supreme Court*, Hyderabad: Orient Black Swan 2014.

Shankar, Shylashri and Pratap Bhanu Mehta, "Courts and Socioeconomic Rights in India," in *Courting Social Justice: Judicial Enforcement of Social and Economic Rights in the Developing World*, Varun Gauri and Daniel M. Brinks (eds.), Cambridge: Cambridge University Press 2008, 146.

Sood, Avani Mehta, "Gender Justice through Public Interest Litigation: Case Studies from India," 41 *Vanderbilt Journal of Transnational Law* 833, 2008.

Supreme Court of India website, http://supremecourtofindia.nic.in/, last accessed August 11, 2018.

UNEP (United Nations Environment Program), "CNG Conversion: Learning from New Delhi," 2006.

WHO (World Health Organization), *WHO Air Quality Guidelines for Particulate Matter, Ozone, Nitrogen Dioxide and Sulfur Dioxide: Global Update 2005*, 2006.

World Bank, "International Experience with CNG Vehicles," *World Bank South Asia Urban Air Quality Management Note No. 2*, (2001), http://documents.worldbank.org/curated/en/748641468337184646/pdf/multiopage.pdf, last accessed August 28, 2018

CASES

M. C. Mehta v. Union of India Writ Petition (C) No. 13029 of 1985.

M. C. Mehta v. Union of India AIR 1997 SC 734.

M. C. Mehta v. Union of India AIR 2002 SC 1696.

Peoples Union for Civil Liberties v. Union of India and Others, Writ Petition (C) No. 196 of 2001.

S. Jagannath v. Union of India AIR 1997 SC 811.

S.P. Gupta and Ors. v. President of India and Ors. AIR 1982 SC 149.

Subhash Kumar v. State of Bihar & Ors., AIR 1991 SC 420.

Vellore Citizens Welfare Forum v. Union of India, AIR 1996 SC 2715.

PART IV

Discrimination

11

The Polarizing Face of Law

Religious Conversion Judgments and Political Discourse in India

SHYLASHRI SHANKAR

I. INTRODUCTION[1]

If a judge's function is to balance competing aspirations embodied in laws, then to what extent have judges been instrumental in providing transformative rights to vulnerable citizens? This question is pertinent because there have been many studies on the positive impact of judges, courts and constitutions in deepening and delivering rights to marginalized citizens (Vilhena et al. 2013). "Constitutional law and courts in virtually all such polities have become bastions of relative secularism, pragmatism, and moderation," says a leading scholar on the judiciary, and points to the moderating effect of supreme courts on polarizing issues such as national security and religious freedom(Hirschl 2010). Reasons cited for such behavior by judges include demands from civil society activists and the impetus provided by the urge to recoup the judiciary's legitimacy after authoritarian rule.

However, these progressive interventions and interpretations do not tell the complete story. Older studies are correct to highlight the barriers – political curbs (Dahl 1957), limited constitutional power (Rosenberg 2007) and ideological motivations (Epstein 1997) – faced by judges in performing such transformative acts. While courts have defused inequality for disadvantaged groups in some areas, the same judgments may produce inequality for these groups in other arenas. Some Supreme Court judgments in personal law have diminished the right of a woman to divorce in Judaism, to receive alimony in Islam and until recently to an equal share of inheritance within Hinduism (Jenkins 2001). Another example is from the arena of national security: judgments that increase the security of a citizen could simultaneously limit the

[1] Parts of this chapter have appeared in Schonthal, Moustafa, Nelson, and Shankar 2016, I am grateful to the editors of this book and to the reader for useful comments and suggestions.

civil liberties of some minorities. Thus, law and its interpreters can create equality of opportunity in one arena while simultaneously exacerbating inequality and religious conflict for the same group in another arena. When these judgments are magnified and utilized by groups in the political and social milieu, the court's impact becomes less transformative.

The chapter discusses this dynamic by analyzing how India's judiciary has tackled the right to affirmative action benefits of those among India's historically vulnerable scheduled castes (SCs) who have converted from Hinduism to other religions. In trying to further the interests of these disadvantaged groups subjected historically to discrimination in status, jobs and political power, the higher judiciary's interpretation of the law on affirmative action has created inequality in another dimension, namely in the ability of these groups to choose a belief or a religion.

The chapter makes three arguments:

(1) Progressive court interventions can be precluded by restrictive constitutional provisions, thus reemphasizing the validity of Gerald Rosenberg's (2008) thesis in *The Hollow Hope,* that a dynamic court is constrained by limited constitutional power to engage in progressive social change. India's judges are hamstrung in their efforts to promote the rights of these groups by the embedded contradiction in the law, which, in its pursuit of one legal goal (social justice), has undermined another (religious freedom).

(2) Even if judges aspire to implement the spirit of the law and try to provide an equitable result to these groups, their efforts need not produce positive social change.

(3) Contrary to the view that apex courts produce moderating effects in the arena of religious freedom, judgments have unintended and deleterious consequences and may enhance religious polarization.

The sections portray these arguments. Section II discusses how SCs and scheduled tribes (STs) who exit their low status by converting to other religions struggle with the intrinsic contradiction created by the Indian constitution between the right to access affirmative action benefits and the freedom to choose a religion. Section III focuses on how the judiciary has interpreted the affirmative action rights of SC and ST converts through a discussion of three stylized cases. Section IV explores the unintended consequences, namely religious polarization produced by the reactions and the utilization of court judgments by the Hindu nationalists.

II. CONVERSION AND AFFIRMATIVE ACTION: THE
CONTRADICTIONS WITHIN INDIA'S CONSTITUTION

The decisive factor, which often goes unstated in religious conversion cases, is caste. Caste, a hierarchical system that determines a Hindu's social status, occupational and economic roles, is central to Hinduism, which accounts for 79.80 percent of India's 1.21 billion population (2011 Census). Caste has undergone many transformations from an ancient varna system to a more contemporary jati system. The varna system divided the population initially into four and later into five mutually exclusive, endogamous, hereditary and occupation specific groups: the Brahmins, Kshatriyas, Vaisyas, Sudras and Ati-Sudras. The last two comprised all castes doing menial jobs, with the latter being considered "untouchables," in that even their presence was considered polluting by the upper castes. Rural India, even today, follows the practice of making Ati-Sudras live in separate enclaves and not allowing them to use the community wells and enter the temples of the upper castes. The three higher varnas are often referred to as "caste Hindus" (upper caste Hindus) or as "twice born," since the men of these castes enter an initiation ceremony (the second birth) and are allowed to wear the sacred thread (Deshpande 2006). Together, the upper castes constitute 17–18 percent of the population. Numerically, the largest varna is Sudra, constituting nearly half of the population. The Ati-Sudras, who are legally categorized as SCs, are roughly 20 percent of the population (2011 Census).

Not surprisingly, most religious conversions in independent India are by the 104 million (2011 Census) SCs and STs (indigenous peoples not part of the Hindu religion who too have suffered discrimination and violence at the hands of upper-caste Hindus). To improve their low social standing and reclaim dignity, SCs and STs have converted to Islam and Christianity, which promise equality to their congregants.[2] Many have also converted to Buddhism, but, as we shall see shortly, Buddhism has been treated differently from

---

[2] In addition, caste metamorphosed into the jati system, with features similar to the varna system, but with some differences. The association between jati and varna at the topmost level (Brahmin jatis, most Kshatriya jatis) and at the bottom (Ati-Sudra or former untouchables) is clearer than it is in the middle ranks. Up to the early 1990s, government data was available for three categories: SC, ST, "Others" (everyone who is neither SC nor ST: the residual category). From the mid-1990s, "Others" were divided into OBCs and "Others" (non-SC/ST/OBC residual). The term "OBC'" is supposed to capture Sudra jatis who have been described in the constitution as "socially and educationally backward classes." See Deshpande 2006.

Christianity and Islam by the courts and by political parties and social move-
ments.[3] The reason for converting out of Hinduism is succinctly stated by
Zafrulla, who along with about a thousand other SCs converted to Islam in
Meenakshipuram (South India) in April 1981:

"Why Islam? We knew other religions indirectly. But Hinduism we knew
directly. Buddhism we knew nothing about except that Ambedkar had converted to it. Here in Tamil Nadu, we knew something of Christianity. We
knew it was riddled with caste. My father-in-law was a Christian ... We
discussed the pros and cons of each faith after talking to the elders of those
groups. We took the initiative for conversion. Why did we really want to
convert? We had only one aim: Equality."[4]

Several such accounts demonstrate how the compulsions of untouchability
and its concomitant inequality have driven these groups to convert from
Hinduism.

These conversions would not matter in a conversation about affirmative
action were it not for the fact that those who drafted India's Constitution had a
foundational commitment to social justice for these historically wronged
people. The constitution mandates that only SCs and STs will get affirmative
action benefits in government colleges, administrative services and electoral
constituencies.[5] Despite the protests of the members of minority religions in
the Constituent Assembly, the initial legal definition of an SC as a Hindu (or a
Sikh or Jain, who Indian law defines as part of the Hindu community for these

---

[3] Buddhism is seen as having emanated from Hinduism and hence is perceived by the court as
     an "indigenous religion," whereas Islam and Christianity are viewed as foreign religions. Sikh
     (in 1956) and Buddhist (in 1989) SCs were also included in the Act and given affirmative action
     benefits..

[4] *The Hindu* (newspaper), January 31, 1999.

[5] Constitutional laws dealing with conversion relate to the right to propagate religion (article 25),
     the right to be governed by religious personal laws and the reservation (special treatment) for
     SCs and STs, as well as the ban on untouchability (Article 17). In light of the social disabilities
     suffered by the SCs and STs, the Constitution-makers decided to include clauses that would
     allow the SCs and STs to rise above such discrimination and take an equal place in society by
     assisting in the educational and economic development of these groups. Article 330(1) provides
     that seats shall be reserved in the House of the People for the SCs. Article 332(1) similarly
     provides for the reservation of seats for the SCs in the legislative assembly of every state. SCs are
     publicly notified by the President. In 2005, the Parliament enacted the 93rd Amendment to the
     Constitution and later to Act 5 of 2007 giving SCs, STs, and other backward classes to
     reservation in educational institutions and in public employment. This Act was challenged in
     the Supreme Court in *Ashoka Kumar Thakur v. Union of India* A. K. Thakur v. UOI, 2008(56)
     BLJR1292. The Parliament also has the power to amend the list of SCs/STs. Moreover, while
     the fundamental rights disallow any discrimination, provision was made to allow the
     government to engage in positive discrimination in favor of SCs/STs in educational
     establishments, government jobs and political representation.

purposes), limited the range of beneficiaries to SCs *within* Hinduism. This, Rowena Robinson (2014) argues, was because Christian representatives in the Constituent Assembly traded the inclusion of Christians in the SC list for the right to propagate. She points out that the weight of the Constituent Assembly was against affirmative action for Muslims and Christians because the two entitlements – political representation and economic benefits – were treated together so that relinquishing the one necessarily led to the surrender of the other. Robinson cites the bloody Partition of the country in 1947 into Hindu majority India and Muslim majority Pakistan as a key reason for such a stance on the part of the Constituent Assembly majority. There was an unwillingness on their part to seriously consider the idea that minorities too could be backward. "Indeed, it was not realised by most Christians, especially the influential and privileged leaders who represented the community in the assembly."(Robinson 2014) Robinson notes that SC converts to the Christian community today feel that Christians in the Constituent Assembly sold out their interests for minority rights (Articles 28–30), which only served the elites and their control over church assets and the educational sector.

In legal parlance, any system that has an operational caste system would be termed Hindu. So Sikhs and Jains have been included among Hindus. As we shall see in the next section, the legal test of whether a person is a Hindu starts with ethnic and geographical tests, which means that Hinduness can be rebutted not by proof of absence of belief or presence of disbelief but only by proof of exclusive adherence or conversion to a foreign (i.e., non-Hindu) faith. For purposes of application of Hindu personal law, a Hindu is one who is not a Muslim, Parsi, Christian or a Jew.[6] When the judiciary was tasked with determining who a Hindu was in the initial decade after independence, judgments considered a person to be a Hindu for the purpose of application of Hindu law even if he renounced all religion, renounced idols and joined a cross-caste community that had a purified monotheistic religion, such as the Brahmo Samaj.[7]

The Constituent Assembly's decision to connect an SC's eligibility for affirmative action with Hindu religion has meant that the constitution (and the law) inadvertently installs barriers to conversion from Hinduism. This decision, as we shall see in the next section, has had adverse implications, particularly for SC converts to other religions. First, it has forced them to either remain within Hinduism or convert back to Hinduism. Second, it has prevented the SC person from striving to regain personal dignity. The law fails

---

[6] See the discussion of *Satsangi* case by Derrett 1999.
[7] *Chandrasekhara v. Kulandaivelu* AIR 1963 SC 185.

to take into consideration the fact that social justice, after all, is about restitution of material and non-material parity to these groups. The vulnerability experienced by the SCs is not just from discrimination in the economic and political spheres, but is also a visceral loss of personal dignity that is not compensated by simply receiving a government job or a good education or by occupying the position of an elected village chief.[8] Third, it has eroded their fundamental right to religious freedom, which includes the freedom to choose a belief system.

STs, or the "original" peoples of India who were known historically to have descended from non-Hindus, are treated differently in the constitutional lexicon. STs could not be Hindus for the purposes of the law unless it was shown that they had adopted Hindu customs, habits and beliefs (Derrett 1999: 45). Their access to affirmative action was not connected to Hindu religion but to their status as members of a scheduled tribe group.

The Indian Constitution's provisions thus restrict affirmative action benefits to an SC within Hindu religion and to an ST who was accepted as a member of that tribe. The President of India is vested with the power (under Article 341) to specify certain groups as SC and ST.[9] The next section will assess how judges have interpreted these laws.

III. THE JUDICIARY AND SCHEDULED CASTE/SCHEDULED TRIBE CONVERTS

To recap the argument, even if judges aspire to implement the spirit of the law and try to provide an equitable result for SCs and STs, their efforts need not produce positive social change. Judges in India's High Courts and the Supreme Court have struggled to find governing principles that effectively balance the right to affirmative action with the right to religious freedom without eviscerating either. SCs and STs have approached the courts to demand access to political representation (reserved electoral seats for these two groups), which were conceptualized as a group right, and economic benefits (government jobs and seats in educational institutions), which are treated as individual rights. Judges have to deal with three types of converts among the SCs and STs:

---

[8] For an analysis of the impact of political affirmative action on access to anti-poverty initiatives, see Shankar and Gaiha 2013 .

[9] The Constitution (Scheduled Castes) Order, 1950 lists 1,108 castes across 29 states, and the Constitution (Scheduled Tribes) Order, 1950 lists 744 tribes across 22 states in its First Schedule. Article 341 and 342 provides for classification of SCs (the untouchable lower castes) and STs, while Articles 330, 332 and 334 provides for reservation of seats in Parliament and Assemblies.

converts to other religions; these same converts who "reconvert" back to the Hindu religion;[10] and the rights of non-SC and non-ST spouses.

Let us take three prototypes in the court's docket.

Case 1: The SC person converts to Buddhism, Islam or Christianity, and approaches the court to argue for retention of affirmative action benefits on the grounds that the stigma of caste does not disappear after conversion..

Case 2: An SC convert to another religion converts (reconverts) to Hinduism and wants the affirmative action benefits.

Case 3: The SC person marries a non-SC person, and the latter approaches the court for access to these benefits on grounds that he/she is now a member of the scheduled caste.

In all three cases, the fundamental question for the court is this: are these benefits assigned to an SC and an ST on the basis of economic status only or on the basis of economic *and* social status? If it is the latter, what is meant by social disability? Is it confined to the caste system within Hinduism or would the notion of social disability be applicable if the stigma associated with low caste were to follow them to their new religion?

A related question is whether the court's stance changes when the benefit claimed is political (group right) or economic (individual right).

Case 1: Consider the case of Gangaram Thaware, who had filed his nominations papers in the 1952 elections from an SC constituency. Thaware's nomination papers were rejected on the ground that he had ceased to be a Mahar (SC) when he joined the Mahanubhava Panth (a sect that repudiated the caste system and told its initiates to break off all former ties of caste and religion). The question faced by the Supreme Court in *Vithaldas v. Parashram* was whether the Panth was part of Hindu religion or not. [11] In answering the question three factors - the reactions of the old body, the intentions of the individual himself and the rules of the new order - had to be considered, said the court. If the old body was tolerant of the new faith and saw no reason to excommunicate the convert and the individual retained his old social and political ties, then the conversion was nominal and the view of the new faith "hardly matters."[12] Since the affirmative action pertaining to electoral constituencies was a group right (Article 330(1) reserves seats in the legislature for SCs), the views of the old body had to be considered. "The new

---

[10] I use the term "reconvert" in quotes because it is an ideologically loaded word used by the Hindu Right and challenged by the Left and others in India.

[11] AIR 1954 SC 236.

[12] Id.

body is free to ostracise and outcast the convert from its fold if he does not adhere to its tenets, but it can hardly claim the right to interfere in matters which concern the political rights of the old body when neither the old body nor the convert is seeking either legal or political favours from the new."[13] Saying that the Mahanubhava sect admitted to their fold persons who elected to retain their old caste customs, and pointing to evidence that Thaware was admitted to all functions of his old caste, they ruled in favor of Thaware.

The judgment's rationale followed the pre-independence Privy Council's precedent in *Durgaprasada Rao* v. *Sudarsanaswami* that the religious group decides who belongs to the group, and in making this decision the conduct of the person is key:

"In matters affecting the well being or composition of a caste, the caste itself is the supreme judge. If the caste is found to have given up certain old notions and practices and adopted new ones not in any way repugnant to morality, such usage should be respected. The function of the court is merely to ascertain the law, or the effect of usage having the force of law, and to apply it without being involved in the tangle of policies and expediencies."[14]

Proof of conversion acceptable to the court included following the customs of marriage, birth, death, worship, dress, occupation and the like, coupled with acceptance by the community by showing evidence of intermarriage, interdining, community of worship and residence in a particular place.. Public acceptance of the convert by the community to which he/she had converted assumed vital importance in the Privy Council judgments, and was later echoed in the Thaware case.

Those who retained their SC affiliation even after converting (though the court avoided the question of whether the Panth was another religion) should continue to enjoy their constitutional political privilege to reserved legislative seats, said the judgment in Thaware's case.

Not so, said the court in *G. Michael* v. *S. Venkateswaran*.[15] Michael was a paraiyan (SC) who converted to Christianity but wanted to contest elections from a seat reserved for SCs. The Supreme Court said:

"Once such a person ceases to be a Hindu and becomes a Christian, the social and economic disabilities arising because of Hindu religion cease and hence it is no longer necessary to give him protection and for this reason he is deemed not to belong to a scheduled caste. But when he is reconverted to

[13] Id.
[14] AIR 1940 Madras 517.
[15] AIR 1952 Madras 474.

Hinduism, the social and economic disabilities once again revive and become attached to him because these are disabilities inflicted by Hinduism."

Here, the acceptance or otherwise by the SC caste group did not count. The judgment also implied that SC converts to Christianity and Islam would cease to be eligible for economic and political benefits.

But that too is not the norm. In *Arumugam v. Rajagopal*, the Supreme Court pointed out that

> "[A] caste may consist not only of persons professing Hindu religion but also persons professing some other religion as well, conversion from Hinduism to that other religion may not involve loss of caste, because even persons professing such other religion can be members of the caste. This might happen where caste is based on economic or occupational characteristics and not on religious identity or the cohesion of the caste as a social group is so strong that conversion into another religion does not operate to snap the bond between the convert and the social group. This is indeed not an infrequent phenomenon in South India where, in some of the castes, even after conversion to Christianity, a person is regarded as continuing to belong to the caste."[16]

In the *Michael* case, the judge had dismissed the prevalence of caste in Christianity as being a case of exception, not the general rule. In a recent High Court case, a Muslim man belonging to Banjaras (classified in different Indian states as SC or ST) challenged the state for not allowing him to contest from a reserved constituency. After reviewing the history of Banjaras, the High Court came to the conclusion that Muslims were included in Banjaras and the whole point of reservation was backwardness of class, not caste.[17]

Thus, judges have not been consistent in either denying or allowing SC converts to other religions to access affirmative action benefits in the political arena. Their answer to the question whether benefits were assigned on the basis of economic status only or on the basis of economic and social status varied in these cases. The next section, which deals with a larger number of cases, will help us assess whether there are patterns to court rulings on this issue.

Case 2: Here, an SC person who had converted to another religion converted back to Hinduism, and then claimed political and economic

---

[16] AIR 1976 SC 939, p. 946. See the discussion on Christian Nadars in Robert Hardgrave, 1969, also see Ankur Barua, 2015.

[17] See *Moazzam Ali, Pradhan, Gram Panchayat v. State of U.P. through Special Secretary, U.P. Government and Ors.*, Civil Misc. Writ Petition No. 6152 of 2001 and Special Appeal No. 509 of 2002, Allahabad High Court. In 2013, the Uttar Pradesh state government decided to grant Banjaras ST status.

affirmative action benefits. The question for the court was whether this meant that the person could revert to their old religion and caste.

The higher judiciary's stance is that the reconverts would be considered members of their old religion, but whether or not they were considered part of the caste depended not just on their personal attestation but also required general acceptance by the caste. The main test of reconversion was the manifestation "of a genuine intention of the reconvert to abjure his new religion" and public acceptance by the caste.[18] "The main basis of the decision is that, if the members of the caste accept the reconversion of a person as a member, it should be held that he does become a member of that caste."[19] The point to note here is that courts do not see religious conversion as an individual or personal act (i.e., acceptance by the family), but as a public one (i.e., acceptance by the official group to which the person had converted). This is similar to the stance of the Privy Council rulings.

The most recent judgment on the issue was in *K.P. Manu v. Chairman, Scrutiny Committee for Verification of Community Certificate*, where the plaintiff wanted to retain his government job to which he had been appointed under an SC quota.[20] Manu was born to Christian parents, whose SC grandparents had embraced Christianity. Manu converted to Hinduism and received an SC certificate. The issuance of this certificate was challenged in court on the grounds that no material was brought on record to show that Manu, after conversion, had followed the traditions and customs of the SC community; this was compounded by the fact that Manu, after conversion, had married a Christian lady. The High Court directed the government to sack him from his government job. Manu appealed to the Supreme Court.

The questions posed to the apex court were threefold: (1) whether on conversion and at what stage a person born to Christian parents can, after reconversion to

---

[18] S. *Anbalangan v. B. Devarajan* AIR 1984 SC 413; *Kailash Sonkar v. Maya Devi*, AIR 1984 SC 600 *Arumugam v. Rajgopal* [1976] 1 SCC 863; also see *Principal, Guntur Medical College v. Y. Mohan Rao*, [1976] 3 SCC 411 (whether a person whose parents were SCs before their conversion to Christianity can, on conversion or reconversion to Hinduism, be regarded as a member of the SC and access educational benefits under affirmative action).

[19] *Arumugam v. Rajgopal* [1976] 1 SCC 863. Also see *V.V. Giri. v. D. Suri Dora and Ors.*, AIR 1959 SC 1318 (emphasized the acceptance by the caste community as key to classifying a person as an SC). Ironically, such acceptance does not matter the case of SC converts who claim reservation under the minorities quota. In *Ms. Alka Arun Pagare v. The State of Maharashtra and others* 1999(1)Bom CR 856, the Bombay High Court ruled that one had to be born a Christian to avail oneself of reserved seats for minorities in an educational institution. The plaintiff was a mahar who claimed reservation under the SC quota until class 12, then converted to Christianity and claimed reservation under the minorities quota.

[20] Civil Appeal No. 7065 of 2008.

the Hindu religion, be eligible to claim the benefit of the caste of his grandparents (who were originally SCs); (2) whether after his eligibility is accepted and his original community on a collective basis takes him within its fold, he still can be denied the benefit; and (3) who should be the authority to say that he has been following the traditions and customs of a particular caste or not.

The court's response was as follows. Three things had to be established by a person who claimed to be a beneficiary of the SC certificate: (1) clear-cut proof that he belongs to the caste that has been recognized by the Constitution (Scheduled Castes) Order, 1950; (2) proof that there has been reconversion to the original religion to which the parents and earlier generations had belonged; and (3) there has to be evidence establishing acceptance by the community. The judgment recalled the concept of eclipse from *Arumugam v Rajagopal*: "In our opinion, when a person is converted to Christianity or some other religion the original caste remains under eclipse and as soon as during his/her lifetime the person is reconverted to the original religion the eclipse disappears and the caste automatically revives."

The eclipse rationale is problematic because it answers yes to the question whether stigma associated with low-caste status is confined to Hinduism – and by doing so it encourages conversion back to Hinduism and to SC status for those who want to benefit from affirmative action. We will see how this plays out in the next section, where a larger number of cases are discussed.

Case 3: To the question of whether non-SC spouses can have access to affirmative action, the apex court has denied them these benefits, while the High Courts have been more equivocal.[21] For instance, a Jain woman married to a SC man wanted to contest from a reserved constituency, but the Allahabad High Court did not allow her to do so.[22] But in a case where the petitioner married an SC man and won from a reserved constituency, the Delhi High Court allowed the election, saying "caste sticks" to the spouse.[23] In 1996, the Supreme Court ruled that affirmative action was designed to right historical infirmities attached from birth to SCs; those who were not born as SCs could not benefit from affirmative action.[24]

[21] *Roopa Ravindra Kankanawadi v. Commissioner, Hubli-Dharwar Municipal Corporation*, W. P. No. 7063 of 1981, Karnataka High Court; *Indira v. State of Kerala*, W.P. Nos. 2483, 7039 and 17317 of 2005, Kerala High Court.
[22] *Smt. Sushma Singh W/o Dharam Pal Singh v. State of U.P. through Secretary Harijan and Samaj Kalyan and Ors.*, Civil Misc. Writ Petition No. 38423 of 2005, Allahabad High Court.
[23] *Ms. Sunita Wife of Shri Ghanshyam v. Krishan Lal S/o late Shri Des Raj and Ors*, CM (Main) No. 1241 of 2004, Delhi High Court.
[24] *Valsamma Paul v. Cochin University and Others* (1996), 3 SCC pp. 545–568.

For this category, the apex court has acted as a gatekeeper and ensured that affirmative action benefits are not appropriated by non-SC/ST persons who, it says, do not suffer from the social infirmities of their SC spouses.

For ST converts too, the acceptance of the tribe is key to certifying the tribal status and access to affirmative action. The court in *State of Kerala and Anr v. Chandramohanan* said:

"The question as to whether a person is a member of the Tribe or has been accepted as such, despite his conversion to another religion, is essentially a question of fact. A member of a Tribe despite his change in the religion may remain a member of the Tribe if he continues to follow the tribal traits and customs ... though as a broad proposition of law it cannot be accepted that merely by change of religion person ceases to be a member of scheduled tribe."[25]

In the next section, we will assess the patterns in a larger set of cases and see if the court's judgments encourage conversion to Hinduism and a return to the abject experience of social indignity by SCs.

IV. FINDINGS FROM THE DATASET

The 80 religious conversion cases in the High Courts and the Supreme Court from 1950 to 2006 are classified according to the type of issue:[26] propagation,[27]

---

[25] (2004)3 SCC 429.

[26] In 2007, using a keyword search on an online legal database, Manupatra, I found the cases on religious conversion in the high courts and the Supreme Court from 1950 to 2006. Manupatra is a database used by the High Court and Supreme court libraries and registrars. Manupatra claims to capture 80–90 percent of the cases reported in the Supreme Court Recorder. I then used an Excel spreadsheet to code the cases according to characteristics such as the court (High Court, Supreme Court); description of litigant (government, individual, religious organization, non-religious organization); nature of litigant (SC/ST and other); type of case (affirmative action non-political cases, affirmative action political cases, personal law, propagation and other); nature of case (conversion from Hinduism to Christianity, Hinduism to Islam, to Buddhism; conversion to Hinduism); description of the issue (conversion procedures did not take place, convert is not accepted by community, convert loses benefits after conversion, ineligible for affirmative action benefits); ruling (pro-convert or anti-convert); type of issue related to conversion; religious groups involved. Between 2008 and 2016, I found only three cases in the Supreme Court that dealt with religious conversion and access to affirmative action. *K. P. Manu* is discussed in the paper. *Rameshwar Dabhai Naika v. State of Gujarat* 2012(3) SCC 400 deals with whether children of intercaste marriages take on the lower caste status of the father. *Kodikunnil Suresh @J Monin v. N.S. Saji Kumar* is in the dataset at the high court level, and this case pertained to whether the successful contestant in an election was an SC (his opponent claimed he was a Christian). The apex court agreed with the lower court that the candidate was accepted by the community, hence election stands.

[27] Propagation cases pertain to anti-conversion acts, and to cases where propagation of a religion is challenged. An anti-conversion Act in Madhya Pradesh is challenged by a Christian missionary in court, which dismisses the case. In some of these propagation cases, the litigants are not SCs

TABLE 11.1 *Type of case and nature of litigant*

Type of case	Number	Litigant		
		SC	ST	Other
Personal law	31	0	0	31
Propagation	10	0	0	10
Affirmative Action (government jobs and education)	19	15	2	2
Affirmative action (election cases)	16	15	0	1
Other	4			4
Total	80	30	2	48

personal law,[28] affirmative action (election),[29] affirmative action (non-election cases),[30] other.[31]

As Table 11.1 shows, 35 cases of religious conversion pertained to access to affirmative action benefits, with 19 cases dealing with government jobs and education and 16 cases where the eligibility of the candidate to contest elections from a seat reserved for SC and ST was in question. None of the cases dealing with personal law and with propagation had litigants who were

or STs. For instance, the janitor of a Christian school appealed to the court saying he was given the choice between converting to Christianity or resigning, and that the school had illegally obtained his signature on a resignation letter. The court agreed with the janitor.

[28] A typical case is as follows: a married Hindu man converts to Islam and marries again. The court rules that it is bigamy because in this case Hindu laws apply first since the first marriage was under Hindu law.

[29] A typical case is as follows: Anbalagan loses the Lok Sabha election to Rajagopal and then challenges it on the grounds that the latter is a Christian, not SC. Rajagopal says that he reconverted to Hinduism and is now SC. Court agrees, saying that reconversion is proven if the community accepts him back, and the proof is that they did accept him because they voted for him. In another case, the appellant challenges the election of the respondent from an SC seat on the grounds that the latter has converted to Buddhism. The court agrees with the respondent that there is no proof of such conversion.

[30] Non-election cases include whether children born of intercaste marriage can claim low caste affirmative action. The plaintiff converts to Hinduism, gets a caste certificate, sits an exam as a judge, gets a job under the reserved category, but the State says that he cannot get SC status because his parents were Christians. Plaintiff successfully challenges it and says that the SC community accepted his conversion.

[31] Other cases include the following. A man is arrested under the law on atrocities against tribals for trying to molest a Christian whose family had converted from an ST. He challenges this, saying that the conversion occurred 200 years ago, so the person is not a member of the ST. The court says that a member of an ST may, despite his change in religion, remain a member of the ST if he continues to follow the tribal traits and customs.

from these two vulnerable groups. Over 50 percent of the cases on conversion were decided by the court after 1992.[32]

I will focus on the patterns displayed in the 35 affirmative action cases.

- Of the 35 cases, 10 were decided by the Supreme Court, while the rest were decided by the High Courts. STs were involved in just 3 cases as compared to SCs who were litigants in 32 cases. This could either indicate that retention of affirmative action benefits was not as much of an issue for STs, and/or it was too expensive for the STs to approach courts.
- About 60 percent of the cases were filed in the court after 1992. This means that there were more cases on affirmative action in the last two decades than in the first 40 years after independence, suggesting perhaps that more contention on the issue has occurred in the private, public and political spheres in this period. The next section examines the resonance of conversion related issues in the political and social arenas.
- Six of the 10 apex court judgments did not favor the convert, and a similar trend is observed in the High Court (only 8 out of 25 cases favored the convert).
- 65 percent of the cases pertained to reconversion to the Hindu religion and caste and access to affirmative action. Six cases dealt with conversions to Christianity, four to Buddhism and two to Islam.

My argument is that by limiting the access to affirmative action to those within Hindu religion, the law (and judges) will more likely restore this right to SCs and STs who reconvert to Hinduism, thus skewing the balance with other religions. This issue pertains to Case 2 discussed earlier. Of the 23 cases involving reconversion to Hinduism, 8 pertained to political benefits and 15 to non-political benefits. In both sets of cases, while the rulings favored the reconvert 50 percent of the time; they also went against the reconvert 50 percent of the time. One could argue that this makes it hard to attribute judicial bias toward Hindu religion in the arena of affirmative action.

A more interesting picture emerges when we assess the reasons given by the court for allowing or denying these reconverts the benefits. In over half of the cases involving conversion to Hinduism, the court privileged the attitude of the SC community toward the convert.[33] We see a similar picture in the

---

[32] Over 57 percent of the cases were decided within two years, and 75 percent were resolved within three years. In over 70 percent of the cases the Congress party (or a Congress party-led coalition) was in power at the center when the judgment was delivered, while the BJP was in power at the center for 22 percent of the cases.

[33] In the remaining 10 cases, the benefits were denied mainly on grounds that the person had not been born an SC or tribe: the person was from a higher caste or religion or was the child of a Christian convert but had not become a Hindu.

TABLE 11.2 *Reasons given by court*[34]

Type of benefit	Community acceptance	Non-acceptance by community	Conversion from Hinduism leads to loss of benefits	Conversion did not take place	Ineligibility of person
Non-political	7	1	4	0	7
Political	4	2	4	3	2
Total	11	3	8	3	9

35 cases of affirmative action. As Table 11.2 shows, in almost half of the cases the main reason for allowing the reconvert to access benefits or stop such access was the response of the SC community. What this implies is that one still has to be a Hindu to access these benefits; the court merely got around the silence in Hinduism on reconversion by looking to the reaction of the SC/ST community to accept or deny the convert.

The pattern in Case 3 type judgments is that the court has barred the access of those who were not born into these vulnerable groups. Upper-caste spouses and children of intercaste marriages did not qualify, said the court, acting as a vigilant gatekeeper. However, when it came to children and grandchildren of converts to other religions such as Christianity, they would only be eligible if they could show acceptance by the SC community. Here too, the pattern in the dataset shows that judicial interpretations favor a return to Hindu religion and SC status (and a concomitant loss of dignity).

One can see that the Indian constitution and its interpreters, the judiciary, in their pursuit of one legal goal (social justice) have encouraged a particular interpretation of religious freedom which, in its application to affirmative action, favors Hinduism over Christianity and Islam.[35] Conversion-related cases in India's higher judiciary show a tilt towards limiting conversion activities, particularly when it pertains to conversions to Islam and

---

[34] One case missing in Table 11.2 did not contain any of the above reasons.

[35] The state is aware of the imbalance. Under V. P. Singh's government (1989–1990), the law was amended to extend affirmative action benefits to Hindu SCs converting to Buddhism, but SC Christians and Muslims still remained outside the fold (unless they were included as part of the backward classes in a state). The courts too have issued several judgments that treat affirmative action benefits as accruing to a backward class, rather than a caste. See, for instance, *Moazzam Ali, Pradhan v. State of U.P.*, Writ Petition No. 6152 of 2001, Allahabad High Court.

Christianity. This is not because Indian judges have a pro-Hindu bias.[36] It is the constitutional linking of entrenched social disadvantage with Hinduism that explains the apparent bias of courts.

V. CONVERSION JUDGMENTS AND POLITICAL DISCOURSE

The third part of my argument is that contrary to the view that apex courts produce moderating effects in the arena of religious freedom, judgments have unintended and deleterious consequences for religious toleration, and could enhance polarization.

Courts do not operate in a vacuum. Their impact on the rights of these vulnerable groups is mediated by the response of civil society, political parties and socioreligious organizations to the judgments. Hindu nationalists have had a particularly strident reaction to the issue of conversion from Hinduism, more so when converts have adopted Islam and Christianity. I will focus on the reactions of the Rashtriya Swayam Sevak Sangh (RSS), Bharatiya Janata Party (BJP) and its predecessor, the Bharatiya Jana Sangh (BJS), and the Vishwa Hindu Parishad) to understand how the Hindu nationalists have used court judgments.

The Hindu nationalists, as Cassie Adcock (2013) points out, were among the Indian elites who in the 1920s changed the meaning of shuddi, a lower-caste "ritual-political" struggle for dignity, into the language of religious freedom. The Hindu nationalists questioned whether such freedom should protect proselytizing, and argued that allowing proselytization would be an intolerable threat to peaceable relations between (Hindu and Muslim) religious groups. The rationale was that since Hinduism did not have conversion (one is born a Hindu and within a hierarchical caste structure), allowing proselytizing religions such as Islam and Christianity to operate unhindered would lead to unequal treatment of religions. Their guiding ideology, known as Hindutva, or Hinduness, was defined by V. D. Savarkar (1923) in Who is a Hindu? as "embracing all the departments of thought and activity of the whole Being of our Hindu race." For Savarkar, who was an atheist, Hindus were a race who by definition followed a particular religion (almost akin to Judaism as a religious and ethnic identity), and Hindutva was a means for promoting the superiority

---

[36] Research on judicial behavior in 190 anti-terror cases indicates that on the contrary, judges are more likely to rule in favor of Muslim (and Sikh) minorities as long as they do not harbor secessionist impulses (Shankar 2009). Members of minority communities who were interviewed by the author also reiterated the point that they did not view Indian judges as displaying an "anti-minority" disposition.

of the Hindu race. Following Savarkar's rationale, the Hindu nationalists perceive the exodus of Hindus to other religions as being "dangerous to the security of the nation and the country . . . The majority of the Muslims in India are converts to that faith from Hinduism through force of circumstances." (Malkani and Mathur 1997).

Such notions are also increasingly being applied to the Christians in India, who were targeted in the aftermath of Partition. From 1953 to 1956, there was widespread agitation by Bharatiya Jana Sangh and the Hindu Mahasabha over the proselytizing activities of missionaries. In 1954 the Bharatiya Jana Sangh launched an "Anti-Foreign Missionary Week" protest movement in a regional state (Madhya Pradesh), but the agitation was suspended when the state government set up a committee, known as the Niyogi Committee, named after the chairman, a retired Chief Justice of the High Court. The Committee, appointed by the government of Madhya Pradesh on April 16, 1954 in response to allegations that Christian missionaries were converting members of tribes by fraud and force, released its report substantiating these allegations. Commenting on conversions in Madhya Pradesh, the Committee observed that "most conversions have been doubtless insincere admittedly brought about in expectation of social service benefits and other material considerations" (Niyogi Report: 113). Not surprisingly, the report raised a political storm. The report was to have a major impact on subsequent bills legislated by state legislatures (Jaffrelot 2007: 234). Later, as we shall see in the Stainislaus judgment and as pointed out by Vishwanathan (2007: 336), the Report played an important role in the Supreme Court ruling that the right to propagate religion did not necessarily include the right to convert. The central government shelved the report saying that it conflicted with the fundamental right to religious freedom.[37]

A vivid picture of how a judgment can have an unintended and polarizing effect is evident in the utilization of the Stainislaus case by the Hindu nationalists. In 1978, a Christian missionary named Stainislaus challenged

---

[37] The debate in the Indian Parliament on conversion crossed party lines; there was an intra-party divide within the Congress. For instance, in September 1955, a Private Members Bill, the Indian Converts Regulation and Registration Bill was introduced (and later withdrawn) in Parliament by Jethalal Joshi of the Indian National Congress Party. Provisions of the bill included not allowing anyone to become a convert without first making a declaration to that effect one month prior to the actual date of conversion; licensing of the person or institution conducting conversions; and prohibition of conversion by minors. Also see Bhagawat Jha Azad, Congress, p. 1109, Lok Sabha Debates, December 2, 1955. A similar bill, which targeted the SCs and STs and backward communities for protection against coerced conversion was proposed and later withdrawn in March 1960.

the Madhya Pradesh Freedom of Religion Act (passed in 1968) in the Madhya Pradesh High Court. The Act prohibited conversion by force, fraud or inducement and prescribed one year's imprisonment and a fine for those convicted.[38] Stanislaus objected to the Act on the grounds that the definition of inducement was overly broad. Losing the case in the High Court, Stainislaus appealed to the Supreme Court, where the case was heard with another case from Orissa on a similar anti-conversion law.[39] In its verdict, the Supreme Court of India upheld both acts. The Chief Justice, writing for the court, insisted that there was "no fundamental right to convert another person to one's own religion" because such a right "would impinge on the freedom of conscience guaranteed to all citizens of the country alike." *(Stainislaus* v. *State of Madhya Pradesh)*[40]

Interpreting the judgment as a victory for Hindus (vis-à-vis Christian missionaries), a Bharatiya Jana Sangh member (O. P. Tyagi) introduced the Freedom of Religion Bill in the Indian parliament in December 1978 that sought to prohibit conversion from one religion to another by the use of force or inducement or by fraudulent means. This proposal, which was backed not just by the RSS (see Jaffrelot 2007: 287) but also by the Prime Minister of the ruling coalition, purportedly intended to offer STs the "protection of the state" from the missionaries.[41] The language of the Bill cited the Supreme Court judgment in the Stainislaus case as supporting the constitutionality of the Bill.[42]

---

[38] The framers of the Constitution were aware of the potential of conversion as a political time bomb. A review of the Constituent Assembly discussion on article 25 that extends the right to propagate religion to all persons shows that the framers were divided on whether to extend such a right to citizens. Tajamul Husain urged that religion was a private affair between oneself and one's creator and it had nothing to do with others, and therefore the right to propagate religion was wholly unnecessary. Another member (Loknath Mishra) held that the aim of propagation of religion was political and hence should be deleted from the fundamental and justiciable rights component of the Constitution. However, those in favor of incorporating the right prevailed; they said the right was not absolute, and if any attempts were made to secure mass conversions through undue influence the State had the right to regulate such activity.

[39] The Orissa High Court found oppositely to the Madhya Pradesh High Court. In Orissa, the court held the Act *ultra vires* partly finding with the party who opposed the act, on the grounds that the definition of "inducement" was indeed too vague and, as such, would prohibit too many proselytizing activities.

[40] 1977 2 SCR 611

[41] Mother Teresa wrote to the Indian Prime Minister Morarji Desai on April 21, 1979, expressing her concerns. In response, the Prime Minister urged her to support the Bill on the grounds that the state had to be "particularly vigilant about the Scheduled Tribes whose protection is not only guaranteed by the laws of the land but is also enshrined in the Constitution. It is our duty to preserve every aspect of their way of life along with their religion and ways of worship. No group belonging to any creed should interfere with their religion and rituals." (Goel 1998).

[42] See Organizer, April 15, 1979, pages 1–15 for a full text of the Bill.

The Prime Minister later withdrew his backing because of an agitation by Christian groups and the Minorities Commission, which had been established by the government in January 1978 for the regulation of religious and linguistic minority affairs. Christian leaders highlighted the violence that comparable legislation had triggered in Arunachal Pradesh in northeast India (Goel 1998)[43]

The Stainislaus judgment continued to cast a long shadow in subsequent years, and has given Hindu nationalists new ways to express and legitimize their long-standing opposition to conversion in the language of religious freedom and judicial precedents. For instance, in May 2008, Rajnath Singh (the then president of the BJP) wrote to Pope Benedict XVI (in response to the Pope's criticism about the official attitude to conversion in India) that Indian anti-conversion laws had withstood the scrutiny of the Supreme Court, which had come down heavily on fraudulent conversions in the Stainislaus judgment:

India's Supreme Court in its Judgment had delivered "What constitution grants is not the right to convert another person to one's own religion but to transmit or spread one's religion by an exposition of its tenets" the court had said. According to the country's top court, organised conversion, whether by force or fraud or by providing help or allurement to persons, taking undue advantage of their poverty and ignorance, its anti secular.[44]

The author's interviews with politicians from other political parties, such as the AIADMK in Tamil Nadu, suggest that politicians were aware of the court's disinclination to strike down anti-conversion laws.[45]

The 1990s saw the reemergence of conversion-related issues in political rhetoric, as the BJP became a credible challenger to the hitherto dominant Indian National Congress Party. Another instance where the Stainislaus judgment was used in the political arena was when missionaries were attacked

---

[43] See Jaffrelot 2007: 287 for citations from newspapers.
[44] www.bjp.org/media-resources/press-releases/sh-rajnath-singh-letter-to-pope-benedict-xvi; also see *Hindustan Times*, May 23, 2006.
[45] The Tamil Nadu Prohibition of Forcible Conversion of Religion Act in 2002 banned all religious conversions by force, deceit or allurement. The State Assembly passed it after a heated debate, with 140 members supporting it and 73 opposing it in a House of 234. In 2005, the AIADMK led Tamil Nadu government had to withdraw an anti-conversion Act after suffering electoral losses in the parliamentary elections. Gujarat, Orissa, Chhattisgarh, Madhya Pradesh, and Himachal Pradesh have anti-conversion laws. Although Arunachal Pradesh enacted its law in 1978, the government has yet to frame the rules needed for enforcement. Gujarat has a Freedom of Religion Act (2003) and Rules (2008) that proscribed religious conversions by means of allurement, force, or fraud. The 1992 National Commission for Minorities Act identified Buddhism as a separate religion. In June 2008, the Delhi government decided to accord minority status to the Jain community, and the Union government followed suit in 2014.

in several states and a particularly gruesome murder of a missionary, Staines, and his two young sons in Orissa in 1998 by a Bajrang Dal activist (part of the larger Hindu Right) put the issue of conversion center stage, and the BJP-led coalition government in a bind. On the one hand, as a government upholding the right of all persons to freedom of religion they were forced to condemn the attack. On the other hand, the cause for which the crime had been committed was supposedly in line with the BJP's attitude toward conversion. The BJP chose a mid-path by releasing a resolution that condemned the killing and also reiterated "that preachers of all religions have the right to propagate their faith." Then, citing the Stainislaus case judgment, the resolution said that "however, the Constitution Bench of the Supreme Court has clearly laid down that conversions cannot be treated as a fundamental right."[46] They reiterated Prime Minister Vajpayee's call for a dialogue on conversions as the best way to sort out contentious issues.

Religious conversion, particularly mass conversions, pitted the BJP against the Congress and Left parties. "Who are the VHP or BJP to decide whether something is mass conversion or not," asked Mr. Raja, CPI, in an interview with the author. Additionally, the Hindu Right's implicit assumption that all STs are Hindus has been questioned by the Left, who argue that only some tribes (*adivasis*) may have been Hinduized but the rest do not subscribe to the commonly accepted Hindu pantheon or religious cultural practices. Hence the Hindu Right's term "reconversion" of these STs is a misnomer, they argue, since the change of religion from Christianity to Hinduism is a conversion like any other. Ironically, the judiciary has used the same term to refer to SC and ST converts to Hinduism. Given this history, the rise of political rhetoric surrounding conversion is not surprising.[47]

Part of the blame also lies with the ambiguity in the Indian Constitution, in particular its difficulty in classifying Hinduism, which Constituent framers variously viewed as a religion, culture and a way of life (Shankar 2018).[48]

---

[46] BJP Resolutions - Political 1980–99, Pub No. E6/2000 p. 304.

[47] Other judgments have exacerbated religious tensions. A judgment in the Shah Bano case, which involved a Muslim woman's claim to maintenance from her divorced husband, was upheld over the objection that to do so would undermine Muslim personal law. This important decision precipitated a series of political actions – including the Government's support of legislation to undo the decision. The Chief Justice's remarks about Islam in that judgment triggered a cry that the judges were Islamophobic. Cossman and Kapur (1996) argue that the court did not stop to consider that this uniform "way of life" is one based on assimilating religious and cultural minorities and on reconstituting all Indian citizens in the image of the unstated dominant norm, that is, a Hindu norm.

[48] I discuss this issue of competing imaginaries of Hinduism (as an ancient order, a religion and a culture) in the Indian constitution and the courts in Shankar (2018).

This has contributed to judgments that have blurred the line between religion, ideology, culture and politics, notably highlighted in a set of judgments on the BJP's use of "Hindutva" in election speeches, and provided the proponents of the Hindu Right with "a judicial imprimatur" to use Hindutva in the public and political arenas.[49]

The author's interviews with members of the Hindu Right highlight their favorable impression of the court's rulings on conversion. In their view, the court tried to "minimize the harmful impact of the constitution" and "balanced" the needs of (the predominantly Hindu) society by handing down judgments against conversion and "upholding Hinduism or Hindutva as part of the national character rather than confining it to a religion on par with Islam and Christianity."[50] In 2015, following a Supreme Court judgment (*K.P. Manu v Chairman, Scrutiny Committee for Verification of Community Certificate*) that ST reconverts from Christianity to Hinduism would be eligible for affirmative action benefits, the Vishwa Hindu Parishad described the ruling as "approval" for its controversial ghar wapsi [return home] programme. VHP national joint secretary Surendra Jain told *Firstpost*: "Pseudo secularists who were objecting to our campaign should now change their minds and start supporting us if they have faith in the judicial system of the country" (Anwar 2015).

It is therefore not surprising that in December 2014, RSS members led a mass conversion drive in which 350 Muslims in Agra were "returned home" to Hinduism. This sparked an explosive debate in Parliament and a walk-out by the opposition, who called on the government to protect the constitutional rights of religious minorities. What this episode shows is an escalation of proselytization by the Hindu Right (an irony considering that entry to Hinduism is through birth and not through conversion) aimed at compelling

[49] The Supreme Court classified Hindutva as religious rhetoric and banned its use in election speeches (*Bommai v. Union of India*, 1994 SC 1918), but in a subsequent judgment said that Hindutva "could not be equated with narrow fundamentalist Hindu religious bigotry" and hence cannot be prohibited from being used for political mobilization (*Manohar Joshi v. Nitin Bhaurau Patil*, 1996, 1 SCC). The BJP president promptly issued a press statement saying he was extremely gratified principally because the Constitution Bench has lent its seal of judicial imprimatur to BJP's ideology of Hindutva.

[50] Interview with S. Gurumurthy, an ideologue of the RSS and a coconvenor of the Swadeshi Jagran Manch, an organization for promoting the awareness of Indian tradition. March 6, 2007, Chennai. Others in the BJP echoed these sentiments. Also see Swamy (2012) Subramaniam Swamy, Ban on Induced Religious Conversion Is Constitutional: Himachal Freedom of Religion Act, Organizer, 2012, http://organiser.org//Encyc/2012/9/11/-b-Ban-on-Induced-Religious-Conversion-is-Constitutional-b-.aspx?NB=&lang=3&m1=&m2=&p1=&p2=&p3=&p4=.

Christian and Muslim groups to demand the state's intervention and ironically perhaps even an anti-conversion law. The strategy of the Hindu Right is clear from a comment by a key supporter (Gurumurthy 2015) that the Modi government was "free to bring a law to ban conversions by inducement and fraud, including Agra conversions."

Thus, in trying to achieve the goal of social justice, the court's interpretation of affirmative action rights of SC and ST religious converts from Hinduism has undermined the ability of these groups to adopt new religions where there is promise of equality. In addition, the judgments have been used to legitimize the actions of the Hindu Right in reconverting these groups to their disadvantaged positions within Hinduism and created disaffection among the religious minorities in the country.[51]

VI. CONCLUSION

The complex story of conversion laws in India shows how the authority of the courts can work not just to undermine the social justice goals of the Indian polity but also to further fuel religious nationalism and undercut the religious freedom and personal dignity of vulnerable groups. Law and the courts can simultaneously sustain, reshape and advance social strife while trying to effect positive social change. To see the law's polarizing potential is not to dismiss law out-of-hand. The language and opinions of court decisions cannot be fixed within a liberal politics; they may also be used as political slogans to justify exclusionary politics. In pointing to these dynamics, one must take into account both the benefits and the unintended negative consequences of judicializing disputes over access to affirmative action and to religious freedom, and in doing so to introduce a new spirit of creativity, modesty and humility about the ameliorative powers of law.

---

[51] John Dayal, secretary general of the All India Christian Council and member of National Integration Council, said, "Christian and Muslim communities cannot but be very disappointed with the Supreme Court's two recent judgements – the one yesterday granting Scheduled Caste rights to Muslim and Dalit Christians who convert to Hinduism and the earlier one which referred to a Constitutional bench the demand that this group be given Scheduled Caste rights because they continue to suffer the infirmities and indignities in Indian society. The judgment also seems to legitimise 'Ghar Wapsi', while making it prohibitive and punitive for any Dalit to exercise his or her freedom of faith and convert to Islam or Christianity. Conversions to Buddhism and Sikhism do not invite this punishment" (Anwar 2015).

REFERENCES

Adcock, Cassie. 2013. *The Limits of Tolerance: Indian Secularism and the Politics of Religious Freedom*. London: Oxford University Press.

Advani, L. K.. 1999. *Secularism – Rooted in India's Culture and Traditions*. Bharatiya Janata Party Publication No. E/3/99.

Anwar, Tarique. 2015. "SC Ruling on Reconversion: A Stamp of Approval for Ghar Wapasi, says VHP." Firstpost, February 28, 2015.

Barua, Ankur. 2015. *Debating Conversion in Hinduism and Christianity*. London: Routledge.

Cossman, Brenda and Ratna Kapur. 1996. Secularism: Benchmarked by the Hindu Right. *Economic and Political Weekly*, Vol. 31, No. 38.

Dahl, Robert A.. 1957. Decision-Making in a Democracy: The Supreme Court as a National Policy-Maker. *Journal of Public Law*, vol. 6, p. 279.

Derrett, J. D. M.. 1999. *Religion Law and the State in India*. New Delhi: Oxford University Press.

Deshpande, Ashwini. 2006. Affirmative Action in India and the United States, Equity and Development. World Development Report 2006, Background Papers.

Epstein, Lee and Jack Knight 1997. *The Choices Justices Make*. Washington D.C. CQ Press.

Goel, Sita Ram. 1998. *Pseudo Secularism, Christian Missions and Hindu Resistance*. New Delhi: Voice of India.

Gurumurthy, S.. 2014. Is the Stage Set for Mother of All Debates. *The New Indian Express*, December 15.

Hardgrave, Robert. 1969. *The Nadars of Tamil Nadu: The Political Culture of a Community in Change*. Berkeley: University of California Press.

Hirschl, Ran. 2010. *Constitutional Theocracy*. Cambridge, MA: Harvard University Press.

Jaffrelot, Christophe. 2007. *Hindu Nationalism: A Reader*. Princeton: Princeton University Press.

Jenkins, Laura Dudley. 2001. "Personal Law and Reservations." In Gerald Larson (ed.) *Religion and Personal Law in Secular India: A Call to Judgment*. Bloomington: Indiana University Press.

Malkani, K. R. and J. P. Mathur. 1997. *BJS to BJP: Two Essays on Ideology in Action*, Bharatiya Janata Party publication No. E/6/97.

Robinson, Rowena. 2014. "Minority versus Caste Claims: Indian Christians and Predicaments of Law." *Economic and Political Weekly*, April 5, Vol. 49, No. 14.

Rosenberg, Gerald. 2008. *The Hollow Hope: Can Courts Bring about Social Change*. Chicago: University of Chicago Press.

Savarkar, V. D.. 1923. *Who Is a Hindu?* Bombay: S.S. Savarkar publications.

Schonthal, Benjamin, Tamir Moustafa, Matthew Nelson and Shylashri Shankar. 2016. "Is the Rule of Law and Antidote for Religious Tension? The Promise and Peril of Judicializing Religious Freedom." *American Behavioral Scientist*, Vol. 60, pp. 966–986.

Shankar, Shylashri. 2009. *Scaling Justice: India's Supreme Court, Anti-Terror Laws and Social Rights*. New Delhi: Oxford University Press.

2018. "Secularism and Hinduism's Imaginaries in India." In Mirjam Kunkler, John
    Madeley and Shylashri Shankar (eds.) *A Secular Age Beyond the West: Law,
    Religion and the State in Asia, the Middle East and North Africa*. Cambridge:
    Cambridge University Press, pp. 128–151.
Shankar, Shylashri. (with Raghav Gaiha. 2013. *Battling Corruption: Has NREGA
    Reached India's Rural Poor*. New Delhi: Oxford University Press.
Swamy, Subramaniam, Ban on Induced Religious Conversion Is Constitutional:
    Himachal Freedom of Religion Act, Organizer, 2012. http://organiser.org//
    Encyc/2012/9/11/-b-Ban-on-Induced-Religious-Conversion-is-Constitutional–b-
    .aspx?NB=&lang=3&m1=&m2=&p1=&p2=&p3=&p4=.
Vilhena, E. Oscar, Upendra Baxi and Frans Viljoen (eds.) 2013. *Transformative
    Constitutionalism: Comparing the Apex Courts of Brazil, India and South Africa*.
    Pretoria: Pretoria University Law Press.
Viswanathan, Gauri. 2007. "Literacy and Conversion in the Discourse of Hindu
    Nationalism." In Anuradha Dingwaney Needham and Rajeswari Sunder Rajan
    (eds.), *The Crisis of Secularism in India*, Durham, NC: Duke University Press,
    pp. 333–355.

12

Evaluating the Impact of the Indian Supreme Court Judgment on Sex-Selective Abortion

SITAL KALANTRY AND ARINDAM NANDI

I. INTRODUCTION

Lawyers bring public interest litigation cases (PIL) to the Indian Supreme Court seeking many different types of remedies, including to prevent the construction of power plants that may damage the environment or to prevent violations of rights of a group of people. The Indian Supreme Court (the Supreme Court or Court) sometimes responds by creating guidelines for what the executive branch might do. But in many PIL cases, litigants are not asking for the creation of new rules, but instead they are simply asking the Supreme Court to encourage the government to amend, implement, and enforce laws that already exist.

In this chapter, we investigate one such case: the PIL brought by the Center for Enquiry into Health and Allied Themes (CEHAT), Mahila Sarvangeen Utkarsh Mandal (MASUM), and Sabu George in 2000. These public interest litigants were concerned about the rate of selective abortions of fetuses when the future biological sex of the child was determined to be female. Starting in the 1980s, ultrasound machines became more widely available in India, and this allowed families to detect the future biological sex of their children; and some women chose to abort fetuses when the future sex was predicted to be female. To curb this practice the government passed a law that became effective in 1996 to prevent medical professionals from giving information to pregnant women about the future sex of their children.

The public interest litigants claimed that the law had not been implemented by the Union and State governments of India. The Supreme Court kept jurisdiction of the case for three years until 2003. During this time it asked for various reports from State governments and prodded the Union government to amend and strengthen its anti-sex-determination legislation.

Defining success broadly, it appears that the Supreme Court's intervention was successful: the Union government did indeed amend and strengthen the law. We observe this through the dialogue in Supreme Court hearings with relevant stakeholders and also by examining the discussions in the Indian Parliament about the Supreme Court's orders in this case. Of course, Parliament may have amended the law even without Supreme Court intervention.

However, from a narrow measure of success, the Supreme Court's orders in this case were an utter failure. The ultimate goal of the litigants was to decrease abortions of female fetuses, which they hoped to do by encouraging the Supreme Court to push the Union government to amend the law to close loopholes and to push State governments to implement the existing law. But, according to available data, the rate of abortions of female fetuses did not decrease during the time the Supreme Court held a number of hearings on the case (2000–2003) and did not decrease even after the amendments were made to the anti-sex determination law in 2002. On the contrary, the number of female births decreased every year.

Simply referring to the Indian Census data makes it abundantly clear that that sex ratios (the number of girls to boys born in any given time period) decreased between 2001 and 2011. What is unique about the data set we utilize is that it observes year-by-year variation to track the impact from the initiation of the PIL and immediately after the 2003 decision when the court issued its final order in the case. Thus, while the Indian Census will show the change over a period of 10 years, our data can be used to determine whether there were any improvements during the shorter period of time that the Supreme Court had jurisdiction over the case and year by year after the enactment of amendments to the anti-sex determination law in 2002. Moreover, the Indian census only reports the sex ratio of children from birth to six years of age. Our data set consists of birth data, which would be more immediately sensitive to increased enforcement efforts, for example.

We conjecture that when the Supreme Court intervenes to change deep-seated cultural desires such as the desire for many families who want to have at least one male-child, it may be less successful than when it attempts to intervene in matters that do not relate to deeply held personal views of many people. In addition, given that much of the illegal behavior that the Supreme Court wants to curb takes place outside the scrutiny of the public view, the law is inherently difficult to enforce.

In Section II, we describe the origin of the Indian sex ratio crisis. We then detail the responses of Parliament and the Indian Supreme Court to the excess of males and shortage of females in Section III. In Section IV, we describe the sex ratio trends over time and geography in India. Our analysis of the impact of the PIL is in Section V. The final section (Section VI) examines the causes of the sex ratio crisis and explains why the Indian Supreme Court judgment has not achieved results.

II. THE INDIAN SEX RATIO CRISIS BEGINS

In the 1970s, amniocentesis technology – meant to diagnose genetic abnormalities, but also capable of determining the sex of a fetus – became available in India. Ironically, the All India Institute of Medical Sciences, the country's most prestigious medical school, was the first to offer these tests at its government teaching hospital. Other government hospitals soon followed suit. While the technology was meant to identify genetic abnormalities in a fetus, doctors also used the tests to identify the sex of the fetus and would offer an abortion if the sex was not what the mother desired.[1]

The doctors performing the sex-selective abortions justified them on population control grounds. Indeed, population control is arguably a more important goal in India today than it was then. India has only 2.5 percent of world's land and yet must accommodate and feed 17 percent of the world's people.[2] The population density of India is 377.7 inhabitants per square kilometer compared to only 142.9 in China and 31.85 in the United States.[3]

The doctors who first began performing sex detection tests published an article in *Indian Pediatrics* explaining that they had conducted trials using amniocenteses for sex determination and found that "seven of the eight patients who had tests carried out primarily for the determination of sex of the fetus" aborted their female fetuses.[4] In the past, American foundations actively supported population control efforts in India, including sex-selective abortions.[5] In 1978, the use of amniocenteses for purposes of sex determination was banned in government hospitals, but private clinics emerged to fill the growing demand.[6]

Given that amniocenteses involves the removal of amniotic fluid and a laboratory in which the testing must be conducted, these tests were mostly available in cities and only affordable for middle-class or rich people. A new

---

[1] Mara Hvistendahl, UNNATURAL SELECTION 80 (2011).

[2] Hrishikesh D. Vinod, *Newborn Sex Selection and India's Overpopulation Problem*, 4 MOD. ECON. 102, 103 (2013).

[3] *Id.*

[4] MARA HVISTENDAHL, UNNATURAL SELECTION 81 (2011).

[5] *Id.* at 82–89 (2011).

[6] The Lawyer's Collective, WOMEN'S RIGHTS INITIATIVE, PRE-CONCEPTION & PRE-NATAL DIAGNOSTIC TECHNIQUES ACT: A USERS GUIDE TO THE LAW 1 (Indira Jaising ed., 2004).

technology, however, changed financial and physical access dramatically: the ultrasound.

By the mid-1980s, many clinics in the capital city of Delhi offered prenatal ultrasound exams.[7] With a growing middle class and increasing access to ultrasound machines used to detect the sex of the fetus, more abortions occurred, and the sex ratio became further male skewed.[8]

In the late 1980s, offensive advertisements promoting sex determination tests were commonly visible in India. Commentators often point out that advertisements would state, "Pay 500 rupees now and save 50,000 [in dowry] later."[9] In the state of Haryana, the sex ratio dipped as low as 879 women per 1000 men.[10] Indian feminists quickly took notice.

III. PARLIAMENT AND THE INDIAN SUPREME COURT RESPONSE

A. Parliament bans sex determination (1994)

Unlike in the United States where the push to ban sex-selective abortion is rooted in the anti-abortion movement, India's movement to curb it was initiated by feminists.[11] In 1982, a group of women's organizations protested to demand a complete ban on sex determination tests.[12] In Mumbai, a group called the Forum Against Sex Determination and Sex Pre-Selection was created in 1985.[13] These groups were explicit in their goal – they did not want to place restrictions on abortion access, but instead demanded that medical professionals be prohibited from telling patients the sex of their fetus.[14] The

---

[7] Mara Hvistendahl, Unnatural Selection 49 (2011).

[8] See Christophe Z. Guilmoto, _Characteristics of Sex-Ratio Imbalance in India, and Future Scenarios_ 4–8 (2007), www.unfpa.org/gender/docs/studies/india.pdf.

[9] _Missing Sisters_, Economist, April 17, 2003.

[10] _Sex Ratio in India_, Census 2011, www.census2011.co.in/sexratio.php (last visited Oct. 4, 2013).

[11] See generally Sital Kalantry, _Sex Selection in the United States and India: A Contextualized Feminist Approach_, 18 UCLA J. Int'l L. Foreign Aff. 61 (2013); Sital Kalantry, _Sex-Selective Abortion Bans: Anti-Immigration or Anti-Abortion?_, 16 Geo. J. Int'l Aff. 140 (2015).

[12] Mary John, _Sex Ratios and Gender Biased Sex Selection History, Debates and Future Directions_ U.N. Population Fund (UNFPA), 8 (2014), http://asiapacific.unfpa.org/webdav/site/asiapacific/shared/Publications/2014/Sex-Ratios-and-Gender-Biased-Sex-Selection.pdf.

[13] Mary John, _Sex Ratios and Gender Biased Sex Selection History, Debates and Future Directions_ U.N. Population Fund (UNFPA), 8 (2014), http://asiapacific.unfpa.org/webdav/site/asiapacific/shared/Publications/2014/Sex-Ratios-and-Gender-Biased-Sex-Selection.pdf.

[14] Bijayalaxmi Nanda, _Campaign against Female Foeticide: Perspectives, Strategies and Experiences, in_ Sex-Selective Abortion in India: Gender, Society and New Reproductive Technologies 361 (Tulsi Patel ed., 2007).

state government of Maharashtra, where Mumbai is located, passed legislation to ban sex determination tests in 1988 before any national legislation was passed.[15]

Six years later, in 1994, the Government of India enacted the Pre-Natal Diagnostic Techniques (Regulation and Prevention of Misuse) Act (PNDT). This law, which came into effect in 1996, prohibited the use of techniques (such as ultrasounds and amniocentesis) to determine the sex of the fetus after conception.

B. Public interest litigation in the Indian Supreme Court

Arguing that national and state governments did not take necessary measures to enforce the PNDT, advocates brought a petition to the Supreme Court of India using a mechanism called PIL whereby people without standing are able to bring cases directly to the Supreme Court to enforce social justice issues.[16] In September 2000, the Center for Enquiry into Health and Allied Themes (CEHAT), Mahila Sarvangeen Utkarsh Mandal (MASUM), and Sabu George argued to the Indian Supreme Court that the government had failed to implement the PNDT.[17] The petitioners asked, among other things, that appropriate authorities be appointed at the state and district levels to monitor compliance with the PNDT.

The Supreme Court issued several interim orders with very specific directions to the Union government and State governments to facilitate implementation of the Act.[18] Through an examination of the numerous orders, it appears that the Supreme Court was in dialogue with the State governments and Union government.[19] First, it is ordering State governments to submit detailed reports about its compliance efforts. For example, on April 30, 2002, the Court asked several states to fill affidavits within 15 days reporting a number of things, including why they failed to seize ultrasound machines that were not properly registered pursuant to the PNDT. Second, it drew attention to the issues and

---

[15] Bijayalaxmi Nanda, *Campaign against Female Foeticide: Perspectives, Strategies and Experiences, in* Sex-Selective Abortion in India: Gender, Society and New Reproductive Technologies 361 (Tulsi Patel ed., 2007).

[16] India Const. Art. 32.

[17] *Centre for Enquiry into Health and Allied Themes (CEHAT)* v. *Union of India* (2001) 3 S.C.R. 534 (India).

[18] We found orders published in Manupatra in *CEHAT and Others* v. *Union of India* and Others of the following dates: May 4, 2001, September 19, 2001, December 11, 2001, April 30, 2002, March 31, 2003, August 4, 2003, July 7, 2003, September 10, 2003.

[19] When we refer to State governments, we also include Union territories in that definition.

failure of implementation. The Court noted that "there is a total slackness by the administration in implementing the Act."[20] Third, it asked the body that was appointed pursuant to the PNDT to propose amendments to that PNDT to include newer technology and new methods that could be used to sex select that was not previously included in the prohibition.[21]

Through the course of the three years within which it kept jurisdiction in the case, its interventions served to remind the Union and State governments about the importance of curbing sex selection, about its lack of implementation, and the need for amendments to the PNDT. The Supreme Court kept at this task even though many State governments failed to comply with the Court's requests. Indeed, in one of his orders in the case, Justice Shah laments that "it appears that the directions issued by this Court are not complied with."[22]

In 2003, the Indian Supreme Court issued its final judgment in the case. It repeated many of the recommendations that it had already issued to the various stakeholders involved in prior orders.[23] Following are examples of some of the "directions" issued to each relevant stakeholder. Some of its directions seem to apply even after the date of the final order. After closing the case, though, the Supreme Court had even less ability to ensure that any of its directions were actually complied with than when it kept the case open.

Directions to the Central Government
- Create public awareness against the practice of sex selection and sex determination.
- Implement the Act with all vigour and zeal.

Directions to the Central Supervisory Board
- Call for meetings at least once in six months.
- Review and monitor implementation of the Act.
- Call for quarterly updates from State and Union Territory (UT) Appropriate Authorities regarding the implementation and working of the Act.
- Examine the necessity of amending the Act keeping in mind emerging technologies and difficulties in implementation of the Act.
- Lay down a code of conduct to be observed by persons working under the Act and to ensure its due publication.

---

[20] Order dated September 19, 2001.
[21] See, e.g., Order dated May 5, 2001.
[22] *CEHAT and others* v. *Union of India and others*, W.P. (C) No. 301/2001, September 19, 2001.
[23] *CEHAT* v. *Union of India*, 2003 SOL Case No. 547 (2003).

- Require Medical Professional Bodies/Associations to create awareness and to ensure implementation of the Act.

Directions to State Governments and UT Administrations
- Appoint by Notification fully empowered Appropriate Authorities at the district and sub district levels.
- Appoint Advisory Committees to aid and advise Appropriate Authorities.
- Furnish a list of Appropriate Authorities in the print and electronic media.
- Create public awareness against the practice of sex selection and sex determination.
- Ensure that Appropriate Authorities furnish quarterly returns to the Central Supervisory Board, giving information on the implementation and working of the Act.

Directions to Appropriate Authorities
- Take prompt action against any person or body that issues or causes to be issued any advertisement in violation of the Act.
- Take prompt action against all bodies and persons who are operating without valid Certificate of Registration under the Act.
- Furnish quarterly returns to the Central Supervisory Board about the implementation of the Act.

C. Indian Parliament Amends the PNDT

In examining the transcripts of various committee discussions about sex selection, it is clear that members of the Rajya Sabha, one of the two houses of Parliament, were keenly aware of the Supreme Court's orders. For example, Prema Cariappa, a Member of Parliament from Karnataka, observed that "the hon'ble Supreme Court has passed an order on 4th May, 2001 directing the registration of all bodies using the ultrasound equipment, under the Pre-natal Diagnostic Techniques (Regulation and Prevention of Misuse) Act, 1994."[24] On another day, the Member of Parliament from Tamil Nadu even quoted one of the Supreme Court orders at length.

Over the course of the time the Supreme Court held jurisdiction, the Ministers of Health were often called to testify about the case. For example, on November 25, 2002, the Minister of Health and Family Welfare (Shri Raja)

---

[24] Rajya Sabha Transcripts Dec. 11, 2002 PREMA CARIAPPA from Karnataka.

discussed the Supreme Court orders to State governments in great detail and specifically noted that "the Hon'ble Supreme Court of India has been issuing directions since May 2001 to the Union of India as well as State/UTs." He also points out that implementation of the PNDT rests with the States and Union Territories.

On December 16, 2002, the Rajya Sabha again asked the Minister of Health and Family Welfare to report on the Supreme Court order. He provided a detailed overview of the July 10, 2002 order and indicated that the Supreme Court ordered certain states to act against clinics that were still advertising sex determination tests despite the fact that this was illegal. The states indicated that 305 ultrasound machines were seized. A "National Inspection and Monitoring Committee" was set up to "kept watch on all States and UTs," which apparently made surprise visits to clinics.

The Lok Sabha, the other house of Parliament, also discussed the Supreme Court orders. In its 13th session on December 20, 2002, the Minister of Health specifically noted that "The hon. Supreme Court has further directed amending the PNDT Act" and then went on to make specific suggestions for amendments, which he said were based on the recommendations of the Central Supervisory Board that was constituted under the PNDT. Indeed, this is the entity that the Supreme Court had directed to propose amendments to the PNDT.

The Central Supervisory Board proposed amendments to the PNDT. Thereafter, the Parliament amended the PNDT, changing its title to The Pre-Conception and Pre-Natal Diagnostic Techniques (Prohibition of Sex Selection) Act (PCPNDT).[25] The PCPNDT (among other things) increases the penalties and other regulations targeted at clinics.[26] Even though the amendments were meant in part to address advancements in sex determination technology, the reality is that most people are not likely to use this technology, in vitro fertilization (IVF), for sex selection purposes because it is expensive. IVF together with a test to determine the sex of an embryo costs $5,500 in India.[27]

Medical personnel and individuals who violate the PCPNDT are subject to criminal penalties and fines. Every clinic that uses diagnostic tests that can be

---

[25] The Pre-Natal Diagnostic Techniques (Regulation and Prevention of Misuse) Amendment Act, No. 14 of 2003, INDIA CODE (2003).

[26] The Pre-Natal Diagnostic Techniques (Regulation and Prevention of Misuse) Amendment Act, No. 14 of 2003, INDIA CODE (2003).

[27] *IVF Cost*, GLOBAL DOCTOR OPTIONS, www.globaldoctoroptions.com/ivf-cost/424 (last visited Aug. 13, 2015).

used for sex determination must register them.[28] Each local jurisdiction must appoint a local officer monitor compliance with the PCPNDT.[29] The PCPNDT further requires all clinics, centers, and laboratories to maintain records of all prenatal diagnostic tests they conduct in order to monitor their use. Additionally, the PCPNDT prohibits anyone from selling ultrasound machines to unregistered clinics or laboratories.[30] Likewise, the PCPNDT prohibits any kind of advertising of pre-conception or prenatal sex determination.[31]

The PCPNDT (like the PDNT) does not limit abortion directly, but, instead limits only disclosure of information about the future sex of the child.[32]

IV. MAPPING SEX SELECTION

Before we discuss our findings regarding the impact of the Supreme Court's decision, we briefly outline the history and current state of the Indian sex ratio crisis using data from the Indian Census. Amartya Sen drew attention to the maltreatment of women by coining the phrase "missing women."[33] This created a genre of studies that use sex ratios (the number of women to men in any given society) to calculate the number of missing women. While Sen intended the category to capture the many facets of inequality women face, "missing women" is more commonly used to mean the number of aborted female fetuses.

In the 1980s, estimates ranged from 100,000 to 220,000 "missing women" annually in India. After 2000, some believed that anywhere from 300,000 to 700,000 women were "missing" a year.[34] There are large variations in these estimates owing to different assumptions about the "normal" sex ratio, different mortality adjustments (including adjustments to account for reasons other than sex-selective abortion that impact imbalanced child sex ratios), and the

---

[28] The Pre-Natal Diagnostic Techniques (Regulation and Prevention of Misuse) Amendment Act, No. 14 of 2003, INDIA CODE (2003), ch. VI (18).
[29] *Id.* at V (17).
[30] *Id.* at ch. II (3)(B).
[31] *Id.* at ch. VII (22).
[32] Kirti Singh, *Laws and Son-Preference in India: A Reality Check*, U.N. POPULATION FUND (UNFPA) 58, 73 & n.94 (2013), www.unfpa.org/sites/default/files/jahia-news/documents/publications/2013/LawsandSonPreferenceinIndia.pdf.
[33] Amartya Sen, *More Than 100 Million Women Are Missing*, N.Y. REV. BOOKS, Dec. 20, 1990.
[34] Melissa Stillman et al., *Guttmacher Inst., Abortion in India: A Literature Review* 18 GUTTMACHER INST., (2014), www.guttmacher.org/pubs/Abortion-India-Lit-Review.pdf.

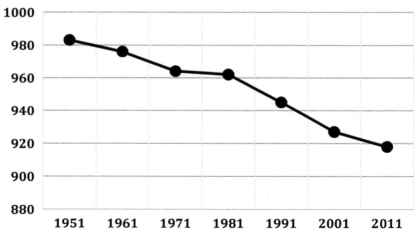

FIGURE 12.1: Child sex ratios in India, 1951–2011

use of different sources of data (e.g., the Indian census, the National Family Health Survey, or the Sample Registration System).[35]

In India, sex ratios are calculated as the number of females for every 1,000 males. We would expect to see at-birth sex ratios anywhere between 930 and 970 women to 1,000 men without any parental intervention. Although most commentators blame sex-selective abortions for causing an imbalanced sex ratio, abortion is not responsible for the entire imbalance. The Guttmacher Institute report notes that ultrasounds can only reliably determine sex during the second trimester of pregnancy, but only 10–15 percent of all abortions are performed after the first trimester.[36] The Indian census calculates only the child sex ratio, which is the ratio of girls to boys from birth to six years of age. Postnatal neglect of young female girls can also be a reason for excess female child mortality and male-biased child sex ratios.[37]

The child sex ratio in India in the 2011 Census was 914, which had dropped from 927 in the 2001 Census. Figure 12.1 depicts the sex ratio of the child sex ratio since 1951 in India.

Although the popular perception is that sex selection prevails throughout all parts of the country, the reality is that there is great regional variation among Indian states and territories. According to the 2011 Indian Census, 10 states or territories had child sex ratios at or above 950 and 19 states had sex ratios above

---

[35] *Id.*
[36] *Id.*
[37] Oster, Emily. *Proximate Sources of Population Sex Imbalance in India.* DEMOGRAPHY 46.2 (2009): 325–339. www.ncbi.nlm.nih.gov/pmc/articles/PMC2831281/.

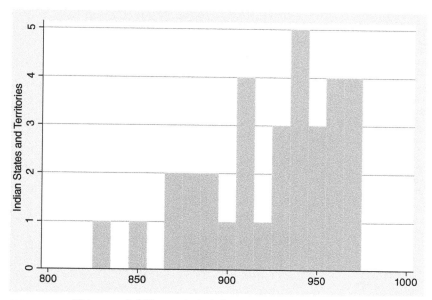

FIGURE 12.2: Histogram of child sex ratios in Indian states and territories.
Source: *Indian Census Bureau,* http://censusindia.gov.in/2011-prov-results/data_files/india/s13_sex_ratio.pdf

930. Figure 12.2 is a histogram showing the distribution of child sex ratios in the Indian states and territories.

The child sex ratios in the states and territories have also changed over the course of 10 years. Figure 12.3 illustrates the changes in sex ratios from the 2001 to the 2011 Indian Census. Child sex ratios improved in eight states, but none reached 950 except for Mizoram and Andaman & Nicobar Islands (which already had sex ratios above 950 in the 2011 Indian Census). Table 12.1 lists the sex ratios in each Indian state and territory in 2001 and 2011.

Having presented an overview of the current data on the child sex ratios in India, we now describe the impact of the Supreme Court's orders in the sex selection case.

V. MEASURING THE IMPACT OF THE SUPREME COURT JUDGMENT

The Supreme Court's intervention helped to push the Central Supervisory Board, an institution created pursuant to the PNDT, to propose amendments to the PNDT to account for new reproductive technologies that allowed people to preselect the future sex of their child and to improve enforcement

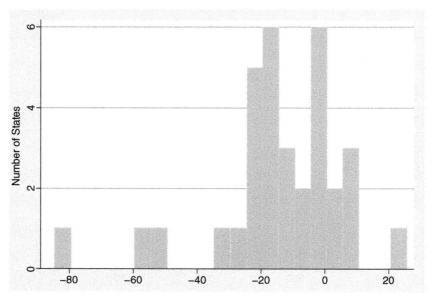

FIGURE 12.3: Figure of changes in child sex ratio in Indian states and territories, 2001–2011.
Source: Indian Census Bureau, http://censusindia.gov.in/2011-prov-results/data_files/india/s13_sex_ratio.pdf

mechanisms of the law (among other things). Parliament thereafter passed amendments to the PNDT.

It is possible that the Parliament would have amended the PNDT without Supreme Court intervention. Even though we cannot prove a casual connection between the Supreme Court's intervention and amendment of the PNDT, we can more firmly conclude that the Court's intervention hastened the process of amendment. The amendments were beneficial because they closed a number of loopholes, increased penalties, and strengthened enforcement. In addition, the State governments were held to task by the Court. They were asked to file compliance reports and encouraged to punish illegal ultrasound operators. We do not have a way of determining whether States actually increased compliance efforts during or after the period that the Supreme Court kept jurisdiction over the case.

Measuring impact in terms of the ultimate goals of the advocates, the Supreme Court's intervention was not successful. The end-goal of the advocates who brought the PIL in 2000 as well as the Supreme Court was to decrease the number of abortions of female fetuses. The litigants hoped that by prodding the Supreme Court, the Parliament would amend the law that banned sex determination tests and would also encourage state governments

TABLE 12.1 *Average annual probability of female-births in India, 1989–2008*

Year	Mean share of female births	Standard deviation	Sample size (number of births)
1989	0.485	0.500	57,176
1990	0.479	0.500	65,615
1991	0.480	0.500	61,873
1992	0.476	0.499	72,728
1993	0.478	0.500	65,990
1994	0.477	0.499	74,826
1995	0.481	0.500	70,493
1996	0.479	0.500	78,077
1997	0.478	0.500	73,591
1998	0.480	0.500	80,662
1999	0.478	0.500	74,735
2000	0.480	0.500	75,324
2001	0.475	0.499	71,157
2002	0.479	0.500	55,391
2003	0.477	0.499	35,201
2004	0.460	0.498	56,801
2005	0.460	0.498	70,353
2006	0.449	0.497	73,218
2007	0.444	0.497	78,953
2008	0.429	0.495	22,055

Source: Data are from DLHS-2 (children born during 19989–2003) and DLHS-3 (children born during 2004–2008). Author's calculations.

to enforce the law. Although the law was amended and perhaps implementation efforts increased, there was no improvement in the male-skewed sex ratio.

It is obvious from Figure 12.3 that the child sex ratios continued to become more male-skewed from the 2001 Indian Census to the 2011 Indian Census. While the Census measures changes over a 10-year period, the question that still remains is whether within that 10-year period there any improvements in the number of female births. The unique data we use allows us to make observations year-by-year in regard to number of female births. We use data from two district level household surveys (DLHS) of India, DLHS-2 during 2002–2004 and DLHS-3 during 2007–2008. The DLHS are large scale nationally representative cross-sectional household surveys covering all districts of

India. The surveys covered 620,107 and 720,320 households respectively. The primary focus of the surveys was on reproductive, maternal, and child health, including pregnancy and childbirth, access to healthcare, child nutrition, immunization, and morbidity and mortality of household members. The primary survey respondents were married women of reproductive age (women aged 15–44 in DLHS-2 and 15–49 in DLHS-3).

A household questionnaire in the DLHS collected information on the demographic and socioeconomic characteristics, including the location, caste, and religion of the household, and age, sex, and educational attainment of each member. A separate questionnaire for the respondent woman collected data on a complete lifetime birth history in DLHS-2, and a truncated birth history since January 2004 in DLHS-3. Birth history data included information on the date of birth, birth order, gender, and age at death (in case the child was not alive at the time of the survey) of children. Additional information on prenatal and postnatal care, pregnancy complications and outcomes was also collected.

We examine the average annual probability of female births among all ever born children during two decades, 1989–2008. From DLHS-2, we obtain data on children born during years 1989–2003, while DLHS-3 provides us child-birth data during years 2004–2008. The sample sizes of children born during each year, along with the average and standard deviation of the likelihood of female births is presented in Table 12.1. The trend in the annual average female birth rate over time is also presented in Figure 12.1.

We find that the share of girls among newborn children has been consistently declining over our study period, from 48.5 percent in 1989 to 42.9 percent in 2008. In comparison, the internationally accepted normal male to female sex ratio (number of boys for each girl) at birth ranges between 930 and 970 girls per boys, which is equivalent to 49.2 percent to 48.3 percent share of girls, respectively.

We would expect that the Supreme Court's efforts at pushing the states to implement the law, which commenced just after the petition was filed in 2000, would likely see positive gains in female births only after 2002. This would give time for the states to actually implement and enforce the law and then it would take at least nine more months to see an impact on the rate of female births. However, there was a sharp decline during the period 2002–2008, which is preciously when we would expect to see the greatest impact of the Supreme Court's interventions.

Several observable and unobservable socioeconomic factors and public policies may determine the trend in female birth probability during our study period. For example, demogeographic transition or changes in income levels

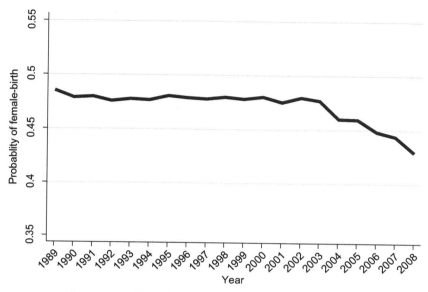

FIGURE 12.4: **Average annual rate of female-birth in India, 1998–2008.**
Source: Data are from DLHS-2 (children born during 1998–2004) and DLHS-3 (children born during 2004–2008). Author's calculations

may lead to changes in the preference for sons over daughters,[38] in turn leading more sex-selective abortion of girls. We can adjust the raw time trend shown in Figure 12.4 by removing the effect of various observable characteristics of the household, parents, and the child in the following way.

We first create a pooled child-level dataset (for all children born between 1998 and 2008) from DLHS-2 and DLHS-3. Then, a state fixed-effect linear regression of the following form is estimated:

$$Female_{it} = \alpha + \beta State_i + \gamma X_{it} + \epsilon_{it} \qquad (1)$$

for the *i-th* child born in year *t*. The outcome variable $Female_{it} = 1$ if the newborn child is a girl, and 0 otherwise. $State_i$ denotes a set of appropriate number of dummy variables for states, and X_{it} is a vector of background characteristics of the household, parents, and the newborn child. Included in X_{it} are the indicators of location (rural or urban), and caste (scheduled caste, scheduled tribe, or other backward classes), religion (Hindu, Muslim, or

---

[38] Monica das Gupta & P. N. Mari Bhat, *Fertility Decline and Increased Manifestation of Sex Bias in India*, 51 POPULATION STUD. 307 (1997); Mamta Murthi, Anne-Catherine & Jean Drèze, *Mortality, Fertility, and Gender Bias in India: A District-Level Analysis.* 21 POPULATION DEV.REV. 745 (1995).

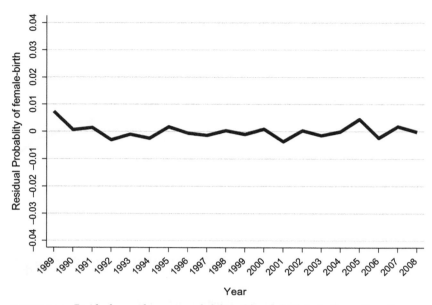

FIGURE 12.5: **Residual annual average probability of female-birth in India, 1998–2008.**
Source: Data are from DLHS-2 (children born during 1989–2004) and DLHS-3 (children born during 2004–2008). Residual probability is estimated from regression equation (1)

Sikh), and age and gender of the household head. Among parental and child characteristics, we include indicators of various levels of education (grades 1–5, 6–11, and 12 and above completed) of the mother and father, mother's age, and the newborn child's birth order in X_{it}. We control for the standard of living of the household by first constructing a composite index of asset ownership (e.g., radio, sewing machine, TV, bicycle, car) and living condition (e.g., construction quality, availability of toilet and electricity, sources of drinking water) using principal-component method.[39] The index is then divided into five quintiles and indicators of the top four quintiles are included in X_{it}.

ϵ_{it} is the error term of the regression. We cluster all standard errors at the district level. The estimated residual error of the regression, $\hat{\epsilon}$, will therefore include factors that are not incorporated in our analysis, including unobservable household and community characteristics and public policies that may affect the secular trend in the female birth probability.

Figure 12.5 shows the time trend of residual probability of female birth obtained from the regression. We find the residual probability to remain fairly

---

[39] Deon Filmer & Lant H. Pritchett, *Estimating Wealth Effects without Expenditure Data- or Tears: An Application to Educational Enrollments in States of India*, 38 DEMOGRAPHY 115 (2001).

stable with a very slight downward trend over our study period. Therefore, we can argue that the Supreme Court judgment is not associated in any improvement in the sex ratio at birth in the short to medium term.

Even if there has been any positive effect that remains undetected in our data, it is clearly not enough to reduce the male bias in the sex ratio. Female births continued to decrease and decreased most sharply during the time we would expect the Supreme Court's efforts to have had the most impact, from 2002 to 2008. Thus, examining only the sex ratio, we are left with the impression that at least in regard to the practice of sex-selective abortion, the Supreme Court's intervention did little to curb the behavior it wanted to prevent.

VI. WHY THE SUPREME COURT'S INTERVENTION DID NOT NORMALIZE SEX RATIOS

As noted above, the Supreme Court's intervention and indeed even the Parliament's intervention was not successful in normalizing the sex ratios. Quite the contrary, the number of female births as compared to all births decreased. Of course, we cannot rule out the possibility that the number of female births could be even lower had the Supreme Court not intervened.[40] In this section, we discuss some of the factors that may help explain why the Supreme Court's order and even an Act of Parliament could not prevent the women who selectively aborted female fetuses from doing so. First, the desire of families to have at least one son is a deep-seated cultural norm in many parts of India. This view combined with changing macroeconomic factors that lead to a desire for smaller families often pushes people to elect selective abortion. People in society are more likely to resist laws that go against cultural norms than laws that support the mainstream view. Second, the behavior that the government has made illegal (e.g., disclosing the future sex of a fetus) is difficult to regulate. It can occur within the privacy of a doctor's office, and people can also gain this information through non-licensed operators of ultrasound machines.

---

[40] Indeed, one of the coauthors (Nandi) has found in another article that the sex ratios in one state (i.e., Maharashtra) that banned sex determination tests before any other state were less male-skewed than the sex ratios in neighboring states that had not adopted bans.

Nandi, Arindam, and Anil B. Deolalikar. *Does a Legal Ban on Sex-Selective Abortions Improve Child Sex Ratios? Evidence from a Policy Change in India.* J DEV ECON 103 (2013): 216–228. http://dx.doi.org/10.1016/j.jdeveco.2013.02.007. See also Nandi Arindam (2014) *The Unintended Effects of a Ban on Sex-Selective Abortion on Infant Mortality: Evidence from India.* OXF. DEV. STUD. 43 (2015):466–482. http://dx.doi.org/10.1080/13600818.2014.973390

A. *Families desire at least one son and smaller family sizes*

Both in the popular imagination and in scholarly work, "culture" is often used to explain the widespread practice of sex-selective abortion.[41] This is often disaggregated into a list of evils in society that essentially place women in an inferior position to men. First, patrilocal marriages, where a couple settles into the husband's family's home, are the norm and are often used to explain "son-preference." As a result of this custom, a daughter is thought to be *paraya dhan* (someone else's wealth). Sons are the ones who are assumed to be breadwinners for the families. A lack of a pension system in India leads parents to rely on the son to provide financial support during old age. On the other hand, there are strong norms against families taking money or any support from a married daughter. To the extent a woman earns an income outside her household, she will often be expected to keep her earnings within the husband's family. For wealthier families, they desire sons because they do not want to share their wealth with daughters who will leave the natal home in the patrilocal system.

Second, dowry is another explanation for sex selection, and this flows directly from the British colonial accounts. Indeed, this factor still remains one of the most cited explanations for sex selection. Although dowry is prohibited under the Dowry Prohibition Act of 1961, the practice continues today.[42] As a result, when a woman gets married, her parents often have to pay money (sometimes large sums in relation to their income) to the groom's family. For poor parents, having to provide a dowry when a daughter marries is often economically challenging.

Third, for wealthier families, while dowry may not be as much of a burden, parents may desire sons to perpetuate their family name and the sons will be the ones that parents leave their money to. Fourth, one Hindu religious tradition is often attributed as a cause for sex selection in favor of boys – many Hindus believe that only sons should light the funeral pyre of their parents. Others believe that *moksha* (liberation from rebirth or reincarnation) is only possible through their sons.[43]

---

[41] MARA HVISTENDAHL, UNNATURAL SELECTION 71–72 (2011).
[42] Mallika Kaur Sarkaria, Comment, *Lessons from Punjab's "Missing Girls": Toward a Global Feminist Perspective on "Choice" in Abortion,* 97 CALIF. L. REV. 905, 910–911 (2009).
[43] *See* Rita Patel, *The Practice of Sex Selective Abortion in India: May You Be the Mother of a Hundred Sons,* THE CENTER FOR GLOBAL INITIATIVES 7 (1996), http://cgi.unc.edu/uploads/media_items/the-practice-of-sex-selective-abortion-in-india-may-you-be-the-mother-of-a-hundred-sons.original.pdf.

Fifth, another factor often cited is the low status of women, which occurs, among other things, because they lack opportunities for paid work (and their unpaid work is not valued) and they generally do not own property. In many places, women do not have economic opportunities or are not permitted to work outside the home. Although inheritance laws have been reformed, a daughter is often expected to give up her rights to her parents' property in favor of her brothers.[44] An Indian government agency has pointed out that in India women own just 10.9 percent of the land.[45] This is because even when they have a right on paper to inherit property, this right gets subverted in a variety of ways. Members of their natal family including brothers are thus able to persuade or coerce them to relinquish their share in the family property.[46]

All of these factors are summarized in the literature as follows: girls are an economic liability to a family, while boys are economic assets. Technology facilitates people's desires to have sons by allowing them to determine the sex of the fetus and abort it if it is a girl.

However, a more nuanced interpretation of the data suggests that Indian people by and large do not have an aversion to having daughters, but want to have at least one son. Birth parity studies from India show that the sex ratio of the first birth of Indian children is skewed in favor of males, but gets progressively worse at second and third parities for parents who have no prior sons. In analyzing a survey of over 1 million households in India conducted in 1998, Prabhat Jha and his coauthors found that the sex ratio for the first child is 871 females to 1,000 males (remember that the standard range is considered to be from 930 to 970 females for every 1,000 males).[47] But in the second birth parity for parents with no prior son, the sex ratio was 759 per 1,000 males; and the ratio decreased in the third birth parity to 719 per 1,000 males for parents with no prior sons.[48] Thus, a great proportion of parents who already have one

---

[44] See, e.g., Ashok Sircar, *Emerging Voices: Ashok Sircar on Women's Right to Inherit Land in India*, LANDESA (June 12, 2013), www.landesa.org/emerging-voices-ashok-sircar-womens-right-inherit-land-india-blog/.

[45] UN Women Expert Group Meeting on Enabling rural women's economic empowerment: institutions, opportunities and participation, Accra, Ghana, Sept. 20–23, 2011, *Women's Access to Land: An Asian Perspective*, 12, TBL. 1, U.N. Doc. EGM/RW/2011/EP.3 (Sept. 2011), www.un .org/womenwatch/daw/csw/csw56/egm/Rao-EP-3-EGM-RW-30Sep-2011.pdf (paper prepared by Nitya Rao).

[46] Kirti Singh, *Laws and Son-Preference in India: A Reality Check* U.N. POPULATION FUND (UNFPA) 51 (2013), www.unfpa.org/sites/default/files/jahia-news/documents/publications/2013/ LawsandSonPreferenceinIndia.pdf.

[47] Prabhat Jha et al., *Low Male-to-Female Sex Ratio of Children Born in India: National Survey of 1.1 Million Households*, 367 THE LANCET 211, 214 (2006).

[48] *Id.*

or two daughters and have no sons are intervening to ensure the birth of a son, whereas a fewer proportion of parents are intervening at the first births (and are willing to have a daughter).

Qualitative studies by Tulsi Patel confirm this view. She states that "female foeticide is not approved and/or practised for the first female foetus."[49] Thus, just because son-preference may be widespread, it does not also mean that "daughter-aversion" is also widespread.[50] Survey results also support the view that the two-child household is the accepted norm and that there is no aversion to having at least one daughter. The Lawyers Collective surveyed 168 households across Delhi,[51] and found that an overwhelming majority of women (79 percent) said that two would be the ideal number of children.[52] While 60 percent of the women said that one male child was ideal, the same percentage said that one female child is ideal. Taken together, it appears that for the women surveyed, the ideal family is two children: one boy and one girl. This micro-study also found that parents who had been married for less than five years had sex ratios that were female-skewed, and these sex ratios became more male-skewed as their time of marriage increased. This again supports the view that parents are willing to have girls, but want to have at least one son.

In Jha's study, we see that a very small number of parents with one or two boy children may actually be selecting for girls. Jha's study finds that the sex ratio of the second child of mothers who have one prior boy is 1102 females per 1,000 males, and the sex ratio of the third child of mothers who have two prior boys is 1176.[53] These sex ratios are slightly female-skewed (they are above the standard range of 930–970 females to 1,000 males). Yet the proportion of parents with boy children that practice female-biased sex selection is much lower than the proportion of parents with girl children that practice male-biased sex selection.

---

[49] Tulsi Patel, *The Mindset behind Eliminating the Female Foetus, in* Sex-selective Abortion in India, Gender, Society and New Reproductive Technologies 135, 143 (Tulsi Patel ed., 2007).

[50] Navtej K. Purewal also points out that much research on son preference also makes assumptions about why people act certain ways on the basis of macro-trend. Navtej K. Purewal, Son Preference: Sex Selection, Gender and Culture in South Asia 14–16 (2010).

[51] Indira Jaising et al., From the Abnormal to the Normal: Preventing Sex Selective Abortions through the Law 108 (2007), www.lawyerscollective.org/publications/abnormal-normal-preventing-sex-selective-abortions-law.html.

[52] *Id.*

[53] Prabhat Jha et al., *Low Male-to-Female Sex Ratio of Children Born in India: National Survey of 1.1 Million Households*, 367 The Lancet 211, 211 (2006).

A new and growing desire of people to have small families when taken together with the desire to have at least one son leads some women to selectively terminate their pregnancies.[54] The United Nations Population Division estimated that the fertility rate in the 1950s was 5.9 children per woman in India, not as high as in many other developing countries at the time where the average was often seven children or more.[55] By 2009, fertility in India had declined to 2.6 children per woman, less than half the rate of the early 1950s. There are a host of reasons for the desire for smaller family sizes. Some argue that as there is a reduction in agrarian modes of production (where the labor of children might have been important), people are having fewer children.[56] In urban areas, increasing prices and cost of living influence people to have smaller families.[57]

Another reason for the changing family size norms has to do with the governmental policies in India. While most people know about China's one-child policy (which it recently announced it will change),[58] few are aware of the coercive policies adopted by Indian state governments to enforce a two-child norm model. In pursuit of the goal of smaller families, certain states have adopted prohibitions barring people with more than two children from holding posts in local governing bodies. Currently, the two-child norm is a part of the population policies in Uttar Pradesh, Madhya Pradesh, Rajasthan, and Maharashtra.[59]

The Indian Supreme Court has found that the two-child norm in the Haryana Panchayati Raj Act, 1994 did not violate the constitution. The Court held that the "disqualification on the right to contest an election by having more than two living children does not contravene any fundamental right nor does it cross the limits of reasonability. Rather it is a disqualification

---

[54] Christophe Z. Guilmoto, Sex *Imbalances at Birth: Current Trends, Consequences and Policy Implications* UNFPA Asia and the Pacific Regional Office 10 (2012), www.unfpa.org/publications/sex-imbalances-birth.

[55] Carl Haub & James Gribble, *Population Reference Bureau, Population Bulletin: The World at 7 Billion* 9 (2011), www.prb.org/pdf11/world-at-7-billion.pdf.

[56] Mary John, *Sex Ratios and Gender Biased Sex Selection History, Debates and Future Directions* U.N. Population Fund (UNFPA) 42–43 (2014), http://asiapacific.unfpa .org/webdav/site/asiapacific/shared/Publications/2014/Sex-Ratios-and-Gender-Biased-Sex-Selection.pdf.

[57] Ravinder Kaur, *Dispensable Daughters and Bachelor Sons: Sex Discrimination in North India*, 43 Econ. Pol. Wkly. 109, 114 (2008).

[58] *See China Reforms: One-Child Policy to Be Relaxed*, BBC, Nov. 15, 2013.

[59] Kirti Singh, *Laws and Son-Preference in India: A Reality Check* U.N. Population Fund (UNFPA) 80 (2013), www.unfpa.org/sites/default/files/jahia-news/documents/publications/2013/LawsandSonPreferenceinIndia.pdf.

conceptually devised in the national interest."[60] Thus, a person's right to have children can be restricted in favor of the larger goal of population control. In upholding two-child norm policies, the Supreme Court may have unintentionally undermined efforts to curb sex selection. By forcing families to have no more than two children, some may sex select to ensure that one of their children is a male.

B. Challenges in enforcing the PCPNDT

There are several reasons for the failure of the PCPNDT to reduce sex-selective abortions. First, it is inherently difficult to enforce the PCPNDT. Ultrasound technology is not completely banned under the law and, on the contrary, it is now a common part of prenatal care practices. It can be used to detect the sex of the fetus. It is difficult to prevent medical professionals from conveying the sex of fetuses in the privacy of their patient rooms. Indeed, medical professionals who convey the sex of the fetus do so in coded terms.

Additionally, while licensed medical professionals using registered ultrasound equipment can illegally disclose information about the future sex of the fetus, there are also unlicensed people using unregistered ultrasounds for the purposes of sex determination. A robust black market for sex determination and sex-selective abortions has developed.

We have presented two potential factors that explain why it is difficult for the Supreme Court and even for an Act of Parliament to prohibit sex-selective termination of pregnancies. The demand to reduce family size while at the same time have a male heir is strong in parts of India. At the same time, the illegal activities occur in private and the law is easy to evade – it requires only access to an ultrasound machine.

VII. CONCLUSION

The child sex ratio in India became starkly more male-skewed starting in the 1980s. Technology that gave pregnant women information about the sex of their fetuses became widespread. A desire by many parents to have at least one male child, while at the same time wanting to have fewer children (than their predecessors) all led to many women to abort female fetuses. In 1994, Parliament reacted by (among other things) prohibiting medical professionals from

---

[60] *Javed v. State of Haryana*, A.I.R. 2003 S.C. 3057 (India).

revealing to pregnant women the sex of their fetuses. This law to prevent sex determination went into effect in 1996. Four years later, a group of litigants brought a PIL to the Supreme Court arguing that the State governments had yet to implement the law by appointing authorities to enforce it. The Supreme Court kept jurisdiction for three years in this case, and in those three years a panel of three judges led primarily by Justice Shah focused the attention of State and Union governments on the problem of the widespread selective abortion of female fetuses.

In a dialogue that lasted nearly three years with the State governments and the Union government, the Supreme Court hauled into its courtroom in New Delhi representatives from State governments and Union government to question them about enforcement of the legislation. The Supreme Court also demanded that the State government representatives file compliance reports and called out by name those governments that had failed to file such reports on a timely basis. In addition, the Supreme Court ordered the body that was appointed pursuant to the legislation that banned sex determination tests to consider amendments to the law that would places restrictions on using newly emerging technology for the purposes of preselecting the sex of a child.

During the time period that the Supreme Court kept jurisdiction in this case, transcripts of discussions in the Rajya Sabha reveal an acute sense of awareness of the orders of the Supreme Court. Indeed, amendments were drafted by the Central Supervisory Board and were eventually enacted by Parliament. Thus, the Supreme Court's prodding certainly hastened the process of strengthening the legislation aimed at curbing sex-selective abortions.

However, an analysis of unique annual sex ratio data from 1998 to 2008 reveals that the Court decision was not associated with any improvements in the relative number of female births. On the contrary, there was a sharp decline in the number of females born exactly when we would expect the Supreme Court's interventions to have had the most impact. Indeed, even the legislation did not work to prevent sex ratios from becoming more male-skewed. This is because it is very difficult to regulate activity that occurs within the privacy of a medical professional's office, to prevent illegal operators from providing a service that is highly in demand, and to change the views of people who believe that their families will not be complete without at least one male child. Thus, the PIL was successful in pushing for law reform, but was not able to impact social change.

REFERENCES

CEHAT and Ors. v. *Union of India and Ors.* 2001. W.P. (C) No. 301/2000 (The Supreme Court of India, Sept. 19).

CEHAT and Ors. v. *Union of India and Ors.* 2001. W.P. (C) No. 301/2000 (The Supreme Court of India, Dec. 11).

CEHAT and Ors. v. *Union of India and Ors.* 2003. Writ Petition (Civil) No. 301 of 2000 (The Supreme Court of India, Sept. 10).

CEHAT and Ors. v. *Union of India and Ors.* 2000. Writ Petition (Civil) No. 301 of 2000 (The Supreme Court of India, May 4).

CEHAT and Ors. v. *Union of India and Ors.* 2002. Writ Petition (Civil) No. 301 of 2000 (The Supreme Court of India, Apr. 30).

CEHAT and Ors. v. *Union of India and Ors.* 2003. Writ Petition (Civil) No. 301 of 2000 (The Supreme Court of India, Mar. 31).

CEHAT and Ors. v. *Union of India and Ors.* 2003. Writ Petition (Civil) No. 301 of 2000 (The Supreme Court of India, Aug. 8).

CEHAT and Ors. v. *Union of India and Ors.* 2003. W.P. (C) No. 301 of 2000 and W.P. (C) No. 339/2002 (The Supreme Court of India, July 7).

Census Organization of India. 2011. "Sex Ratio in India." CENSUS 2011 INDIA. Accessed Aug. 24, 2018. www.census2011.co.in/sexratio.php.

Centre for Enquiry into Health and Allied Themes (CEHAT) v. *Union of India.* 2003. Writ Petition (civil) 301 of 2000 (Supreme Court of India, Sept. 10).

Filmer, Deon, & Lant H. Pritchett. 2001. *Estimating Wealth Effects without Expenditure Data-or Tears: An Application to Educational Enrollments in States of India.* DEMOGRAPHY, Vol. 38, No. 1 115–132.

Global Doctor Options. n.d. Accessed Aug. 13, 2015. www.globaldoctoroptions.com/ivf-cost/424.

Guilmoto, Christophe Z. 2007. *Characteristics of Sex-Ratio Imbalance in India, and Future Scenarios.* Oct. 29–31. Accessed Aug. 24, 2018. www.unfpa.org/sites/default/files/resource-pdf/india_o.pdf.

2012. *Sex Imbalances at Birth: Current Trends, Consequences and Policy Implications.* UNFPA ASIA AND PACIFIC REGIONAL OFFICE. www.unfpa.org/resources/sex-imbalances-birth-trends-consequences-and-policy-implications.

Gupta, Monica Das, and P.N. Mari Bhat. 1997. *Fertility Decline and Increased Manifestation of Sex Bias in India.* POPULATION STUD., Vol. 51, No. 3 307–315.

HATTON, CELIA. 2013. CHINA REFORMS: ONE-CHILD POLICY TO BE RELAXED. Beijing, Nov. 15.

Haub, Carl, and James Gribble. 2011. *The World at 7 Billion.* POPULATION BULLETIN, Vol. 66, No. 2.

HVISTENDAHL, MARA. 2011. UNNATURAL SELECTION: CHOOSING BOYS OVER GIRLS, AND THE CONSEQUENCES OF A WORLD FULL OF MEN. New York: World Affairs.

JAISING, INDIRA, ED. 2004. PRE-CONCEPTION AND PRE-NATAL DIAGNOSTIC TECHNIQUES ACT: A USER'S GUIDE TO THE LAW. New Delhi: Universal Law Publishing.

JAISING, INDIRA, C. SATHYAMALA, AND ASMITA BASU. 2007. *FROM THE ABNOR-MAL TO THE NORMAL: PREVENTING SEX SELECTION ABORTIONS THROUGH THE LAW.* New Delhi: Lawyers Collective.

Javed v. State of Haryana. 2003. Writ Petition (Civil) 302 of 2001 (Supreme Court of India, July 30).

Jha, Prabhat, Rajesh Kumar, Priya Vasa, Neeraj Dhingra, Deva Thiruchelvam, and Rahim Moineddin. 2006. *Low Male-to-Female Sex Ratio of Children Born in India: National Survey of 1.1 Million Households.* THE LANCET, Vol. 367, No. 9506 211–218.

John, Mary. 2014. *Sex Ratios and Gender Biased Sex Selection.* U.N. POPULATION FUND (UNFPA), Accessed Aug. 24, 2018. https://asiapacific.unfpa.org/sites/default/files/pub-pdf/Sex-Ratios-and-Gender-Biased-Sex-Selection.pdf.

Kalantry, Sital. 2013. *Sex Selection in the United States and India: A Contextualist Feminist Approach.* UCLA J. INT'L L. & FOREIGN AFF 61–85.

Kaur, Ravinder. 2008. *Dispensable Daughters and Bachelor Sons: Sex Discrimination in North India.* ECON. POLIT. WKLY., Vol. 43, No. 30 109–114.

Murthi, Mamta, Anne-Catherine Guio, and Jean Drèze. 1995. *Mortality, Fertility, and Gender-Bias in India: A District-Level Analysis.* POP DEV REV, Vol. 21, No. 4 745–782.

Nanda, Bijayalaxmi. 2006. *Campaign against Female Foeticide: Perspectives, Strategies and Experiences.* In *SEX-SELECTIVE ABORTION IN INDIA: GENDER, SOCIETY AND NEW REPRODUCTIVE TECHNOLOGIES,* ed. Tulsi Patel. SAGE Publications, India.

Nandi, Arindam. 2015. *The Unintended Effects of a Ban on Sex-Selective Abortion on Infant Mortality: Evidence from India.* OXF. DEV. STUD, Vol. 43, No. 4 466–482.

Nandi, Arindam, and Anil B. Deolalikar. 2013. "Does a legal ban on sex-selective abortions improve child sex ratios? Evidence from a policy change in India." Journal of Development Economics 103: 216–228.

Oster, Emily. 2009. *Proximate Sources of Population Sex Imbalance in India.* DEMOGRAPHY 46.2 (2009): 325–339. Accessed Aug. 24, 2018. www.ncbi.nlm.nih.gov/pmc/articles/PMC2831281/.

Patel, Rita. 1996. *You May be the Mother of a Hundred Sons: The Practice of Sex Selective Abortion in India.* CAROLINA PAPERS IN INTERNATIONAL HEALTH AND DEVELOPMENT, Vol. 3, No. 1.

PUREWAL, NAVTEJ K. 2010. SON PREFERENCE: SEX SELECTION, GENDER AND CULTURE IN SOUTH ASIA. Berg.

Rajya Sabha, Synopsis of Debates. 2002. December 11. Accessed Aug. 2018. http://164.100.47.5/newsynopsis1/Englishsessionno/197/11122002.htm.

Rao, Nitya. 2011. *Women's Access to Land: An Asian Perspective.* 12, TBL. 1, U.N. DOC. EGM/RW/2011/EP.3. Sept. 20–23. Accessed Aug. 25, 2018. www.un.org/womenwatch/daw/csw/csw56/egm/Rao-EP-3-EGM-RW-30Sep-2011.pdf.

Sarkaria, Mallika Kaur. 2009. *Lessons from Punjab's Missing Girls: Toward a Global Feminist Perspective on Choice in Abortion.* CAL. L. REV., Vol. 97, No. 3.

Sen, Amartya. 1990. *More Than 100 Million Women Are Missing.* N.Y. REV. BOOKS. Dec. 20. Accessed Aug. 24, 2018. www.nybooks.com/articles/1990/12/20/more-than-100-million-women-are-missing/.

Singh, Kirti. 2013. *Laws and Son Preference in India: A Reality Check.* U.N. POPULA-TION FUND (UNFPA). Aug. Accessed Aug. 24, 2018. www.unfpa.org/sites/default/files/jahia-news/documents/publications/2013/LawsandSonPreferenceinIndia.pdf.

Sircar, Ashok. 2013. *Emerging Voices: Ashok Sircar on Women's Right to Inherit Land in India.* LANDESA. June 12. Accessed Aug. 25, 2018. www.landesa.org/emerging-voices-ashok-sircar-womens-right-inherit-land-india-blog/.

Stillman, Melissa, Jennifer J. Frost, Susheela Singh, Ann M. Moore, and Shveta Kalyanwala. 2014. *Abortion in India: A Literature Review.* Dec. Accessed Aug. 24, 2018. www.guttmacher.org/sites/default/files/report_pdf/abortion-india-lit-review.pdf.

The Economist. 2003. *MISSING SISTERS.* Rohtak, Apr. 17.

2003. "The Pre-natal Diagnostic Techniques (Regulation and Prevention of Misuse) Amendment Act, No. 14 of 2003, India Code, Chapter II (3)(B)."

2003. "The Pre-natal Diagnostic Techniques (Regulation and Prevention of Misuse) Amendment Act, No. 14 of 2003, India Code, Chapter V (17)."

2003. "The Pre-natal Diagnostic Techniques (Regulation and Prevention of Misuse) Amendment Act, No. 14 of 2003, India Code, Chapter VII (22)."

2003. "The Pre-natal Diagnostic Techniques (Regulation and Prevention of Misuse), Amendment Act, No. 14 of 2003, India Code."

2003. "The Pre-natal Diagnostic Techniques (Regulation and Prevention of Misuse) Amendment Act, No. 14 of 2003, India Code, Chapter VI (18)."

Tulsi Patel. 2007. *The Mindset behind Eliminating the Female Foetus.* In *SEX-SELECTIVE ABORTION IN INDIA: GENDER, SOCIETY AND NEW REPRODUCTIVE TECHNOLOGIES,* ed. Tulsi Patel, 135–143. SAGE Publications India.

Vinod, Hrishikesh D. 2013. *Newborn Sex Selection and India's Overpopulation Problem.* MODERN ECONOMY 102–108.

Conclusion

Neither a Silver Bullet Nor a Hollow Hope

GERALD N. ROSENBERG, SHISHIR BAIL,
AND SUDHIR KRISHNASWAMY

The preceding chapters explored the effects of leading decisions of the Indian Supreme Court on the lives of India's marginalized citizens. They addressed the question of whether the Indian Supreme Court is an effective agent of progressive social change or is constrained in furthering the rights of the relatively disadvantaged. We suggested in the Introduction that the Indian Supreme Court might be capable of playing a progressive role because it has several advantages that other national high courts, particularly the US Supreme Court, lack. These include the broad sweep of constitutional rights in the Indian Constitution, the procedural improvisations the Court has made such as its public interest litigation (PIL) docket, its *suo moto* jurisdiction, its continuing *mandamus* process, and its heightened structural independence from the other branches of the central government. These suggest that Indian Supreme Court decisions might have the ability to make a real difference in the lives of India's most disadvantaged citizens.

On the other hand, we noted that the Indian Supreme Court, like all courts, depends on the actions of others for its decisions to be implemented. We suggested that this dependence might be a significant barrier for three reasons. First, the often antagonistic relationship between the Supreme Court and the national government potentially limits the willingness of the government to fully promote Supreme Court orders. Second, the resource constraints of the Indian state are likely to make it reticent, if not simply unable, to implement judicial orders prescribing wide-ranging and expensive reform. Sadly, in addition, the Indian state is riddled with inefficiency and corruption, creating barriers to successful implementation. Third, the significant heterogeneity of individual states within the Indian nation suggests widely differing willingness and capacity to implement Supreme Court orders. Lastly, we drew attention to the complicated social contexts in which Supreme Court orders are implemented, marked by a persistence of traditional religious and caste animosities which are often hostile to external intervention.

We concluded the Introduction by suggesting that while there was a potential for Indian Supreme Court decisions to bring about progressive social change, there were also obstacles that might prevent it from doing so. This "mixed account" of the Indian Supreme Court's role inspired us to encourage and bring together the empirical studies in the preceding pages. Although their research questions, methodologies and theoretical frames differ, the author(s) of each study seriously engage with the underlying question of the actual effects of the Court's decisions on the lives of the relatively disadvantaged. What did they find?

In many ways, their findings mirror the mixed account presented in the Introduction. That is, under some conditions the Indian Supreme Court emerges as an effective agent of progressive social change. Its decisions improve the lives of those most in need. Yet under other conditions the Court's decisions do little.

One perhaps useful way of thinking about the findings of the individual chapters is to organize them around two primary kinds of impact attributable to Supreme Court decisions; judicial or direct effects and extrajudicial or indirect effects. The direct effects of judicial decisions, in their original characterization by Rosenberg, focus on the direct outcome of judicial decisions and examine whether the change required by the courts was made.[1] The study of the direct effects of court decisions is based on a direct causal pathway. The question is, simply, did what the court ordered in fact occur? To use an example drawn from this book, if the Court ordered all transport vehicles in Delhi to change fuels, did this indeed take place?

By contrast, the study of the indirect effects of judicial decisions is more complex. Rather than focusing on whether behavior changed in the short run, a study of indirect effects asks about the Court's ability to influence public opinion, to enable previously ignored issues to be framed in legal terms, or to embolden disadvantaged social groups by providing an avenue for their grievances to be aired.[2] The argument that the US Supreme Court's most celebrated decisions had minimal extrajudicial effects was, perhaps, one

---

[1] Gerald N. Rosenberg, *The Hollow Hope: Can Courts Bring about Social Change* 7 (1993) [hereinafter *Hollow Hope*].
[2] Id.

of the most controversial features of Rosenberg's original study of the US Supreme Court.[3]

Rosenberg's study is notable for its empirical approach. His approach is based on verifiable evidence, on carefully examining causal claims on the basis of that evidence, and investigating alternate explanations. However, others have questioned whether this approach is the best way to study the effects (particularly the extrajudicial effects) of Court decisions. Perhaps the best known of these studies is Michael McCann's *Rights at Work*.[4] McCann argues against a purely social scientific understanding of the impact of judicial decisions in favor of one that pays more attention to the "cultural interpretation of law as a constitutive element of social life."[5] Through a study of the pay equity movement in the United States, McCann brings attention to the ability of courts to help disadvantaged social groups understand their predicament through legal conventions and discourses, in other words, to foster *rights consciousness*. Rights consciousness, in turn, allowed these groups to mobilize the discursive and symbolic forms of the law to further their agenda in interactions with the state and to influence the creation of public policy. Whereas *The Hollow Hope* focuses largely on aggregate data, *Rights at Work* adopts a more context-specific approach that consciously shies away from making claims about causality. This approach includes in-depth interviews and qualitative case-study, among other sources.[6]

A conscious departure point of this volume is the acceptance of both approaches as useful and necessary to understand the impact of decisions of the Indian Supreme Court.[7] While we have an eye firmly on whether Supreme Court decisions tangibly, measurably, affect the lives of the relatively disadvantaged, we also take seriously the potential symbolic and discursive effects of these decisions. This is evident from the chapters in the book that address both these kinds of impact through diverse empirical studies. In these concluding pages we review what these chapters tell us about the impact of

---

[3] This approach is best illustrated in Rosenberg's study of the indirect effects of the lauded US Supreme Court decision in *Brown v Board of Education* in helping the cause of desegregation through extra-judicial influence. See *Hollow Hope* 107–156.

[4] Michael W. McCann, *Rights at Work: Pay Equity Reform and the Politics of Legal Mobilization* (1994).

[5] Id. at 282.

[6] Id. at 14–22. For a debate between Rosenberg and McCann on the strengths and weaknesses of their competing approaches, see "Review Section Symposium: Gauging the Impact of Law," 21 *L. & Soc. Inquiry* 435 (1996).

[7] Rosenberg acknowledged the need for a combination of both approaches to fully understand the effects of judicial decisions in his 1996 review of *Rights at Work*. See Gerald N. Rosenberg, "Positivism, Interpretivism, and the Study of Law", 21 *L. & Soc. Inquiry* 435, 455 (1996).

the Indian Supreme Court both in the direct, judicial sense, but also in the discursive, indirect, extrajudicial sense.

The chapters in Part I provide an empirical foundation for the Indian Supreme Court's potential role as an effective agent of progressive social change. They outline the very distinct institutional character of the Indian Supreme Court across a range of indices. For example, the Indian Supreme Court hears exponentially more cases than, for instance, the Supreme Court of the United States. Though this may partly be a product of India's much greater population, Robinson demonstrates that the Supreme Court's caseload has in fact expanded on the basis of an explicit desire on the part of the executive and the judiciary to increase access to courts. Further, not only does the Court hear a large number of cases, it is also often willing to intervene and overturn the orders of courts and other institutions below it, as Chandra, Hubbard and Kalantry demonstrate through their remarkable and original data set. They find, in part, that the Court reverses lower court decisions close to 60 percent of the time. However, importantly, they also find that almost 90 percent of Court decisions are the work of two-judge benches. These panels are not typically authorized to decide constitutional questions.[8] Thus, Chandra, Hubbard, and Kalantry raise the question of whether the "rush of thousands of routine cases ... detracts from the time and energy that the Court can devote to high-profile cases or the elaboration of broad rules to govern Indian society."[9] The Court's openness to the relatively disadvantaged may work, in practice, to lessen its ability to help them.

PIL is a procedure that most easily allows relatively disadvantaged individuals and progressive interest groups to file lawsuits and gives the Court the opportunity to order sweeping change. In terms of their visibility, PILs are by far the most prominent emblem of the Supreme Court's self-understanding as a "court of the people." Yet, as Chitalkar and Gauri demonstrate, after an initial surge of activism in the 1970s and 1980s, the increasing institutionalization of PIL has seen it become more and more of a venue for advantaged social groups. Chitalkar and Gauri suggest that this might be driven by the Court no longer needing to win back public legitimacy, as it needed to do

---

[8]   Article 145, Section 3 of the Indian Constitution specifies a minimum bench size of five judges to decide "any case involving a substantial question of law as to the interpretation of this Constitution." However, in practice, most cases heard by benches of two judges involve substantial questions of law involving interpretation of the Constitution. See Chintan Chandrachud, "Constitutional Interpretation", in *The Oxford Handbook of the Indian Constitution*, eds. Sujit Choudhry, Madhav Khosla & Pratap Bhanu Mehta, 1st ed. (Oxford University Press 2016), 86.

[9]   See Chapter 2

after Indira Gandhi's imposition of emergency rule in the 1970s. In turn this might be leading the Court to use a language of deference to the executive or legislature more frequently, signaling a shift towards a more conservative interpretation of the separation of powers. In addition, Chandra, Hubbard, and Kilantry find that PILs are uncommon. They constitute less than 4 percent of the cases in their data set.

Another procedural innovation that attracts a great deal of publicity is the Court's *suo moto* jurisdiction. In Chapter 4, Galanter and Ram examine the practice of *suo moto* by which the Indian Supreme Court has the jurisdiction to initiate cases at the instigation of the justices without a party first filing a suit. They show that the Court has used its *suo moto* jurisdiction in dramatic fashion. However, their findings suggest that use of *suo moto* jurisdiction is not a reliable tool to help the relatively disadvantaged. It is used episodically, inconsistently, and without supporting lower level executive and judicial institutions that interact with the relatively disadvantaged every day and whose support is essential for change to occur.

The final chapter in Part I examines Indians' views of the judicial system. A crusading Court in which no one has faith is unlikely to foster change. However, Krishnaswamy and Swaminathan find that trust in the Indian judiciary is relatively high and cuts across diverse social and cultural groups. Interestingly, this high degree of trust is *not* driven by lack of trust in other governmental institutions as it is, for example, in Pakistan.[10] Nor is it driven by faith in the Court's ability to act in countermajoritarian ways to help the relatively disadvantaged. Rather, Krishnaswamy and Swaminathan find that trust in Indian courts is correlated with trust in *all* the institutions of the state including the legislature and the executive. What this chapter leaves open is the link between the actions of the Indian Supreme Court and their effects on trust in the judiciary as a whole. This is an important area for future research.

JUDICIAL (DIRECT) IMPACT

The chapters of this book that most clearly address the ability of the Indian Supreme Court to directly bring about change in social conditions through its decisions are those by Dixon and Chowdhury, Moog, and Kalantry and Nandi. Each of these chapters studies the question of whether the Supreme Court has been able to bring about measurable social change through explicit

---

[10] For a fascinating exploration of trust in the Supreme Court of Pakistan, see Asher Qazi, "A Government of Judges," JSD Dissertation, University of Chicago, 2018.

judicial activity aimed at doing so. The picture they paint is, perhaps unsurprisingly, mixed.

In two of the cases, the Supreme Court was in fact largely successful in having its orders implemented. As Moog describes, in the Delhi pollution case the Supreme Court was successful in overseeing a massive overhaul of the transportation infrastructure of one of the largest cities in the world. Over a roughly two-year period (2001–2003) all the auto-rickshaws and buses in Delhi switched from petrol/diesel to compressed natural gas. To achieve this, the Court relied on its full arsenal of judicial innovations. The case itself was registered as a PIL on the application of a lawyer-environmentalist, and thereafter remained with the Court for over 30 years, during which time it passed multiple orders and kept abreast of developments on a regular basis. Intervening squarely in matters of policy, the Court sought and used expert evidence, and appointed monitoring agents to provide the justices regular reports on the status of implementation. In doing this, the justices stepped quite clearly out of the formal adversarial structure of most judicial adjudication and assumed the role of positive generators and monitors of policy. To go back to Rosenberg's original formulation, the Delhi Pollution Case seems to be a textbook manifestation of a *dynamic court*.[11]

It should be clear that Moog is at pains to point out the exceptional circumstances that gave the Court the ability to adopt this position in the Delhi pollution case. The problem of pollution in Delhi was one that had immense public visibility, since Delhi is the national capital. It is also the location of the Supreme Court, not to mention the residence of all the judges themselves. The problem was, therefore, one that the judges felt first hand. The localness of the case, as Moog describes, also meant that the implementing authorities were easily at hand and could be overseen by the judges in a way that may not be possible elsewhere in the country. However, even with all these qualifications in mind, it is difficult not to see the Delhi pollution case as a clear example of the Indian Supreme Court using the full force of its procedural dexterity to tangibly change social conditions. At the very least, it demonstrates that when some (admittedly demanding) background conditions are met, the Court can indeed move things "on the ground," almost entirely by itself. On the other hand, air pollution in Delhi continues to worsen. For all the Court's momentous effort, air quality is worse than when the case

---

[11]   See *Hollow Hope* 21–30.

started. The Court, focused as it was on one case and one cause of air pollution, only addressed one part of the problem.[12]

A somewhat similar instance is highlighted by Dixon and Chowdhury in the *Right to Food* case. In this case, too, the Court maintained the case on its docket for 16 years and appointed Commissioners to oversee implementation of its orders. The Court's freehand approach to addressing pressing issues of social policy is also apparent in the fact that what began as a PIL to address starvation deaths subsequently turned into one equally concerned with educational policy. However, in this case, as opposed to the Delhi pollution case, it is more difficult to isolate the precise impact of Supreme Court intervention. This is because the Court's intervention arose alongside widespread legislative and executive activity on midday meals, most of which predated the Court's orders. In addition, elections brought a supportive government to power which favored expanding the program. Dixon and Chowdhury wrestle with the difficult question of attributing causality to the Court's interventions. Ultimately, they conclude by arguing that though it would be difficult to attribute the entire success of the midday meal program to the Supreme Court, its intervention had important consequences in terms of increasing the coverage of the scheme, as well as removing *burdens of inertia* that stymied its full implementation. And, similarly to the Delhi pollution case, Dixon and Chowdhury argue that the active monitoring of implementation by the Supreme Court contributed in no small measure to its success in improving nutritional outcomes. Although we may never be sure of the extent to which the Indian Supreme Court's Right to Food decisions made a difference in the program's implementation, it seems likely that they contributed to improving the lives of the relatively disadvantaged.

In contrast to the two cases described above, the chapter by Kalantry and Nandi paints a more sobering picture of the lack of direct impact of Supreme Court decisions. Kalantry and Nandi study the case of prenatal sex determination, an important issue in India where female feticide is still widely prevalent. In this case, the Supreme Court admitted a PIL that sought the appropriate implementation of an already enacted law (the Pre-Natal Diagnostic Techniques (Prevention of Misuse) Act) that banned the procedure. The Supreme Court passed directions to the Union Government as well as all the States, and periodically summoned representatives of these various governments to enquire as to the status of the implementation of these directions. The Supreme Court held on to this case for three years, during which time

---

[12] For a classic study of the structural constraints that limit the ability of courts to make good policy decisions, see Donald L. Horowitz, *The Courts and Social Policy* (1977).

the Parliament of India amended the law in question and strengthened its punitive provisions substantially. The Supreme Court's orders were repeatedly cited in Parliament as reason to amend the law, and in this respect it appears that its interventions did bring about a legislative change. However, both during the litigation, and subsequently after the passage of the amendment, sex-ratios across the country continued to fall. If the ultimate aim of the Supreme Court was to curb female feticide and improve India's imbalanced sex ratio, as it undoubtedly was, it was unsuccessful.

Kalantry and Nandi attribute this failure to two main causes: the rise of cheap and accessible ultrasound technology that enables quick sex-determination, carried out in the private spaces of the home and the doctor's office, and deeply held beliefs concerning family structure. These conclusions point to a more general difficulty in enforcing this law by all the institutions of the state, rather than a deficiency particular to the Supreme Court. However, this being said, it is notable that the Supreme Court held on to this matter for only three years, as opposed to those cases discussed above, which ran for decades, and are still running. It is difficult to surmise whether there may have been a better outcome if the Supreme Court had engaged with this issue over a longer period; the evidence of the cases above certainly seems to suggest that it might have. Then again, there was strong popular support for improving the quality of the air in Delhi and for feeding hungry children. In contrast, the preference of many Indians for sons rather than daughters is a powerful obstacle to change.

These three cases suggest that when the Supreme Court adopts a front-and-center role as a generator and monitor of policy, where the policies have wide support, and, in the *Right to Food* case, where the national government has acted, its interventions can make a difference. In these cases, the Supreme Court is at its most dynamic, transcending nearly all of the implementation constraints traditionally attributed to judicial institutions and functioning more like an executive agency. Thus, when these conditions are met the Indian Supreme Court seems able to improve the lives of the relatively disadvantaged.

EXTRAJUDICIAL (INDIRECT) IMPACT

If there is cause for some optimism in the case of the judicial impact of Indian Supreme Court decisions, the case of extrajudicial impact furthering the interests of the relatively disadvantaged is somewhat more ambiguous. The symbolic, discursive effects of Indian Supreme Court decisions are most clearly dealt with in the chapters by Bhat, Rao-Cavale, Brierley, and Shankar, and also briefly by Galanter and Ram. Bhat, Rao-Cavale, and Brierley provide three accounts of how interventions by the Supreme Court can be used by civil society activists to mobilize on behalf of the disadvantaged. However, the precise mechanics of this process are distinct in each case.

Brierley's chapter offers a complementary analysis of the *Right to Food* case to that provided by Dixon and Chowdhury, and describes the manner in which large-scale mobilization by civil society activists amplified and strengthened the implementation of the Supreme Court's orders. Brierley's study describes a feedback loop that was created between civil society activists and the Court, where the former supplied the Court with the technical knowledge needed to intervene effectively, as well as functioning as monitors of the implementation of Court orders. Brierley suggests that the Court's success in this case was in no small part thanks to the presence of a well-organized and committed civil society movement which utilized the Court's orders to pursue its agenda vigorously. Importantly, Brierley contrasts the success of the *Right to Food* case with an earlier case involving similar issues that failed to have the same effects, largely because it was not backed by an organized movement. Rather than the Court's actions *leading to* legal mobilization, Brierley argues that in the *Right to Food* case the prior mobilization in fact shaped the nature, extent, and efficacy of the Court's interventions. In this case, it seems, judicial and extrajudicial impact were mutually reinforcing. Brierley's research suggests that the Indian Supreme Court can improve the lives of the relatively disadvantaged where organized social movement groups can both pressure and monitor government bureaucrats. Where state bureaucracies are either unwilling or unable to implement decisions, existing organized social movements can step in.

Whereas in Brierley's case a muscular and well-developed civil society mobilization formed the context of the Supreme Court's intervention, Bhat describes an instance where a decision of the Supreme Court provided the ground for a hitherto fragile movement to gain strength. He discusses the manner in which the Supreme Court decision in *Indra Sawhney v. Union of India* served to embolden the struggle of *Dalit* Muslims to have their status as lower castes recognized, and thereby gain access to the benefits of reservations in public employment. This is especially interesting because the final decision of the Court in this case did not include any relief aimed directly at *Dalit* Muslims; instead it was curiously silent on their status. However, in the hands of a group of creative activists in the State of Bihar, a few lines of the Court's reasoning became rallying points. Activists in the Morcha movement recognized a potential entry point for their demands in the words of the Supreme Court, and managed to construct both a political as well as legal strategy around it, a process Bhat describes as interpretive framing. This had consequences for the nature of subsequent mobilization, which ultimately culminated in a separate PIL filed by a group influenced by the activism of Morcha. Bhat's chapter describes the ways in which the altogether uninspiring language of the Supreme Court in the *Indra Sawhney* case provided the activists of Morcha, and the *Dalit* Muslim movement generally, a platform on which they could mount an effort to better their condition. As with the *Right to Food* case, Bhat's study shows that existing civil society groups can make use of Supreme Court decisions to mobilize supporters.

If Bhat's chapter points to the potential of the Supreme Court's language to frame and provide legitimacy to the struggles of disadvantaged groups, Shankar's chapter provides a sobering counterpoint. Her research shows how the Court's judgments can also provide legitimacy, perhaps unwittingly, to reactionary social forces. This is especially apparent in Shankar's discussion of the Supreme Court's approach to anti-conversion legislation in the *Stanislaus* case onwards. The Supreme Court's refusal to strike down the State of Madhya Pradesh' anti-conversion legislation was seen by Hindu majoritarian groups as a major victory, a vindication by the Supreme Court of their aversion to proselytizing religions such as Islam and Christianity. Shankar describes how this judgment was seen by such groups as the Court's way of remedying the anomalous position of religion in the Constitution, which treats Hinduism on a par with other religions, rather than according the Hindu way of life primary status. Though the Court may have been trying to protect the religious freedom of those thought to be undergoing forced conversions, its pronouncements were weaponized by groups with a decidedly less egalitarian outlook.

Both Bhat's and Shankar's chapters point to the discursive and symbolic impact of Supreme Court decisions. The unpredictability of the discursive effects of these decisions echoes McCann's emphasis on the indeterminacy of all social interaction.[13] The two cases illustrate this nicely: in the first, a judgment that was not necessarily concerned with *Dalit* Muslims became a central plank for their mobilization, while in the second, a judgment intended to protect religious freedom became a rallying cry for reactionary religious groups.

In contrast to the chapters above, Rao-Cavale moves away from the discursive realm to describe how disadvantaged groups can make use of even partial judicial victories to further their goals. Rao-Cavale describes how street vendor groups, faced with an inhospitable political climate and executive harassment, turned to the courts in Bombay and Madras (as they were then known) to

---

[13] *Supra* note 4 at 15.

protect their livelihoods. In this case litigation was a defensive move to preserve the status quo in a changing political environment that had previously favored them, as opposed to a move to establish new rights in an environment that had always been unfavorable to them. Though they did receive some substantive relief from the courts, the implementation of the court orders did not safeguard their livelihoods. It would, therefore, seem that they were out of options, with no support from any of the branches of the state. However, Rao-Cavale finds that from this seemingly moribund position the street vendors were able to leverage judicial decisions to gain some protection. Through temporary injunctions against the government, and appeals drawn out in court, street vendor associations were able to stave off imminent threats to their existence from the state, which allowed them to carry on their occupations, however provisionally. Rao-Cavale's chapter highlights how in some cases judicial insistence on process and the slowness with which the judicial process moves, can be useful for the relatively disadvantaged, at least in the short run.

THE INDIAN SUPREME COURT AND PROGRESSIVE SOCIAL CHANGE

The Indian Supreme Court, like all courts, lacks the power of implementation and "must ultimately depend," as Alexander Hamilton wrote so eloquently about the US Supreme Court, "upon the aid of the executive arm even for the efficacy of its judgments."[14] Its decisions will be implemented to the extent that governmental officials and the public are willing to follow them. The Delhi High Court acknowledged as much in April 2014, in a filing about preventing men from urinating in public. The justices admitted that they could not effectively require that every man who walks out of his house put a "lock on his zip."[15] Though admittedly trivial and silly, this case underscores the reliance of the judiciary on the support of government and the people.

The case studies in the preceding chapters provide evidence for a limited ability of the Indian Supreme Court to further the interests of the relatively disadvantaged. Proponents of judicial efficacy can stress those examples where judicial decisions made a difference in the lives of the relatively disadvantaged while opponents can highlight those where it didn't. The case studies in this book suggest that when the Indian Supreme Court adopts a front and center role as a generator and monitor of policy, where the national government has

[14] *Federalist 78.*
[15] Ayesha Arvind, "Even Deities Can't Stop Men from Urinating in Public, Says Court," *India Today,* April 12, 2014.

acted and is supportive, where preexisting organized social movement groups can both pressure and monitor government bureaucrats, and where the policies have wide support, interventions can make a difference. In contrast, where these conditions are missing, decisions of the Indian Supreme Court in support of the rights of the relatively disadvantaged will not materially improve their lives. Importantly, these conclusions echo the findings of both Rosenberg and McCann who find that in a limited set of conditions the US Supreme Court can further the interests of the relatively disadvantaged.[16]

In sum, it appears that when the Indian Supreme Court decides a case furthering the interests of the relatively disadvantaged, that decision can materially improve their lives if the following conditions are present:

- the Indian Supreme Court keeps the case for many years and continuously monitors progress;
  AND
- the national government is supportive and either has or does legislate on the issue;
  AND
- preexisting civil society groups use the decision to mobilize supporters and pressure, and
- incentivize bureaucrats to implement the decision;
- there is public support.

In addition, preexisting civil society groups can utilize legal decisions to temporarily protect their interests. And, in some cases, these groups can use judicial decisions to reframe their grievances.

In conclusion, the Indian Supreme Court has much in common with its US counterpart. Under some conditions it can be an effective agent of progressive social change. Its decisions can improve the lives of those most in need. Yet in the absence of these conditions, the Court's decisions do little. The Indian Supreme Court is neither a silver bullet nor a hollow hope for Indian's relatively disadvantaged population. The challenge to progressive forces in India that are considering litigation is to identify whether the conditions necessary for decisions to improve the lives of the relatively disadvantaged are present. And the challenge to scholars is to carefully examine the conditions under which this is possible. We hope this volume helps to better understand both of these challenges.

---

[16] *Hollow Hope* at 36; McCann, supra note 4 at 136–137.

REFERENCES

Arvind, Ayesha, "Even Deities Can't Stop Men from Urinating in Public, Says Court," *India Today*, April 12, 2014.

Chandrachud, Chintan, "Constitutional Interpretation." In *The Oxford Handbook of the Indian Constitution* (Sujit Choudhry, Madhav Khosla & Pratap Bhanu Mehta eds., 1st ed. India: Oxford University Press 2016).

Hamilton, Alexander, Federalist No.78, in *The Federalist Papers*, ed. Clinton Rossiter (New York, NY, New American Library, 1961).

Horowitz, Donald L., *The Courts and Social Policy* (Washington, D.C., Brookings, 1977).

McCann, Michael W., *Rights at Work: Pay Equity Reform and the Politics of Legal Mobilization* (Chicago, University of Chicago Press, 1994).

Qazi, Asher, "A Government of Judges," *JSD Dissertation*, University of Chicago, 2018.

Rosenberg, Gerald N., *The Hollow Hope: Can Courts Bring about Social Change?* 2nd ed. (Chicago, University of Chicago Press, 2008).

Positivism, Interpretivism, and the Study of Law, 21 *L. & Soc. Inquiry* 435, 455 (1996).

"Review Section Symposium: Gauging the Impact of Law," 21 *L. & Soc. Inquiry* 435 (1996).

For EU product safety concerns, contact us at Calle de José Abascal, 56–1°,
28003 Madrid, Spain or eugpsr@cambridge.org.

www.ingramcontent.com/pod-product-compliance
Ingram Content Group UK Ltd.
Pitfield, Milton Keynes, MK11 3LW, UK
UKHW020807190625
459647UK00032B/2266